DATE			
FEB 1 2 1999			
			.

THE BATTLE OF BATAAN

THE BATTLE OF BATAAN

*A History of the 90 Day Siege
and Eventual Surrender of 75,000
Filipino and United States Troops
to the Japanese in World War II*

by

Donald J. Young

McFarland & Company, Inc., Publishers
Jefferson, North Carolina, and London

British Library Cataloguing-in-Publication data are available

Library of Congress Cataloguing-in-Publication Data

Young, Donald J., 1930–
    The Battle of Bataan : a history of the 90 day siege and eventual
surrender of 75,000 Filipino and United States troops to the
Japanese in World War II / by Donald J. Young.
        p.   cm.
    Includes bibliographical references and index.
    ISBN 0-89950-757-3 (lib. bdg. : 50# alk. paper) ∞
    1. Bataan (Philippines : Province), Battle of, 1942.   I. Title.
D767.4.Y69   1992
940.54'25—dc20   92-50326
                                                              CIP

Manufactured in the United States of America

McFarland & Company, Inc., Publishers
  Box 611, Jefferson, North Carolina 28640

Dedicated to
Col. Ambrosio P. Peña,
Philippine Army, retired,
without whose help this
story would be incomplete,
and
to the preservation of
the memory of those who
sacrificed their lives
in this battle

ACKNOWLEDGMENTS

The loss of Bataan and the subsequent loss of most of the records the U.S. Army usually relies on when compiling the official history of a campaign, is one of the reasons, after 40 years, so few books have been written on this battle. There will never be an "official" history of the battle of Bataan. Even Dr. Louis Morton's 1953 book *Fall of the Philippines,* done as part of the government's voluminous series of official histories of the U.S. Army in World War II, could be considered "unofficial." Among other things, he failed to consult Philippine Army records or include the role of the U.S. Army Air Corps or Navy in the book.

Along with the usual sources from which the material for this book was drawn, such as published and unpublished works and diaries, one of my major contributing sources, unlike Dr. Morton, came from the Philippines. Filipino historians, led by Col. Ambrosio Peña, former chief historian of the Philippine Army, have compiled their own "unofficial" history of the battle, which, up to this time, has remained virtually untapped by American writers and historians.

I have also included the history of the U.S. Army Air Corps and Navy on Bataan. Of great help with the air corps story was Allison Ind's book *Bataan: The Judgment Seat,* written from the diary he kept as an aid to Bataan air corps commander Gen. Harold George; fighter pilot Capt. Edward Dyess' book *The Dyess Story;* the diaries of three pilots who flew on Bataan, lieutenants Ben Brown, David Obert and Stewart Robb; two USAF studies on air action in the Philippines and the Dutch East Indies; and several interviews with retired Brig. Gen. Richard Fellows, who, as a captain on Bataan, flew with the Bamboo Fleet. The biggest aids in compiling the story of the U.S. Navy's role on Bataan came from W. L. White's book *They Were Expendable,* written for Capt. John Bulkeley and Lt. Robert Kelly of Motor Torpedo Boat Squadron Three; Robert Bulkley's *At Close Quarters: PT Boats in the U.S. Navy;* Cmdr. Earl Sackett's 24-page paper on the USS *Canopus;* and the *16 Naval District War Diary.*

A great aid in adding a personal as well as historic touch to parts of the story came from the monographs written after the war by 16 different officers who fought on Bataan. These papers, written of their experiences for various advanced U.S. Army officer schools (infantry, armor, command, etc.) from 1946 to 1949, exposed incidents and occurrences down to the platoon and company levels, while at the same time pointing out just how confusing and, in most cases, hopeless U.S. efforts were.

Along with the major task of gathering and refining information on the various battles of the campaign, I worked especially hard on trying to capture the atmosphere that existed on Bataan during its brief and tragic 90 days in history. To accomplish this I leaned heavily on some of the early published works of survivors, namely Carlos Romulo, Edward Dyess, Clark Lee, Alfred Weinstein, Ernest B. Miller, Juanita Redmond, and Allison Ind. Their reflections of life on Bataan, I felt, represented the true feelings of most of the men and women who suffered through the ordeal.

★   ★   ★

All of the poems and excerpts from poems used throughout this book are the work of 1st Lt. Henry G. Lee, of the U.S. 31st Infantry on Bataan. Collected in his book, *Nothing But Praise,* these poems were found buried under a Nipa hut at Cabanatuan Prison in February 1945. Just 21 days before American Rangers liberated the Bataan and Corregidor P.O.W.s from Cabanatuan, Lt. Lee lost his life on board a Japanese prison ship en route to Japan. The poems were forwarded to his parents, who had them published. Special thanks are extended to Lee's sister, Frances Lee, of Pasadena, California, for allowing the impressive and sensitive work of her brother Henry—the Bataan Poet—to be used throughout this book.

> I see no gleam of victory alluring
> No chance of splendid booty or of gain
> If I endure—I must go on enduring
> And my reward for bearing pain—is pain
> Yet, though the thrill, the zest, the hope are gone
> Something within me keeps me fighting on.
>   —Lt. Henry G. Lee
>   Bataan, 1942

CONTENTS

PREFACE

My interest in the story of the battle of Bataan goes back over 40 years to when, as a young man in high school in 1945, I began reading about it in such books as *They Were Expendable, I Saw the Fall of the Philippines, They Call It Pacific,* and Allison Ind's *Bataan: The Judgment Seat.* For the next 30 years I searched out everything in print on the subject, and decided in 1980 to write my own version of the story. There were a number of things that influenced this decision. The main one came from what I felt were several voids in the existing and accepted history of the battle. With the unprecedented surrender of the American army on Bataan also came the loss of pages of punctiliously kept records and daily reports from which official histories of battles are compiled. Much of the existing "official" history of the battle for Bataan, therefore, up to that time had come from "unofficial" sources, everything from diaries to survivor recollection. Based on my research, many of the accepted versions of how, why and when certain things happened during the battle have now been changed, and are revealed for the first time in this book.

One of the most significant revelations involved the Philippine army: I found that every American account of the campaign I came across shortchanged the role of the Filipinos in the battle. Of the accomplishments of the nine Philippine Army divisions on Bataan, little, if anything, was written. Yet, not only had the Philippine Army made up over 75 percent of the 75,000-man army on Bataan, but it had also entirely manned, with the exception of one small corner of the first and final battle lines, every inch of the peninsula's two main lines of defense. Since my best source for information in this area was probably in the Philippines, before writing the story, I, of course, had to visit the battlefield itself. So in the early summer of 1981, with my good friend Warner Boone of Honolulu accompanying me as photographer, I headed for the Islands. Preliminary inquiries put me in touch with a retired Philippine Army colonel, Ambrosio Peña, whom I contacted upon my arrival. Of the Filipinos I could have sought for help with my research, Col. Peña was, by far, the most knowledgeable on the subject: He had fought on Bataan as a third lieutenant in the artillery, was retired in 1968 as chief historian of the Philippine Army, and had authored books

The author with Col. Peña in the jungles of Bataan in 1981.

on two of the Filipino divisions that took part in the campaign. As the recognized authority on the role of the Philippine Army in the battle, my several days of touring Bataan with Col. Peña were to prove indispensable, as was the material on the Filipino side of the story he provided.

Another major reason for writing of the battle was to bring all facets of the story together by incorporating the role of not only the Filipinos, but also the U.S. Army, Air Force, and Navy. In further effort to make this the most complete book on the battle, I have added over 50 photographs, many never before or rarely seen, to the usual dozen or so pictures associated with the campaign. Also included are some 30 photographs taken in 1981 by Warner Boone showing Bataan is it looks today. The book also includes 29 maps of the campaign covering different phases of the battle.

BATAAN UNIT DESIGNATIONS AND ABBREVIATIONS

U.S., P.S., and *P.A.:* Units of the American Army's long-established Philippine Division, composed of Americans and Philippine Scouts, when abbreviated in this book will be *U.S.* for American and *P.S.* for Philippine Scout units. Philippine Army units, although officially sworn into the U.S. Army on July 26, 1941, remained entirely separate from the Philippine Division and are abbreviated as *P.A.*

P.C.: Reporting to Bataan prior to the outbreak of hostilities there were three regiments of Philippine Constabulary. Although officially designated as the 2nd Regular Division, Philippine Army, they are abbreviated in this book as *P.C.*

51st C.T.: Following the disintegration of the 51st Division on Bataan in late January 1942, a remnant force organized, designated, and referred to as the 51st Combat Team (*C.T.*) took its place.

Although technically representing the United States in this battle yet fighting alongside the Philippine Army, the army on Bataan is referred to as either *U.S.* or *Fil-American* in this book.

Inf.–infantry; *Q.M.*–quartermaster; *Eng.*–engineers; *F.A.*–field artillery; *C.A.*–coast artillery; *A.A.*–antiaircraft; *C.P.*–command post; *C.O.*–commanding officer; *M.L.R.*–main line of resistance/main battle line.

JAPANESE LANDINGS AND THE WITHDRAWAL INTO BATAAN

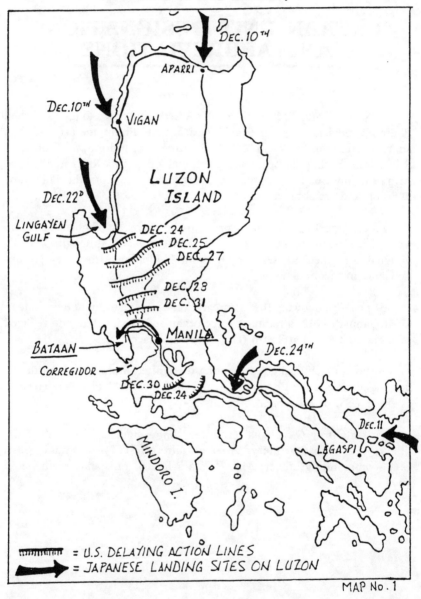

DEC. 10TH

APARRI

DEC. 10TH

VIGAN

DEC. 22D

LUZON ISLAND

LINGAYEN GULF

DEC. 24
DEC. 25
DEC. 27

DEC. 28
DEC. 31

MANILA

BATAAN

CORREGIDOR

DEC. 30
DEC. 24

DEC. 24TH

DEC. 11

LEGASPI

MINDORO I.

= U.S. DELAYING ACTION LINES
= JAPANESE LANDING SITES ON LUZON

MAP No. 1

INTRODUCTION

The Retreat into Bataan

The sad result of American unpreparedness for war in the Pacific in 1941 needs no comment, other than to note that it took until December 1944, some two and a half years, to regain what had been lost in just six months. The only existing United States Army unit of any size in the western Pacific was in the Philippines when the war broke out. Although some 30,000 in number, it was caught in a state of partial preparedness when war came and, along with a fledgling Philippine Army, was unable to stop the tough, China-hardened Japanese from gaining footholds at five different places on the island of Luzon during the first 14 days of hostilities.

On December 23, without air and naval support and facing a rapidly advancing enemy on two major fronts, Gen. Douglas MacArthur, overall commander of the American and Filipino forces in the Islands, ordered his army withdrawn to Bataan. (See Map 1.)

The idea of retreating into the jungled fastness of this mountainous peninsula which jutted down to form the western shore of Manila Bay did not originate at that moment, however. Several years before, a plan was initiated that dictated such a move should a military situation occur between the United States and Japan that isolated the Philippines from help. Called War Plan Orange-3 (WPO-3), it directed that Bataan and the island fortress of Corregidor should be built up, supplied, and equipped in advance to block the Japanese from having the use of Manila Bay for a period of approximately six months. Application of this well-anticipated plan would give the isolated Filipino-American garrison its only chance.

But it was not to be. The plan, which preacknowledged the eventual loss of the Philippines, was not accepted by Gen. MacArthur. The optimistic American commander, who had been working in the Philippines putting its army together since 1935, was convinced that recent U.S. military buildup in the Islands precluded the need for WPO-3. His plan to discard WPO-3 for a more aggressive tack, one that was to overcommit his unprepared army to defending the Luzon beaches against possible enemy invasion, was approved by the War Department in Washington in late

1

Top: This aerial view of the Bataan east coast shows the general location of the first MLR on Bataan. Known as the Abucay line, this flat, open, eastern end of the line began a few hundred yards to the right (north) of the barrio of Mabatang (left edge of the picture). The maze of fish ponds in the foreground, separated by the East Road, prevented the Japanese from flanking the II Corps from Manila Bay (below). *Bottom:* General MacArthur on his inspection tour to Bataan with Gen. Albert Jones, on the right, and Gen. Richard Sutherland, his trusted chief of staff, center background, on January 11. This was the only time MacArthur set foot on the peninsula during his 60 days in command during the battle. *Opposite, top:* Bombed-out Quarantine Station and dock area as it looked in 1945 after Bataan was recaptured from the Japanese. *Opposite, bottom:* Bataan as it looks from above Corregidor. Sisiman Bay and Mariveles can barely be seen in the upper left of the picture.

October 1941. This change preempted all military preparation on Bataan:
No roads would be ready; there would be no stockpiles of food or medicine;
no defense lines would be established or built, and no airfields constructed.
Nevertheless, the sixteenth day of the war found MacArthur's army on its
way to the peninsula and in desperate need of everything WPO-3 could
have provided. Despite MacArthur's frantic attempt to reestablish WPO-3
on December 23, it was too late.

And thus Bataan was born—out of the blunders of unpreparedness and the overconfidence of its commander. But despite these handicaps, the forces at Bataan would put up a fight like no other army in American and World War II history, while at the same time dying a slow, agonizing death—or as one of the soldiers who was there would write:

> Our war—our own little rat trap
> The hopeless defense of Bataan
> A rear guard with no main body
> But a thorn in the flesh of Japan.

Although technically part of the U.S. Army, the 75,000-man army on Bataan, in reality, was seven-eighths Filipino, barely half of whom had completed basic training before being called to their country's defense. Also, not many more than one-third of the Filipinos carried weapons newer than World War I vintage.

The Philippine Division

The only regular U.S. Army division in the Philippines when the war started was the Philippine Division. Established in the early 1900s, and manned entirely by Filipinos but officered and trained by Americans, the Philippine Division was composed of three infantry regiments, the 31st, 45th and 57th; two field artillery regiments, the 23d and 24th; one regiment of engineers, the 14th, plus service units. Not until 1919 did an American regiment, the 31st Infantry, become part of the division. The Philippine Scouts, making up the remainder of the outfit, were products of highly selective recruiting efforts throughout the Islands, which produced in the end a soldier whose loyalty to duty, honor, and country were paralleled by few military units of that size in history. The Philippine Scout record in the U.S. Army showed long and creditable service; retirement was the rule, and the court-martial as a means of enforcing discipline was a nearly nonexistent exception. Of the Scout soldier, American Capt. Ernest L. Brown of the 57th Infantry, wrote: "They were well-known to the rest of the United States Army for their proficiency in marksmanship and their love of soldiering. Court-martials were rare and venereals unheard of. Their standard of discipline was among the highest in the army. Their willingness and immediate obedience to orders provided inspiration to their American officers in combat."[1] Lt. Col. Adrianus Van Oosten of the 45th Infantry wrote that just the "knowledge that the Scouts were fighting in the same action" gave inspiration to Philippine Army troops.[2] Hard-put for replacements during the battle, the Scouts were forced to seek help from Philippine Army units. Many an officer in the Philippine Army jumped at the chance to give up his bars for a Scout private's uniform. These lines from Lt. Henry G. Lee's poem "Abucay Withdrawal" further describe "the lean, efficient Philippine Scout" on Bataan:

> Polished and trained and weeded out;
> Pick of the best of the Philippines
> Perfect precision fighting machines,
> Polished and trained since nineteen four
> To be expended in four months war.

The division made up approximately 10,500 of the estimated 75,000 troops on Bataan at the time of the first battle. With about 2,300 of its men assigned before the war to the Philippine Army as instructors, the 45th and 57th Philippine Scout Regiments totaled slightly over 2,100 men each; the U.S. 31st Infantry, some 1,600; and the 14th Engineers, 800.

Special mention must be made of the only all–American fighting unit in the Philippines at this time — the 31st Infantry. Of the 2,300 men of the Philippine Division assigned to instructor duty with the young Philippine Army before the war, the officers and noncommissioned officers of the 31st far outnumbered all others (no Scout officers were assigned this duty). Although an infantry regiment, before the war it led a soft, garrison-type existence in the very heart of Manila itself. When war broke out, the regiment not only found itself barely over half-strength but also overloaded with young ROTC officers and 12-month trainees fresh from the States. The record of the U.S. 31st on Bataan will, of course, be found in this book: It has nothing to be embarrassed about other than that it was the least-used and least-exposed infantry regiment on Bataan. Although this is something over which the men of the regiment had very little control, it was something that affected the morale of other not-so-lucky combat units. Morale within the regiment — which was down to less than 50 percent effectiveness throughout the last month of the battle due to malaria and dysentery — remained exemplary. "Gradually," wrote Maj. Eugene Conrad of the regiment's 2d Battalion, "the men began to believe they were doomed. When the full impact of the situation hit [them] it seemed to help their morale. They became more determined."[3] Underexposed or not, morale of the 31st would remain "American" to the end. In respect to the 31st, Lt. Henry Lee included these descriptive lines in his "Abucay Withdrawal" poem:

> Tall and dirty and very thin,
> With a two week's stubble on every chin
> Covering ground but watching the sky,
> An American rifle platoon goes by.
> They look efficient but show the signs
> Of fourteen days on the fighting lines
> And their shredded trousers are black with dirt

And salt dries white on their khaki shirt,
And the tilted helmets show new scars
And the only officer has no bars.

The only all-Philippine Scout combat regiment not attached to the
Philippine Division was the 26th Cavalry, last of the traditional horse-
cavalry regiments ever to go into battle in an American war. One of the
most exposed units in the early stages of the war, by the time it reached
Bataan, the 26th had lost nearly one-fourth of its original complement of
800 in the early battles and during the painful withdrawal into the
peninsula.

The Philippine Army

The nine Philippine Army divisions on Bataan were to assume, by far,
the most important role in the defense. Except for a small but key sector
on the right of the first main battle line on Bataan (manned by 57th Infantry
Scouts), and a small sector on the final MLR (manned by Americans of the
Provisional Air Corps Regiment), both the first and the final main line of
resistance were every inch manned by men of the Philippine Army.

The seven Philippine Army divisions—11th, 21st, 31st, 41st, 51st, 71st,
and 91st—which fought on Bataan were organized under the greatest of
handicaps: the lack of time. Because of the absence of training facilities,
cadre, and equipment, the first third of each division was not called into
service until September 1, 1941. The middle third reported about two
months later and the final third, just hours before the war started. Division
artillery, signal, medical, transportation—all were mobilized
simultaneously, but they too found the time and equipment obstacles too
great to overcome. The training was conducted in cycles, with the early in-
ductees getting the most exposure to army life and training, and later arrivals getting proportionally less. When the war started on December 8, as
many as half the infantry regiments in some divisions had yet to fire a live
round in their World War I Enfield or 1903 Springfield rifles. The Philippine National Defense Act of 1935 was perhaps the one redeeming factor,
however, that gave the Philippine Army a chance in the field. It directed
that all Filipino males between the ages of 21 and 50 were liable for military
service. All, therefore, would be put through five and a half months of training and then released back to civilian life as part of a reserve force. Many
of the Filipinos called up in 1941 had been through this training cycle. Also,
many of the officers and enlisted men in the regular Philippine Army at the
time the war broke out had become regulars after their mandatory five-and-
a-half-month exposure.

There was much criticism made of the Filipino soldier both before and during the campaign; Brig. Gen. William E. Brougher, commanding officer of the Philippine Army's 11th Division on Bataan, however, felt that when properly trained and led, the Filipino was as good a soldier as there was in the Far East. To fight, said Brougher, as he did on Bataan, "all day and fall back at night only to fight again on the morrow—he's a tough soldier."[4] Colonel Russell Volckmann of Brougher's 11th Infantry added that they "found that the Filipino [had] an excellent mind, [was] attentive, and quick to learn a new subject."[5] Major William E. Webb of the 41st Division's 41st Infantry added that the "Filipino soldier did not have to be motivated to fight. Knowledge that they were to hold at all costs gave those members of the regiment who were fighting for their homeland an additional incentive."[6]

And so the Philippine Army, although young and green and short on almost everything, took to the field against the Japanese invader. Perhaps what it lacked in skill and training, it worked hard to make up for because they were fighting in the Philippines, for the Philippines and for a way of life whose pursuits were the same as the Americans': liberty and happiness.

Because of the acute shortage of personal equipment in the Philippine Army, the Filipino soldier, when in uniform, stood his tallest in a brightly shellacked, coconut-palm fiber covered pith helmet, crudely shaped to resemble the American and Scout World War I–type steel helmet; unmistakable blue denim fatigues; a pair of cheap, usually ill-fitting canvas tennis shoes—very often seen dangling from the end of his rifle; and a light canvas pack. A problem with the rifles issued to the Filipinos, no doubt common within all the Philippine divisions, was noted with respect to those issued to the 11th Division. Colonel Volckmann of the 11th Infantry wrote that over 500 rifles issued to his regiment had broken extractors: "Each rifleman with a broken extractor carried a piece of split bamboo that he used as a ramrod. After the round was fired, the bamboo ramrod was inserted into the muzzle end of the rifle in order to push out the expended cartridge case."

Part of Henry G. Lee's poem's "Abucay Withdrawal" briefly sums up how the Philippine Army looked on Bataan as it "straggled past":

> obsolete rifle without a sling,
> and a bolo tied with a piece of string,
> coconut hat and canvas shoes,
> and shoddy, dust white, denim blues.

To each division, the U.S. Army assigned approximately 40 American officers and 20 American or Scout noncommissioned officers to serve as instructors. At the division level, things functioned quite smoothly under these conditions. At lower (battalion and company) levels, however, where an American ROTC officer of five months might act as instructor to regular Filipino officers of higher rank, resentment often built up within the ranks of Filipinos. The language barrier, too, was never completely overcome, even by Filipinos whose many dialects often remained foreign to their own comrades and officers. In the 11th Infantry Regiment, for example, there were more than 11 different dialects spoken. In one 11th Infantry company of less than 100 men, five different dialects were spoken.

Two Philippine Army divisions somewhat separate from the aforementioned seven, were the 1st Regular Division and the 2d Philippine Constabulary Division.

The 1st Regular Division was the only peacetime regular army division maintained by the Philippine government. Functioning mainly to supply cadre for the training of reservists, 40 percent of its 1st Regiment reported between December 15 and 19 with almost no training. Its 3d Regiment was literally recruited within days after the war's start from civilian volunteers, dock workers, stewards, elevator operators, and the like. The division had no artillery, and its 2d Regiment, in operation on Mindanao when the war broke out, remained there throughout the campaign.[7, 8]

The 2d Philippine Constabulary Division (officially designated as the 2d Regular Division) was not actually formed or designated as such until its elements reached Bataan in early January 1942. Its three regiments, the 1st, 2d, and 4th (there was no 3d), were composed almost entirely of Philippine Constabulary troops. The 1st and 2d regiments were regular prewar constabulary regiments. As such, they were better equipped and organized, due to their training and military-like duties in the Philippine countryside, than were any of those within the Philippine Army. The 4th Regiment was made up of various Luzon Constabulary companies, including the elite, highly selected Malacanan Palace Guards, who were released for duty after Philippine President Manuel Quezon moved to Corregidor on December 24. (Malacanan Palace was the official Manila residence of the president.)[9]

The role of the individual Philippine Army divisions prior to Bataan varied greatly. It must be said, however, that close to 90 percent of the fighting that took place during the unsuccessful defense and then withdrawal periods involved Philippine Army units. Only the 31st and 41st divisions escaped seeing some action during the pre–Bataan period. Of the remaining seven, the 11th, 71st, and 91st divisions, initially assigned to coastal defense in northern Luzon, were to become, along with the 26th Cavalry, an integral part of the important withdraw-delay tactics implemented on December 23.

All three suffered terrible losses during the withdrawal period, the figures of the missing, wounded, and dead going above 10,000. (Although desertion to the green, undisciplined Filipinos was first thought to be the cause, it was found later that most of those who failed to make it into Bataan, including C Troop of the 26th Cavalry, had been cut off in northern Luzon by the rapidly advancing Japanese army. Finding themselves separated, they took to the hills where they became seeds for the soon-to-be highly organized and effective Philippine guerrilla army.)

The Air Force on Bataan

The stunning loss of 17 B-17s and 53 P-40s, exactly half of the Far East Air Force, on the first day of the war gave the Japanese immediate air superiority in the Philippines. With the remaining American bombers momentarily safe at Del Monte Field on Mindanao, the few fighters still on Luzon found the going very rough, and by January 4, were down to a mere ten planes. In the meantime, in anticipation of the coming battle, the air force moved into Bataan. There the tiny force found itself spread amongst three dusty little airstrips near the southern tip of the peninsula. The fields, little more than dried-up and smoothed out rice paddies, were known as Bataan, Cabcaben, and Mariveles. In addition to the army planes, a small collection of antiquated, nonmilitary planes, nicknamed the "Bamboo Fleet," also operated out of Bataan Field. From here it made daring medical, supply, and VIP runs back and forth to the southern islands throughout the last part of the campaign.

While they were few in number, the infrequent appearance of American planes over Bataan throughout the battle led most to believe that there were fewer than there actually were. Army nurse Lt. Juanita Redmond referred to "our P-40" as keeping them "just short of disaster," and of "*the* P-40," which bombed "*a* Japanese ship in the Gulf." There were actually five P-40s involved in the raid on the Gulf, which occurred on March 3, and which resulted in the sinking of at least four enemy ships. The last two P-40s, along with a couple of P-35s, in fact, did not leave Bataan until the night of April 8, just hours before the surrender. Sergeant Abie Abraham of the U.S. 31st Infantry, one day caught a glimpse of an American P-40 "through a hole in the jungle ceiling." "American," he yelled in utter disbelief. "We jumped out of our foxholes. Men cried, laughed, yelled and cheered," he said.[10] Captain Allison Ind, at the sight of "our own P-40s," remembered a "tremendous surge of emotion" going through his body. "A leaping desire to smash bare-fisted into the enemy. A swelling intoxication of patriotism." United Press correspondent Frank Hewlett, wrote that "[he] saw his first dog fight since arriving on Bataan in view of thousands of troops. [They] saw a Curtiss P-40 fighter overtake and riddle a Japanese plane. I learned later that those troops, cheering and shouting, waded into

Aerial photograph of barrio and engineer dock at Cabcaben as it looked in 1945.

battle with renewed vigor. The loss of that enemy plane was costly to the enemy in more ways than one."[11]

The function of the adventerous little Bataan air force was limited primarily to reconnaissance. On several occasions, however, usually at the cost of one or two of the precious fighters, they were able to reap a little vengeance against a usually surprised and unsuspecting enemy.

Because of the diminutive size and needs of the functioning part of the air corps on Bataan, the demand on pilots and ground personnel remained at

Two unidentified Filipino naval officers on board a Philippine Navy Q-boat in action in Manila Bay.

a bare minimum. This allowed for the release of five "grounded" air corps pursuit squadrons to the infantry. Nearly 1,000 strong, the First Far Eastern Air Force Combat Team, as it was unofficially known, was called to duty on the west coast in early January, where it soon found itself in the thick of probably the most bitterly fought battle of the campaign.

Another group of approximately 1,200 men, mostly ground and bomber personnel, were formed into the Provisional Air Corps Regiment. Divided into two battalions, they later made up part of Bataan's final main line, controlling a 2,000-yard sector near the east coast.[12] This small regiment had the distinction of being the only all–American unit to serve on either of the two Bataan fronts during the battle.

The Navy on Bataan

With the "official" abandonment of the Philippines by the U.S. Navy on December 10, 1941, the few suitable ships left functioned only as long as Bataan remained in friendly hands. Thus, on December 10, the unofficial Bataan Navy formed. Its list of ships included, among others: five PT-boats, two Q-boats (British-built, Philippine-owned, PT-type boats), three minesweepers, three river gunboats which had escaped from China just prior to the war, one submarine tender, and two pleasure yachts that had been converted into patrol boats.

Prewar photograph of the old sub-tender, USS *Canopus*.

The only ships equal to the task or risk of combat were the PTs, Q-boats, and river gunboats, to which the assignment of Inshore Patrol went. On the PTs fell the greatest responsibility — that of keeping a Japanese invasion force off of the west coast of Bataan and out of Subic Bay. Later, of course, they were called on to take Gen. MacArthur, his family, and staff to Mindanao and out of the encircling grasp of the Japanese. To the Q-boats and river gunboats went the assignment of patrolling Bataan's east coast and as much of Manila Bay as risk would allow.

On December 29, with the docking of the submarine-tender USS *Canopus* at Mariveles, there began one of the greatest human interest stories to come out of the campaign. Try as they might, the Japanese could not sink the old ship, even after she docked, where damage from several bomb hits just gave her the look of being sunk. Even with no subs left to tend, she continued to function until the end, utilizing her beautiful, well-equipped machine shops at night to repair almost anything for the army. She was remembered most fondly, however, by the officers, nurses, and men who were near enough to benefit from her generous supply of long forgotten but oft dreamed of luxury items: homemade ice cream with chocolate sauce, cigarettes, candy, hot showers, soap, a well-cooked meal served on white linen covered tables, hot bread, and real butter. You name it, and the *Canopus*, if it didn't have it, could probably make it.[13] Nurse Lt. Redmond, who, along with all the nurses, had a standing invitation for dinner on board the old ship, summarized as well as anyone what a visit to the *Canopus* meant: "we were almost overcome by nostalgia at the sight of the silver and table linens. They gave us wonderful food and lots of cigarettes,

Commander Francis "Frank" Bridget, commanding officer of the Naval Battalion on Bataan.

and after dinner we played bridge. . . . When the Chaplain said goodnight he handed us each a lollypop; we could hardly believe our eyes."

In November 1941, Adm. Thomas C. Hart, commander of the 16th Naval District (Asiatic Fleet), fearing that war was near, pulled the 4th U.S. Marine Regiment out of Shanghai and brought it to the Philippines. Arriving in early December, the fully equipped regiment of 750 officers and men boosted the existing Philippine Marine complement to about 1,600. What was left of the U.S. Navy picked itself up from the rubble of Cavite Naval Base—regarded as untenable after the devastating air attacks of December 9 and 10—and moved, along with the Marines, to Corregidor, except for a small detachment that was sent to Mariveles on Bataan.

Because of the shortage of qualified fighting men on the peninsula, a small group of about 120 Marines and 480 variously skilled shipless sailors were formed into what was called the Naval Battalion. Under the able leadership of Cmdr. Frank Bridget, it was responsible for coastal and antiaircraft security of the immediate Mariveles area. In late January, the battalion found itself involved in beating off a small, lost, but determined Japanese invasion force that had gained a foothold less than a mile from Mariveles itself. Although the Japanese were only lightly touched by the rifle-carrying sailors the battalion played a key role in defense against the threat of seaward invasion.

Please see Appendix B for information on the following: 192d and

GENERAL FEATURES AND ROADS

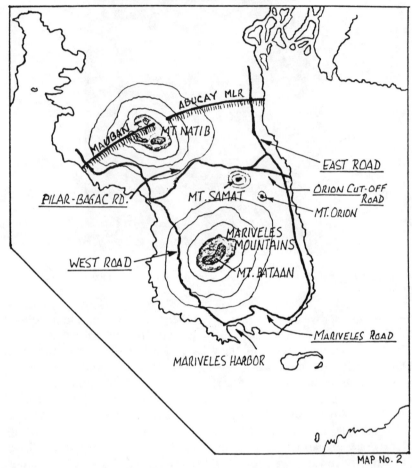

MAP No. 2

194th Tank Battalions; Bataan Artillery; Bataan Engineers; Bataan Quartermaster and the Supply Situation; the Bataan Ration; transportation; Bataan hospitals and the medical situation; refugees; and communications.

Physical and Military-Related Geography of Bataan

Bataan was selected for its role in a war with Japan many years before it was actively employed. As was projected under War Plan Orange-3, it was to be part of a delay-and-defend tactic that was designed to keep the Japanese out of Manila Bay for a period of approximately six months. The peninsula was selected not only because of its strategic location, but for its rugged terrain as well.

Three key features immediately qualified it for the defensive role it was to play. (See Map 2.) They were (1) a rugged interior, dominated by two 4,000-foot-plus volcanoes, Mt. Natib in the north and Mt. Bataan and the Mariveles Mountains in the south; (2) a nearly impenetrable jungle (its most awesome feature) covering over 75 percent of its 420 square mile area; and (3) a rugged, cliff-lined, tide-ripped west coast, which made the most likely spot for a large scale seaward invasion by the enemy all but impossible. Erosion of the two extinct volcanoes left the peninsula with still another austere feature. Gentle slopes of alluvium that began at the foot of the ancient cones and ended at the sea were gouged by steep, deep, brush and jungle infested ravines that, too, would make organized fighting within their entangling confines virtually impossible. The presence of the two mountains at opposite ends of Bataan split it for all practical purposes into two parts. In between lay a low, swampy, malaria-infested valley that formed a physical belt-line across the peninsula. Running east and west, it formed the best natural line of defense on Bataan.

The dominating terrain and defense feature of the valley was 2,000 foot Mt. Samat, rising abruptly from the northeastern slopes of the Mariveles Mountains. The only relatively flat area on Bataan was its upper, northeast corner. This flat, swampy, barrio-lined part of the Pampanga River delta made up a little less than one-fourth of the peninsula. It was here, home to about three-fourths of Bataan's prewar population, that 90 percent of this poor province's rice and sugar cane was grown. Also, lining this part of the Manila Bay shoreline for several miles were a series of man-made fish ponds. These not only helped increase the productivity of the area but also offered natural defense barriers during the early phase of the battle.

Roads

With the rapid movement of men and equipment integral to the defensive role chosen for the army on Bataan, a frantic build-up and improvement of existing roads by army engineers began immediately following the December withdrawal decision. Prewar roads consisted of the East Road, a lightly paved, two-lane road running down the east coast from the north, some 40 miles to Mariveles Harbor on the southern tip; a rough, gravel-paved West Road that paralleled the South China Sea coast to its end, some three-quarters of the way up the peninsula; and an east-west connecting road that linked the East and West Roads by traversing through the valley separating the two mountain ranges. (See Map 2.)

The Japanese Army

The four successful Japanese landings on the island of Luzon on December 10, 12, 22, and 24 sent the inept American and Filipino defenders reeling. Realizing on December 23 that his army was facing disaster, Gen. MacArthur issued orders for it to be withdrawn into the confines of Bataan peninsula. From that day on, Fil-American troops appeared, if anything, even more submissive to the Japanese. In reality, however, the invaders were facing a preplanned series of delaying actions designed to give the defenders as much time as possible to complete the difficult withdrawal maneuver. The rapid, passively contested advance by the Japanese on Manila, just 20 short days after the first landings, mistakenly led the Japanese Southern Army Command to believe that the battle for Luzon, and for that matter, the entire Philippines, was as good as over. With all avenues of escape and reinforcement blocked, the Japanese anticipated the Americans and Filipinos would make their last stand in the city of Manila. Based on these assumptions, a decision was made on January 2 to advance the invasion of the Dutch East Indies (specifically Java) ahead one whole month. This meant making an immediate transfer of the Japanese 14th Army's crack 48th Division and 5th Air Group to the Java Invasion Force. This left only one combat division, the 16th, plus the newly arrived 65th Brigade, the 7th Tank Regiment, and a freshly assembled 10th Independent Air Unit, with fewer than 70 planes (including only 11 fighters and 36 bombers). The "swap" of the battle-tested, 15,000-man 48th Division for the smaller, 6,600-man 65th Brigade, a garrison unit whose ranks swelled with draftees with little more than a month's training, did much, at least temporarily, to swing the scales in favor of the Fil-Americans on Bataan.

Japanese Strategy for the Battle of Bataan

Following the relief of the 48th Division on January 8, the untried Japanese 65th Brigade plus one regiment from the 16th Division, the 9th, stood poised at the "gates to Bataan," ready to strike the one final blow that would give the Japanese total victory in the Philippines.

Lt. Gen. Masaharu Homma, commanding general of the Japanese 14th Army, relying on intelligence and aerial reconnaissance reports, estimated the strength of the remnant army on Bataan to be no more than 25,000 men. It was thought that both morale and physical condition were poor, and that the desertion rate was high among Philippine Army units. Also, after locating the three American air fields on January 5, it was further believed that the presence of an air defense force on Bataan was nearly, if

LOCATION OF BARRIOS, AIR FIELDS & MILITARY INSTALLATIONS

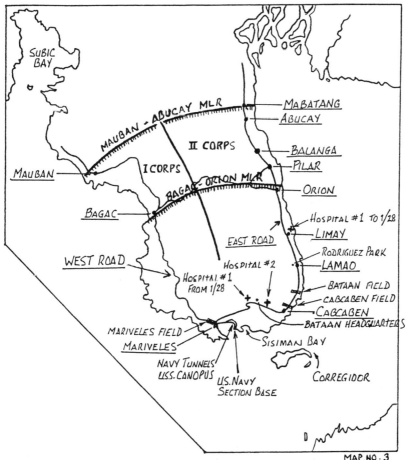

MAP NO. 3

not totally, improbable. In summary, Homma believed that the Bataan campaign would amount to little more than a mopping-up operation, with the only real resistance anticipated coming from the island of Corregidor.

Unworried about the 65th Brigade's ability to handle the anticipated confrontation, Homma split its three, two-battalion regiments, sending two, the 141st and 142d plus the 16th's 9th Infantry, down the East Road into Bataan. The 65th's 122d Regiment was ordered to cross over the peninsula in the north to the abandoned U.S. Navy base at Olongapo, in Subic Bay. From there, this single regiment was to move by foot trail down the west coast of Bataan to the barrio of Bagac, apparently expecting little if any resistance above that point.

CHAPTER ONE

Overture to the Beginning

"When they come tomorrow—"

By January 1, 1942, 11 days before the battle that would open the bitter 90-day seige of Bataan, only half of the 28 combat regiments that would take part in its defense had arrived on the peninsula. Although it was the late arrivals who had been involved in the exhausting delay and withdrawal fighting since December 10, most were allowed less than 24 hours to rest and reorganize before they were assigned to "dig in" on the new line.

As the scrambling army on Bataan hurried its final preparations, enemy air activity over the peninsula began to pick up. It started on December 29, following the occupation of Manila. That day the Imperial Japanese Air Force turned all its efforts toward Corregidor and eastern and southern Bataan, where they mistakenly believed the disorganized remnants of the U.S. and Philippine armies had withdrawn.

After declaring Manila an open city on December 26, along with the military, many of whom chose not to rely on the mercy of the Imperial Japanese Army, sought refuge on Bataan. At almost any time up to the day Manila was occupied, the 29th, boats of all sizes and shapes could be seen making the 30-mile run across the bay to one of the docks at Limay or Cabcaben on Bataan.

Because of this, on January 2, Japanese dive-bombers decided to pay a visit to the heavily congested waterfront at Limay. Although damage from the raid was minimal, in the course of the bombing a Philippine Constabulary medical unit bivouacked just outside the tiny barrio took several hits, despite the presence of a large, appropriately placed red cross panel in the middle of the camp clearing. Two Filipino officers and 17 corpsmen were killed in the resulting attack. This, sad to say, was a harbinger of things to come—during the battle pilots of the Imperial Japanese Air Force ignored red cross markers.[1]

After several days of bombing against only light U.S. antiaircraft

U.S. defensive positions built along the edge of Manila Bay that would never be challenged by the Japanes.

opposition, the Japanese attacks had not only become very predictable, but, because there had been no American fighter intervention, the bombers were flying without escort.

Following the raids on January 3, which again followed the same pattern, information on the Japanese predictability was forwarded to the air corps, whose last remaining 18 P-40s had just moved onto two dusty little auxiliary fields near Pilar and Orani in northeastern Bataan. That evening Col. Harold George, commanding officer of the air corps on Bataan, gathered his staff and pilots at the temporary campsite of the 17th Pursuit Squadron. "When they come tomorrow," George told his pilots, "we're going to try to mess them up."

The plan was for the 18 fighters to rendezvous at 11 A.M. over Del Carmen, some 20 miles north of Bataan, go up to 20,000 feet, and, according to Lt. Dave Obert, one of the pilots, "shoot down the entire formation of bombers, then land, refuel and take off for Del Monte Field, Mindanao, 520 miles south."[2]

"It seemed," remembered Obert, "that the Japs were rapidly advancing down the upper part of Bataan, and, as there was some doubt as to whether they could be stopped, it had been decided to evacuate all planes to Mindanao after first bolstering the morale of the American and Filipino troops by shooting down a couple of dozen heavy bombers. Interception," they were told, "would be no problem, because just about any time of the day heavy bombers could be seen above Bataan."

As scheduled, the nine planes of the Pilar group, under Lt. Fred Roberts, arrived over the Del Carmen assembly point at 11 A.M. where they circled for the next hour waiting for the Orani fighters.

"After being in the air an hour none of [us] had sufficient gas to climb to 20,000 feet and engage in combat," said Obert, "so our nine planes returned to the airfield and landed."

Ironically, it was while all his planes were in the air attempting to ambush the Japanese, that Col. George was ordered by USAFFE (United States Army in the Far East) headquarters on Corregidor to retain his fighters on Bataan for reconnaissance purposes. The order directing the two flights to Mindanao was immediately rescinded, but for some unknown reason, Roberts did not receive it in time, and, after refueling, led his group south as originally planned.

The Orani fighters, led by Capt. Ed Dyess, who had skipped the Del Carmen rendezvous when, after taking off, he spotted 12 enemy bombers, were able to at least make the intercept and give chase, but little else. Other than breaking up the attack, the overworked P-40s never got close. "When they spotted us," lamented one of the pilots, "twelve Japanese planes went in twelve different directions. We simply couldn't catch them . . . they held such a pace that [we] never got within shooting distance."

Interestingly, of the 18 fighters involved in the planned American attack, 9 of the planes waited at the rendezvous and missed the Japanese, and the others couldn't catch them when they did rendezvous. The only positive thing to come out of the mission was that the Orani group received the order canceling their transfer to Mindanao and did not leave.

Except for the unscheduled return later of one of Roberts' Mindanao-bound P-40s with engine trouble, by sundown of January 4 nearly half of what would have become Bataan's air force had left without as much as firing a shot in its own behalf.

The next day, on the heels of the surprise visit by American planes, the Japanese spent most of their time pinpointing the locations of the air fields on Bataan. From then on, few if any days would pass without the three dusty little strips receiving a visit or two or three from planes of the Japanese Air Force.

The results of the first heavy bombings of Corregidor and southern Bataan six days earlier on December 29, also opened the history of the U.S. Navy on Bataan with a story of the old submarine tender, USS *Canopus.*

Although the navy had withdrawn all of its key surface ships from the

Islands during the first few days of the war, its submarines, which could still continue to operate in hostile waters, needed a repair and supply vessel. The 23-year-old *Canopus* was chosen. On Christmas Eve she pulled out from the burning Manila waterfront and moved some thirty miles across the bay to Mariveles on Bataan, tying up at the edge of Lilimbon Cove along the harbor's eastern shoreline. There, for the next three days, the crew, with camouflage netting and green paint, worked diligently at blending the old ship in with her new surroundings. Unfortunately, green was far from the right color for her at her mooring in Lilimbon as, just behind the road that bordered the eastern edge of the bay, was a huge white-faced cliff from which most of the rock used for road repair and construction on Bataan was quarried. When finished, *Canopus* stuck out like a big green thumb, or as one of her crew more accurately put it, "like a cruiser," against the chalky white background of the quarry.

He was right. *Canopus'* ploy would, in fact, last through just two enemy air attacks. Of the Japanese planes involved in the three raids launched against Corregidor and southern Bataan on the 29th, those in the last raid went after the *Canopus.* But that one was almost enough. Although amazingly escaping with only a single bomb hit, a near miracle was still needed to pull her through. The one armor-piercing enemy bomb that did find its mark tore through three decks before finally exploding and starting a fire just beneath the powder magazine.

Undaunted by the obvious danger of the situation, the ship's courageous crew battled headlong with the fire until it was put out. Later, an inspection of the magazine showed that the *Canopus* had done more than her share in helping to save herself. The bomb explosion, it seems, had ruptured several water pipes near the deadly magazine blaze. Unknown to the crew at the time, the water and steam from the shattered pipes had thrown up such a wall of moisture that the fire was actually held-off from moving into the area where the explosives were stored before being brought under control.

The old ship was still a long way from being out of the woods, however. On January 5, the Japanese struck again. Although totally bracketed by enemy bombs, whose concussion literally lifted her out of the water, only one actually found its mark. This one, a fragmentation bomb, exploded against the smokestack, raining shrapnel down on the decks. Although several of the crew were wounded in the explosion, damage to the ship was only superficial. But superficial or not, it had become sadly apparent that under the existing circumstances, her days were indeed numbered. Or were they? After inspecting the damage above decks, which appeared far worse than it actually was, her resourceful skipper, Cmdr. Earl L. Sackett, had an idea: Why not make use of the existing damage along with a little added "make-up" of their own to fool the Japanese into believing that *Canopus*

Men who made the "Voice of Freedom" from the communications lateral on Corregidor: (from left to right, sitting) Lt. Salvador Lopez, Maj. Kenneth Sauer, Capt. Ince, and Capt. Carlos Romulo. Standing is Sgt. Conover Nichols. It was Lt. Lopez who had the unenviable task on the night of April 8 of writing the script which was read by Lt. Norman Reyes, announcing the fall of Bataan.

was foundering and abandoned. They had to work fast in order to trick the Japanese "Photo Joe" reconnaissance plane, when he came over the next morning, into thinking that the last attack had finished her.

Taking advantage of the damage caused by the previous bombings, oil-soaked rags were placed in small cans and strategically placed near areas of greatest damage. When lit, they expelled wafts of black smoke that gave the appearance of fires smoldering inside her hull. Cargo booms were then cut loose and left hanging lifeless over deserted holds. Probably the most effective ploy was the list. Although struck by only one bomb, concussion from the blanket of the day's near misses had ruptured a seam below the water line. Although quickly repaired, enough water had seeped in to give the old girl a list, which conformed perfectly to Cmdr. Sackett's scheme. Finally, all the antiaircraft guns were removed and relocated on nearby hills so as not to draw attention to her when used later to ward off attacking Japanese planes.

Apparently the disguise worked, as only one other half-hearted attack was launched against *Canopus* during the campaign. But that was far from the end of the "Old Lady," as she had been affectionately labeled by her

Major Gen. Jonathan Wainwright along with aides, Lt. Col. John Pugh (at his left) and Maj. Tom Dooley (in front), returning from an inspection of I Corps positions on Bataan.

crew, as from that day forward she assumed the role of super repair shop. Working mostly at night, her resourceful officers and crew kept the ship's beautiful, fully equipped machine shops repairing or replacing weapons, engine parts, or what-have-you for the army, air corps, artillery, navy, and engineers.[3]

On the afternoon of January 5, the first of over 300 broadcasts was made over the "Voice of Freedom" radio on Corregidor. The announcer, right up to the fall of Bataan, was Capt. Carlos P. Romulo, who opened this and all his broadcasts with "People of the Philippines, you are listening to the Voice of Freedom from the battlefront of Bataan." In reality, it was originating, as it did throughout the battle, from the USAFFE headquarters tunnel on Corregidor. The main target for these broadcasts were the people of the Philippines, who anxiously and, of course, secretly listened on hidden radios throughout the Islands. Although popular with the troops on Bataan too, most of the Americans considered many of their programs propaganda.

At 2 A.M. the next morning, January 6, the predawn peacefulness of northern Bataan was broken by a thundering explosion. As witnessed by Gen. Jonathan Wainwright, the big, steel-span Layac Bridge at that moment crashed into the sluggish waters of the Culo River, over which had just crossed the last of what would soon become the Bataan Army. With the bridge's destruction came the severance of the only road leading into Bataan from the north and a temporary delay of the Japanese Army not far behind.

A half-mile or so below, behind a short, temporary line established across the East Road, U.S. and Filipino troops apprehensively awaited what was to be their eighth and final delaying action since December 23. By 10 A.M., this battle, the final overture to the first battle of Bataan, would be joined.

At dawn that same morning, as troops already on the peninsula lined up for chow, they were greeted with orders and portions officially placing them on half-ration. Meals were cut from that day not only in portion, but in number, too. The troops would eat just twice daily, at dawn and just before dark.

Just three days earlier, the chief quartermaster, Brig. Gen. Charles Drake, had astounded MacArthur's chief of staff, Gen. Richard Sutherland, with information indicating that there were presently 20,000 more mouths to feed on Bataan than had been originally estimated. More startling was the fact that if they were to remain on full ration, unsupplemented from outside sources, Bataan could run out of food in less than 30 days. Despite Sutherland's claim that some of the strength reports had been padded, orders were cut immediately for the issuance of what was to become ignominuously and controversially known throughout the campaign as the "Bataan Ration."[4]

At about the time the troops had finished their first rationed meal that morning, two lone P-40s took off from dusty Pilar Field on a reconnaissance flight to the north with orders to observe the scale of Japanese troop movements above Bataan. On the return leg of their flight the two planes gave chase to six Japanese dive-bombers returning from a strike over the peninsula. While none of the enemy was destroyed, Lt. Elmer Powell's Kittyhawk was hit with return fire, forcing him to bail out. The other plane, piloted by Lt. William Rowe, was forced to land at Orani, as Pilar had been severely damaged by the Japanese planes he had just chased away.[5]

Around 10:30, as the lead elements of Japanese troops hit the temporary U.S. line below Layac Junction, guns from the Philippine Scout 23d and 88th Field Artillery Regiments opened up on them. Within minutes, their accurate fire had forced the enemy column off the road and into the fields. A half-hour later the Japanese had their own artillery in position, along with something else — unmolested aerial reconnaissance — that before long was directing murderous counter-battery fire down on top of the Scouts.

Particularly hard hit during the fierce exchange, was Battery A of the Scout 88th, which lost nearly an entire crew from a near direct hit. A

An American support unit—perhaps quartermaster, signal, or ordnance—stand morning formation somewhere on Bataan on January 10. Notice that a few of the men have fallen out with their mess gear. This was the fourth day of the Bataan ration.

hundred or so yards from the unlucky gun position, Battery B mess sergeant, Jose Calugas, was watching when the crew got hit. Tearing off his apron, Calugas took off running toward the now silent Scout gun. He didn't have a chance—or so it appeared as he started across the now heavily interdicted open field. But the stocky little Filipino sergeant, running and dodging like a halfback, safely made it with a headfirst dive into a battery slit-trench on top of two surviving gunners.

The first lull in enemy fire found Calugas up out of the trench, pulling wounded to safety while at the same time ordering the surviving members of the crew along with several volunteers to get ready to put the silenced 75 back into action. Within minutes, he and the makeshift gun crew had the big gun firing.

For this heroic deed, at complete disregard for his own safety, Sgt. Jose Calugas, Philippine Scout 12-year veteran, would be awarded the American Congressional Medal of Honor.[6]

By late afternoon, the battle to delay the Japanese from entering Bataan had gone from bad to worse for the defending Fil-Americans. With continued help from unchallenged aerial reconnaissance, Japanese artillery had maintained complete dominance over the open, hastily established U.S. line. By nightfall, it was decided that under the existing circumstances the position could no longer be held. Orders for its abandonment were issued before midnight.

With the passing, early the next morning, of the last of the delaying action forces through the main battle line, some 11 miles to the south, formation of the Bataan Defense Force was completed. The next shot fired from this position would officially announce the opening of the historic battle for Bataan. With the arrival of the last friendly troops on the peninsula, finishing touches were hurriedly put on key frontline positions near the tiny coastal barrio of Mabatang. Along with a final touching-up of positions along the front line, what was left of the barrio itself was burned to the ground to avoid the confusion of its being destroyed during the ensuing battle.

At dawn on January 8, the final day of peace on the peninsula, the last flight of P-40s to take off from unprotected Pilar Field roared out over Manila Bay. Pilar was being abandoned. Upon return from their reconnaissance mission over northern Bataan, the three fighters were ordered to land at Bataan Field, where they could be concealed in the newly completed camouflaged revetments and suitably protected by antiaircraft.

Although under orders to avoid aerial combat, the mission was not completely uneventful. After purposely dodging a fight with six enemy dive-bombers north of Bataan, Lt. William Rowe led his fighters in a couple of strafing runs against Japanese troop columns moving down the East Road before heading for home. In maneuvering out over Manila Bay for their first approach into Bataan Field, much to the pilot's dismay, they found it under attack from the same six enemy planes they had avoided earlier. Throttles this time were pushed forward and the three P-40s took off in pursuit. But again the Japanese were able to outrun the overworked American fighters, who, after a couple of unsuccessful and frustrating long-range bursts at the tails of the fleeing enemy, broke off the chase. After landing, the men of Bataan's tiny air force, like those of the friendly army around it, pondered what history had in store for them as they awaited the arrival of the Japanese.[7]

The Battle for Bataan Is Joined

**"A basic training company gone crazy
on an Infiltration Course!"**

With relief of the 48th Division completed on the 8th of January, under Lt. Gen. Akira Nara, the next day Japanese units moved unchal-

Camouflaged antitank gun position near the first MLR at Abucay on Bataan.

lenged down the East Road into Bataan to a position some five miles above the U.S. main line at Mabatang.

Nara, because of the delaying action fight put up by the Americans and Filipinos south of Layac two days earlier, anticipated that what would probably be the final U.S. stand on Bataan would be made from the next suitable high ground position just south of the barrio of Hermosa. So confident was the Japanese command of this, and of the likelihood of there being nothing more than moderate opposition, that a reconnaissance of the U.S. position was not even thought necessary prior to the attack. By 2:30 in the afternoon of the 9th, Nara had his artillery in position, and at 3 P.M. opened fire on what he was sure was the main Fil-American line at Hermosa. An hour later, on the heels of the unanswered 60-minute-long bombardment, the Japanese 141st Infantry jumped off confidently but blindly down the East Road toward what they anticipated would be the first and probably last major battle of Bataan.

Unknown to the enemy, however, their appearance on Bataan's main highway had been detected by sharp-eyed II Corps artillery observers from the slopes of nearby Mt. Natib. With weapons already zeroed in off prewar established registration points along the road, moments later two dozen U.S. 155-mm. "Long Tom's" unleashed a massive barrage that totally interdicted the startled enemy force that was moving up the road. Nevertheless, and to the delight of the U.S. artillerymen, firing every 15 seconds, the Japanese continued their advance along the open road for another 15 minutes before finally scattering into the fields on either side.

Convinced by the intensity of the shelling that he had hit the main U.S. line, Col. Takeo Imai, 141st Infantry commander, halted to regroup, and within an hour was on the move again. Although not able to completely stop the Japanese advance, II Corps artillery had guaranteed at least one thing: The East Road had seen the last of the 141st Infantry that day.

By nightfall, the leading elements of the enemy force, their advance having remained nearly unchallenged since the U.S. interdiction of the East Road earlier, jubilantly returned to report the Fil-American line at Hermosa had been abandoned. General Nara's concurrence was even more profound, claiming that the Americans and Filipinos had left the line and "fled into the jungle without putting up a fight." As expected, the first and probably only battle on Bataan had gone to the Imperial Japanese Army. But had it? Unknown to them, with the Fil-American lines still over two miles away, the Japanese had taken no ground not already conceded to them. Furthermore, they were still over 24 hours away from engaging in what even their own history books would later record as the opening battle for Bataan.

Perhaps it was their "phantom" victory at Hermosa that encouraged the Japanese, the next day, January 10, to air-drop to the troops on Bataan copies of the personal message sent from Gen. Homma to Gen. MacArthur earlier that day. Based on their own intelligence estimates of U.S. strength, coupled with the rout at Hermosa the day before, Homma politely "advised" MacArthur, in a rather lengthy 160-word message, "to avoid needless bloodshed" and surrender.

Unfortunately for the Japanese commander, the timing of his ignored "epistle," as Gen. MacArthur referred to it, couldn't have been poorer. First of all, the yet to be tested army of Bataan was completely unaware that it was thought by the enemy to have fled from a battle that it had never been in. To the contrary, at no time since the war started was American and Filipino morale higher or anticipation greater now that the withdrawal was complete. Second, MacArthur himself had just returned to Corregidor from what would be his first and only trip to Bataan. After a predawn PT-boat crossing, he proceeded to meet with both I and II Corps commanders, Wainwright and Parker, near their respective frontline positions. Before long, news of the General "himself" being at the front spread throughout the command, giving yet another boost to the morale of the already sanguine troops.[8]

An incident occurred on the way to visit Gen. Wainwright's I Corps, by the way, that was to be the trademark of Gen. MacArthur's courage under fire throughout the war. While on an open stretch of the Pilar-Bagac road immediately in front of Mt. Samat, the General's four-car motorcade came under heavy enemy artillery fire. Without much urging, everyone

Mauban Ridge (in the background) as it looks today, cleared of its dense jungle. A single battalion of Japanese infantry was able to infiltrate behind the U.S. I Corps lines on the ridge and establish a small roadblock across the West Road where it passed through the trees in the left foreground. This single battalion of enemy soldiers forced the entire I Corps (some 5,000 men) to abandon the line by working their way south along the edge of the South China Sea to safety.

abandoned their vehicles for ditches alongside the road. That is everyone except MacArthur, who, despite the pleadings of generals Sutherland and Arnold Funk, refused. "There's no Jap shell with MacArthur's name on it," said the helmetless Philippine commander. He was right. There never would be.[9]

Ironically, it was while inspecting I Corps positions that Gen. Richard Sutherland, MacArthur's chief of staff, made what would later prove to be a portentous statement to Gen. Wainwright that in his opinion more troops should be placed in the upper Mt. Natib area to not only beef up the nearly nonexistent upper end of the line, but to physically link it up with the dangling western end of the II Corps as well. Despite past performances, he feared the Japanese "would attack down the center of the peninsula over the roughest terrain and not along the coast where the roads were located." Wainwright, on the contrary, believed that the difficult terrain would deter rather than invite an attack, and, being shorthanded, would make no major effort to either build up or join with Gen. Parker's II Corps.[10]

The I and II Corps on Bataan had been officially established only three days before, on January 7. Picked to lead the I Corps on the rugged west coast was Maj. Gen. Jonathan Wainwright. Command of the immensely important II Corps went to Maj. Gen. George F. Parker.

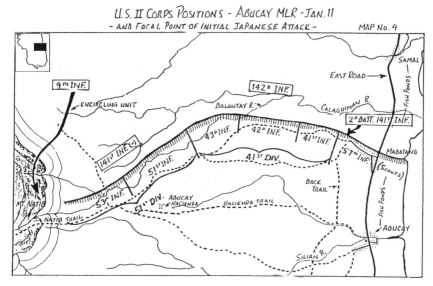

U.S. II CORPS POSITIONS - ABUCAY MLR - JAN. 11
- AND FOCAL POINT OF INITIAL JAPANESE ATTACK -   MAP No. 4

Officially the two corps formed what was called the Mauban-Abucay MLR, but realistically they remained physically divided from one another by the rugged mountainous interior of 4,000-foot Mt. Natib.

The site chosen as the westernmost anchor point of the I Corps end of the Mauban-Abucay line began near the barrio of Mauban on the shores of the South China Sea. After a rather abrupt 60-foot climb the line followed what was called Mauban Ridge eastward for about five miles before literally disappearing into the uncharted jungled vastness of Mt. Silanganan and Mt. Natib.

General Wainwright's command consisted of approximately 15,000 troops. Much of it was made up, unfortunately, from those units of the army on Bataan that had been exposed to the roughest part of the fighting both before and during the December withdrawal. The Philippine Army's contribution to the I Corps was the greatest. In it was Brig. Gen. Fidel Segundo's 1st Regular Division, Brig. Gen. Luther Steven's 91st Division, and combat elements of the 71st Division. Simultaneous to its assignment to the I Corps, the 71st, badly mauled during the withdrawal, was absorbed into the 91st Division, and its commanding officer, Brig. Gen. Clyde Selleck, was put in charge of the defense of Bataan's west coast. The only Philippine Scout unit available to Wainwright was his old regiment, the 26th Cavalry, but they too, were tired, battered, and reduced from losses suffered during the withdrawal.

On the left of this narrow, four-and-a-half-mile wide front that began at the edge of the South China Sea, was the 1st Division's 3d Infantry Regiment, yet to be tried in combat. In the center, fighting as infantry,

The U.S. MLR near Abucay liberally strung with double-apron barbed wire and antitank obstacles.

was another untested unit, the 31st Philippine Army Field Artillery Regiment. Holding down the dangling, unconnected right flank on the forbidding, jungled slopes of Mt. Silanganan was single Company K of the battered, newly arrived 1st Infantry Regiment of the 1st Division. In assigning this single, poorly trained, and nearly expended rifle company to a job that a well trained, rested, and fully equipped battalion would have found almost impossible, Wainwright had unknowingly placed the fate of the entire I Corps in jeopardy.

As for defenses, the mile-and-a-half wide sector fronting the 3d Infantry was the only area along the entire four-mile wide front protected by something other than that provided by nature. In addition to a screen of double-apron barbed wire, antitank mines and log barriers were placed at strategic locations. Additional wire was also strung and underwater obstacles placed along the shoreline for about a mile as protection against possible seaward invasion.

On the II Corps side of the peninsula (see Map 4), the important eastern end of the Mauban-Abucay line began on the edge of Manila Bay by crossing a three-quarters of a mile wide maze of man-made fish ponds. Restricting travel over them to the narrow footpaths on top of the numerous dikes that separated them offered a natural defense barrier that would be too much even for the dogged Japanese to challenge. Where the

Two Filipino plantation workers walk in after a day's work in sugar cane fields of Abucay Hacienda. The fields of "hated" cane look today as they did 50 years ago.

fish ponds ended at the East Road, the line continued west over relatively flat ground for a mile or so inland before beginning a gentle climb up the middle slopes of 4,000-foot Mt. Natib. Much of this first mile was open, dried-up rice paddies—natural in the January dry season—with an occasional clump of bamboo, jungle, or sugar cane field thrown in to complete the landscape. Responsibility for this important sector was given to the highly trained, fresh, 57th Infantry, whose anxious Scouts had yet to see action in the war. Their deployment at this vital spot was based on knowledge of the well-known Japanese tactic of attacking down the main roads when making their initial assault against an enemy position. If unsuccessful, then a systematic probe of the entire line could be anticipated until a weakness was found.

About a mile inland from the East Road, the line began its steady climb up the lower slopes of ancient Mt. Natib alluvium. The landscape began its transformation from rice to cane field, interrupted only by occasional clusters of trees and bamboo thickets. It was from here, for the next

General Vincente Lim, left, at one of his makeshift 41st Division command posts on Bataan. This one was in an old pigpen.

five miles, that the line traversed the large Abucay Sugar Plantation, known locally as the Abucay Hacienda. It was for this hacienda that the line itself was named.

The most deadly terrain feature of this area was in the form of a network of suddenly appearing, steeply eroded ravines. From the edge of a cane field the earth would open up into a densely overgrown gorge that, in spots, made infiltration easy and defense extremely difficult. The strength of the line as it crossed the fields of the hacienda came in the presence of one of those ravines, called the Balantay River gorge. Linking together about two and a half miles inland from the East Road, both the MLR and the steep-sided Balantay gorge paralleled each other until totally enveloped by the dense jungle of Natib's upper slopes.[11]

Defense of this three-and-a-half-mile wide sector went to another untried but well-rested unit, the Philippine Army's 41st Division. In command was the Philippine Army's only West Point graduate, Brig. Gen. Vincente Lim. All three regiments of Lim's division, the 41st, 42d, and 43d, were on line, from right to left, in that order. It was near the center of the 42d Regiment's sector, by the way, that the MLR joined the Balantay for its journey up Mt. Natib.

The final two and a half miles of the Abucay line was manned by Brig. Gen. Albert Jones' untried, very green, and very tired 51st Philippine Army

Fiery Brig. Gen. Albert Jones, 51st Division and later I Corps commander on Bataan.

Division. Since December 24, the 51st had been involved, although avoiding heavy combat, in the strenuous 200-mile withdrawal of the South Luzon Force. Three days after literally dragging itself into the peninsula, it was ordered to move up to positions on the MLR. It had time to neither rest nor reorganize before Gen. Parker ordered Jones into his new positions.

General Vincente Lim, one of the four Philippine Army generals on Bataan, was a West Point graduate. Lim commanded one of the toughest Philippine Army divisions on Bataan—the 41st.

The most serious problem, due to its late arrival, was the lack of opportunity to take advantage of its defensive positions. Without realizing it, Parker had mirrored Gen. Wainwright's I Corps decision in placing the fate of the entire MLR in the hands of the unit probably least qualified or prepared for the job.

Upon reaching his assigned sector, Jones placed the division's 51st and 53d Regiments on line, from right to left, respectively. Where it took over from the 43d Infantry on the north side of the Balantay River gorge, the 51st Infantry found itself faced, for the most part, with the same terrain problems as that of the 43d on its right. The difference, however, was in the preparation of the troops and positions. The 51st would be in position less than a week prior to the first attack; the 43d, over two weeks prior. The 51st was exhausted from nearly a month of pressure as part of the South Luzon Force; the 43d rode into Bataan in trucks in late December to begin work on the positions it now manned.

Where the 53d Regiment sector began on the 51st's left, cane fields had long since given way to the irregular and rugged slopes of Mt. Natib. Organization, communication, and control of the 53d soon became less and less possible. Before long, the thin, scattered string of fox holes, dug sometimes as far as 50 yards apart, disappeared completely into the almost haunting vastness of Natib's dense jungle.

U.S. antitank obstacles laid across the dried rice fields near the eastern edge of the Abucay line.

Man-made defenses along the II Corps line, like the troops who manned them, ran the gamut for completeness and effectiveness. (See Map 5.) In the 51st Division sector they were nonexistent. Neither time, tools, nor terrain had allowed for anything other than what nature and a well placed foxhole could offer. On the opposite end of the line, however, great pains were

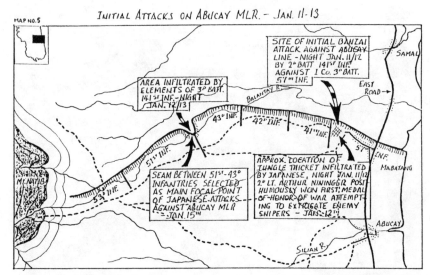

MAP NO.5

INITIAL ATTACKS ON ABUCAY MLR. - JAN. 11-13

taken to adequately fortify the routes of probable attack. From the impassable fish ponds, II Corps engineers, with help from the 57th Infantry and 41st Division troops, had fortified their positions as far west as was thought necessary. The four and a half miles between the East Road and the 41st–51st division boundary was strung with continuous strands of double-apron barbed wire. Again, only up to the boundary between the two divisions, cane fields were burned and clumps of bamboo and brush cut down in effort to clear fields of fire. In the 41st Division sector, where the natural terrain gave way to deep ravines, machine gun and antitank positions were placed on well located strong points overlooking them. The area of major concern, since it was accessible to tanks and motor vehicles, ran from the East Road inland through about a mile and a half of dry rice fields. To combat the tank threat to this area, engineers patterned the entire distance with homemade antitank mines. In addition to destroying all bridges for several miles north, the East Road was literally severed above Mabatang by four large dynamite craters.[12]

The unit held in general reserve, available to committment by need to either the I or II Corps was the Philippine Division, less the 57th Infantry, on line at Abucay. The remaining American 31st and Scout 45th Regiments could be committed only on orders from USAFFE headquarters itself.

By three o'clock on January 11, advance elements of Col. Takeo Imai's 141st Infantry, advancing steadily since their "victory" at Hermosa two days before, had reached the south bank of the Calaguiman River, less than half a mile above the actual U.S. main line at Mabatang. Although only lightly contested, the enemy's movements had not gone unobserved or unheeded. By late afternoon, word had been passed all along the II Corps front of the strong probability of an attack sometime that night.

After a last minute inspection of his II Corps' positions near the East Road that afternoon, Gen. Parker decided the tiny barrio of Samal, a mile and a half north of the MLR, should be burned to avoid its use by the Japanese as an assembly point during the upcoming battle. Since it was now inside the area of enemy control, it would not be a job without hazard. The man volunteering for the mission was a burly captain from the 1st Battalion, 57th Infantry—Arthur Wermuth, a man who was on his way to becoming a legend for his behind-the-lines and antisniper ventures.

With a five-gallon can of gasoline strapped to his back, Wermuth moved out from friendly lines shortly after 3 P.M. Staying well inland of the flat, open terrain along the East Road, by dusk he had reached the village. Finding it void of Japanese, within minutes he had its few remaining nipa huts and buildings enveloped in flames and was on his way back. To cover his return, as prearranged upon seeing the village go up in flames, II Corps artillery lobbed a dozen-or-so shells in behind him along the East Road to discourage possible pursuit by the enemy.[13]

As American and Filipino troops watched the last of Samal's fires flicker out from behind what they were confident was a well prepared position, they unknowingly had left yet another potentially dangerous assembly point to the use of the Japanese. About a mile inland from the East Road, and only 150 yards in front of the MLR, there remained an overlooked seven-acre field of uncut sugar cane that by 11 P.M. had been infiltrated by close to the entire 2d Battalion, 141st Japanese Infantry.

Holding down the half-mile wide sector directly in front of the cane field were the Philippine Scouts of I Company, 3d Battalion, 57th Infantry, with K Company on its right and the 41st Infantry of the Philippine Army's 41st Division on its left.

At eleven o'clock, I Company began receiving artillery and mortar fire from Japanese positions opposite the main line. As a precaution against a possible tank assault, a battery of U.S. 75-mm. guns, placed just behind the MLR in I Company's sector, countered almost immediately with direct fire into the now bustling cane field. Suddenly, in groups of ten and twenty, Japanese soldiers burst onto the open field, yelling "Banzai! Banzai!" as they charged.

Within seconds, the battlefield was ablaze with gunfire as every I Company weapon, including the 75s whose trails had been quickly propped-up for point-blank fire, opened up. Accurate Scout gunners soon had the onrushing Japanese tumbling in clusters. Despite this, however, the frenzied charge continued, "looking," remembered a startled American officer with 3d Battalion, "like a basic training company gone crazy on an Infiltration Course." The Japanese, although staggered, were not noticeably slowed until they reached the line of barbed wire. At this point the charge ground to a near standstill, as the first waves slowly, almost deliberately began picking their way through. Fil-American gunners were quick to take advantage of the slowdown, and within minutes had both ground and wire stacked with enemy dead. As later waves reached what was rapidly building into a wall of corpses, they were able, with little hesitation, to scramble over the top using the bodies of their own dead and dying and continue on towards the lines of tracers streaming from U.S. positions.

Overpowered by the sheer number of enemy attackers, the Scouts of both I and K Company began to fall back, forcing 3d Battalion commander, Col. Philip Fry, to commit his reserve, Company L, to the fight.

Surprisingly enough, rebounding from the effects of the Japanese breakthrough was easier than expected as once the enemy charge reached the Scout foxholes, according to Capt. Ernest Brown of the 3d Battalion, "they seemed to lose organization. . . . When they were among us they ceased to yell, the only sound we heard was their officers and noncommissioned officers shouting. However, soon there were no more officers or sword wavers to shout as their drawn Samurai swords made them most conspicuous." After the hand-to-hand struggles over individual positions, the enemy's initiative faltered, making it relatively easy to retake the lost ground. [14]

As the remaining enemy soldiers disengaged themselves and withdrew back into the darkness, firing gradually waned to an occasional shot or machine gun burst, and before long, for all practical purposes, the most desperately fought 40-minute battle of the young Pacific war was over. With senses still reeling from the noise and commotion that continued to come from the cane field for several minutes afterwards, exhausted 3d Battalion troops cautiously moved back into their foxholes to wait for daylight, still some four hours away.

The first crack at the "official" U.S. line on Bataan by the Japanese had failed as had the unusual tactic used in the attempt: the first organized Banzai attack of World War II. In fact, despite the plaguing cane field from which a battalion-scale assault had come, the Japanese had been repelled by little more than two Philippine Scout rifle companies.

With daylight, came mute evidence of the bulldogged Japanese efforts of the night before. Although the entire area in front of the cane field was littered with enemy dead, the greatest toll was visible at the barbed wire—in some places, the bodies were stacked three high. Many had been killed while trying to negotiate the barbed wire's treacherous strands or in suicidal lunges across it in efforts to form human bridges for those who followed. Inside I Company's line, particularly within the perimeter foxholes, the figure was also high. The unusually large cache of Samurai swords indicated that few Japanese officers, once past the wire, ever returned to the safety of their own lines. Perhaps the confusion that took place during the wild, close-quarter fight following the brief enemy breakthrough can best be imagined after an examination was made of the splinter shields on the battery of 75s. They had not only been peppered with bullets from in front, but from behind as well.

In one of the many wild melees that took place in the trenches that night, Scout Cpl. Narcisco Ortilano of the 57th, while working to unjam his rifle, was forced to take on a bayonet-wielding Japanese soldier with his bare hands. The charging enemy soldier lunged at Ortilano who parried by grabbing the bayonet. The tough Scout then yanked the rifle away from the startled Japanese, cutting his own little finger off in the process, then turned it on his assailant and killed him. By that time a second enemy soldier was upon him, slashing and cutting him several times before he could recover enough to kill him with the same rifle.[15]

The number of enemy dead was estimated at between 250 and 300. Although U.S. casualties had remained surprisingly low, Japanese efforts of the night were not without some reward. During the melee, a handful of enemy soldiers had successfully infiltrated a heavily jungled area behind the 3d Battalion line, and with daylight came yet another unconventional tactic the Japanese would soon become known for: sniping. No longer was there safety behind one's own lines as enemy sniper activity that morning was reported as far behind the main line as one mile. The Japanese, at times, seemed everywhere: in every tree, behind every bamboo clump, around every curve in the trail—and yet nowhere, blending in with every branch and thicket they hid behind.

By noon, following the sniper-caused deaths of several men, including two officers, a group of volunteers from the 57th's anxious but yet to be tested 1st Battalion, formed an antisniper unit that began combing the deadly thickets. "In the ensuing two trips," wrote Lt. John E. Olson, 57th Personnel Officer, "the antisniper group killed a large number of the enemy but suffered so heavily themselves that Maj. Royal Reynolds, the 1st Battalion commander, ordered them to desist." According to Olson, the officer in charge of the squad of 1st Battalion volunteers, Lt. Arthur Nininger, "rushed back for a third try." Whether it was that he sensed the location of many of the Japanese still hiding in the forbidding position, or simply that he was incensed with a fanatic determination to end the deadly harassment, unheedful of risk to his own life, no one knew. Ordering his battered squad to stand down, it soon became apparent that this young West Point officer was making a personal sacrifice that would be far above the normal call of duty.[16]

Since Nininger worked alone, much of what he did could only be surmised. What was known, however, is that most of his dangerous

Lieutenant Arthur Nininger, first Medal of Honor recipient in World War II— awarded posthumously.

task was done with hand grenades, as the only other weapon he carried was a .45 pistol.

It was also known that several Japanese positions were wiped out and that he was carrying at least two wounds before receiving the fatal shot, all in turn, indicating the reckless abandon with which he worked. Last, it is known that he received his third and fatal wound while making a headlong charge at a Japanese automatic weapon position, but not before lobbing his final grenade into it, killing the two man gun crew and an officer.[17]

Lieutenant Nininger was not found until the next day when a Scout patrol, under Cpl. Manuel Mabunga, under fire from enemy snipers still active within the thicket, discovered his still, bloodied body in the clearing in which he fell.[18]

For his heroic effort, 2d Lt. Arthur "Sandy" Nininger posthumously received the first Medal of Honor voted by Congress in World War II. (The second medal issued during the war was given to Cpl. Jose Calugas of the Philippine Scout's 88th Field Artillery Regiment for, as noted earlier, action that took place six days earlier during the delaying action near Layac Junction.)

By nightfall of the 12th, activity once again swung back to the Abucay front. To confuse and frighten the already edgy Fil-American troops, firecrackers were set off in the jungle by infiltrating enemy soldiers. This method of harassment was also accomplished from within the confines of their own lines. To do it, two small firecrackers were stuffed into cartridges in place of the bullet. A single shot aimed towards U.S. lines moments later would be interpreted by friendly troops as a pair of rifle shots fired from somewhere behind them. Although the firecracker trick was soon recognized, and before long ignored by most of the troops, the method of how and by whom they were set off continued to baffle men throughout the campaign.

By midnight, Japanese activity in and around the cane field again reached the noisy, preattack level of the night before. This time, however, the attackers were facing a much more disciplined Scout defense than they had the first time, one which would not be drawn into exposing its vital automatic weapon positions until the last second to keep the enemy from focusing their assault on them as they had on their initial attack.

Again, as on the first night, fire from Scout 75s ripped into the cane field in an attempt to smash the assault before it could be mounted. But the attack came too late.

Again the Japanese broke from the cane towards the waiting Fil-American defenders, but this assault would not attain even the minor success of its forerunner of the night before. Within minutes, the better disciplined 1st Battalion defenders, with help from several well placed artillery rounds, had the Japanese reeling and the second Banzai attack in as many nights brokenup.[19]

But the night was far from over. About an hour before dawn, the silence along I Company's front was again broken. Amidst the rumble of what sounded like hoofbeats, explosions began to occur from the U.S. mine field.

Antitank mines were being set off, but not by tanks. The Japanese instead had stampeded a herd of massive carabao, or water buffalo, across the field in front of them as they themselves came on for the second time. Banzai! Banzai! they yelled as they crossed the field amongst the confused water buffalo.

Again I Company found itself the center of the bull's-eye and was soon enveloped by a massive wave of Japanese that swept through its perimeter foxholes. The Scouts, with three officers and several NCOs dead or wounded, began to fall back.

For the moment, the line appeared broken. Anticipating the situation moments before it occurred, however, Col. Fry already had his reserve Company L moving forward when the cry for help came. His timing couldn't have been better, for as L Company troops moved forward they met the retreating I Company, whom, within minutes, they caused to turn and move forward in a skirmish line with them.

The simultaneous arrival of daylight with Company I and Company L's counterattack forced what was left of the Japanese assault force back toward their own lines. But not before a large number of enemy troops had scrambled into a densely wooded area between the 57th and 41st Infantry positions with enough men to force a small salient between the two regiments.[20]

Earlier that day, Col. Takao Imai, 141st Infantry commander, whose 2d Battalion had been involved in the unsuccessful Banzai attack the night before, repositioned his regiment some three miles further west to a position opposite the 43d–51st Infantry boundary.

Although not part of a planned coordinated effort, about the same time as the men of the Japanese 142d Infantry were making their unsuccessful charge out of the cane field against the 57th, an Imai patrol located and successfully penetrated a small gap in the outpost line between the two Filipino regiments. (See Map 5.)

Operating in small groups, the Japanese were ordered to carry on a series of hit-and-run raids as far behind the line as possible, in an effort to unnerve and confuse the defending troops into believing they were being hit by a force of major proportion.

Ironically, if there was a better place for the Japanese to have initiated such a tactic, it would not be found in this campaign. The dense, irregular, ravine-scored terrain between the two Philippine army regiments made it all but impossible to detect the infiltrators, let alone ferret them out. Also, if there was a regiment more susceptible to overestimating or overreacting to the scale of the harassing attacks than the shaken 51st, it might only have been the 53d, farther up on the rugged slopes of Mt. Natib.[21]

When word of the Japanese infiltration reached the 51st Infantry command post, its leader, Lt. Col. Loren Stewart, at dawn led a small squad into the densely wooded area after them. It didn't take long to discover why the line had been so easily penetrated. By mid-morning, the deadly combination of jungle, ravine, and enemy hit-and-run tactics had proved insurmountable to the tiny Filipino patrol. Aside from failing to accomplish their mission, the small squad also lost the courageous Col. Stewart. As he had been all morning, the regimental commander was far out in front of his men when the end came. Unfortunately, the area in which he fell remained under such intense enemy sniper fire that his body was never recovered.

Unknown to the fine 51st Infantry commander, waiting for him upon his return were orders from Gen. MacArthur elevating him to full colonel—the first battlefield commission to come down in the young battle for Bataan—as well as a Silver Star later for gallantry in the action that had taken his life.[22]

Despite the rout of some of the Japanese with a battalion-scale sweep of the dense ravines later in the day, the leading edge of what would bring about the disintegration of the entire 51st Division a few days later had penetrated the Abucay line.

By the morning of January 13, five of the six U.S. regiments on the Abucay line plus two of the three from corps reserve's 21st Division had been committed to the fight.

In reaction to the small bulge the Japanese had pushed into the line between the 57th and 41st Regiments, Gen. Parker early that morning released the 21st Infantry from II Corps reserve to Col. George Clark, commanding officer of the 57th. With the fresh 21st plus his own 2d Battalion, Clark counterattacked the enemy salient at 6 A.M. behind one of the few rolling barrages to be fired by U.S. artillery on Bataan. The attack moved along favorably until just before noon, when it was held up by the first rounds of what was to be a three-hour-long interdiction of the area by enemy artillery. At 4 o'clock, unhindered by the Japanese fire, the U.S. attack resumed and by dusk all but the final 150 yards of ground lost the night before had been regained.

For all intents and purposes, the Japanese attempts to breach the eastern end of the Abucay line, two days after it had begun, had already seen its high-water mark. The lack of success against the capable 57th and 41st, dug-in behind the best prepared positions on the entire Abucay front, brought Gen. Nara to redirect the focal point of his attacks further inland.

A further deterrent to enemy buildup behind the flat, readily observable eastern end of the line was the extremely accurate fire of the II Corps artillery.

Particularily effective was the Philippine Scout 24th F.A. Regiment, whose forward observers, directing fire from the tower of the old Abucay church, had contributed greatly to discouraging large scale troop and supply movements during daylight hours.

As the U.S. counterattack against the small salient between the 57th and 41st opened up on the morning of the 13th, elements of Col. Imai's 141st Infantry were, in the meantime, butting heads for the first time with the 51st Infantry near the opposite end.

Thinly spread along the middle slopes of Mt. Natib, Brig. Gen. Albert Jones' green, tentative outpost troops, who, along with everything else, had been in positions less than a week, were quickly forced back to the MLR on the north side of the Balantay River gorge.

The increase in enemy activity in the II Corps, meanwhile, had not gone unnoticed by Gen. Richard Sutherland back on Corregidor, particularly since his recommendation to join the Mauban-Abucay flanks had gone unheeded. The situation as it appeared at the moment prompted him to order the Scout 45th Infantry and the Philippine Army's 31st Division, on beach defense in Gen. Wainwright's I Corps, transferred immediately into II Corps reserve.

Action against the Abucay line the next day, although relatively light, was again directed against the 51st near its eastern boundary. Here, moderate pressure from the Japanese 141st Infantry forced both the 51st and the 43d, to the right of the 51st, to withdraw back across the Balantay to new positions on the south bank.

The results of the enemy's probing attacks that day had brought the Japanese command to decide that they would make their run at breaking the Abucay line at that point between the two Filipino regiments. Accordingly, dawn of the next day, January 15, saw a sharp increase in enemy pressure at the chosen spot. The seriousness of the Japanese intentions, however, had not gone unheeded by the II Corps. Both Filipino regiments had been quickly reinforced earlier that same morning, and were able, therefore, to hold the Japanese throughout the entire exhausting day to a mere toehold on the south side of the river.

Despite the unusual quiet along the Abucay front that night, things were happening on both sides of the line that would have a significant effect on the outcome of the battle.

Of the few shots fired that night on the U.S. side of the line, perhaps it was the psychological "shot in the arm" message read throughout Bataan from Gen. MacArthur that had the most effect. Although gibed at by many of the Americans, influenced no doubt by the lingering hunger pains that existed following the evening's edition of Bataan ration, most of the Filipinos throughout the command hung on the General's every word:

> Help is on the way from the United States. Thousands of troops and hundreds of planes are being dispatched. . . . No further retreat is possible. We have more troops in Bataan than the Japanese have thrown against us; our supplies are ample; a determined defense will defeat the enemy's attack. . . . I call upon every soldier in Bataan to fight in his assigned position, resisting every attack. This is the only road to salvation. If we fight, we will win; if we retreat, we will be destroyed.[23]

In the meantime, Gen. Parker, following a discouraging conversation with the 51st Division Commander, Gen. Albert Jones, who convinced him of the immediate need for reinforcements in his sector, called Gen. Sutherland. The II Corps commander was in for a surprise. Following his request for help he was told by Sutherland, who had unwittingly failed to notify him of the order that had been issued two days earlier, that the 45th Infantry and 31st Division had already been released to him. He was also told that the U.S. 31st Infantry had broken camp and was heading for the II Corps area. Parker was delighted. Envisioning, apparently, their availability the next day if necessary to back up in the 51st 43d sector, he called Gen. Jones. The 51st Division commander was ordered, with immediate support from a nearby battalion of 21st Infantry troops, to attack and restore the MLR to its original position the next morning.

Dumbfounded at first, the outspoken Jones, despite the anticipated back-up from the 21st, exploded in protest at the order, claiming that "the present position [was] being held only with great difficulty," and insisting that a counterattack would be "extremely hazardous." Despite his vociferous efforts, Parker held firm. The "weakened" 51st would go.

When Gen. Nara laid his plans for the assault against the U.S. II Corps, he assigned a reinforced regiment from the 16th Division, the 9th Infantry, under Col. Susumu Takechi, the initial job of "overwhelming" Gen. Parker's left flank. Since launching their general attack against the phantom U.S. line at Hermosa on the 9th, Takechi had literally disappeared off Japanese maps. For seven days he and his regiment had thrashed about in the jungle on the confusing eastern slopes of Mt. Natib, looking for the elusive western end of the Fil-American line. By midnight of the 15th, unknown to Takechi, he was in a position where he would reach his objective before noon the next day, in time to play an integral role in the day's events. In fact, timely appearance of the 9th Infantry would do more than make up for the seven days it spent "lost" in the Natib forest.

Dawn of January 16, the most important day thus far for either side, brought light to an interesting occurrence behind the 1st Battalion, 57th Infantry sector of the line. It was prompted by an incident that took place the morning before, after Capt. Arthur Wermuth had been shot in the leg by a sniper while walking through his battalion area.

Ever since their first attack against the eastern end of the MLR on January 11–12, the Japanese had been able to infiltrate small groups of snipers in behind the Fil-American lines. In the days following, more allied men were killed and wounded from these snipers' harassing tactics than in the actual combat that had taken place in that sector.

Evidence that this was more than meaningless harassment, however, was indicated by an examination of the equipment each sniper carried. Most brought enough food to last five days, including hardtack, a small sack of rice, a package of dehydrated or concentrated foods, coffee, rock candy, water, and vitamin pills. Items of equipment included a water purifier, quinine tablets, first aid kit, mosquito netting, gas mask with spare lenses, climbing rope, extra socks, toothbrush, gloves, and a flashlight equipped with rotating, multicolored lenses for signaling. A sniper's helmet, face, and gloves were usually camouflaged to blend in with the branches of the tree into which he customarily tied himself. Like most of the Japanese on Bataan at this time, they also carried the smaller .25-caliber rifle, whose report resembled little more than the snapping sound of an American .22-caliber target pistol. In fact, the damage inflicted, unless striking its victim in a vital spot, was often more annoying than effective. Some men on Bataan were known to have fought while carrying two or three fresh wounds. The smokeless powder used in the Japanese small arm weapons used in sniping also made detection more difficult.

Wermuth had become so infuriated by the "goddamn snipers," that on that very day he formed what he called the "Bataan Anti-Sniper Association." Over 80 eager Scouts quickly volunteered to follow the "One Man Army"—as he was becoming known because of his frequent behind-the-lines ventures—on his latest escapade.

At first light on the 16th, limping leader and all, the "Association" began the first of what was to be a week-long, systematic probe into every possible sniper position. Every tree, bush, and bamboo clump was combed. Twelve of the enemy were felled by 8:30 the first morning, and by the end of the week over 230 more, along with two machine gun positions, would be eliminated. By the end of the week, the sniper threat behind the 57th sector of the line had ceased to exist.[24]

At about the time Wermuth's special hunting party was completing the first hour of its sniper-shoot on the 16th, air corps Lt. Bill Rowe was leading five American P-40s off of Bataan Field. His mission was to fly cover over the Abucay sector while the 45th and 31st Infantries and 31st Division moved into position behind the MLR.

Swinging in from Manila Bay over the fish pond–lined shore near Abucay, who should they spot but old "Photo Joe" himself, heading for his usual perch over the U.S. line. Unfortunately for the Americans, the Japanese pilot saw them first and, before they could get within range, had disappeared into the clouds over Mt. Natib.

Although it did not appear very significant at the time, the incidental spooking of the Japanese reconnaissance plane from the sky over Abucay may have contributed more to the Fil-American cause that day than was realized. Its not being able to help direct the Japanese assault later that morning, probably contributed much to the confusion that followed.

As the five American fighters continued across the enemy side of the line, everything seemed quiet. After strafing a small convoy of trucks moving down the East Road near Orani and exchanging fire with an antiaircraft gun or two, the first flight of American fighters in over seven days returned to Bataan Field.[25]

Not long after the Americans landed, four men traveling up the East

Road near Orion were chased from their truck by a strafing Japanese fighter. In the event that followed, it is hard to say who was the most surprised, the Americans or the enemy pilot.

The men, on their way to the west coast of Bataan to pick up spare rectifier bulbs for their secret U.S. Marine–operated Air Warning Service radar, had seen the plane and made it safely to a ditch alongside the road before the first pass. Noting the fighter turn to make a second run, one of the men, army PFC "Barney" Oldfield, suddenly jumped up, aimed his rifle at the Zero—approaching this time at treetop level—and fired. As witnessed by the driver, Marine Cpl. Ted Williams, "the pilot slumped forward in the seat and the plane slammed into the ground . . . just to the left of the road," coming to a stop at the edge of a nearby cane field.

In the two years and seven months of war left against the Japanese in the Pacific, it's possible that Barney "One-shot" Oldfield's feat was never equalled.[26]

Back at the General Hospital at Limay where casualties from the fighting at Abucay had been increasing since the battle started, the surgical staff had been finding something very puzzling in some of its bullet wound cases—wooden slivers. Instead of finding the usual brass slug, doctors had extracted evidence that the Japanese were actually firing hardwood bullets that would splinter upon contact with bone. The mystery was solved one day when a souvenir-hunting ambulance driver brought in a Japanese .25-caliber rifle. Upon examination of the clip, the bullets were found to be made of wood.

For the first four days of fighting, the U.S. line at Abucay had remained relatively intact against all the Japanese could throw at it. January 16 marked the beginning of its end. But for a day that would be Japan's biggest since the battle began, it is ironic that all indications at the start pointed toward just the opposite.

Before dawn, as he had been ordered, the still-reluctant Gen. Albert Jones moved his 51st Division out against the Abucay line across a three-mile-wide front. Despite some initial heavy resistance, the 51st was quite successful. In fact, even without the expected help from the 21st, which apparently wasn't notified of its assignment and didn't show up at all, the division's 51st Infantry alone was able to force a mile-wide gap in the line to a point several hundred yards beyond their old positions on the Balantay. But their success was to be short-lived.

With the 43d Infantry on its right uncommitted in the attack and the 53d on its left bogged down near the old MLR due to the dense, impassable terrain, the 51st's aggressive advance had gullibly although innocently placed not only its own, but the entire II Corps' head into a Japanese noose. Colonel Imai, quick to recognize what the Filipinos were doing to themselves, at the appropriate moment struck at the exposed "neck" of the advance from the east, pushing a wedge of enemy soldiers in the now-exposed seam between the 51st and 43d.

About the same time on the other side of the salient, who should accidently but appropriately blunder into the exposed left flank of the 51st but Col. Takechi's no longer lost 9th Infantry. The 51st, suddenly realizing that it was being pincered, began to fall back. In fact, by noon, all semblance of what started out as a well disciplined withdrawal had given way to that of a rout. The reeling 51st, in fact, didn't so much as slow down when they reached their old positions on the MLR, leaving the Abucay line with an undefended mile and a half wide gap near its western end. (See Map 6.)

It was at this point that the rugged terrain and dense jungle of Mt. Natib's eastern slopes moved in to play their role. In the 53d Infantry sector, the regiment's commanding officer, Col. John Boatwright, in order to avoid envelopment, had been attempting the physically insurmountable task of pulling back his troops in sequence with the reeling 51st. But at every turn the terrain and jungle made it impossible to maintain contact with his troops or those of the rapidly disappearing 51st.

To allow the 53d to remain on the end of the Abucay "limb" had all the marks of a disaster. For lack of a better solution, Gen. Parker ordered Boatwright to cross over the top of Mt. Natib and join with the I Corps on the other side. And so, for all practical purposes, as it began groping its way west in search of the upper end of the I Corps line, the entire 53d Infantry ceased to exist as a fighting unit.

On the Japanese side, due to the lack of both physical and radio communications and aerial reconnaissance information, Col. Imai was hesitant to strike out after the disintegrating 51st for fear of walking into a similar trap. In fact, because of the confusing terrain, he had already been engaged in a brief fire fight with members of Col. Takechi's eager 9th Infantry, which, after seven days in the Natib forest, like a blind, hungry rattlesnake, were striking at anything that moved. He was leary too of the situation in the 43d sector, since any attempt to counterattack would no doubt come from there. Also, not knowing clearly what was happening on the 53d side of the gap brought him to make the decision to pivot east against the exposed flank of the 43d. Conceivably, had Imai continued after the 51st, it is possible that he could have forced a U.S. abandonment of the entire Abucay line within 24 hours.

After its timely attack against the exposed left flank of the 51st that afternoon, Col. Takechi's 9th Infantry was ordered to continue on as an encircling unit and to work its way in behind the II Corps line through the Silian River valley—a valley whose waters eventually emptied into the bay near Abucay. But this time their movement would be disputed in an action high up on the rugged slopes of Mt. Natib, an action that possibly saved the entire corps. (See Map 7.)

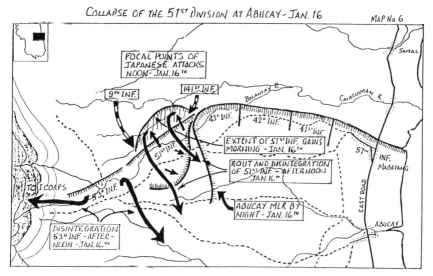

COLLAPSE OF THE 51ST DIVISION AT ABUCAY-JAN. 16   MAP No. 6

It was a maverick, makeshift unit under Lt. Ferdinand Marcos, composed of a few 21st Infantry troops, some division headquarters personnel, and a handful of 51st Division stragglers, that stopped Col. Takechi's movement down the Silian. In fact, so stubborn was the Marcos-inspired stand that the Japanese commander was forced to abandon his Silian objective altogether for the next undefended valley a few hundred yards south.

Unknown to the mapless 9th Infantry, this, the Abo Abo River valley, would lead them toward Balanga, some five miles south of their original objective, while at the same time almost neutralizing them as a major threat to the II Corps. As minor as it may have appeared at the time, the importance of this skirmish may be best understood by noting some of the reactions that followed. For his role in this action, Lt. Marcos was recommended for the Congressional Medal of Honor by his division commander, Gen. Matao Capinpin. Although never awarded because of lost affidavits during the last hectic days of Bataan, the unissued citation, prepared by the 21st Division, made note that had this action failed, the entire II Corps "would have been routed and Bataan might have fallen."

General Wainwright, as commanding general of the forces on Bataan, after hearing of the story some two months later, telephoned Marcos from Corregidor and promoted him to captain.[27]

Neither Takechi nor Marcos knew, of course, that the two men would meet again in an action almost equally as important within a few days.

And so the dense, infamous Bataan jungle, on this most important day, contributed decisively to successes and failures on both sides. It helped the Japanese position by bringing about, for all practical purposes, the disintegration of the entire 51st Division. But also it not only helped send

KEY BATTLE ON UPPER SILIAN RIVER
-JAN. 17

SITE OF KEY BATTLE ON SLOPES OF MT. NATIB BY ELEMENTS OF 21ST DIVISION. DEFLECT ENCIRCLING 9TH INFANTRY REG. FROM SILIAN RIVER OBJECTIVE TO ABO-ABO RIVER - JAN. 17TH

the enemy 9th Infantry Regiment on another temporary wild-goose chase, it forced Col. Imai, who had gained the advantage in the fight, into the predicament of not knowing quite what to do with it. Ironically, had corps, division, or Boatwright suspected that the Japanese would not push their advantage in the abandoned 51st Infantry sector, the 53d along with an uncommitted reserve battalion from the 21st Infantry, who quietly sat out the entire battle bivouacked behind the 51st Division area, could have possibly linked up with the 43d.

By noon Gen. Parker, realizing the impending seriousness of the situation, ordered the U.S. 31st Infantry Regiment to move up from their bivouac west of Balanga to a position on the left of the 43d. Within fifteen minutes, the only all–American regiment on Bataan was on its way to what was to be an exhausting seven-hour, sixteen-mile long forced march to its first and almost only combat of the entire campaign.

Later that afternoon at about the same time as the 31st reached the halfway point of its march, about twenty-five miles to the south at Mariveles, the relocated antiaircraft guns off the USS *Canopus* were frantically engaged in beating back the biggest Japanese air raid on the navy since Cavite.

By the time it was over, the section base was a shambles; one man was dead and six were wounded, four buildings were totally destroyed and six others, including three that were being used to store ammunition that miraculously did not explode, were badly damaged.

In addition, the main water line servicing the base was severed from the concrete tanks on the hill above. From then on, little that couldn't be stored inside one of the five tunnels on the base was of much value. Like the navy at Corregidor, for all practical purposes the navy at Mariveles moved inside too.

Since January 16 had gone to the Japanese, the 17th had better go to the Fil-Americans. Or so must have been the thoughts of Gen. Parker on the night of the 16th as he made preparations to restraighten the bent but not yet turned western end of the Abucay line.

At no more appropriate time in the entire campaign could two more appropriate regiments—the U.S. 31st and Philippine Scout 45th—have been called upon. Hinging on the success of their counterattack was the fate of not only the II Corps, but Wainwright's I Corps as well. An immediate major effort to regain the 51st sector before the enemy could strengthen its position and renew the attack—which would not be launched until January 22—was vital.

Unfortunately, Parker, still some 15 hours away from H-hour, had already erred. At noon he had ordered the 31st Infantry to move up to the MLR to a position on the left of the 43d. There, along with the 45th, it was to prepare to attack the next morning. For some unknown reason, however, Parker failed to notify the 45th of its role until five o'clock that afternoon.

Temporarily bivouacked near the tiny barrio of Bani and without transportation except for its heavy weapons, the 45th suddenly found itself faced with a 15-mile march on a dark night with, as quoted by Capt. Louis Besbeck of the 3d Battalion, "no moon, no stars, no signs and in places, no road."[28]

The 45th did not make it in time. In fact, it was not only late but lost—as was, therefore, the entire day's cause.

By failing on the 17th to make anything more than a piecemeal attack by one instead of both capable regiments, the fate of the Abucay line had been sealed. It was not delivered, however, until seven days later following a series of spirited but confusing and unsuccessful attempts to regain the former 51st Division positions.

Counterattack in the II Corps

"I am not sure ... just what the objective was ..."

At 8:15 A.M. on the morning of January 17, the U.S. 31st Infantry opened what was to be the first of a series of five different counterattacks involving itself and the 45th Infantry in an attempt to restore the MLR to its original position.

About an hour before the Americans reached their line of departure, the early Saturday morning quiet was interrupted by the roar of planes from the "dawn patrol" taking off from Bataan Field. Under Lt. Marshall Anderson, the flight of four P-40s' mission read: Reconnaissance and destroying installations and aircraft on Bataan.

Like the morning before, the plan was to make their initial pass over the Abucay front in an east-west direction in hopes of catching the unsuspecting Japanese out in the open. Right away they were in luck. A big dust trail was spotted in the distance rising from a back road leading to the front. Anderson and his wingmen broke off and headed for the telltale signs of what they hoped was convoy. Down below, a small, six-truck Japanese supply column was winding its way through the dry, dusty cane fields of the Abucay plantation. Suddenly the driver in the lead truck, to the astonishment of the rest of the column, swerved off the road. Before the next driver ever understood why, he was struck with a rain of .50-caliber bullets coming from two diving American fighters flying head-on at treetop level. So much dust and debris was kicked up that the convoy appeared to the two pilots, as they looked back over their shoulders, to have been blown clear off the road. The second pass left every vehicle either burning or destroyed.

In the meantime, the other two pilots, still eagerly searching for their first targets, had circled back for their second sweep over the line. This time they too were in luck. For the second day in a row, an unsuspecting Japanese reconnaissance plane had run smack into American fighters. Unlike the day before, however, there would be no escape for old "Photo Joe" this time, as the first burst from the lead P-40 sent him plummeting into the Bataan jungle.

With appetites whetted, the four planes regrouped and continued on. About twenty minutes later, with fuel and ammunition low, they spotted six enemy bombers heading down the coast, probably for Bataan Field. Unfortunately, as the Americans moved in they were seen, causing the Japanese squadron to scatter in six different directions out over Manila Bay. The best the overworked Kittyhawks could do was get in a few bursts at the departing enemy before they disappeared into the bright morning sunlight. For all their effort and anticipation, the net result of the chase was

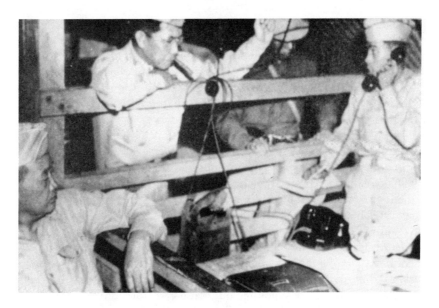

Group picture of ground crewmen and pilots of Bataan Field in front of a P-40D "Kittyhawk" taken by Gen. Harold George just before leaving Bataan in March 1942.

disappointingly recorded officially as: "Drove bombers away; Claims: 1 probable."[29]

As Anderson led his little group back to Bataan Field a few minutes later, he was shocked to see that a big white chalk circle had been placed in the middle of the runway. Although the tiny airfield had been bombed no less than 18 times since the first of January, not one Japanese bomb had hit a plane, destroyed any equipment, or wounded or killed anyone. In mockery of the enemy's accuracy, the groundcrew had placed the circle for them to use as an aiming point. It wouldn't help.[30]

That afternoon, the Japanese were back. The opposition this time would come from the Philippine Navy, not the Bataan air force. Represented solely by two British-built Q-boats, *Abra* and *Luzon*, the tiny Philippine Navy was involved in a 20 minute running gun battle with Japanese planes along the western shoreline of Manila Bay that would earn its commander, Capt. Alberto Navarette, his country's second highest award for valor—the Distinguished Conduct Star.

Navarette, witnessing a squadron of Japanese dive-bombers working over targets along the east coast of Bataan, maneuvered his two boats into position and began firing at the enemy planes.

The Japanese soon turned their attention toward the two Q-boats. It was a spectacle. The streaking, zig-zagging torpedo boats broke the serene waters of Manila Bay with half a dozen enemy dive-bombers in their wakes.

In the end it was no contest. The Q-boats were too quick for the slow to maneuver Japanese dive-bombers, and, with three of their number trailing smoke, after a few minutes they broke off the fight and headed for home.[31]

Meanwhile, over on Corregidor, intelligence personnel in the USAFFE headquarters tunnel were busy coding a long and important radio message for the chief of staff in Washington, D.C., Gen. George C. Marshall.

Two days earlier, on the evening of January 15, Gen. MacArthur, it will be recalled, had his "help is on the way" message read throughout the command. In truth, however, the troops had been more easily convinced that help really was coming than had the General himself. Although the imminent crisis that faced his command should the Japanese blockade not be penetrated had been made clear in an earlier message to Gen. Marshall, little result was yet evident. Impatient for news of what progress had been made, on January 17 he sent another message to Marshall. In this one he mentioned, among other things, that the "food situation here is becoming serious," but that he was sure that the enemy's "so-called blockade [could] easily be pierced." He also pointed out that it was "incredible" that nothing so far appeared to have been done to alleviate the critical situation.

Contrary to MacArthur's conclusions, Marshall had been working hard on the problem. In fact, on January 12 he notified MacArthur that the War Department had taken over seven converted World War I destroyers from a fruit shipping company in Louisiana. They were to be loaded with food and medicine on the west coast and sent, via Honolulu, directly to Corregidor. But that was still long-range. To placate the impatient USAFFE commander, 24 hours later Marshall sent a message notifying MacArthur of the assignment of former secretary of war Gen. Patrick Hurley to Australia with "practically unlimited funds" ($10 million in credit, to be exact), plus a $1 million reward fund for the successful blockade-running ships' crews.

Money could buy the ships and supplies all right, but could it fuel the courage of the captains and crews to go with them, and the luck needed to make it through? Time would tell. But time was something Bataan was already running out of.[32]

As mentioned earlier, the launch of the U.S. 31st Infantry counterattack at Abucay on the 17th marked the first of five consecutive days of similar attacks in that area. The action during this period was confused and repetitious.

The initial counterattack on January 17 can be summarized as follows:

January 17: U.S. 31st Infantry counterattacked in the vicinity of Abucay Hacienda on the left of 43d. [The Abucay Hacienda referred to was a small cluster of huts in a clearing near the center of the old 51st Infantry sector, used as living quarters for natives working in the surrounding fields.]

Assignments: 1st Battalion on left; 2d Battalion on right; 3d Battalion in reserve.

Action and Results: First Battalion reached objective on Balantay River; 2d Battalion met stiff resistance, falling short of same objective.

Comments: Major Eugene Conrad of the 31st's 2d Battalion commented on his battalion's progress that day: "We knew practically nothing of the terrain . . . the attacks were never coordinated. I personally do not believe the actual position of the enemy was ever discovered. The brunt of the attack was carried by the 2d Battalion but [it] was never able to restore the MLR in its sector."[33]

Major John I. Pray, commanding officer of Company G of the 2d Battalion, commented on the confusion that existed during the battalion's assault: "As soon as we crossed the line of departure, we received mortar and sniper fire. In addition a terrific cracking and banging was heard all around us. We later found it to be firecrackers developed to sound like rifle and machine gun fire. They created the impression that we were surrounded. Also it was very difficult to locate the actual snipers. We went forward about 400 yards when my left platoon was stopped by enemy machine guns sited down lanes in the sugar cane field. The right platoon, also under fire from the edge of the cane field, continued forward and finally got around the Jap flank and into a deep ravine—which was not shown correctly on the battalion commander's map. Maps were very scarce and those available were inaccurate. About five or six men had been hit. All were walking wounded since the Japs were using a .25-caliber rifle. Taking a runner, I set out to establish contact with B Company, who were supposed to be about 200 yards on the left of Trail 12. Lt. Franklin joined me. We went laterally along a cane field for about 300 yards and then turned toward the ravine [probably ravine of Balantay River]. About 10 yards from the edge of the cane field I saw an abandoned automatic rifle belt. I stopped to exchange it for my pistol belt so I could carry rifle ammunition for the rifle I had picked up. Lt. Franklin walked on ahead. He called back, 'There are two dead bodies here.' Suddenly a burst of automatic fire . . . caused me to look up. I saw Lt. Franklin stagger off to the left clutching his chest. [Later] taking two hand grenades, I went back up the trail to a slight bend and threw [them] in the general direction of the previous firing. [They] had no apparent effect for the [captured] BAR began firing. These bursts were several feet off the ground and I could crawl up to the bodies without danger. However, when I reached a point about 10 yards from [them], a sniper from a tree across the ravine also started firing. His fire was too close so I returned. I couldn't hear any sound from Lt. Franklin."[34]

Like the day before, Sunday, January 18 dawned to the sound of P-40s taking off from Bataan Field for the front. The army was scheduled to move a large supply convoy over an exposed section of the Pilar-Bagac Road at eight o'clock and had requested the air corps to cover it. As scheduled, Lt.

Bill Rowe's two-plane flight picked up the convoy's dust trail on the road near Orion.

Except for the usual cloud buildup over Mt. Natib and Mt. Bataan, the morning was clear as the planes climbed to a higher vantage point. Twenty uneventful minutes later as the tail end of the column disappeared into a jungle covered part of the road for the last two miles of its journey, the two fighters banked northward toward Abucay, "looking for trouble." It wasn't long in coming. Three Japanese planes, two dive-bombers and a fighter, working over the area behind the II Corps were jumped by the two Americans. Apparently too surprised to stay and make a fight of it, the Japanese immediately made for the clouds over Mt. Natib, but not before Rowe and his wingman scored. All three enemy planes were trailing smoke as they disappeared into the safety of the clouds over rugged Mt. Natib.[35]

The American fighters' return to the field around nine o'clock marked the beginning of what was to be a busy Sunday for not only the air force on Bataan, but the navy as well. The navy's involvement that day, in part, stemmed from the fact that lookouts on Corregidor four days earlier had spotted a convoy of Japanese heavy artillery being towed into position on the southern shore of Manila Bay. Realizing immediately what threat enemy artillery would pose on Corregidor and the other Manila Bay forts fewer than 12 miles away, Col. Paul D. Bunker, commander of the island's Seaward Defense, directed the area be shelled. But his order was overruled for fear, apparently, that indiscriminate artillery fire from that range might land in a civilian populated area by mistake. It was suggested that aerial photographs be taken so that the gun positions could be pinpointed first. On the 16th, a lone P-40 made a photo-reconnaissance run over the area, but the pictures revealed nothing.

So, on the 18th, the job of locating the guns was dropped into the navy's lap. At 5:30 that afternoon, PT-41, under the command of Ens. George Cox, after stopping at Corregidor's south dock to pick up army artillery observer Maj. Stephen Mellnik, sped across the South Channel to the southern shoreline.

For fifteen minutes, with binoculars scanning every conceivable terrain feature for the enemy guns, the 41 boat moved boldly along the shore "tempting the Japs." "When they opened fire at us," said Cox, "the major would take careful note of their position." But there was nothing—not a shot fired. Just before returning, however, an unusually large number of native bancas on a nearby beach drew the spotters' attention to a group of unsuspecting Japanese soldiers playing what appeared to be volleyball on the sand near the edge of the jungle. "A whole company of Jap infantry, no hats, stripped down to their waists, wearing white underdrawers," commented Cox. "We thought at first they were natives, and then noticed every man had on glasses, which always [gave] them away. Instead of running,

Ensign George Cox, skipper, PT-41.

curiosity got the better of them—they crowded down to the water, pointing at us, and then they began to laugh and jeer, showing their crooked monkey teeth." In seconds, the 41's .50-calibers swung into action. According to an army intelligence report the next day, guns from the 41 boat left 8 dead and 14 wounded on the beach. They also brought rather a decisive end to a volleyball game and an otherwise uneventful patrol.[36]

Back on January 1st, navy Lt. John D. Bulkeley, at that time commanding officer of Motor Torpedo Boat Squadron Three, was placed in charge of establishing a PT-boat patrol of both the west coast and Manila Bay sides of Bataan. Using the five boats of his own squadron for the former and the two remaining Philippine Q-boats for the latter, he began the official operation of his "Inside and Outside Patrol" the next night.

For that and the subsequent 15 nights, patrols remained uneventfully routine. But the 18th promised something different. Throughout the day, reports had it that a convoy of Japanese ships had pulled into Binanga Bay

Lieutenant John Bulkeley, commanding officer of Inshore Patrol and Motor Torpedo Boat Squadron Three.

near the entrance to Subic Bay in northern Bataan. Rumors placed the number of ships as high as 20, including aircraft carriers, but this number was later "officially" changed by a reconnaissance report from Gen. Wainwright's I Corps to three transports and two warships, one of which was thought to be a cruiser.

The air corps had been assigned earlier to the job of attacking the enemy ships, but delays and the arrival of darkness brought about a switch in plans. The assignment went to the PTs. Although the 31 and 34 boats were scheduled for the patrol, Bulkeley couldn't miss this one, so he assigned himself to go along on the 34 "for the hell of it."

The patrol left Sisiman at 11:30 P.M., reaching the entrance to the big bay an hour later. There the boats separated. The 31 boat, commanded by Lt. Edward DeLong, veered right along the western shore and Ens. Barron Chandler's 34 boat, with Bulkeley, moved up the eastern side. The boats were scheduled to rendezvous at the entrance to Binanga at 1:00 A.M. for the attack.

Moving in at 18 knots, the 34 was immediately challenged by a light from Biniptican Point off to the left: dash, dash, dash—the international

Lieutenant Ed DeLong, skipper of PT-31 lost on the night of January 18 in the first air raid on Subic Bay.

signal meaning "identify yourself." Chandler, throttling back a little to cut down the engine noise, continued on. Seconds later, the crew of the 34 heard what sounded like a Japanese 3-inch gun opening up from Ilinin Point on the opposite shore, and Bulkeley guessed that the 31 boat must be the target.

He was right, it was the 31. Moments after the boats separated, two of its engines stalled out from wax-sabotaged gasoline, a familiar problem the crews had been fighting since moving to Bataan. Dead in the water, within a few minutes the current had carried the 31 boat onto a nearby reef, which would become its final resting place. It was about that time that the gun from Ilinin Point, which Bulkeley had heard, cut loose.

The 34 boat, in the meantime, had been challenged by a second light that appeared to come from a small boat off its port beam: dash, dash, dash. But again it was ignored as Chandler turned to cross the bay just below Grande Island. Moments later, Grande Island's light challenged. Same signal, same response. Only this time, in answer to the Americans' disregard, the Japanese responded with fire from several nearby shore batteries. The shots, however, were probing and wild, but flashes from the

Sisiman Bay on the southern tip of Bataan as it looked in 1981. This cove was the home of Lt. John Bulkeley's famous Motor Torpedo Boat Squadron Three, the expendables. The Philippine Navy's Q-boats also docked here.

Sisiman Bay on the southern tip of Bataan. PT boats from John Bulkeley's Squadron Three tied up in the cove on the left.

guns lit up the dark night enough to guide Chandler to the rendezvous point near the mouth of Binanga Bay. It was 1:10 A.M., but no 31 boat. Thirty minutes later, with still no sign of DeLong, Bulkeley ordered Chandler to go in alone.

About a quarter of a mile inside the bay, what appeared to be a large freighter blinked at the PT boat for identification. This time the Americans would answer. With throttles full forward, the 34 leaped in the water toward the enemy ship. Moving within range, Chandler ordered both tubes fired, and then the boat turned and headed out. An explosion behind them about a minute later indicated that the first torpedo had hit the target. But the second torpedo, to the horror of the crew, was still hung up in its tube. In a few seconds, with their way illuminated by the now-exploding enemy freighter, the boat cleared the entrance to the bay and disappeared into the darkness.

Once outside, Chandler throttled back, allowing Chief Torpedoman John Martino to put a bear hug on the still running torpedo, then calmly to close off the air valve leading to the motor's combustion chamber. The propeller sputtered and then stopped. But the possibility of the torpedo exploding while hanging precariously out of its tube like a half-extracted tooth still existed. After a set number of revolutions, like cocking a pistol, it automatically armed itself. Once in that state, a blow with a force of less than 10 pounds could set it off. Again Martino was Johnny-on-the-spot; this time he fed a role of toilet paper into the prop vanes, which in seconds were clogged and stopped for good. To everyone's relief, four hours later the big tinfish broke loose and fell harmlessly into the sea.

It was a little after 7 A.M. when the 34 boat pulled into Sisiman Bay from where it had embarked nearly eight hours earlier. The first venture of the Inshore Patrol into Subic Bay since the campaign opened, as well as being fruitful, had also won its commanding officer, Lt. John Bulkeley, the Distinguished Service Cross.

Fate, meanwhile, had dealt a different hand to the 31 boat. Finding himself hung up on the reef after losing power, Lt. DeLong had spent the next three hours futilely trying to back his ship off the reef. By 3 A.M. with the clutches burned out it was over. As the boat perched conspicuously on a pile of rocks practically in the middle of enemy-held Subic Bay, the crew's fight to save themselves was now against daylight.

Ordering the 31 abandoned, DeLong piled his 12-man crew onto a makeshift raft (actually the engine-room canopy), while he went about setting fire to the ship. Ten minutes later, with the boat ablaze behind him, he prepared to join his crew. To the young lieutenant's surprise, however, the raft and its oarless occupants by then had been carried a hundred or so yards to the south by the current. DeLong yelled out, but heard no reply. He could wait no longer. With the ship's small arms ammunition beginning to explode all around him, he dove into the water and headed for shore.

Ironically, at about that same time, 9 of the 12 crewmen on board the raft, fearing that they would not be able to reach shore before daylight, also decided to swim for it. The remaining three men, including the boat's second officer, Ens. William Plant, were sadly never seen again.

Meanwhile, DeLong, reaching shore after an exhausting swim, started south along a deserted stretch of beach. Around 6 A.M. much to his delight, he came across the footprints left by the rest of the crew where they had come out of the water. Following them up the beach, he soon discovered the nine men hiding behind a clump of bushes.[37]

A few hundred yards south of where the exhausted crew was holed-up, a fire-fight erupted that went on throughout most of the day. The battle PT-31's crew was hearing had actually been going on for nearly four days.

Because of the stiff resistance the Japanese were meeting in their attempts to crack the Abucay side of the U.S. line, Gen. Homma, on January 13, decided to double his efforts against the west coast, making the I Corps his main objective. Orders were for his army, after reaching Bagac, to complete an encirclement of the II Corps by driving east across the Pilar-Bagac Road—an action that could force abandonment of the entire east coast.

On the morning of January 16, a beefed-up 5,000-man enemy force, made up principally of one regiment of the 65th Brigade, the 122d, and the 2d and 3d Battalions of the 16th Division's 20th Infantry, prepared to move into assault positions near the small barrio of Moron, northernmost of the road-connected villages on Bataan's west coast. Under the command of Maj. Gen. Naoki Kimura, the plan was simple: The 122d would strike at the center of the U.S. line along the West Road, while at the same time the 3d Battalion, 20th Infantry, would move high up into the Natib-Silanganan forest and work its way in behind the I Corps positions on Mauban Ridge.

Early that morning, as the lead column of the 122d Infantry neared Moron, it was spotted. Elements of the 1st P.A. Division's 3d Infantry were ordered to attack the village, with a mounted troop of 26th Cavalry Scouts, under the command of Capt. John Wheeler, moving in as advance guard.

The tiny village of Moron was considered vital because of the Batalan River that emptied into the South China Sea immediately above it. It was the only sizeable river between Japanese and U.S. lines on the entire Bataan west coast. General Wainwright felt that if Moron could be secured before the Japanese arrived, the natural defense obstacle it presented could help stop the enemy advance.

With Wheeler in command, E Company of the 26th Cavalry moved out on horseback for Moron just after noon. Sharing command with Wheeler was Lt. Edwin Ramsey, whose platoon of 27 exhausted, but game, Scouts led off up the trail toward the village.

Japanese troops move past an abandoned sector of the U.S. Pilar-Bagac line. The sharp, pointed bamboo stakes were used in place of barbed-wire.

As the men riding point reached the village, Ramsey ordered the remainder of the company to follow. Moron, which a few minutes earlier had been blasted by a preattack bombardment, was deserted and hauntingly still. Just as the point men disappeared behind the Catholic church in the center of the village, there was an outburst of rifle and machine gun fire that sent the Scouts galloping back. They had run headlong into leading elements of the Japanese 122d Infantry who themselves had just crossed the river and were entering the village.

Ramsey quickly deployed his platoon into foragers, a cavalry formation similar to an infantry skirmish line. Seconds later the Scouts charged. Suddenly, as the unsuspecting Japanese moved forward toward the center of the village, over two dozen mounted horsemen, guns blazing, came charging around the corner of the church launching what would be the last cavalry charge in United States military history; within seconds the startled enemy was scattering in all directions.

The impetus of Ramsey's unexpected assault took them clear through the village to the edge of the river, where they quickly dismounted. Leaving a squad to block the Japanese from escaping, the young lieutenant led the rest of his men back into Moron to search for stragglers. Finding themselves under heavy sniper fire from both sides of the street as they worked their way back through the village, Ramsey sent a rider back to Capt.

Wheeler for help. It wasn't long in coming, as Wheeler had already begun moving up at the unmistakable sound of Japanese machine gun fire.

An interesting event occurred as Wheeler reached the wall of the church. Unbeknownst to Ramsey, Gen. Wainwright had his trusted chief of staff, Col. William Mahar, ride in with E Troop to report on the results of the assault. Under heavy fire, Ramsey saw an unidentified American officer against the wall of the church. "Hey, you yellow son of a bitch, get over here and fight," he yelled, at which point the man quickly disappeared.

Although Ramsey unknowingly yelled at Mahar, there only as an observer, Wheeler thought it was directed at him. "This prompted me," he said later, "to try to get myself shot just to prove Ramsey wrong."

At this point, the story of what followed is from the official "action report" filed by Capt. Wheeler himself, who, by the way, would not only get the wound he wanted, but the Distinguished Service Cross as well:

> Ramsey had taken cover in a ditch behind some coconut trees. One man was dead and three wounded.
> At that point Pvt. Pedro Euperio, a 19-year-old Scout, spotted three soldiers wearing Philippine Army uniforms. He moved forward until they saw him and fired, then he shot quickly—they were Japanese disguised as Philippine officers. Euperio was shot in the arm. The last time I saw him he was drenched with blood, propped against a house, pistol in his good hand, directing us how to move up, indicating points under enemy fire.
> We attacked first straight through to the beach. We fired where we heard fire and were happy to see when we went through the bushes that there were dead Japanese. We got straight through to the water, reorganized and attacked around Ramsey, using him as a pivot, sweeping south and killing them under houses, in trees and under bushes. About 20 broke, throwing down all equipment, even guns, in the high grass. I was surprised to see two of my men with bullet holes through their helmets, yet unscratched. I had Private Gonzalez behind me and as I went along I grabbed the Jap maps, compasses and so forth, handing them to Gonzalez. Then there was a lull.
> Ramsey and I saw three inert Japanese. Two were dead—the third had been hit in the thigh and shoulder. He would make a begging sign, pull open his shirt and pull a bayonet point toward his chest. He may have been told we killed all Japanese by torture, but I think he was just in terrible pain. We tried to give him water, and I left him my canteen.
> Suddenly we heard a machine gun from the river and all hell broke loose again. We realized that we had been fighting an advance group and that a battalion was forming across the river. We fought in small groups, every man for himself. Sergeant Tolentino ran forward under heavy fire and threw a grenade into a house that had been giving us lots of trouble. Later he grabbed a light machine gun and began chasing a squad of Japanese down the road, moving in on them alone and without fear. I grabbed a rifle and followed him. We had no cover but it seems to me if you run around and fight hard you don't get hurt—you keep moving aggressively and it's the best defense.

I hit one Jap who was trying to shoot Tolentino. He twisted, squirmed and finally ended hanging over a fence. Sergeant Tolentino closed in on one flank while I went around the other, shooting another Jap. Just then his companion leaned around behind a tree and shot me in the leg. Sergeant Tolentino had been shot too. About that leg wound of mine, have you ever been kicked in the leg by a horse? It felt just like that. Knowing how it feels is a great satisfaction—doesn't leave anything unknown to fear.

Moron became a hail of bullets that never stopped. There were so many in the air that if you put out a sheet in five minutes it would have been riddled. We were outshooting them and could, any day. We fought all day. I can remember running through fire behind some little houses trying to get a drink but all the pumps were dry. Our lips were so swollen we could hardly talk. The Scouts were loyal to the *n*th degree. All they said were things like: "Don't go there, sir, I will go," and "They are shooting from that, sir, be careful." Late that afternoon my mission had been accomplished, the town was held adequately and I was to fall back again in reserve.

We slipped out on a trail south along the beach. Moron was held for 24 hours after our withdrawal, and the final withdrawal was by order, not by Japanese action.[38]

Meanwhile, with the battle below them still raging, Lt. DeLong and his crew waited hopefully for the opportunity to skirt the section of enemy-controlled beach between them and safety. But it would not come. Before the afternoon was over it was obvious that the Japanese lines had held firm, bringing the young lieutenant to all but "abandon any hope of making it around the beach" that day. Spirits were buoyed again later though after two small native bancas were discovered hidden amongst the bushes on the edge of the shoreline.

At 8 P.M., with a Japanese patrol spotted moving up the beach in their direction, they shoved off. Jury-rigged for sail with pieces of rope, barbed wire, and hunks of canvas scrounged up off the beach, in a few minutes the boats were safely through the surf and heading south. About an hour later, however, escape efforts were dampened when a sudden gust of wind capsized both boats. After a great deal of effort the bancas were finally righted. With masts and sails gone, and only two paddles left, DeLong placed the smallest boat in tow and headed south once again.

For six agonizing hours, alternating paddlers on the half hour, the 31 boat crew crept along Bataan's western shoreline. Finally, at 3 A.M., pointing toward the dark headland he recognized as Napo Point, the skipper ordered the exhausted crew to at last turn for the beach. A few feet off shore the men slipped over the sides and waded onto a narrow ribbon of sand below what they hoped was Napo Point. Although Napo Point, if that's where they were, was well behind friendly lines, DeLong decided to wait for daylight before attempting to make contact with anyone on shore.

Filipino soldiers of the 2d Battalion of the 92d Infantry Regiment, who had moved into position on Napo Point seven days earlier, had just finished their morning ration of rice and salmon gravy when the report came in that two native bancas and a small group of men had been spotted on the beach below. A few minutes later when the sailors neared the top of the trail they were greeted by a grinning Filipino soldier, whose first words were "Hey, Joe—got a cigarette?" They'd made it. An hour later, as guests of the 2d Battalion, they sat down to their first meal in almost two days.[39]

By dawn that same morning high up in the rain forest of Mt. Silanganan, 700 Japanese soldiers from the 3d Battalion, 20th Infantry, as ordered, had successfully worked their way in behind the I Corps line at Mauban Ridge. Under the command of Lt. Col. Hiroshi Nakanishi they had slipped unchallenged during the night between the abandoned foxholes of a company of the Philippine Army's 31st Field Artillery, in position as infantry, and single Company K of the 1st Infantry, 1st Division, anchoring the easternmost end of the line. (See Map 8.) The error of having left the responsibility of defending the vital upper end of the entire I Corps MLR to just two Philippine Army rifle companies would prove disastrous. Under building enemy pressure from both flanks that night, the two companies had withdrawn without orders from their positions without as much as firing a shot. Their commanders, each accusing the other of "withdrawing first," would later be court-martialed for "misconduct in the face of the enemy," resulting in their dismissal from the Philippine Army right on Bataan.[40]

The presence of the single battalion of Japanese, at that moment preparing to throw a roadblock across the West Road, would itself do much to decide the fate of the entire I Corps just five days later. (See Map 9.)

While things began to unfold on the western side of the peninsula on the 18th and 19th, results of the second and third U.S. and Scout counterattack against the Abucay line, in the meantime, had gone like this:

> *January 18* [second day]: Patrols report sighting Japanese troops [9th Infantry Regiment] on upper Abo Abo River.
> Assignments: 31st and 45th Infantry resume counterattack in hacienda area with 31st on right and 45th on left.
> *Action and Results:* 1st Battalion 31st and 3d Battalion 45th reach objectives on Balantay River; 2d Battalion 31st and remainder of 45th still short of river by nightfall.
> *Comments:* As was noted earlier, the Scout 45th Infantry Regiment, who was ordered to attack with the U.S. 31st Infantry on January 17 to straighten out the line in the 51st Division sector, did not make it in time. Captain Louis Besbeck, executive officer with the 45th's 3d Battalion,

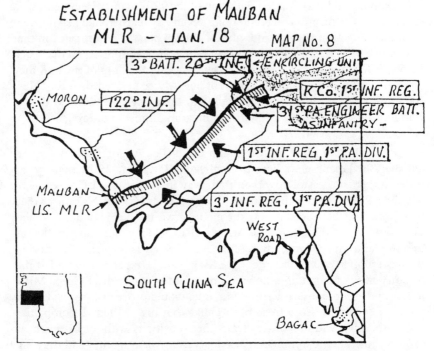

ESTABLISHMENT OF MAUBAN
MLR - JAN. 18   MAP No. 8

commented on the trials of his unit on the 17th and 18th: "On the morning of 17 January, [when the] 31st Infantry attacked, the 3d Battalion 45th Infantry still had some three and a half miles to go over rough country to arrive at the battle position. The 3d Battalion was a singing outfit. The soldiers liked to sing Filipino rice-planting songs as they marched. But with the long march across rough hills, dry rice paddies, rocky streams, each soldier carrying 80 pounds of machine gun ammunition, there was no singing. At 1200 the 3d Battalion moved out with the 2d Battalion a half mile to the east and the 1st Battalion lost far to the west. For the next seven days the 3d Battalion had no contact with any other combat unit of the regiment.

"At dawn on the 18th, the leading column of the 3d Battalion 45th Infantry moved out to an assault position to the rear of the 31st Infantry, 1,000 yards east of the hacienda. The second column on the trail was awake at daybreak to see two P-40s [Lt. Bill Rowe's action already noted] jump three Japanese planes and shoot down one over Abucay. The Air Force was visible for the first time and things looked brighter.

"Though the plan had been to commit the three battalions on the right of the 31st, enemy pressure made it necessary to send the 3d Battalion, 45th Infantry to the left. Leading elements were to reach and clean out the seven one-story buildings of the hacienda, then turn 90 degrees to the right and attack due north on a total front of about 500 yards.

"The attacking battalion moved out at 12:00 as planned. The point had moved out about 300 yards across open fields when a single shot from

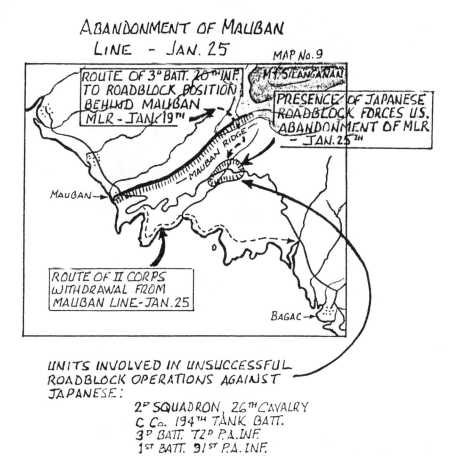

ABANDONMENT OF MAUBAN
LINE - JAN. 25   MAP No. 9

ROUTE OF 3ᴰ BATT. 20ᵀᴴ INF.
TO ROADBLOCK POSITION
BEHIND MAUBAN
MLR - JAN. 19ᵀᴴ

MT. SILANGANAN

PRESENCE OF JAPANESE
ROADBLOCK FORCES U.S.
ABANDONMENT OF MLR
- JAN. 25ᵀᴴ

MAUBAN RIDGE

MAUBAN

ROUTE OF II CORPS
WITHDRAWAL FROM
MAUBAN LINE - JAN. 25

BAGAC

UNITS INVOLVED IN UNSUCCESSFUL
ROADBLOCK OPERATIONS AGAINST
JAPANESE:

        2ᴰ SQUADRON, 26ᵀᴴ CAVALRY
        C Co. 194ᵀᴴ TANK BATT.
        3ᴰ BATT. 72ᴰ P.A. INF.
        1ˢᵀ BATT. 91ˢᵀ P.A. INF.
        2ᴰ BATT. 92ᴰ P.A. INF.

the left front brought the point man down with a hole in his head. The point pulled back and a flank patrol was sent out. The point moved out again and completed the occupation of the buildings without resistance. The three rifle companies faced north and attacked. Under the impetus of eighteen firing machine guns and 550 determined Philippine Scouts, the battalion gained its objective by 1630. The first meal in 36 hours arrived about 2100."[41]

Captain Henry Pierce of the 3d Battalion's Company L, felt differently about the operation: "The lack of adequate maps of the area and the fact that all communications were by runner brought about the complete failure of the operation, even though the objective was finally secured."

Late that afternoon, just 100 yards short of their objective, L Company along with the rest of the 3d Battalion was abruptly ordered to break off the attack. Wrote Pierce of the puzzling order: "The 45th Infantry Regimental Headquarters, upon hearing that the objective was about to

Captain Henry Pierce with the 45th Infantry Regiment on Bataan.

be taken, had ordered the battalion to withdraw. The reason for this decision was never discovered. Only timely intervention by II Corps Headquarters, who ordered the attack reopened, saved the day for the 3d. By
nightfall, the old 51st Infantry foxholes along the Abucay line were once
more occupied by friendly troops.

"Enemy fire was very heavy for the rest of the night. There was no
possible way of evacuating the wounded soldiers that night because contact with the battalion CP had been completely broken. Their screams,
easily heard over the small arms fire, was hard on the morale of the troops.
When an attempt was made to remove the company dead, effective [en-
emy] automatic weapons fire was heard from the high ground to the left
flank. The men [had to be] buried in their foxholes."[42]

January 19 [third day]: Second sighting of troops on Abo Abo.
Requested tank support for counterattack. Refused, unsuitable terrain.
[This was the third time during this battle that a request for tanks was
denied.]

Assignments: 31st and 45th Infantry Regiments renew attempts to
straighten line.

Actions and Results: 3d Battalion, 45th Infantry, on exposed left flank of line, under increased pressure all day; 2d Battalion 31st and remainder of 45th reach Balantay. [Entire line now restored up to south bank of river.]

Comments: Major Eugene Conrad of the U.S. 31st, wrote the following comments about the days activities on the Abucay: "On January 19th we made what was almost a coordinated attack. [It] started about 1600 and ended at 1900 in much confusion. The objective was not taken. I am not sure to this day just what the objective was except the enemy. The attack was not coordinated. Communication, as always, was extremely poor. The terrain was rugged and heavily wooded and for communication we had to depend almost entirely on messengers. We received no artillery support whatsoever, our mortars were extremely ineffective and we had requested tank support but it was refused. We were attempting to fire three-inch mortar ammunition in 81mm. mortars. If three rounds out of ten detonated we were very lucky. Eighty percent of the hand grenades we received were practice grenades. Half of the remaining 20 percent had faulty detonators and would not explode."[43]

Captain John Pray of Company G of the 31st, wrote of the confusion that occurred within the company level that day and night: "G Company moved out between E and F Company's. By noon E and G were in the ravine and F was on the near side in contact with the 3d Battalion, 45th Infantry. We waited about an hour and nothing happened. I sent a runner to E Company to see what was happening. After another hour I went myself to see what was happening. When I reached E Company, I found only about a squad. They didn't know where the rest of the company was. A while later Major O'Donovan, Battalion Executive Officer, came back and said 'Attack at once.' It was now about 1700. By 1800 the squad columns started up the side of the ravine. At one point we scaled vertically about 20 feet . . . using rifles to hoist or pull each other up. It was dark when we arrived at the top. Time now about 2100. We were directly on the flank of a mango grove in a draw about 15-feet deep and could hear Japs talking. I sent a runner back with instructions to go to the other group, give them the information we had and to tell them that when they were ready we would join in. We could also hear the other group. The runner went part way back through the draw then stopped, and called 'Sergeant Fortune, Captain Pray is in the draw over here. When you are ready he is.' A burst of fire caught the runner in the leg. He tumbled into the draw and had to be evacuated. A Jap voice said in good English, 'Over this way, Sergeant'."[44]

During the five nights the Americans and Filipinos spent in the old 51st positions at Abucay, the Japanese waged a continuous war of infiltration and harassment. Of one of those nights, January 19, Maj. Louis Besbeck of the 45th's 3d Battalion wrote: "Small groups infiltrated into the center of the battalion area and fired tracer bullets from automatic weapons during the night. Other Japs to the rear of the position then replied with more tracers, emulating a fire fight. They discharged large firecrackers which produced the hollow sound of discharging mortar projectiles. Japs blew bird whistles all night long. Fires started up in the sugar cane to the rear. Long range machine gun and mortar fire fell on the rear areas. Long strings of Jap firecrackers dropped by airplane with delayed fuses would start popping at different times from all parts of the position.

The firecrackers duplicated the crack of the Japanese small-bore ammunition. The Filipino soldiers were disturbed by these tricks the first night. But by the second night, the veteran garrison soldiers had become battle veterans. Firecrackers and bird-calls were wasted on them. The Japanese fired many red flares at night from all about the battalion position. Whenever they fired a flare, Company I fired several more."[45]

Throughout the campaign, "official" communiqués were sent daily from Gen. MacArthur to the War Department in Washington as part of the normal routine. Although these reports supplied the main source of information on what was happening on Bataan and Corregidor, wartime censorship altered or concealed many of the details from the public. It is interesting because of this to occasionally match one of these "watered down" versions with the real thing. MacArthur's report number 64, of January 18, in contrast to the activity of that same date reported above, read like this at home:

> Enemy pressure on American and Philippine positions in the Bataan Peninsula has lessened. Combat operations, which have been very active for the past two days, have largely subsided. Repeated enemy thrusts have been parried. Several sharp skirmishes to reestablish our troops' positions were successful.[46]

That evening, men listening to Maj. Carlos Romulo's nightly Voice of Freedom radio broadcast on Bataan heard the story of the heroic but tragic death of air corps Lt. Marshall Anderson earlier that day.

Two days earlier, information was received at Col. George's headquarters above Bataan Field of the arrival of four P-40s from Mindanao sometime within the next 48 hours. Anticipating that they would arrive low on fuel and therefore impotent to enemy fighter attack, George assigned two P-40s to fly a daylight reconnaissance south of Bataan and escort them in when they arrived.

Having failed to show up on the 19th, Anderson and Lt. Jack Hall took off from Bataan Field the next morning to patrol again for the incoming planes. About ten minutes out, the two men were jumped by three Japanese fighters. Hall immediately paired off with one of the enemy planes, leaving Anderson on his own with the other two. Giving up his tail to one while he concentrated on the other, the young lieutenant quickly scored. But doing so cost him his own plane.

The air battle, in the meantime, had drawn considerable attention from the ground. Troops had cheered wildly when the first Japanese plane burst into flames. The appearance of a little white parachute moments later from out of the smoking American fighter, however, brought sudden silence from the spectators. As Anderson floated slowly down toward his

Lieutenant Marshall Anderson, machine-gunned by a Japanese fighter while floating to the ground in a parachute.

beckoning comrades, the Japanese fighter came roaring in toward the helpless pilot with all guns blazing, its gunfire collapsing his chute. Moments later, amidst an outburst of four-letter words and fist-shaking gestures directed toward the fleeing enemy plane, the lifeless body of 1st Lt. Marshall J. Anderson of Oklahoma City, Oklahoma, already the holder of a Distinguished Flying Cross, was picked up by some American soldiers near Real Point on Bataan. The next day he was buried in the small military cemetery located less than 50 yards from the edge of the fighter strip at Mariveles.[47]

It was a sad moment for the little Bataan air force. Anderson, a quiet, serious young man of 26, would be missed. And so, for that matter, would his plane. Its loss had momentarily cut the number of available P-40s to seven. But the day was not to be entirely without its bright side for the air corps.

At 8:30 that same night, guided by two rows of landing flares marking the outer edges of tiny Bataan Field, three of the anticipated four Mindanao P-40s that were due to arrive earlier set down on the gently sloping red earth runway of the recently converted rice valley.

For the planes' pilots, lieutenants Ed Woolery, Bob Ibold, and Dave Obert, this had been a return flight. Originally they had been part of the nine plane group that was mistakenly ordered to Mindanao from Bataan following the unsuccessful intercept of Japanese bombers over Corregidor back on January 4. In fact, following their totally unexpected arrival at Mindanao, where, according to Lt. Obert, they were treated like "truant schoolboys," they did nothing but work on their planes and fly long, uneventful reconnaissance missions.

On January 18, an order came down to Del Monte Field on Mindanao from Gen. MacArthur's headquarters on Corregidor to send four P-40s back to Bataan immediately. Although most of the eight pilots believed it would be a one-way trip, all drew cards to see who would go. Since it was a job nobody wanted, it would go to the four holders of the lowest cards.

The next morning, the four "unlucky" pilots took off. Somewhere north of Cebu, the plane piloted by Lt. Gordon Benson lost power, forcing him to bail out. If anyone could make it though, it was Benson. This was the third P-40 the luckless young American had lost since the war started. About 250 miles later near the southwest corner of Mindoro Island, the three remaining pilots made plans for an emergency fuel stop at Waterous Field, San Jose. Unsure that the airstrip was still in friendly hands, they buzzed the field, bringing a group of waving Americans out onto the runway. On the ground they were warmly greeted by Lt. Ed Baggett, who, with a detachment of 60 men, had been assigned to Waterous in mid–December and then seemingly forgotten. These were the first planes to use the field since that time.

The refueling process at the little field was slow, delaying the take off until late afternoon. The arrival of the three Kittyhawks on dimly lit Bataan Field that evening boosted the combat aircraft availability of the tiny air force by a whopping 30 percent.[48]

As the two Philippine Division regiments struggled to restraighten the western end of the Abucay line, another regiment was engaged in equally interesting activities—the 41st Division's 41st Infantry was undertaking the defense of the "quieter" eastern end of the line. For its bulldogged efforts against the Japanese between January 15 and 18, the regiment would earn itself a Presidential Unit Citation.

Specific comments about the 41st come from Maj. William E. Webb, an American instructor with the regiment, who noted that its very first exposure to combat, on the morning of January 12, was nearly marred by tragedy. While counterattacking to regain ground lost to the Japanese the night before, the regiment just barely missed being shelled by friendly artillery. The blue denim uniforms worn by Philippine Army troops "presented an unfamiliar sight in the adjacent 57th Infantry sector and at first were believed to be enemy forces by artillery observers."

Japanese air and artillery attacks throughout the daylight hours of January 14 "became so devastating on the exposed positions of the regiment, that its frontline companies were withdrawn to the support line south of Dalahetan Creek. By 2000 hours, 550 casualties had been taken by the regiment. It was estimated that 400 enemy 105-mm. shells had fallen within a 400-yard circle of the regimental CP during the day."

Three times in three consecutive days, the regiment vainly tried to regain their positions on the MLR, each attempt meeting with failure. The report for January 16 was typical of how things had gone: "The counterattack jumped off at 0600 hours and was partially successful. The 1st Battalion [on the right] regained its positions on the MLR, but the 2d and 3d Composite Battalions, reinforced by the 3d Battalion, 32d Infantry, was unable to advance. This was partly due to the lack of friendly artillery and mortar support. Enemy attacks by artillery and air increased intensity. All requests for air support and antiaircraft protection were answered with 'not available.' Again the 1st Battalion was withdrawn."

The Japanese, who had successfully infiltrated the heavily wooded bottom of Dalahetan Creek, could not be driven out until U.S. artillery could be brought into use. It finally came on the morning of January 18. Only five minutes of fire from the regiment's field artillery battalion was needed. "At 0625," wrote Webb, "a forward observer in a very exposed position brought the fire down with excellent results. Five minutes later the assault forces rushed both flanks. The fight was short-lived. The enemy was driven out leaving over 300 dead. . . . The main line was back in the hands of the 41st Infantry Regiment.

"The Presidential Unit Citation was awarded the 41st . . . for its action in the defense of the Abucay line."

Webb later wrote in a criticism all too familiar to those versed in the futile defense of the Abucay position: "It was never anticipated that unhampered air activity on the part of the enemy could be so effective in denying the infantry their most valuable and powerful support arm, the artillery."[49]

The achievements of January 18 and 19 in the Hacienda sector of the Abucay line by the 31st and 45th Infantry Regiments unfortunately were to become the high watermark of the U.S. counterattack in the II Corps.

For the next two days, neither regiment could successfully mount or maintain a counterattack over the irregular, confused, densely vegetated terrain. The one attack that nearly materialized on January 20 served to show again the futility of trying to conduct offensive operations under the existing circumstances. Lieutenant Henry Pierce of the 45th Infantry wrote of the attack:

> On 20 January, one company of the 3d Battalion, 31st Infantry, was ordered to clear out the ravine by an enveloping movement around the left

flank of the 1st Battalion of the 31st Infantry. Due to the lack of communications, the [3d/31st] Battalion was not told that the 3d Battalion,
45th Infantry was on the left flank, nor was the 3d Battalion, 45th Infantry
told that the attack was going to be made. This resulted in an element of
this battalion engaging in a fire fight with Companies I and L of the 45th
Infantry. This action failed to clear the ravine.[50]

The disappointing failure to restore the line by what was thought to
be the best the Bataan Army could offer was frustrating as well, of course,
as critical. For several reasons, however, the "best" really hadn't had it that
way. Most damaging to their efforts was the lack of organic support. Of
these, probably the most glaring inadequacy was in communications. In the
dense, baffling terrain, radio or telephone communication between units
was c rucial. Yet most if not all frontline messages had to be hand carried
by runners. All arrived late; many failed to be delivered; few were
acknowledged. Therefore, few attacks remained coordinated beyond their
H-hour. Another void, of course, was the lack of supporting artillery.
Mostly because of the continuous presence of Japanese planes overhead,
not one single counterattack during the entire five day period was prefaced
or supported by U.S. artillery. "If friendly artillery," commented Maj.
Everett Mead of the 31st, "so much as fired a round, the Japanese were on
them like a swarm of bees."[51] Tank suport also was neither made available
nor offered by its commander, Brig. Gen. James R. N. Weaver, during this
most crucial time. The combination of sparse cover and total domination
of the air by the Japanese Air Force would be like "sending an elephant to
kill flies," wrote Weaver.

While making plans for his counterattack against the western flank of
the Abucay line, Gen. Nara had purposely omitted the 9th Infantry Regiment. To be exact, at that particular moment, he wasn't really sure where
they were. In fact, it is possible that the 9th Infantry didn't either. But the
Americans and Filipinos did. On January 18 and 19 the Japanese, as stated,
were spotted moving down the Abo Abo River, well behind the II Corps
line.

With the first sighting on the January 18, Gen. Parker brought Brig.
Gen. Clifford Bluemel's 31st Division along with a battalion from the 21st
Infantry, both from corps reserve, up to intersecting positions west of the
barrio of Guitol. There they joined remnants of Gen. Jones' 51st Division,
who, since their flight from Abucay three days before, had become the
covering force in that area.

Of all places for Takechi's force to come out, the Guitol barrio, within
a half a mile of the junction of five key trails, posed the most serious threat
to the Fil-American front at Abucay. In fact, the only north-south military
roads in the II Corps, save the East Road itself, junctioned there. If the
Japanese were to capture or block these, all traffic would be confined to the

wide open East Road—meaning 25,000 men would have to withdraw down this single two-lane road should evacuation of the II Corps become necessary.

From the afternoon of the 19th to the evening of the 21st, the battle to confine the Japanese 9th Infantry to what II Corps engineers showed on their maps to be the "Guitol-Natib Pack Trail" raged west of the Guitol barrio. It was during this period that a small Philippine Army patrol, under the command of Lt. Ferdinand Marcos, successfully destroyed a 9th Infantry artillery position whose accurate fire was jeopardizing the entire U.S. perimeter blocking the Guitol road junction. (See Map 7.)

Marcos, a 21st Division intelligence officer, had convinced his commander, Brig. Gen. Matao Capinpin, that a small patrol stood the best chance of destroying the artillery position. Within an hour, Marcos and three hand-picked enlisted men were off. After hours of working their way through the dense Japanese-controlled jungle, the four men came across the bodies of several of their comrades. They had been captured, tortured, and then beheaded. It was a sickening sight that would not be forgotten. Not far away, a trail was discovered that, after an hour or more of dangerous and difficult going, led them straight to their objective.

On a grassy plateau halfway up the southeastern slops of Mt. Natib, they found what appeared to be a sparsely manned, four-gun battery of 75-mm. field pieces along with a well-stocked ammunition dump.

The four Filipinos, after crawling to within 50 yards of the unsuspecting enemy, who were busy preparing for a fire mission, opened up with grenades and rifles. "The Japs were never so confused," remembered Pvt. Jose Salindong. "Their first instinct was to run away, but the Japanese officers whipped them into some semblance of order." However, with Marcos "attending to the officers," it wasn't long before the handful of enemy soldiers that were still alive were routed from the plateau. The four men made quick work of the enemy guns. "[They] were hurriedly dropped to the bottom of the cliff," said Salindong.

Not long after that, the Japanese, in greater number than first thought, counterattacked, forcing the tiny patrol back into the jungle. At dark, after first blowing up the enemy ammunition dump, they started back, at times hanging on to each other's belts to keep from becoming separated in the dense jungle. By dawn they were back, having lost one man, Pvt. Agustin Espinosa, who had slipped and fallen to his death from the edge of a trail high above a precipitous ravine.

By evening of the third day, helped no doubt by the results of Marcos' patrol action, the Japanese had been confined to the top of a small hill just south of the trail overlooking the Abo Abo River valley. But much danger still existed. Should Takechi be able to effect a breakout against the shaky Filipino defenders, the entire junction and perhaps the East Road itself, less

Brig. Gen. Mateo Capinin, commanding general, 21st Division, Philippine Army.

than two miles to the east, stood in jeopardy. Had the Japanese, in fact, known what was at stake, it is more than probable that they could have achieved that very goal.[52]

At noon the next day, January 22, the main Japanese force struck as scheduled at the exposed left flank of the United States MLR at Abucay five miles north of Guitol. On the heels of a combined air and artillery bombardment, the enemy's 141st Infantry, fighting at full strength for the first time in the battle, forced a small salient near the western end of the line.

By late afternoon, the bulge, extending into the 31st Infantry sector, brought the Americans, along with the 3d Battalion, 45th Infantry on the extreme left flank, to abandon their hard-won positions on the Balantay. By nightfall, bent but still unbroken, the extreme western end of the Abucay line had been hammered into a shape resembling that of a reverse question mark. The gains of five days of hard, confusing fighting had been relost back in just six hours.

Crisis in the I Corps

"You'll get your damn head shot off!"

Although not by design, it was during this same 48-hour period in the I Corps, that the situation also turned in favor of the Japanese. On the morning of January 21, two American colonels, both artillerymen, were unknowingly traveling toward each other on the West Road between Moron and Bagac. They would never meet.

Colonel Halstead C. Fowler, heading south from the I Corps front to his division command post, was shot out of the seat of his jeep by an enemy sniper when he reached the vicinity of kilometer post 167. I Corps artillery officer Colonel Jones Haskins, upon reaching the same area from the opposite direction an hour or so later, met a similar fate, except Haskins was killed instantly.

Badly wounded, Fowler was picked up by a 1st Division ambulance that happened to be passing through the area — a bit of good fortune that would save his life.

Unbeknownst to the Fil-American command, the ambush of the two American officers was the "informal announcement" of the arrival of Lt. Col. Hiroshi Nakanishi's 3d Battalion, 20th Infantry to a position astride the West Road immediately behind the I Corps front. Ironically, what Col. Takechi's 9th Infantry had been threatening to do to the East Road behind the II Corps front, Col. Nakinishi had just done in the west.

For all practical purposes, the I Corps had been without an actual reserve division since the transfer of the Philippine Army's 31st Division to II Corps four or five days earlier.

Therefore, the important first attempt to dislodge Nakinishi's force, made later that day by little more than two platoons of infantry, was piecemeal and ineffective. It was Gen. Wainwright himself, in fact, who upon learning of the roadblock led a makeshift party of 20 men in the attack from the south while another platoon of similar size struck from the upper end. Both groups fell far short of their objective of dislodging the Japanese, let alone of penetrating the dense, entangling jungle through which the road passed.

The wall around the church at Abucay is still pockmarked with shrapnel from the intense poundings the area took 50 years ago.

The battle-scarred but indestructable Abucay church tower 50 years after the battle. While the Fil-Americans occupied the Abucay line, U.S. artillery observers used this tower to direct fire against the Japanese. After the withdrawal from Abucay, the Japanese, in turn, used it for the same purpose. Despite the concentrated efforts by U.S. artillerymen to destroy it, not one direct hit was ever registered.

It was while Gen. Wainwright was "personally commanding the detachments," that he narrowly missed death. He was standing near the edge of the road right "in the midst of an order to a junior officer," when his orderly, Sgt. Hubert "Tex" Carrol, suddenly grabbed "two fistfuls of the seat of [his] pants," yanking him to the ground. "God damn it, General, get down or you'll get your damn head shot off!" Seconds later a Philippine Army officer and an enlisted man standing less than ten feet away were shot dead by enemy sniper fire.

That evening, realizing full well that the fate of his entire Corps depended on a quick reopening of the West Road, Wainwright was at last able to secure a company of tanks from the 194th Tank Battalion to lead the thrust the next morning. In addition, he brought up a motorized squadron (battalion) of 26th Cavalry Scouts plus a regimental-size Philippine Army force from the 91st–71st Division.

Plans for the attack early the next morning were laid by an anxious Wainwright. The tanks, under the command of Capt. Fred Moffitt, were to be preceded by a 100-yard-wide infantry skirmish line. The soldiers' job was to clear the jungle on both sides of the road of Japanese to assure against their favorite trick of slipping a mine under the treads of the tanks as they passed by.

The attack jumped off as scheduled. Within a hundred yards of its line of departure, however, it stalled. The jungle on both sides of the narrow dirt road was fiercely dense, making it almost impossible to sweep clear of the well-concealed enemy. By infiltrating behind the passing line of infantrymen, just as Capt. Moffitt had anticipated, the Japanese were able to slip charges under the first two tanks. Both were knocked out, and along with them, the only real hope of breaking the roadblock. Blocked from effectively using the remainder of the tanks, all Fil-American efforts made throughout the day failed to dislodge the enemy force from their positions within the towering trees and deep ravines through which the vital section of road passed.

To Wainwright, news of the failure came as a shock, because as of that moment, he was a commander cut off from his command, as was food, ammunition, and reinforcement. News of the failure of the tanks, considered "gross mishandling" by the executive officer of the Provisional Tank Group, brought a singeing report from the officer to Gen. MacArthur's headquarters on Corregidor. Wainwright was "severely criticized," Col. Ernest Miller later wrote, for "allowing such asinine use of the tanks."

The situations in both corps had obviously not gone unnoticed by Gen. MacArthur. On January 22, with the fate of perhaps the entire campaign in the balance, he ordered his trusted chief of staff, Gen. Richard Sutherland, to Bataan to get "a clear picture of the situation." Sutherland, whom MacArthur later wrote "[had] the most comprehensive grasp of the situation," was given the authority to issue withdrawal orders on the spot if he saw fit.

Sutherland's first stop was at Gen. Parker's II Corps Headquarters at Limay. Finding the situation even less tenable than expected, and before even talking to Wainwright, Sutherland issued verbal orders to withdraw within the next day or so to new positions on the newly constructed Bagac-Orion line. Later that night, both corps commanders were officially notified to initiate the plan for the general withdrawal the next night.

For Parker, if all went well, the withdrawal would be close to a "text book" retrograde movement. But in Wainwright's I Corps, unless the roadblock could be forced, fate of the 5,000 men on the Mauban front was definitely in doubt. In fact, whereas Parker had issued the withdrawal orders to his various division commanders early the next day, Wainwright, who was completely cut off from his subordinates at the front, never did issue them.

Reacting to the orders for the general withdrawal, Col. George stepped up the frequency of the air corps' aerial reconnaissance missions over the II Corps. On the 24th, the routine two-plane patrol flown by lieutenants Earl Stone and John Posten was pleasantly interrupted when they caught four unsuspecting enemy dive-bombers busily at work over Abucay. Both pilots scored on their first pass, making it relatively easy for them to finish off the two slow, underarmed survivors. All four were shot down "within sight of our ground forces," noted Lt. Dave Obert, who had been sharing the patrol duties with the two happy pilots. "This was quite an achievement in [our] worn out P-40s."[53]

As the battle for Bataan entered its fourth week, the behind-the-line rumors that could be counted on to make an appearance by then certainly had. That is what one would think after reading an entry for that week in the Bataan diary of Lt. Thomas Garrity, an air corps liaison officer with Gen. Jonathan Wainwright's staff. "Major Montgomery," he wrote, "invented a yardstick for measuring the terrific crop of rumors we've been hearing lately: 'many bombs' really means one bomb; 'many airplanes' really means two planes; 'a fleet of Japanese ships' really means one native banca; and 'many parachutists' really means a batch of Jap leaflets."[54]

With five times as many men involved, plans were for the II Corps to begin its pull-back almost immediately, while the I Corps was to wait and make their move on the night of January 25. The only difference was that the I Corps situation by then, according to the frontline commander, Col. Kearie L. Berry, had become "desperate" and was "growing worse."

By nightfall of the 24th, results of over three days of counterattacks by superior numbers against the Japanese roadblock, had netted the Fil-Americans only a few moments of success. That came on January 23 when a battalion of the Philippine Constabulary, led by P.A. Maj. Jose Arambulo, was able to effect an opening long enough to allow a handful of trucks full of 1st Division wounded to pass through to the rear.

Effects of the enemy's tenacious hold on almost the entire back side of Mauban ridge, coupled with a desperate shortage of food and ammunition, caused Col. Berry that night, without consulting Wainwright, to order the line abandoned. With the road blocked, however, there would be no orderly military withdrawal.

It would be difficult to call it anything less than a rout. It meant destroying everything that couldn't be carried, including artillery and vehicles. In fact, 25 field pieces, including the irreplacable 75s, had to be spiked and left behind. It meant that the only semblance of organization would be in keeping the troops moving in the right direction. It meant that the only form of discipline would be to make sure each man brought out his own weapon, which close to 1,000 men failed to do.

The next morning, January 25, behind a covering force from the 3d Infantry, withdrawal from I Corps positions began. (See Map 9.) Following the line of dense jungle to the shore line, the entire force had successfully slipped away from under the very noses of the Japanese by nightfall. Fortunately, the only daylight threat to the long line of stragglers along the beaches, the Japanese Air Force, failed to show up in force. Had they, their planes could have rained havoc on the helpless troops strung out for miles along the open beach.

By noon, Col. Berry's party had reached Bagac, where he by coincidence ran into Gen. Wainwright. Ironically, the corps commander was on his way to order Berry to do the very thing he had just done. A little hesitant at facing the general for what he might say about withdrawing without orders, Berry, standing barefoot with a 1903 Springfield slung over his shoulder, saluted. "Berry," said Wainwright, reaching out to shake hands, "I'm damn glad to see you." Berry relaxed. It was over. Orders or no, his intuition and good judgment had been responsible for bringing over 5,000 men back to fight another day. Orders or no, Wainwright would recommend him for the Distinguished Service Cross later that same day.

It wasn't until five o'clock that evening that the rear guard from the Third Infantry caught up with the rest of their division near Bagac. There, the tatterdemalion little Filipino soldiers, according to their commander, Maj. Alfredo Santos, "threw themselves to the ground from sheer exhaustion; canned foods were served and the men ate greedily for the first time in days."[55] Lieutenant Tom Garrity, air corps liaison officer with Gen. Wainwright, upon seeing the Filipinos, added that "a quarter of them wore only underwear, and none had eaten in four days."[56]

Withdrawal from Abucay

"Saved for another day."

On the II Corps side of the line, where the failure of 25,000 men to successfully slip away from the front would mean disaster for the entire

A U.S. roadblock on the West Road north of Bagac.

command, a much more sophisticated plan was necessary. The withdrawal of the main body would start during the night of January 25. With a covering shell consisting of no more than a single platoon of riflemen, a handful of machine guns, and a four-gun artillery battery per line regiment, one by one, from right to left, the seven infantry regiments were ordered to slip away from their positions.

In the meantime, the main covering force, under the command of Brig. Gen. Max Lough, commanding officer of the U.S. 31st Infantry, had moved up into a blocking position in the shape of a reverse L on roads running from Abucay south to Balanga and from Balanga west to the Guitol junction. (See Map 10.) The backbone of this force was Gen. James Weaver's tanks and 75-mm.–carrying half-tracks, which were spread out along the East and so-called Back roads, the only two north-south roads in eastern Bataan. In position on the line running east to west was a makeshift infantry force composed of units from the P.A. 31st and 51st divisions, the Scout 57th and U.S. 31st Infantry Regiments, whose combined firepower roughly amounted to that of about seven battalions.

The key to the entire operation evolved around the expediency with which the MLR could be abandoned during the hours of darkness. By dawn of the 25th it was vital that the Japanese wake up to a "ghost front," or the entire withdrawal could be facing disaster.

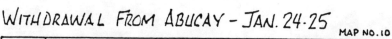

WITHDRAWAL FROM ABUCAY - JAN. 24-25

MAP NO. 10

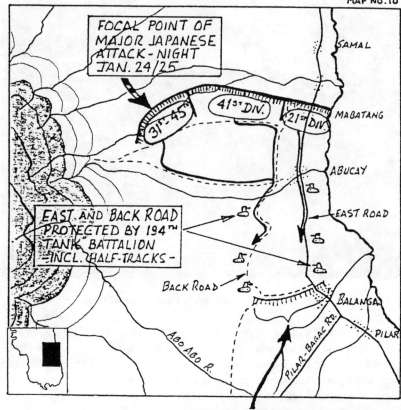

FOCAL POINT OF
MAJOR JAPANESE
ATTACK - NIGHT
JAN. 24/25

31st-45th

41st DIV.

21st DIV.

SAMAL

MABATANG

ABUCAY

EAST AND BACK ROAD
PROTECTED BY 194th
TANK BATTALION
- INCL. HALF-TRACKS -

EAST ROAD

BACK ROAD

BALANGA

ABO ABO R.

PILAR-BAGAC RD.

PILAR

US. II CORPS COVERING
FORCE POSITION, NIGHTS -
JAN. 24, 25:

33rd INF. REG.
REMNANTS - 51st DIV.
ONE BATTALION EACH OF:
US. 31st INF.
PS. 57th INF.
PA. 31st INF.

Beginning at dusk, every available source of transportation within the II Corps, from trucks to open-sided commercial buses, was moved into marshalling areas behind the MLR. By seven o'clock, troops from the 21st Division, who had replaced the 57th Infantry on the eastern end of the line on January 21, began to fall back.

The 21st Division was followed closely by troops of Brig. Gen.

Wounded Filipino soldiers on the floor of a converted commercial bus being used as an ambulance. Buses were taken from various Manila bus companies by prearrangement with the Philippine Army when the war started and were used throughout the battle.

Vincente Lim's 41st Division, who abandoned the positions they had doggedly but successfully held on to throughout the entire Abucay fight.

By 10 P.M., the scene in the area immediately to the rear of the two divisions had become one of near chaos. First of all, few of the roads or road junctions were controlled or regulated by military police. Soon, the intermingled mass of men on foot and in trucks and buses had so slowed that those walking were actually moving faster than those riding. Fortunately, however, the dark night, which had acted to compound the problem for the Filipinos and Americans, had at the same time afforded them protection against enemy detection. Had the Japanese chosen that moment to interdict the area with artillery fire, they would have ignited the troops into a cattle-like stampede to the rear, aside from causing hundreds of casualties.[57]

In the meantime, troops in the 31st and 45th Infantry sectors, who had the farthest to go and who had been facing almost continuous enemy pressure since January 22, had also begun to move back.

At 7 P.M., as troops of the 31st began to extricate themselves from the extreme western end of the line, the Japanese, as if with a foreknowledge of what was going on, launched perhaps their heaviest night attack of the campaign. Major Everett Mead of the 31st wrote of the attack: "Just as the regiment was preparing to withdraw, the Japs seemed to sense it and launched a terrific night attack. After, Japs were piled [so] high in front of machine gun emplacements, [it] was almost too high to fire over."[58]

Thus began the eight hour withdrawal of "Bataan's best" that was to become such a melange of unrelated experiences that no single version of what happened could be agreed upon afterwards. Because of the simultaneity of the Japanese attack, which was launched as a complete coincidence, units that were supposed to pull back couldn't, and those that did pull back weren't supposed to. Because of the confusion, the covering shells, who were supposed to leapfrog their way to the rear, often didn't know where to establish or reestablish themselves. Possibly all that prevented the withdrawal operation in the western sector from becoming a complete disaster were the personal efforts of a few of its officers. In fact, according to Capt. Clarence Bess of the 31st, only one company of his regiment, Company G, under the command of Maj. John Pray, as part of the shell "properly performed its mission, and [even] it had been left alone with no contact with our forces." What's more, except for a last-second intervention by Capt. Bess himself, G Company would have mistakenly been fired upon by friendly troops for having "performed its mission" as it fell back in the dark towards the embarkation point.[59]

Major Everett Mead, regimental supply and evacuation officer with the U.S. 31st Infantry, was stunned that night when he saw the men of his regiment for the first time in nine days as they came out of the cane fields of Abucay. "As [they] came out of the line," he wrote, "marching slowly and laboriously, they looked like walking dead men. They had a blank stare in their eyes, and their faces, covered with beards, lacked any expression. Their clothes were in shreds ... they looked like anything but an efficient fighting force, and little wonder, considering the days just past and their state of malnutrition."[60]

The last unit out of Abucay was the 3d Battalion of the 45th Infantry, which under the calm and reassuring leadership of its commander, Maj. Dudley Strickler, had remained intact during the entire eight-hour ordeal. "Armed with only a pistol and wearing an old khaki cap instead of his helmet," wrote Capt. Louis Besbeck of the 3d Battalion, "[Strickler] worked up and down the screen and kept the two companies working together. About six hours later he brought his entire force through the tank position to the east."[61]

It was 3 A.M. when the 31st reached the truck-loading point, which by then was receiving heavy enemy sniper fire. To protect the trucks, a platoon of tanks had convoyed them up to the pick-up point on the road. Hurriedly, as the tankers began to return fire against the Japanese, the last two companies of 31st Infantry boarded and pulled out. Unfortunately, however, the transportation that was promised to the 45th Infantry did not arrive. And so the tired, Scouts began the final leg of their 14-hour ordeal that would end an exhausting 12 miles and 7 hours later.

No sooner had the 45th disappeared down the road, than a large column of Japanese, now on the trail of the retreating Fil-Americans, appeared. The first enemy troops to reach the road were greeted by a fusillade from the American tanks and armored half-tracks, forcing them to quickly duck back into the jungle. With those shots, the tanks, representing the last living defenders on the Abucay line, also began to withdraw.

Despite the successful abandonment of the Abucay front, the withdrawal was still far from complete. Dawn of January 25 found thousands of II Corps soldiers still lining the open roads leading south. What the enemy artillery had failed to capitalize on during the night, their air force attempted to make up for throughout the day. Unopposed as usual, for 12 hours Japanese planes rained havoc and death upon the slow-moving, dust-covered columns of Philippine Army and Philippine Scout troops as they staggered across the wide open roads of east-central Bataan.

A few lines from Lt. Henry G. Lee's 241-line poem, "Abucay Withdrawal," may give the best capsule picture of that dreadful day's happenings:

> Along the shoulder in a staggered file,
> Picking their cover in every mile,
> And watching with apprehensive eyes
> For the first far speck of death that flies,
> These are the men who have fought and fled
> And fought again and have left their dead...
> The white men sprawled in the inch-deep dust
> Curse in a tone of hurt and disgust
> And slander the noble Japanese
> With four letter Saxon obscenities...

The morning of January 26 dawned at last to emptied roads. Except for the Provisional Tank Group, which was still in the process of withdrawing from their position southwest of Balanga, the rest of the Bataan Army was preparing to move into their newly assigned positions on the Bagac-Orion line to, according to MacArthur, "fight it out to complete destruction."

The tankers' first action of the battle of Bataan was, in the meantime, taking shape on the southernmost link of what was called the Back Road, between the village of Bani and the Pilar-Bagac Road.

General Weaver, who was not with the group, had held up its withdrawal that night until a wrecker could be dispatched to help pull one of

First Lieutenant Henry G. Lee

the tanks out of a ditch. Daylight found Col. Ernest B. Miller, commander the tank group, on the radio to Weaver explaining that since the wrecker still hadn't shown up and daylight would bring enemy planes, "the whole situation was being jeopardized for the sake of getting one tank out of the ditch." To his disgust the reply came back, "You will bring back all Chesterfields [tanks], repeat—all Chesterfields," meaning: Stay put until you get the tank out.

At 10:30, with still no wrecker in sight, the column was struck from the west by the Japanese 141st Infantry. An hour later, the enemy's up-until-then ineffective small arms fire was being supplemented with artillery and mortars.

Word of the new threat brought Gen. Weaver himself to the radio, ordering Miller to "infiltrate to the rear, bring all Chesterfields." So incensed by the General's maladroit use of the word "infiltrate," Miller ordered his operator to "Tell that old sonofabitch to go to hell and turn off that damn radio."

Although the situation with the tanks was becoming serious, it was a long way from being critical. In fact, it was now the Americans' turn to "put some points on the board." Before dawn, Miller had smartly placed his 75-

Colonel Ernest B. Miller, 194th Tank Battalion.

mm.–toting half-tracks on a small knoll near the south end of the road. From their slight, high ground advantage, the Americans could easily bring the west side of the road under fire, which they did. "Wherever cover was afforded in which there might be Japs," wrote Miller later, "they dropped their shells. The result was astonishing. The Nips poured out like fleas off a dog. As they appeared, they were picked off by the tankers," who had jumped out of their tanks and began blazing away with submachine guns.

By noon, except for increasing enemy artillery fire, things quieted enough for Miller to order the column to begin its withdrawal to the south. Their movements, however, had soon drawn the attention of enemy planes, which literally swarmed on the tanks and half-tracks as they lumbered over the dusty, wide-open stretch of road. Fortunately, every vehicle in the group made it back to friendly lines, save the tank in the ditch and the wrecker, whom they passed parked off the side of the road on the way out. In fact, it was the officer in charge of bringing up the wrecker, Lt. Russell Swearingen, who added a little comedy to the tank group's last act. Hearing heavy artillery fire up ahead earlier, Swearingen left his wrecker about a half-a-mile below the tank column and proceeded the rest of the way on foot. It was at that time that Miller ordered the group to withdraw and also

An American captain gives a Japanese soldier, wounded during the battle at Abucay, a drink of water.

about the same time that they were jumped by enemy planes. "Everyone was concerned with hostile aircraft," said Miller, "and nobody saw Swearingen." Miller's half-track was the last one out. "We were firing at a plane which was diving at us. Above the roar, a weird sound penetrated our ears," he wrote. It was Swearingen running like "Billyhell" after Miller, "bellowing at the top of his lungs: 'Hey you guys, wait for me!'" Miller stopped and picked up the thankful and exhausted lieutenant, who appeared not too pleased at "being left behind to take on the whole Jap army and air force all alone."

With the withdrawal now completed, Gen. MacArthur's daily "fairy tale" communiqué to the War Department covering the same time period read, in part:

> Number 75—January 25, 1942:
>   General MacArthur launched a heavy counterattack on his extreme right, scoring a smashing success. His powerful concentration of 155-mm. artillery fired with deadly accuracy on enemy lines. American and Filipino troops then charged. They found the Japanese infantry completely disorganized. Enemy troops fled from their positions, leaving hundreds of dead and large quantities of supplies and equipment on the battlefield. The effect of the success of this brilliant maneuver was to relieve the pressure on the left. The situation is now temporarily stabilized. However, a re-

A Philippine Scout private displays his captured Japanese officer's Samurai sword to his medical corps comrade.

newed attack by the enemy may be expected as soon as a reorganization had been effected.[62]

Lieutenant Lee, in the meantime, had written a much more realistic close to the Abucay withdrawal. Bataan, he scribbled, had been saved,

> . . . saved for another day
> Saved for hunger and wounds and heat
> For slow exhaustion and grim retreat
> For a wasted hope and sure defeat. . . .

CHAPTER TWO

Invasion from the Sea

"The Japs are down there, Sir!"

On January 22, the same night that Gen. Sutherland ordered the abandonment of the Mauban-Abucay lines, the Japanese coincidentally launched a seaward invasion against the west coast of Bataan. A small, battalion-size force of some 1,200 men was ordered to effect a landing at Caibobo Point, some five air-miles below Bagac. After denying the Fil-Americans use of the West Road, they were to link up with Col. Nakanishi's "roadblock" battalion, who they were sure would by then be in Bagac. With the I Corps line then severed, plans were to move east across the Pilar-Bagac Road and take the II Corps from behind.

For the invaders, however, the night, almost from the start, became one of nightmarish confusion. Navigating in rough seas, in overcrowded landing barges on a moonless night without adequate maps, while trying to isolate Caibobo Point from the other dozen or so similar looking headlands, was an impossible task.

Under the command of Lt. Col. Nariyoshi Tsunehiro, the 2d Battalion, 20th Infantry, shoved off from Mayagao Point near Moron shortly before ten o'clock. Their maps had placed the distance to Caibobo at 15 miles. With help from the current, it was calculated that they would be abreast of the landing beach at 1 A.M.

As scheduled, three hours later, assuming that the point looming up off the port beam was Caibobo, Tsunehiro ordered the boats turned toward shore. Suddenly, the flotilla was illuminated by half a dozen searchlights located on Saysain Point, some three miles north of Caibobo. In seconds tracers from automatic weapons along the shoreline filled the night, forcing the invaders to scatter and to remain scattered. Obviously, they had overestimated the distance they had gone. Caibobo was still farther south. But how far?[1]

The Japanese did not then realize that their first mistake had just doomed the mission. The melee had caused the force to become fatally separated. The bulk of the boats, under the direction of Col. Tsunehiro, rejoined and began again to work their way south. The remaining one-third, however, unable to find the rest of the 20th Infantry, began probing its way down the Bataan coast in a hopeless search for the larger group.

Earlier that night, Lt. John Bulkeley shoved off from Sisiman Bay aboard PT-34 on his routine, graveyard-shift patrol of the Bataan west coast. The 34 boat was accompanied, for the first time, by the converted yacht *Fisheries II*. In order to save wear and tear on the overworked PTs, Bulkeley ordered that beginning that night either the launch *Fisheries II* or *Maryanne* would accompany one of the PT boats on the nightly patrol.

At 4:30 A.M. about 12 air miles up the coast, the quiet monotony of the patrol was momentarily broken when the 34 boat was fired on from the vicinity of Canas Point. It was the guns of the Philippine Constabulary who, unbeknownst to Bulkeley, had been alerted by the sounds of motor-boats earlier that night and ordered by their commanding officer to "Open fire when [they] heard those sounds again." More exasperated from being fired at by friendly guns than worried about being hit, Lt. Robert Kelly, fresh out of the hospital on Corregidor, calmly altered the course of his 34 boat to mutterings of "Half the time those dumb bastards don't know friend from foe."

Minutes later, lookouts on the 34 picked up a faint light sitting low in the water some distance away. Kelly moved to investigate, holding fire in case it was the three men from the 31 boat who were still missing from the Binanga Bay raid four nights earlier. At the sound of the PT's engines, the light began flashing in a series of unreadable dots and dashes, and then suddenly went out.

Bulkeley, who in the meantime had ordered general quarters, grabbed a megaphone and yelled, "Boat ahoy." His reply was a volley of machine gun fire that splattered against the plywood side of the 34 as the uniden-tified vessel began heading for shore. In response, the entire deck of the PT boat simultaneously erupted with return fire as everybody, including the engine room crew, "had grabbed rifles and come up to fire over the sides." Before long they could make out the silhouette of a Japanese landing barge, crammed with troops and obviously part of a larger group, that was in the process of affecting a landing on Bataan's west coast.

Within minutes, the one-sided running gun battle had reached its ob-vious conclusions, as the superior fire power of the PT's four .50s soon had the landing barge dead and settling in the water.

During the exchange, however, Ens. Barron Chandler, the boat's sec-ond officer, was hit by a bullet that tore through both ankles. He was badly in need of medical care. But since the patrol couldn't negotiate through

Longoskawayan (on right) and Lapiay points, landing sites of some 300 Japanese during the night of January 22, 1942. The discovery of enemy troops on Mt. Pucot (behind Lapiay Point) the next morning led to what was called the battle for Longoskawayan Point, carried out by U.S. sailors, Marines, and Philippine Scouts. Both Longoskawayan and Lapiay points were shelled by Corregidor's Battery Geary during the battle. (Note Mariveles in the background.)

Corregidor's minefield until daylight, according to Kelly they "fooled around until almost dawn and were headed for home when Bulkeley happened to glance back." It was another landing barge, only this one, empty of troops, was heading out to sea.

Kelly quickly turned about, and within minutes tracer fire from the PT boat, which in the meantime had closed to within ten yards of the target, exploded its gas tanks.

In one final, suicidal gasp the Japanese tried to ram the 34 as it came alongside, which prompted Bulkeley to underhand a couple of grenades into her burning hull. Then, with .45 in hand, he jumped across into the now rapidly sinking barge and rescued its only two survivors, one of them an officer. Along with saving two of the enemy, Bulkeley also salvaged an official-looking dispatch case, which, upon later examination, revealed plans for the entire Japanese landing operation that night, including ultimate objectives.[2]

Of course, what Bulkeley had earlier assumed to be an attempted

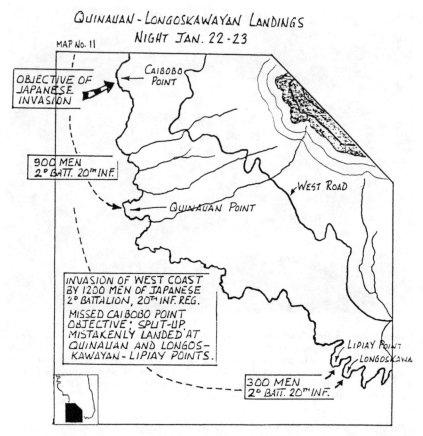

QUINAUAN - LONGOSKAWAYAN LANDINGS
NIGHT JAN. 22-23

MAP No. 11

OBJECTIVE OF JAPANESE INVASION

CAIBOBO POINT

900 MEN 2° BATT. 20™ INF.

WEST ROAD

QUINAUAN POINT

INVASION OF WEST COAST BY 1200 MEN OF JAPANESE 2° BATTALION, 20™ INF. REG.

MISSED CAIBOBO POINT OBJECTIVE : SPLIT-UP. MISTAKENLY LANDED AT QUINAUAN AND LONGOS- KAWAYAN - LIPIAY POINTS.

LIPIAY POINT
LONGOSKAWA

300 MEN 2° BATT. 20™ INF.

invasion of the west coast was actually two of the boats of Col. Tsunehiro's force. A little before 4 A.M. the largest part of the once-thwarted invasion fleet turned again for shore toward the promontory that had to be Caibobo Point. It wasn't. This time they had gone too far and were approaching the cliff-lined shore of Quinauan Point, some three miles south of their planned destination.

The smaller Japanese force, since the separation from the group, had in the meantime been groping its way south vainly looking for the main body. Around 6:30 A.M. the confused, leaderless group finally turned for shore. They too had overshot their destination, but not by a mere three miles. Astonishingly, they had drifted no less than ten miles too far and would land on a narrow, fingerlike projection of land known as Longoskawayan Point, only one mile west of Mariveles. (See Map 11.)

In charge of defending this rugged, jungle-enveloped section of Bataan coast at this time was Brig. Gen. Clyde Selleck. With priority on qualified combat troops, of course, going to the I and II Corps, Selleck had put

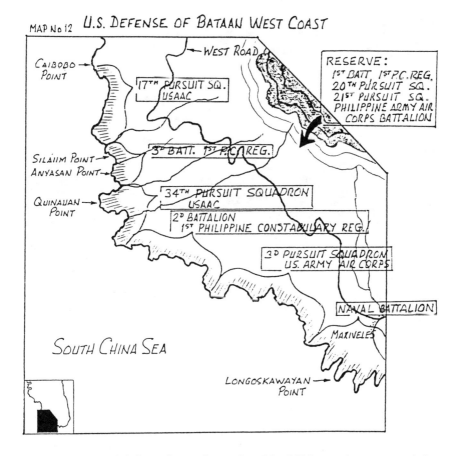

MAP No 12 U.S. DEFENSE OF BATAAN WEST COAST

CAIBOBO POINT

←WEST ROAD

17TH PURSUIT SQ. USAAC

RESERVE:
1ST BATT 1ST P.C. REG.
20TH PURSUIT SQ.
21ST PURSUIT SQ.
PHILIPPINE ARMY AIR CORPS BATTALION

SILAIIM POINT→
ANYASAN POINT→

3D BATT. 1ST P.C. REG.

QUINAUAN POINT

34TH PURSUIT SQUADRON USAAC

2D BATTALION 1ST PHILIPPINE CONSTABULARY REG.

3D PURSUIT SQUADRON US. ARMY AIR CORPS

NAVAL BATTALION

MARIVELES

SOUTH CHINA SEA

LONGOSKAWAYAN→ POINT

together a coastal defense force of questionable skill from whatever was left. Alternately placed from Mariveles north to Caibobo Point, the limit of his area of responsibility, were the following makeshift coastal defense units: Cmdr. Frank Bridget's Naval Battalion; U.S. Army Air Corps, 3d Pursuit Squadron; the 2d Battalion, 1st Philippine Constabulary Regiment; a second air corps squadron, the 34th; the 3d Battalion of the 1st Constabulary Regiment; and last, the 17th Pursuit Squadron. (See Map 12.)

The Quinauan Point sector, where the bulk of the Japanese had come ashore, happened to be the responsibility of the 34th Pursuit Squadron, whose 200 or so members were thinly spread along the edge of over two and a half miles of cliffs and beaches. Without searchlights or adequate sound detectors and against the noise of the surf, the Fil-Americans didn't hear the enemy barges when they first reached the shore, nor were the Japanese themselves discovered until they had already ascended the precipitous cliffs and were on top of the defenders' positions. They had also

Isolated Quinauan Point as it looks today. Now completely denuded of its heavy jungle, some of the bitterest of fighting on Bataan took place on this broad finger of land, ending with the Japanese throwing themselves off of its cliffs into the sea.

fooled the air corps defenders. "They did not land on the sandy beaches as we had predicted," commented Lt. Stewart Robb of the 34th, "but on little peninsulas where they were required to climb abrupt cliffs as high as 60 feet."[3]

Denied effective use of their machine guns, the surprised American airmen, with as little commotion as possible, abandoned their positions with little more than firing a shot. A few minutes later, an out-of-breath air corps PFC burst into the 34th's command post frantically pointing in the direction of the water's edge. "The Japs are down there, Sir!" he gasped.

It wasn't until an hour later that word that the Japs were "down there" reached Gen. Selleck at his command post above Quinauan. After literally being handed the Quinauan beachhead at 1:30 in the morning of the 23d, Col. Tsunehiro was to be given nearly nine more hours to prepare his defenses before the Americans and Filipinos could strike back.

In fact, a surprise attack by a platoon of constabulary troops at 4 A.M. was the only opposition they would have until almost noon. That opposition, interestingly, coming from men of the 1st Battalion, 1st Constabulary Regiment, was vigorous enough to push the surprised Japanese back from the Agloloma Bay side of Quinauan Point to the cliffs just above the main landing site. Aggressively led by Lt. Paciano Capalongan, the constabularymen were able to recapture three American .50-caliber machine gun positions with guns intact, several boxes of hand grenades, and other

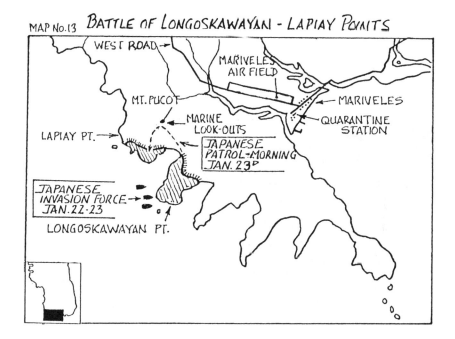

MAP No.13 BATTLE OF LONGOSKAWAYAN - LAPIAY POINTS

pieces of equipment left by the 34th Pursuit Squadron some three hours earlier. Ordered later that morning to pull back some 600 yards to the new main assault line across the point, the 1st Constabulary regiment unknowingly gave up terrain that would take 14 long, hard, bloody days to retake.[4]

The situation for the seven Japanese officers and 249 men who had landed on Longoskayawan Point near Bataan's southern tip was quite different. Beaching their barges just minutes before daylight, they were quickly up the cliffs and into the jungle. By dawn, a small patrol had ventured up the slopes of the sugarloaf shaped mountain just above the landing site known as Mt. Pucot. From there, the lost enemy force's confusion quickly turned to dismay, as below them, not more than 2,000 yards away, sat busy little Mariveles Harbor, hub port of the entire Bataan defense operations. As for the Americans, the last place they could allow the Japanese to be was on 617-foot-high Mt. Pucot, because its heights not only dominated the Mariveles area, but also the West Road, which passed little more than half-a-mile from the base of its slopes. (See Map 13.)

Although the Naval Battalion had been given the responsibility of defending the Mariveles area against sea and air attack, Cmdr. Bridget chose to set up a 24-hour lookout on top of Mt. Pucot itself instead of occupying positions along the cliffs. It was this three-man lookout that received first warning that the enemy had landed on the morning of the 23d. At about 8:30 A.M., Marine PFC Robert McKechnie, perched with binoculars

This picture of the eastern edge of Mariveles Harbor was taken looking south along
what was known as the U.S. Navy Section Base. The road at left fronted the five navy
tunnels as it led past the open-faced rock quarry and ended at Sisiman Bay. The edge
of the bay in front of the quarry, known as Lilimbon Cove, was the docking site of
the USS *Canopus.*

and field telephone on the limb of the most prominent tree he could find
on Pucot, was shot at from a clump of bushes a few yards away. He quickly
rang Cmdr. Bridget. "Longoskawayan, Lapiay, and Naiklec Points are
crawling with Japs, Sir. We're gettin' the hell out of here, right now!"
McKechnie then dropped the phone and, on the heels of his two companions who had already started down the hill, sprinted the entire mile back
to the Quarantine Station.

Bridget, upon receiving the frantic call from McKechnie, alerted nearby
Marine Lt. William F. Hogaboom of the presence of the enemy force and
told him to take the two platoons of grounded sailors he commanded and
make a sweep of both Pucot and Mt. Mauankis. He then called Lt. Wilfred
"Willie" Holdredge, in position at the upper end of Mariveles Field with
two platoons of Marines from Battery A of the 3d Battalion, 4th Marines,
and told him to do the same thing.

As Lt. Hogaboom prepared his 60 or so bluejackets to take to the bush,
one of the most colorful pages of Bataan history began to unfold. Of all the
pis aller units organized to fight on Bataan, this one, along with about fifty
more assigned to Lt. Holdredge, appeared by far the least likely to succeed.

The 4th Marines, as part of Cmdr. Frank Bridget's Naval Battalion, have fallen in to receive individual decorations for their role in the battle for Longoskawayan and Lapiay Points.

Their "sickly, mustard-yellow" uniforms, which were nothing more than navy whites boiled in coffee grounds to make them blend in more with the jungle, gave them an identity separate from friend and foe alike.

By midmorning, Hogaboom's two platoons of three-day wonders— they had only completed the equivalent of three days of infantry training when called into action—had left their Quarantine Station bivouac for mts. Mauankis and Pucot. Simultaneously, the two platoons of Marines under Lt. Holdredge, manning an antiaircraft battery north of Mariveles Field, shoved off to reconnoiter the same area. With Holdredge were the other 40 sailors under the immediate command of Ens. William Grundels. His group had received only half the infantry training of Hogaboom's—one and a half days.

With the presence of the bluejacket soldiers, along with Bridget's failure to coordinate his attack, the first day of what would later be referred to as the battle for Longoskawayan Point had all the indications of being an interesting if not historic one. (See Map 14.)

Lieutenant Hogaboom, upon examining his map, decided to split his force, sending one platoon of sailors and a few Marines, under navy Lt. Les Pew, straight to Pucot. Hogaboom planned to reconnoiter Mauankis himself with the remaining platoon and, after dropping off a squad to patrol the 580-foot hill, would follow the ridge line across to Pucot.

Lieutenant Holdredge, like Hogaboom, split his force, sending Ens.

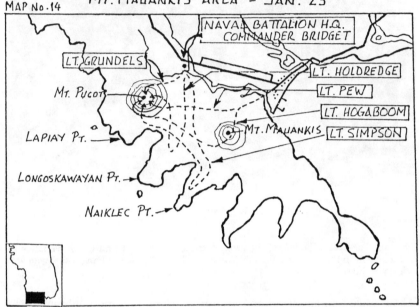

NAVAL BATTALION "SWEEP" OF MT. PUCOT —
MT. MAUANKIS AREA — JAN. 23

MAP No. 14

Grundels and a platoon of sailors, as had been done with Pew, straight to Mt. Pucot. He planned to take the remaining platoon of sailors across the ridge connecting the two little mountains to take a look at Longoskawayan Point. Last, he ordered a platoon of Marines from his battery, under Lt. Carter Simpson, to check out Naiklec Point, the small finger of land immediately south of Longoskawayan. Like Holdredge, Simpson would also be crossing paths with Lt. Hogaboom on his way to Naiklec.

Grundels, with about half as far to go as Pew, arrived at Pucot first. After an uncontested sweep of the top of the little mountain, his sailors were fired upon as they came down over the southeastern slope by a small enemy force. Grundels and a Marine sergeant-major were wounded in the first volley, triggering his bluejackets to open up with everything they had in the general direction of the enemy. Despite the absence of return fire, the sailors continued to blast away at the jungle.

Meanwhile, Pew, approaching Pucot from the northwest, deployed his platoon after hearing shots from the other side. Nearing the top, his sailors came under fire from a small enemy force that was actually between them and Ens. Grundels' platoon. Outgunned, the Japanese quickly withdrew.

By this time, Lt. Hogaboom, who had literally double-timed it across from Mt. Mauankis upon the sound of gunfire from Pucot, had begun to advance on the mountain. Interpreting what he was hearing as meaning that the Japanese were "between the firing and the water, we immediately cut down the hill to get on the Japanese rear," said Hogaboom. "Deployed and sweeping up toward the firing, we came on the rear of Ensign Grundels' patrol . . . on the deck and firing at random into the bushes." Both men were surprised to see each other. Grundels was equally surprised to learn that yet a third platoon of sailors was on the hill—Lt. Pew's. Judging by the light volumn of small arms fire coming from the top of the mountain, Hogaboom assured Grundels that Pew would soon be joining them. The two officers did not know that before the day was over one more platoon and two more officers from the Naval Battalion would be joining them on top of the little mountain.

Lieutenant Simpson, returning empty-handed from his reconnaissance of Naiklec Point, like Hogaboom heard the firing from Mt. Pucot. By the time he and his men neared the base of the 617-foot mountain, all was quiet. Deploying his men for action, he began moving up. Suddenly, at the edge of a clearing appeared a soldier dressed in an unmistakable "mustard yellow" uniform. Unbelievably, Simpson, like Hogaboom, Pew, and Grundels, had avoided an almost certain run-in with one of the other units. But there was still a platoon unaccounted for.

Lieutenant Holdredge, who commanded that platoon, like the others altered his plans when he heard firing from Mt. Pucot. Instead of continuing on to Longoskawayan, he dropped off his men in position on the ridge between Pucot and Mauankis and headed on to see what all the shooting was about.

When he walked out of the jungle and joined the other four officers a few minutes later, it was a sign that the operation to clear the Pucot-Mauankis area of Japanese had been successful. The sailors had performed well. In each case when they ran into an enemy force, the Japanese quickly withdrew without firing a shot in return. Perhaps more amazing was the fact that not one of the five platoons of sailors and Marines probing the dense jungle on top of and around mts. Pucot and Mauankis mistook each other for the enemy.

It was at this time, apparently, that the actions of the sailors influenced the Japanese into thinking that they were fighting a "new type of suicide squad." Evidence of this came from a diary later found on the body of a dead enemy soldier. These "squads," he wrote, "which thrashed about in the jungle wearing bright-colored uniforms and making plenty of noise, would attempt to draw [our] fire by sitting down, talking loudly and lighting cigarettes."[5]

While the small group of isolated Japanese who had landed on Longoskawayan, incorrectly estimated to be "about a platoon," were attempting to organize themselves below Mt. Pucot, the remaining two-thirds of the

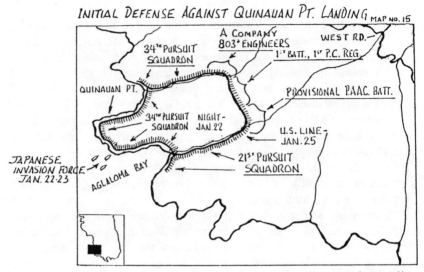

INITIAL DEFENSE AGAINST QUINAUAN PT. LANDING MAP NO. 15

battalion on Quinauan Point had dug in and were under attack on a line some 600-yards inland. (See Map 15.) Nothing could have worked more in favor of Col. Tsunehiro's force than allowing its advance to go all but unchecked throughout most of the day. By the time the first U.S. counterattack was mounted late that afternoon, the adroit enemy force had secured a virtual bastion in the thick jungle. Along with a series of deep, well-placed foxholes that had been dug among the trees, boulders, and thick tropical underbrush, mines and booby traps had also been set and automatic weapons placed so as to bring a heavy concentration of fire onto the only two roads leading into the area.

It wasn't until 5:30 that afternoon that the enemy line was seriously challenged. Although the challenge came from the game and capable 1st Battalion of the 1st Philippine Constabulary Regiment, it failed to as much as budge the well dug-in enemy from their positions.

For Gen. Clyde Selleck, January 23 became, to say the least, the most perplexing day in his short military career as a general on Bataan. Selleck, who just 13 days before had been given the job of creating and training an army out of thin air while at the same time defending the coastline, suddenly found his unprepared charges being put to the test.

For Selleck, the 23d, which was to be both his first and last day as commander of a force in action, began very early. At 2:30 A.M., he was awakened to the report that the Japanese had successfully effected a landing on Quinauan Point, just a few hundred yards below his command post on the West Road. At 8:30, he received a call from Gen. Richard Sutherland on Corregidor with information, given to him by Lt. Bulkeley, that the Japanese had landed at Caibobo Point.

About an hour later, Maj. Gen. Allen C. McBride, commanding gen-

A lull in the fighting gives the men a chance to catch-up on weapon and equipment maintenance. Here, American and Philippine Scout soldiers clean and oil a water-cooled .30-caliber machine gun. It was not uncommon for weapons to rust overnight from the combination of extremely high humidity and dense jungle on Bataan.

eral of the service command and Selleck's immediate superior, showed up along with Brig. Gen. Richard Marshall, MacArthur's deputy chief of staff on Bataan. Together the three men, after agreeing that the Caibobo information was probably a deception, began working on the trouble at hand. Despite their good intentions, however, the delayed efforts made at dislodging the Japanese on Quinauan over eight hours after their initial landing failed. Later that night, Selleck received a phone call from Marshall from his Bataan Echelon Headquarters at Little Baguio informing him that Gen. MacArthur expected him to take personal charge of the Quinauan attack the next morning.

But the wheels were not through turning. Working under the misapprehension that the enemy force on the Point was much smaller than it was, Marshall was able to convince Sutherland that Selleck had failed to dislodge the Japanese by not pushing his initial counterattack aggressively enough. In reaction, no doubt, to Marshall's opinion, Sutherland later that same night phoned Col. Clinton A. Pierce, commanding officer of the 26th Cavalry, at his regimental command post just north of Bagac. Pierce was told that effective as soon as he could get there, he was to relieve Gen. Selleck as commanding officer of the forces along the west coast.

Brig. Gen. Clinton Pierce interrogating a handful of Japanese prisoners captured during the battle of the Points.

At 4:00 A.M., Col. Pierce soberly entered Selleck's command post and reported to him that Gen. MacArthur had ordered him to immediately assume command of the sector. Within slightly more than 24 hours since the first shot was fired on Quinauan Point, hardly enough time to even fairly analyze the situation, Gen. Selleck had the jolt of having his command yanked out from under him. But there was more. He would lose his star too. From that time on, until the end of the battle of Bataan, it would be Col. Clyde Selleck.*

Throughout all of the next day and into the morning of the 25th, the battle to dislodge what was, according to Marshall, the "small number of Japanese" who had come ashore on Quinauan had netted the constabulary attackers absolutely nothing.

The situation in the south, during the same time period, found the Japanese resistance stiffening, too. A daytime reconnaissance of that area by sailors and Marines had placed the enemy in two isolated groups, one on Longoskawayan and the other on adjacent Lipiay Point. But piecemeal efforts failed to oust them before dark on the 24th.

At a few minutes before ten o'clock that night, just when it appeared that the only hope of reaping any kind of battle success at all against the Japanese had gone with the setting sun, things began to warm up. Hampered by the lack of fuel, only one boat from the Inshore Patrol, Ens. George Cox's PT-41, had come out to patrol the west coast that night. On board were lieutenants Ed DeLong and, of course, red-bearded and red-eyed John Bulkeley, who had yet to miss a run since the patrols were instated.

By 9:45, the boat reached a point just off the western entrance to Subic Bay, bringing Cox to cut down to one engine in an effort to eliminate as much noise as possible. Minutes later, lookouts spotted a Japanese ship silhouetted against the background of Sampoloc Bay. It appeared to Bulkeley to be an auxiliary aircraft carrier because of its modern, streamlined shape.

Closing quietly to about 2,500 yards, with all hands now poised at general quarters, Cox shoved the throttles up against the instrument panel. The 41 responded with a leaping roar toward the enemy ship. With DeLong on the torpedos, Cox bore in: 1,800 yards, 1,200, 800, then "fire one." Undaunted by the heavy return fire now coming from the enemy ship, it was 300 yards more before the second torpedo was fired. This one, however, caromed off the deck before entering the water, forcing it awry of the target.

Now no less than 400 yards from the target, Cox turned hard to port, bringing his four .50s along with rifle fire from the entire uncommitted

After the war, a special War Department Board of Officers investigation restored Selleck, retroactive to January 25, 1942, to the rank of brigadier general.

Top: U.S. Marines muster on the edge of Mariveles Field prior to moving out to Longoskawayan Point area—their only action on Bataan. *Bottom:* A truckload of 4th Marines debark for Longoskawayan Point in late January 1942. Most of the Marines were brought to the Philippines from Shanghai, China, a few weeks before the war broke out.

crew, who had come topside, broadside to the target. About then, the first torpedo, according to Bulkeley, "struck home, and pieces of wreckage fell in the water all around us."

At that, the skipper completed his 180-degree turn away from the now burning Japanese ship, only to be bracketed suddenly on both sides by geysers of water thrown up by shells exploding from the enemy's nearby 3-inch shore battery. Executing a maneuver aptly described by Bulkeley as "getting the hell out of there," the 41 began her zigzagging exit from Sampoloc Bay, just barely clearing an antisubmarine net strung part way across the entrance.

Although the auxiliary carrier later turned out to be a 6,000-ton transport ship, the successful action of Motor Torpedo Boat Squadron Three on the night of January 24, 1942, had salvaged at least something from the day's efforts.[6]

In anticipation of its being needed the next day, sometime during the night of the 24th, Corregidor sent one of its U.S. Marine 81-mm. mortar sections to the Naval Battalion at Bataan, which Cmdr. Bridget promptly placed in a position where they could shell Lipiay Point the next morning. This decision proved to be a wise one, as, under the excellent direction of Lt. Hogaboom, fire from the two 81s had forced the Japanese completely off their position on the point by the afternoon of the 25th. The only remaining force, estimated to be around 200 in number, was now concentrated on Longoskawayan.[7]

Lieutenant Holdredge, who in the meantime had been assigned to clear Longoskawayan, had found the going very tough. Attacking with two platoons of sailors and Marines, all had gone well until they were about halfway down the 700-yard-long peninsula. At that point, Holdredge and the lead element of his platoon were caught in the open by a Japanese machine gun. Thirteen of the 15 men in the group were hit, including its commanding officer. Unable to continue, Holdredge turned command of the remaining sailors and Marines over to Ens. Lowell Williamson. Although a PBY pilot when the war started, Williamson acted with the coolness of a veteran infantry officer. Instead of pulling back, he ordered the advance to continue, alternately leapfroging half his men forward while the other half covered them. They had worked their way down the point about 100 yards against moderate opposition when suddenly all hell broke loose. Finding himself pinned down under intense enemy fire, Williamson quickly ordered his men to pull back. Unfortunately, in attempting to recross the open spot on the ridge where Lt. Holdredge had been ambushed, they again found the Japanese waiting. There was no cover and the enemy fire was on target. Many of those who chose to run for it never made it. The smart ones crawled. It was nearly dark before the last man reached the safety of the positions they had left earlier that day on the Pucot–Mauankis ridge. Twenty-nine men who had been with them that morning had been lost.[8]

By now, stories about the fight taking place on the two nearby points were being passed around by some of the wounded sailors and Marines recovering in the navy's Mine Tunnel Hospital on the Section Base at Mariveles. Stories of their adventures triggered sailors from all over the area to draw rifles and ammunition and head for the action in groups of two and three. Of this bold, strange looking "soldier," yet another Japanese soldier was to write in his diary, "We have encountered a new kind of enemy. They come walking to the front yelling 'Hey, Mac, where the hell are you?' They are completely without fear."

There were other stories, too—stories about Japanese trickery. A Japanese soldier, it was told, stepped out of the jungle in front of Marine positions on Longoskawayan with his hands above his head, muttering something like "me surrender, me surrender." Four Marines stepped out to bring him in when suddenly a Japanese machine gun opened up, killing two of them instantly. This was the first of several incidents that helped convince Americans and Filipinos that the word "surrender" was not part of the Japanese vocabulary.[9]

Commander Bridget's request for help from Corregidor on the night of the 24th, which resulted in the release of the 81s, had also reached the ears of Col. Paul Bunker, commander of the Rock's Seaward Defenses. The former two-time football All-American from West Point was, needless to say, ready, able, and anxious to pitch in. On hand, especially for this type of fire mission, were a couple of hundred 670-pound, 12-inch antipersonnel mortar shells with an effective bursting radius of 5,000 yards.

After his initial "disappointment of having to wait over 18 hours for the okay," the anxious Bunker was turned loose just after midnight on the 26th. Finally, for the first time since the American Civil War, a major caliber coast artillery battery fired, lobbing sixteen 12-inch rounds onto Longoskawayan. According to Hogaboom and Lt. Dick Fullmer, who were directing the fire by field telephone, the historic first-fire mission, anticlimatically, was nowhere near the mark.[10] The efforts to dislodge the enemy from the point made during the same day failed, as well. As on the 25th, the last entry on Cmdr. Bridget's "official report" on the actions of the 26th would read "no change in position."[11]

That evening, however, prospects for a more successful action against the enemy on Longoskawayan on the following day increased. Just after dark, a battery of 75-mm. guns from the Philippine Scout 88th Field Artillery Regiment, who just two nights before had withdrawn from their positions behind the Abucay line, arrived.

While the tired but efficient Scout gunners began the arduous task of moving their weapons into position for the next morning, eight miles away on the opposite side of the peninsula seven army air corps lieutenants were preparing to take off on a special, long-awaited mission that they themselves had been allowed to plan.

For the first time since the battle of Bataan began, the air corps was going to "come out of hiding" to launch an offensive air attack on the enemy. The targets were Nichols and Nielson Fields south of Manila, which according to intelligence reports were loaded with enemy planes. It would be a low-risk raid made under the cover of darkness.

Loaded with three 100-pound fragmentation bombs under each wing, the first of seven P-40s lifted off dusty Bataan Field at 8:10 P.M. Bob Ibold, piloting the second fighter, overestimated the length of the blacked-out, dust-shrouded runway and ground looped at the far end of the field amidst a flash of exploding fragmentation bombs.

As the shocked and saddened rescuers, apprehensively sick at what they might find, reached the wreckage, much to their amazement and relief, they found the pilot still alive. Despite the detonation of three of the 100-pound bombs, Ibold, although in shock and badly burned, would survive.

The remaining pilots, although shaken, got off safely. After passing over darkened Corregidor, the six planes, flown by lieutenants Woolery, Hall, Stinson, Obert, Baker, and Brown, headed for Manila, whose brightly lit shoreline and city, almost sneeringly ignoring air raid blackout precautions, literally beckoned them to their targets.

Because of a light tule-fog the flight was down to less than 3,000 feet when they came screaming in over the two fields. The six American fighters were carrying out the most successful offensive air attack against the Japanese since the war started. Time after time the planes, almost without opposition from the ground, roared over the brightly lit fields, stealing scene after scene from any one of half a dozen of Hollywood's old World War I flying films. One by one the planes returned, leaving the flames from burning fuel dumps, hangars, and aircraft behind, lighting up the sky so brightly that it could be seen from Bataan itself.

One of the pilots, Lt. Dave Obert, on his way back, spotted "a wonderful target—a long [enemy] convoy with all lights on driving toward Bataan." Concentrating on "shooting out all the ... lights," Obert barely missed flying his P-40 straight into the road behind the last truck. With bombs and ammunition gone, but luck still holding, he too headed for home.

Two of the first planes back landed at Cabcaben, refueled, reloaded and actually took off again. The success of the first attack had created so much smoke, however, that no targets could been seen, so happily the pilots returned home.

Thirty-seven enemy planes were estimated to have been destroyed and numerous others damaged. The Japanese claimed in the Manila newspapers the next day that there were over 300 casualties from the raids. Finally, and perhaps most gratifying to the Bataan flyers, from the next night on the "cocksure little bastards blacked out every military installation in and around Manila."[12]

By the time the last of the six American fighters had been pushed safely back into their well-hidden revetments on the edge of Bataan Field, orders had come down for the Naval Battalion to attack the enemy positions on Longoskawayan again the next morning. Only this time it would be on the heels of the biggest coordinated artillery barrage that could be put together.

At 7:00 A.M. on the 27th, the newly positioned Scout 75s, along with the two Marine 81-mm. mortars, a 2.95-inch pack howitzer from the 71st F.A., and 12-inch mortars of Battery Geary on Corregidor simultaneously shattered the morning's silence with the first rounds of what would be an hour-long interdiction of Longoskawayan Point. Within minutes the entire target area was engulfed in dust and smoke. Reports from Lt. Fullmer, spotting from atop Mt. Pucot back to Corregidor, led Col. Bunker to believe that nobody would be left alive afterwards.[13]

For the enemy, the effect was terrifying. A Japanese soldier who was later captured said, "We could not know where the big shells or bombs were coming from. They seemed to be falling from the sky. Some of my companions jumped off the cliff to escape the terrific fire."

Although "terrified," the Americans soon discovered, once the barrage lifted, that the Japanese spirit as well as their defenses were still intact. In fact, the attacking sailors and Marines soon found themselves in trouble, having inadvertently left a gap in their lines that the wily enemy troops took quick advantage of, causing a near split of the battalion.

Commander Bridget, in telephone communication with Lt. Hogaboom from his field headquarters a few yards off the end of Mariveles fighter strip, however, was immediately onto the problem. It was at that exact moment, in fact, that Associated Press correspondent Clark Lee stopped by to say hello to his old friend and was able to record the following series of events. "From his conversation on the phones," began Lee, "I could tell I'd arrived at a crucial time...."

"What's that Hogey?" Bridget yelled into one of the receivers. "You can't hold them? You've got to hold them Hogey old boy!"

Quickly on another phone to one of the Scout 75s. "Perez, you've got to lay a few shells in there in front of Lieutenant Hogaboom. ... You have nine rounds, right? ... You've got to make every one count."

Back to "Hogey. Watch this now. Perez is going to throw one over for you. Tell me where it lands."

Again to Perez. "Okay. Let the first one go." Off to the right somewhere in the jungle, the 75 roars.

MOP-UP OPERATIONS ON LONGOSKAWAYAN PT.
JAN. 27 - FEB. 1

MAP No. 16

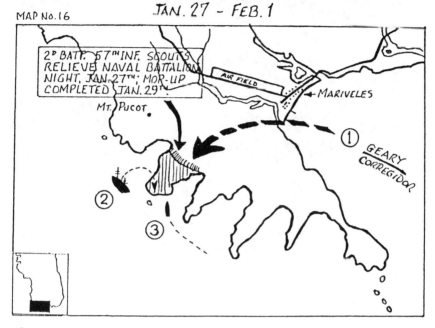

① BATTERY GEARY SHELLS JAPANESE ON LONGOSKAWAYAN POINT FROM CORREGIDOR - JAN. 27, 28.

② MINESWEEPER USS. QUAIL DIRECTS FIRE FROM BATTERY GEARY AND SHELL JAPANESE ON LONGOSKAWAYAN CLIFFS - JANUARY 28.

③ "MICKEY MOUSE BATTLESHIP" GUNBOAT FROM CANOPUS MOP-UP ALONG LONGOSKAWAYAN CLIFFS - JAN. 31, FEB. 1

"Hogey. How was that? A little off? Okay. Hold everything."

"Perez. ... Just ten yards more elevation, son. ..."

"Hogey. How was that? On the nose. Swell kid."

"Perez. That was just right. Fire the rest of them." Perez did "fire the rest" and although staggered, the Japanese were still able to continue their push against the weakened Naval Battalion center.[14]

It wasn't long, however, before Hogaboom was able to regroup his reeling forces and stop the enemy thrust. Although saved momentarily by the accurate fire from Perez's 75, a report came through to Cmdr. Bridget indicating that without reinforcements, the battalion could not continue the attack or, for that matter, even hold their existing positions. Bridget's

Captain Arthur Wermuth (right) with a Philippine Scout, possibly his Bataan sidekick, Cpl. Crispin "Jock" Jacob.

terse reply to "dig in and prepare to continue the attack tomorrow morning," meant that again, for the third time in as many days, the dogged Japanese had bested the U.S. attempts to push them off of Longoskawayan.

Unbeknownst to the 65 or 70 Marines and 130 or so sailors of the Naval Battalion, they wouldn't be the ones to "continue the attack" the next morning after all.

After his reply to Hogaboom, Bridget got on the line to headquarters on Corregidor where he got permission to relieve his beleaguered battalion with 57th Infantry Scouts, bivouacked just a few kilometers up the West Road. Less than 30 minutes later, half a dozen open-sided red buses full of the eager fighters pulled up. Quietly and efficiently, the first of 500 men from the 57th's 2d Battalion detailed to the battle moved out. Around midnight, with a tap on the shoulder and an "Okay, Joe. You go now. I take over . . .," the Naval Battalion was relieved. The Scouts were moving in.

Lieutenant Hogaboom, who guided the 57th into position, "was thoroughly impressed by their efficiency, discipline, and precision. . . . They were every inch first class fighting men going in to take over a situation they knew how to handle."[15]

Among those taking over for Hogaboom's company of sailors and Marines, was Capt. Arthur Wermuth, who had brought his now famed "Sniper Company" with him. Under the command of Lt. Col. Harold C.

Silaiim (on left) and Anyasan points as they look today. Twice, attempting to rein-force their troops on adjacent Quinauan Point, the Japanese mislanded on these two similar-looking headlands on the west coast of Bataan. No Japanese soldiers involved in the battles of the points—Longoskawayan, Quinauan, Silaiim, and Anyasan—are known to have escaped.

Granberry and spearheaded by Wermuth's snipers, the 2d Battalion, by nightfall of the next day, had the Japanese bottled up within 300 yards of the tip of the tiny peninsula.

In preparation of what was hoped would be their final attack the next morning, a second coordinated 30-minute artillery barrage in as many days was scheduled to begin at 7 A.M., involving the Scout 75s, Geary's 12-inch mortars plus the guns of the minesweeper, USS *Quail*. The responsibility of spotting the mission was taken by Cmdr. Bridget himself, who, from the *Quail*, would be in radio contact with both Corregidor and the Scouts on the point. (See Map 16.)

As scheduled, the minesweeper shoved off from Corregidor at 5 A.M. with Bridget and two army artillery observers on board. An hour later, while heading up the west coast, the ship was illuminated by two friendly searchlights located on the cliffs above, which Bridget, needless to say, sternly ordered turned off.

Arriving off Longoskawayan at close to 7 A.M., contact was established with Battery Geary, which, seconds later, opened up. Results of the mission read like this in *Quail* commander John Morrill's official report:

Top: **Two very rare items on Bataan: Japanese prisoners and bread.** *Bottom:* **Japanese prisoners being led to a POW compound on Bataan. Japanese soldiers usually preferred suicide to being taken prisoner.**

0700 Corregidor mortars open up. First salvo was in water close off point. Commander Bridget spotted this fire to top of ridge on point. Believe there were four salvos of heavy mortars. Cease fire 0723.

At 7:25, the minesweeper's 3-inch guns were put into use. While Geary was firing, several Japanese were spotted moving into a small cave just off the beach. *Quail's* gunners cut loose from 2,200 yards. In fact, for the next 20 minutes, according to Morrill, who had moved in to 1,300 yards, her guns "systematically searched out every cave, clump of bushes, or tree on the west and south slopes of the point and put one or more bursts in each."[16]

In the meantime, on the heels of the fire from Geary, the Scouts, who had withdrawn back up the point some 500 yards before the shelling began, started back. To their surprise, however, sometime during the barrage a handful of Japanese had actually slipped back into many of the same positions they had been forced out of the day before.

It was while fighting their way back through this area that Wermuth, whose exploits on Bataan had by now made him a legend back home, was struck down by enemy machine gun fire. The single bullet, which entered his side, passed between two ribs and exited through his back. After being pulled out of the clearing where he fell by his half-American, half-Filipino Scout sidekick, Cpl. Crispin "Jock" Jacob, Wermuth remained conscious to witness his friend's successful destruction of the enemy position. When Jock returned to the side of his fallen companion, he too was hit, twice, with both bullets passing clean through the thigh of his right leg. Nevertheless, Jock, a big man and some three or four inches taller than Wermuth, hoisted the still-conscious captain over his shoulder and managed somehow to get them both down to the aid station.

Wermuth would live through what was the third wound received during the battle, and, along with Cpl. Jacob, would be out of the hospital and back with the 57th less than 20 days later.[17]

As for the remainder of the 2d Battalion Scouts, they had the battle of Longoskawayan concluded by three o'clock that afternoon, when all three companies gained possession of the point itself. Although matter-of-factly described in Cmdr. Bridget's official report to Admiral Rockwell dated 29 January 1942 — "Final destruction of the Japanese on Longoskawayan Point was completed in the late afternoon by 2d Battalion of the 57th Infantry" — unofficially, he was delighted it was over. To express his gratitude to the 2d Battalion, a special truck loaded with a generous supply of canned salmon and rice was sent back with them to their regimental bivouac up the West Road.[18]

Losses in the seven-day battle for Longoskawayan and Lipiay Points amounted to the following: United States: Marines and Navy — 11 dead, 26

This decaying concrete-covered rock pyramid marks the U.S. Marine Corps'
cemetery site in the jungle just off the West Road. The six Marines killed in the battle
for Longoskawayan Point were buried here. Their bodies, as in all of the temporary
battlefield cemeteries on Bataan, have been removed to the American Military
Cemetery in Manila or returned to the United States.

wounded; Army (all from 57th)—11 dead, 27 wounded. Japanese: (estimated)—256 dead. Because of the character of the enemy, determined to
fight to the death, even to commit suicide rather than surrender, the job of
mopping-up on the two points was to continue for another four or five days.
For example, on January 30, Lt. Hogaboom and a small detachment of
men ambushed and killed seven enemy soldiers north of Lipiay.

Other Naval Battalion search parties, since January 29, had also
received gunfire from Japanese soldiers who had moved in among the
numerous caves and crevasses on the cliffs behind Longoskawayan. A comment made by Cmdr Bridget one night that the "Japs should be shot out
of their holes from the sea," sent the resourceful crew of the USS *Canopus*
to work on a solution.[19]

There were three 40-foot motor launches on board the "Old Lady"
that, with some conversion, could do the job. In less than 12 hours, the
Bataan Navy's first "Mickey Mouse Battleship" was ready for action. Converted, it looked like this: three-eighths-inch thick armor plating bolted on
the bow and over the engines; sandbags stacked around the gas tank; a

Wounded Filipino soldiers await transportation from this battalion clearing station near the Abucay front to the general hospital at Limay. In late January after the general withdrawal, the Limay hospital was reestablished as Hospital No. 1 in Little Baguio.

captured Japanese 37-mm. antitank gun lashed to the bow; two .50-caliber machine guns set up just behind the bow plating; two .30-caliber machine guns positioned at the waists.

The next morning, Saturday, January 31, the first miniature "battleship," amid shouts of encouragement from a group of envious well-wishers from the *Canopus*, pushed off for Longoskawayan. Under the command of Lt. Cmdr. Harold "Hap" Goodall, executive officer of the *Canopus*, the little boat was to make two 30-mile round-trips to the cliffs and back before the day was over. On the last trip, as evidence of their success, they brought back five emaciated enemy soldiers, three of whom died of wounds en route.

Sunday, February 1, dawned on Bataan just like any other day. The war knew no Sundays or holidays. For the navy that day, another and what was to be the last straggler sweep of Longoskawayan was launched with two boats this time instead of one. After a thorough combing of the area resulted, according to Bridget, in sending "only four more Japs after their ancestors," the gunboats were temporarily mothballed. Unbeknownst to Goodall and his "Irregulars," as they tabbed themselves during this action, the Longoskawayan cleanup was just a warm-up for what was to come eight days later in a similar action off Quinauan Point, some seven miles farther north.[20]

Sunday was also like any other day for the Japanese Air Force. Their target that morning was a cluster of barrack-looking buildings along the edge of the bay near the barrio of Limay. The 20-minute uncontested raid left the barracks a burning shambles. Fortunately, however, they were empty at the time—but barely. From the early part of January up until just ten hours before the raid, they had been the site of Bataan's General Hospital. Along with the doctors, dentists, nurses, and technicians, there were close to 1,000 patients in various stages of recovery housed in the prewar Philippine Scout barracks, now used as wards.

The general withdrawal from positions on Abucay to positions on the Bagac-Orion line on January 25 had left Hospital No. 1 less than three and a half miles from the new front. A search was immediately begun for spots most ideal for the needs of a large hospital. On the 27th, it was decided that an old prewar motor-pool site nestled among the tall trees of what was soon called Little Baguio would fill the bill. Most of the buildings in the area could be converted to hospital use, water was nearby, and it was cool in comparison to most of the peninsula.

The next day, January 28, the entire hospital was ordered evacuated, according to nurse Lt. Juanita Redmond, "further back in the jungle and high in the mountains." It wasn't until just before midnight of the 31st that the last truck, loaded with miscellaneous pieces of equipment, pulled away from the darkened, empty buildings and small cemetery where 64 white crosses marked the final resting place of soldiers who had died despite the efforts of the hospital staff. By 10 A.M. the next day, little except the cemetery was recognizable from what just 24 hours before had been the largest and busiest hospital on Bataan.

The Little Baguio site was picked to minimize the threat of bombing, but in fact a worse site could not have been found short of the front line itself. After a few days of getting their bearings, everyone on the hospital staff realized that they had placed themselves right in the center of one of the choicest military targets on Bataan. On the left sat a huge II Corps ammunition dump; on the right, a motor pool; on the hill behind, a unit of antiaircraft; across the road in front, a large quartermaster supply dump; and down the road a few hundred yards, USAFFE's important Bataan Echelon Headquarters. Wrote Dr. Alfred Weinstein of the situation that came to exist, "We heard the deafening crash of falling bombs day after day."

The site offered yet another annoyance: The hospital stood adjacent to a rather steep part of the Mariveles Road, which had to be negotiated over a series of switchbacks known as the zigzag. Heavily laden vehicles gearing down to negotiate its sharp turns actually caused the very ground under the hospital to shake. Worse than that, trucks "grinding up this steep grade," according to Weinstein, "sounded exactly like Nip bombers...." Everytime it happened, everyone stopped what he was doing, "listening to the grind of the motor, praying for the change in the sound when the truck driver shifted his gears into second."

In the meantime, a summary of the results of the action against the Japanese on Quinauan on January 25, like that on Longoskawayan on the same date, also showed a "no change in position" situation. Ground activity by the constabulary against the well dug-in enemy on the point during that period, however, had left one of its officers with not one but two eerie and somewhat providential experiences.

While operating as temporary commander of the 1st Battalion, Capt. Louis Marohombsar had volunteered to deliver a supply of hand grenades to one of his company commanders, who had requested them especially for use against a nearby enemy machine gun nest. Arriving just in time to witness the operation, the lieutenant, with Marohombsar crouched nearby, lobbed one of the grenades in the direction of the enemy position. Hugging the ground, the two men began silently counting off the seconds before the explosion when suddenly, "Thud!" Horrified, both men looked down to see the very same grenade spin to a stop between them. It had been hot-potatoed back to them by one of the Japanese machine gunners. But, to the astonishment of the two terrified officers, it did not explode. It was, of all things and of all times, a dud.

While still in shock from the first incident, less than 24 hours later, Marohombsar would walk away from his second "flirt with death" in as many days. It came while visiting another company of his battalion. An enemy position was in the process of being bombarded by mortar fire when he arrived. No sooner had the first round been routinely loaded and fired, than "thud," it was back again at the feet of the startled gun crew. Again, however, there was no explosion. For Marohombsar, it was another dud, this one having ricocheted off of the limb of one of the giant banyan trees that surrounded the position before plummeting back to earth not ten feet from where he was standing. Needless to say, it was a much more religious Filipino captain that happily turned the battalion back to its original commander, Capt. Jose Tando, the next day.[21]

It was not until the afternoon of the 26th, almost four full days since the enemy landing at Quinauan, that the Fil-Americans were able to make any headway against the Japanese. Even more makeshift in character than the Naval Battalion on Longoskawayan, the Quinauan force jumped off that day at 3 P.M. in its biggest attempt thus far to dislodge the determined invaders. To the left of the 1st Battalion, 1st Constabulary Regiment, which had remained in the thick of the battle since the 23d, Col. Pierce had assigned a battalion of Philippine Army Air Corps. Like its big brother U.S. Army Air Corps units, the small force of PAAC boys had been training as infantrymen in the Rodriguez Park area on the east side of Bataan since arriving on the peninsula in early January. The day before, January 25, a handful of the Filipino airmen got their baptism of fire on Quinauan while reconnoitering the extent of enemy gains on the point. Although easily chased off by the Japanese, the operation resulted in one man receiving the U.S. Army's Distinguished Service Cross and two others receiving the Silver Star.

Major Pelagio Cruz, commanding officer of the regiment, picked up a Silver Star through a "personal display of extraordinary courage and leadership" while under fire. Time and time again, according to his citation, "despite heavy machine gun fire, he crawled forward to where his foremost riflemen were, thus inspiring leadership."

Captain Eustacio Orobia, executive officer of the PAAC, like Cruz, received his Silver Star for a similar display of courage and leadership while "coordinating the efforts of his men advancing through the thick Quinauan jungle." It was because of the fiercely thick jungle, however, that no one was around to see Orobia get hit by enemy sniper fire. In fact, so intense did the enemy fire become that no one was able to stay around long enough to see anything. The subsequent hurried withdrawal of the PAAC back to their line of departure of that morning would have been fatal to the badly wounded Orobia, except for the courage of another man of the unit.

The Distinguished Service Cross citation of PAAC Capt. Pedro Molina reads: "Observing that an officer lying about 20 yards to his front was seriously wounded and bleeding profusely, [he] rushed to the aid of the man without considering the hail of enemy machine gun fire in the area, and carried him to safety. . ."

It is doubtful that Capt. Molina himself was any more proud of the DSC he had won than was the man he saved while earning it.[22]

On the constabulary right was Company A of the U.S. 803d Aviation Engineer Battalion, who, inopportunely, had been working on widening the West Road through the Quinauan area when the Japanese landed. Although only 90 strong, they were handed the responsibility of anchoring the entire right side of the line, keeping them, as well as the PAAC, close to the middle of the bitter fight almost from the beginning.[23] The responsibility of protecting the extreme ends of the line along the edge and face of the cliffs, was given to two U.S. Air Corps squadrons, the 34th on the north and the 21st on the Agloloma Bay side.

Launched without the usual preliminary artillery and mortar assault that had thus far announced the U.S. attacks, the unorthodox assault caught the Japanese in the frontline foxholes completely by surprise. Aside from an occasional isolated burst of small arms fire, the fight became, for the most, a quiet although deadly hand-to-hand, bayonet-to-bayonet, and in some cases, fist-to-fist series of individual duels. By nightfall, the Japanese had been pushed out of their frontline positions, which were discovered to be a remarkable series of cleverly placed, mutually supporting foxholes and trenches—one of the reasons why they had remained unbreachable for four full days.

As the constabulary organized their new perimeter within the freshly captured enemy positions that night, they did so with the knowledge that they had registered the first gain against the Japanese since their landing on January 23.

Early the next morning, after the usual night-long struggle against the counterattacking and infiltrating Japanese, the Fil-Americans struck again. And again, despite an initial setback, with the constabulary leading the way, the assault was successful. By noon, the stubborn enemy had lost another 50 yards of line along with a second network of foxholes. But the cost to the Fil-Americans was high, particularly within the spearheading constabulary units. It was doubtful, in fact, that the assault could be continued without reinforcements.[24]

Ironically, at almost that very moment, Scouts of the 3d Battalion, 45th Infantry were making preparations to reinforce the constabulary. Although the timing couldn't have been better, it had not been the situation on Quinauan that brought it about. The changes were the result of an attempt made by the Japanese earlier that morning to reinforce their position on the point. Like the entire 2d Battalion that had gone before them, the single reinforcing company of 200 Japanese soldiers from the 20th Infantry's 1st Battalion, had also failed to land on the proper point. Instead of Quinauan, the combination of a dark night and poor seamanship put the enemy ashore at yet another unplanned location. This one, Silaiim Point, a headland rarely identified on most maps, was some 2,000 yards short of their intended objective.[25]

Regardless of the size or location of the landing, the Japanese intention to reinforce themselves was enough to draw the special attention of Gen. MacArthur on Corregidor. Convinced with this landing that the enemy now posed a serious threat to Bataan's west coast, MacArthur, that night, phoned Gen. Jonathan Wainwright at his newly established headquarters on the West Road.

With completion of the withdrawal from the Mauban-Abucay positions two days earlier, overall command of the west coast, from Bagac to Mariveles, had been given to Wainwright. In reaction to MacArthur's concern, Wainwright ordered Maj. Dudley Strickler's 3d Battalion, 45th Infantry Scouts to Quinauan that afternoon.

Army Air Corps pilots at Bataan Field headquarters eating, but not necessarily enjoying, breakfast. Captain Ed Dyess is second from left.

By midnight, the 3d Battalion had taken position across the entire 900-yard-wide point in anticipation of attacking at dawn. Soon, for the efficient Scout soldiers, Quinauan Point would become one square mile of living hell, as it already had to the constabulary, engineers, and airmen.

After five days fighting over the same small patch of ground, the putrid stench of rotting jungle and decaying human flesh permeated the stifling blanket of humid air that hung over it. Bodies of dead enemy snipers dangling grotesquely from the trees into which they had tied themselves, were everywhere, as were the maggot-covered carcasses of their dead comrades on the ground. It was not that the Americans and Filipinos had preferred it that way, but rather that almost any attempt at policing the battlefield of enemy or friendly dead was met by sniper fire from somewhere nearby. In fact, until the defending troops caught on to their tricks, many "dead" Japanese soldiers rose up and shot an American or Filipino in the back during an unguarded moment within friendly lines. Soon, according to air corps Capt. Ed Dyess, commanding officer of the 21st Pursuit Squadron on Quinauan, "we countered this by never passing a 'dead' Jap without shooting him to make sure he was hors de combat."

One gruff young sergeant with Dyess "was particularily adept at spotting 'possuming Japs'." One day, after staring at a "dead" one lying against a nearby tree, he said, "Cap'n, I don't think that buzzard's dead." Dyess

Captain Ed Dyess led the attack on Subic Bay on March 3.

told him to shoot him and find out. He did. "The Jap bounced to a sitting position then fell over." He was shot twice more "to make it official."

Later that same day while moving into a "particularily dense jungle sector," one of Dyess' men, with a little "whistling in the dark" humor, asked the captain how to tell "which are Japs and which are monkeys?" The same sergeant, answering for Dyess, replied that we "eat the ones that ain't got uniforms on."

For the untrained, poorly equipped air corps squadrons, their Quinauan experience, although only temporarily over, had been a bitter one. In fact, wrote Dyess, "before the sleepless days and nights had ended, we were so weary, dirty, and starved, we didn't care whether we were shot or not."[26]

For inauspicious Company A of the 803d Engineers though, the battle was over. Although suffering over 50 percent casualties during the five days and nights of fighting (of the 90 men of the company, 47 were casualties, 9 of whom had been killed), more of the engineers came out of the jungle cussing their inadequate equipment and homemade hand grenades for failing to explode than did those who seemed to care about being relieved.[27] A week later, what was left of the company—according to Capt. Allison Ind of the air corps "as tough a fighting outfit as ever set foot on Bataan"—was transferred to Corregidor for the duration of the battle.

By noon of their first day of battle, January 28, Maj. Strickler's hardy Scouts were already well aware that they were up against an even tougher if not more fanatical enemy soldier than they had faced earlier on the Abucay line. It seemed to the Filipinos that, for all practical purposes, the Japanese had conceded all chances of victory in lieu of killing as many men as possible before being killed themselves. Enemy positions seemed also to lose all semblance of the organization they once had. Their strategy had changed. There were no more counterattacks, and little infiltrating. Fighting had narrowed down to search-and-destroy tactics against an enemy that had concealed itself in a stinking mass of matted and entwined tropical underbrush. In fact, a comment made by an American sergeant attached to the 45th that he "believed the goddamn jungle had even gone over to the Japs side" may best describe the jungle's effects.

For four days, despite the addition of a company of 57th Infantry troops, the tough Scouts could only account for gains of little more than 40 yards. As an indicator of how rough the going was, the casualty rate for the adept veterans for the four day period was a staggering 50 percent.

After analyzing the reports of the meager gains recorded by the Scouts on the evening of January 31, a worried Gen. MacArthur phoned Gen. James Weaver at Tank Group Headquarters on Bataan. For the first time in the battle, for the first time in World War II for that matter, close coordination between American tanks and infantry in jungle warfare was going to be attempted.[28]

While the tanks of the 192d Tank Battalion readied for their movement across the peninsula the next morning, the 3d Battalion Scouts struck again. Aiming at the center of the line where resistance had remained the stiffest despite an especially heavy preliminary mortar concentration, the attack again waned. The casualties, again high, this time sadly included the 3d Battalion's popular commander, Maj. Dudley Strickler. Few, if any, field-grade officers on Bataan had performed any more efficiently under fire. Even when confusion had become the rule during the withdrawal from Abucay on the dark, difficult night of January 25, Strickler's leadership kept his battalion the exception. Seven days later, on the last day of the battle for Quinauan, the major's partially decomposed body was found well inside the enemy position. He had been shot in the head.

Despite the loss of their beloved commander, February 2 dawned with new hope for the battered 3d Battalion. By midmorning, the first tanks arrived, much to the elation of the newly arrived battalion commander, Capt. Clifton Croom. At 3:30 that afternoon, the initial attack, with the tanks well out in front, got under way. Probing blindly about the matted undergrowth and huge fallen trees, the tankers, with the Scouts lagging cautiously behind, failed to gain. Four more times that day the tanks went in, and four more times they came out empty-handed and frustrated.

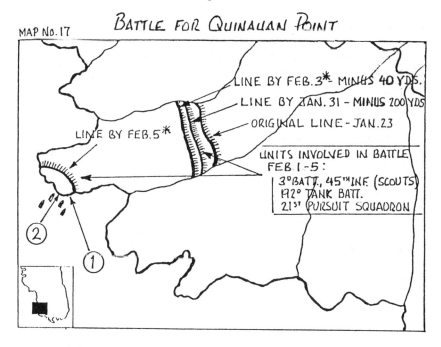

MAP No.17 — BATTLE FOR QUINAUAN POINT

* = FEB. 3 - FEB. 5 - FIRST COORDINATED USE OF TANKS AND INFANTRY ON BATAAN.

① = FEB. 5 - JAPANESE SOLDIERS, TO AVOID CAPTURE, COMMIT SUICIDE BY LEAPING FROM CLIFFS OR DROWNING SELVES IN SURF.

② = FEB. 7 - CDR. GOODALL AND CAPT. DYESS LEAD MOP-UP OPERATIONS WITH 2 GUNBOATS AND 2 WHALEBOATS AGAINST JAPANESE ON CLIFFS. ALL BOATS SUNK BY ENEMY PLANES; GOODALL WOUNDED; OPERATION STILL SUCCESSFUL.

Throughout the next day, the trial-by-fire assaults continued with the same maddening results registered each time. Even when the jungle, which in some places had been trampled down and shot away, ceased to become a factor, the tankers were unable to effectively spot the elusive enemy.

That night a meeting of the frustrated infantry and tank commanders was held. Colonel Donald Hilton, who had assumed command of the entire Quinauan operation the day before, at the pleadings of the perplexed tankers agreed to attempt to coordinate the next day's attacks with radios. Part of the answer to the effective use of tanks in jungle warfare was about to be found.[28]

For additional support for the battered Filipinos, Hilton ordered Capt. Ed Dyess and his 70-man strong 21st Pursuit Squadron, who were bivouacked nearby, back onto the battlefield. For the airmen, who had been off the line for six days, the front presented a slightly different picture this time. Although much of the thick, impenetrable undergrowth had been blasted away or smashed down by the tanks, the line itself appeared no more than 50 yards nearer the point than it had six days before. "The stench of death," magnified by the unbearable heat and humidity, appeared, according to Dyess, "everywhere." Even the Scouts, normally perky and confident, seemed dispirited. But rightfully so: Their casualty rate, with little to show for their efforts, had reached the incredible figure of 60 percent.[29]

Early the next morning, February 4, the first truly coordinated tank and infantry attack of the young Pacific war began. For the first time since the constabulary had recorded gains ten days earlier, success was achieved. Following behind in his radio control car, Hilton, in walkie-talkie contact with both tank and infantry commanders, had so effectively coordinated the attack that by nightfall the Japanese had literally been pushed to the very edge of the point.

On the morning of February 5, with the blue waters of the South China Sea reflecting at last through the trees, the attack was resumed. Tanks, with the infantry close on their heels, began moving up, while blasting away with everything they had. Soon the Japanese, jammed into an area about the size of a football field, could be seen moving around like ants just flushed from their nests. (See Map 17.)

"Suddenly," wrote Dyess, "above the noise of gunfire, we could hear shrieks and high-pitched yelling. Scores of Japs were tearing their uniforms and leaping off the cliffs." Within minutes the Americans and Filipinos who had worked their way to the cliff's edge became witness to yet another enemy spectacle. The narrow stretch of rocky beach some 75 to 100 feet below was littered with the bodies of those who had chosen suicide rather than surrender. Those Japanese who had apparently lacked the courage to jump to their deaths were "running wildly up and down plunging into the surf." Before long, American and Filipino automatic weapons had joined in helping the Japanese speed up the process, "annihilating all who moved. ... Presently," concluded Capt. Dyess, "the waves were rolling in stained with blood and dotted with dead Japs."[30]

Throughout the remainder of that day and into the next, efforts to extricate the handful of remaining enemy soldiers who had taken cover below the cliffs continued. Despite their efforts, however, the Americans and Filipinos found it impossible to make any headway from the beach, which forced them into the very difficult maneuver of ferreting out their fanatical opponents from above.

Meanwhile, Gen. Wainwright, who found it "hard to believe" when notified that the Japanese were actually refusing to surrender, wasted no time in taking steps to end the battle. On the afternoon of the 5th, he placed a call to Lt. Cmdr. "Hap" Goodall on the *Canopus* requesting that he standby with his armored motor launches in case he was needed to help mop-up on Quinauan. If he was needed his orders would be sent down to him with an infantry spotter and a small landing party from one of the units fighting on the point.

Next, Wainwright contacted his I Corps chief engineer, Col. Harry Skerry, and ordered him to lead a platoon of explosives engineers down to help blast the Japanese out of the caves on Quinauan Point.

Skerry and a platoon from the Philippine Army's 71st Engineer Battalion were on the job bright and early the next morning. Most of the enemy by then were holed-up somewhere between a brushy ravine and two large caves at the base of the cliff. Skerry went right to work, getting a Scout volunteer to work his way down the cliff face and swing a 50-pound box of dynamite into the mouth of one of the caves. On his second descent, however, the scout was shot and killed by a sniper from somewhere down below. This brought the engineers to seek another solution. Lashing four sticks of dynamite around a 30-second fuse was the answer. Throwing the "homemade" grenades, the engineers' and Scouts' accuracy soon flushed about 50 of the enemy from the ravine into one of the large caves. With most of them bottled-up inside, the engineers lowered an entire case of explosives down the front of the entrance, which, according to Skerry, promptly "blew the place to pieces."

Despite the success achieved by the engineers, Scout patrols continued to be fired upon throughout the day by scattered remnants of Japanese still hidden along the cliff face. Later that afternoon, Capt. Dyess was given orders to report with 20 of his men to Cmdr. "Hap" Goodall at the Navy Section Base at Mariveles. Orders were for him to direct fire the next morning for the navy's gunboats against the cliffs, and then to personally lead from the beach below his 20-man landing party against the remaining few enemy.

That night Dyess and his men were taken by truck to Mariveles, where, over a hot meal on the *Canopus*, he and Cmdr. Goodall discussed the coming operation. Among other things, Dyess mentioned that the Scouts would have white sheets lowered to a point just above the known enemy positions on the cliff for them the next morning.

With Dyess on board one of the "Mickey Mouse Battleships" with Goodall, the tiny flotilla of two homemade gunboats followed by two motor whaleboats carrying the 20 airmen shoved off from Mariveles at 6 A.M. (See Map 17.)

Two hours later they were off Quinauan Point, where the two captured Japanese 37-mm. guns, lashed to the armor plated bows of the little gunboats, were promptly put to work. After about ten minutes of shooting, the cry came that "enemy planes [were] approaching from the east!" Goodall, standing next to Dyess, calmly retorted, "to hell with the airplanes. Where do you want the next shot, Captain?"

But the "next shot" was to be the last, as, with four enemy dive-bombers closing in, Goodall frantically signaled for the boats to take off for shore. Before it had gone 20 yards, one of the whaleboats was upset from a near miss, dumping most of its air corps occupants over the side. Then one of the gunboats, lashing out at the enemy planes with its two .30-caliber machine guns, was struck.

The last thing Dyess saw before a near miss overturned the boat with him and Cmdr. Goodall on board was the second whaleboat full of airmen getting clobbered. It was a mess. In less than three minutes, all four boats had been either overturned or destroyed. As the survivors dragged themselves onto the shore, the sailors counted three men dead and four wounded. One of the dead was Gunners Mate Charles Kramb, who had bagged one of the enemy dive-bombers before losing his life. Among the seriously wounded was Cmdr. Goodall, who had taken hits in both legs and couldn't walk. For their action that morning, the United States Army awarded both Kramb, posthumously, and Goodall its highest honor—the Distinguished Service Cross.

Dyess, meanwhile, after taking muster of his bedraggled men, who amazingly had all made it to shore, moved out against the few remaining Japanese on the cliffs. By noon, with help from the Scouts who cleared the troublesome ravines, the book on the battle for Quinauan Point was officially closed, as also was the history of the entire 2d Battalion, 20th Infantry of the 16th Japanese Division, which, according to Gen. Homma, had been "lost without a trace."[31]

Losses on the U.S. side in the Quinauan battle were also high. "The 3d Battalion [45th Infantry]," wrote Gen. Wainwright, "went into action with a major, four captains, a full complement of lieutenants and 600 men. When it was withdrawn 12 days later, after driving the Japs into the China Sea, it was commanded by a second lieutenant and its force had been hacked down to 212 men."

Not long afterwards, Associated Press correspondent Clark Lee walked the battlefield with Clinton Pierce. He, however, couldn't stay too long; "the stench of death drove me away," he wrote.[32]

The Battle for the Points Continues

"Somewhere between asinine and quinine points."

Although the battle for Longoskawayan and Quinauan Points had been concluded, yet a third chapter to the battle of the points was still to be added.

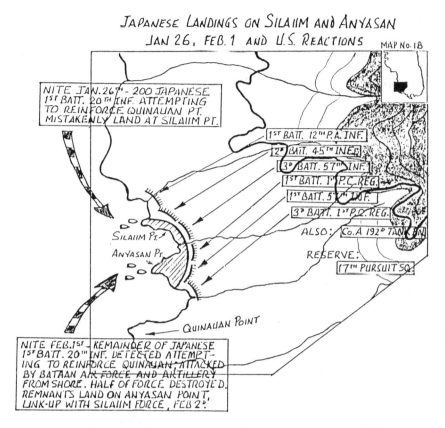

JAPANESE LANDINGS ON SILAIIM AND ANYASAN
JAN 26, FEB.1 AND U.S. REACTIONS   MAP No.18

NITE JAN.26ᵀᴴ - 200 JAPANESE
1ˢᵀ BATT. 20ᵀᴴ INF. ATTEMPTING
TO REINFORCE QUINAUAN PT.
MISTAKENLY LAND AT SILAIIM PT.

1ˢᵀ BATT. 12ᵀᴴ P.A. INF.
2ᵈ BATT. 45ᵀᴴ INF.
3ᵈ BATT. 57ᵀᴴ INF.
1ˢᵀ BATT. 1ˢᵗ P.C. REG.
1ˢᵀ BATT. 5ᵀᴴ INF.
3ᵈ BATT. 1ˢᵗ P.C. REG.

SILAIIM Pt.
ANYASAN Pt.

ALSO: Co.A 192ᵈ TANK BN

RESERVE:
17ᵀᴴ PURSUIT SQ.

QUINAUAN POINT

NITE FEB.1ˢᵀ - REMAINDER OF JAPANESE
1ˢᵀ BATT. 20ᵀᴴ INF. DETECTED ATTEMPT-
ING TO REINFORCE QUINAUAN ATTACKED
BY BATAAN AIR FORCE AND ARTILLERY
FROM SHORE. HALF OF FORCE DESTROYED.
REMNANTS LAND ON ANYASAN POINT,
LINK-UP WITH SILAIIM FORCE, FEB 2.

As mentioned earlier, the Japanese, in an attempt to strengthen their position on Quinauan, had dispatched a company of troops by boat to that point on the night of January 26. It will be remembered also that this company of 200 men of the 1st Battalion, 20th Infantry, came ashore a little over a mile short of Quinauan, on a headland identified later as Silaiim Point. (See Map 18.)

The beach where the Japanese landed about 3 A.M. on the morning of the 27th was similar in topography to that below Quinauan. Perhaps it was for this reason that the enemy was able to land undetected, and, in a near repetition of the original Quinauan landing, frighten the defenders into abandoning their defensive positions without firing a shot. Fortunately for the handful of 17th Pursuit Squadron and 3d Battalion Constabulary troops who had almost dutifully yielded their beach, the Japanese chose not to move inland. Believing, of course, that they had reinforced the 1st Battalion on Quinauan, they fully expected at any moment to be greeted by Col. Tsunehiro himself.

It was not until well past dawn on the 27th that word reached Col.

Pierce at his headquarters on the West Road that an enemy landing had taken place in the Silaiim-Anyasan area. In absence of information on the size or exact location of the invaders, Pierce sent the 17th Pursuit Squadron, under the command of Capt. Ray Sloan, down the only trail leading into the area to investigate.

A hundred or so yards below the West Road, Sloan's men came across the abandoned 3d Constabulary Battalion command post. The sight was almost eerie. The Filipinos, at word of the Japanese landing, had obviously left in a hurry. The morning's rice was, in fact, still simmering in its pots, and it was made quick work of by the hungry airmen. Other than a smashed telephone switchboard, everything had been left intact. After sending a runner back to Col. Pierce with word of the abandoned command post, Sloan resumed his single file march down the trail towards Silaiim.

Meanwhile, with daylight the Japanese invasion party had moved up off the beach. About a half a mile inland, confused yet still confident of meeting Col. Tsunehiro, they halted and began to dig in. While the main body went about preparing their positions in the jungle, a squad was dispatched in search of the 2d Battalion.

It was this squad that Capt. Sloan and his men stumbled on less than a quarter of a mile from the abandoned constabulary command post. The Japanese, startled at the sight of the single file of Americans, quickly withdrew with the army air corps close on their heels.

About 20 minutes and a half-mile later, the chase came to an abrupt halt when the airmen unwittingly blundered into the main body of the Japanese landing party. The brief clash that followed was initiated by one of the most unusual scenes recorded in modern military history.

Amongst the miscellaneous array of weapons the American airmen carried were two air-cooled .50-caliber machine guns that had been salvaged from a wrecked P-40. Since there were no mounts for the bulky weapons, each gun was first loaded and then strapped to the back of a man, who, in turn, was followed closely down the trail by the gunner. To go into action, the man carrying the 95-pound .50 literally became a human gunmount, dropping to all fours and then aiming himself in the general direction of the enemy. The gunner, in the meantime, would crawl up behind and begin firing.

As the American column unknowingly reached the now alerted Japanese main body, they were hit with automatic weapon fire, sending the lead machine gun team sprawling. But the enemy gunner, startled perhaps at what he was seeing, fired high, which allowed the airmen to scramble to safety.[33]

Although joined later by the Constabulary's 3d Battalion, an attack launched that afternoon by the Americans and Filipinos failed to make headway against the dug-in Japanese.

Sometime during that night, the small enemy force decided to improve their positions and, when the attack was resumed by the defenders the next morning, the constabulary were able to move unopposed all the way to the tip of Silaiim Point on Anyasan Bay. The airmen, on the other hand, found the going much tougher and were routed from their positions that night by a vigorous Japanese counterattack.

Reports, meanwhile, had reached Col. Pierce that the Japanese had broken through 17th Pursuit Squadron positions and were heading unimpeded, except by the jungle, for the West Road. It was not only the strength of the enemy force that was still unknown, but its whereabouts too, that triggered Pierce to immediately send out a call for help.

By daylight the next morning, January 30, two additional battalions, including the 2d Battalion of the 45th Infantry and a battalion from the 12th Infantry of the Philippine Army's 11th Division, had arrived in time to block the Japanese from reaching the West Road. That afternoon, the Fil-Americans counterattacked. With nothing more than an American captain in charge, the regimental-size force jumped off on the heels of a 75-mm. artillery barrage from the Philippine Scout 88th Field Artillery.

An unfortunate error in the placement of the barrage, however, magnified by the dense jungle and absence of a forward observer, brought havoc to the leading element of Scout attackers as they got started. Of the battalion of 45th Scouts spearheading the attack, four were killed and 16 wounded before the "friendly" fire could be lifted, the results of which brought a quick halt to further efforts that day.

That night, "General" Pierce, who had pinned on his brigadier star earlier that same evening, ordered the 57th Infantry to the Silaiim area. At the same time he "advertised" for a qualified infantry officer from the same unit with the rank of major or higher to take over operations in the field against the newest enemy threat.

At 7:30 that night, Maj. Harold K. Johnson, recently relieved operations officer of the 57th, with "nothing else specific to do," reported to Pierce, volunteering himself for a situation still pregnant with unknowns. The inept attempts thus far to corral the invaders had left the Fil-Americans without the slightest knowledge of the size or location of the enemy force. Wrote Johnson of the first meeting with his officers:

> Interrogation of the unit commanders disclosed that all of them believed themselves in contact with the enemy, [but] they did not know just where nor did they have any idea of what the enemy capabilities might be. There was no indication of enemy strength in the area.[34]

Unaware he outnumbered the single company of Japanese almost five to one, the uninformed new commander would have to act with caution until the size of the force could be correctly determined.

Action by the Fil-Americans throughout the next day was therefore soft-pedaled in lieu of firmly locating the elusive enemy force, whose position but not strength was finally pinpointed just before dark. Carrying the inconclusive results of the day's reconnoiter with him, Johnson reported to Gen. Pierce that night that in his opinion still more reinforcements would be needed to carry on the fight the next day. After listening, Pierce agreed, but with his concurrence went Maj. Johnson's job as well. At his suggestion, Pierce decided to call up the entire 57th Infantry, less the 2d Battalion. To its commander, Col. Edmund Lilly, also went control of the entire operation.

Although Johnson's inaccurate estimate of the enemy's strength had unnecessarily drawn the bulk of the 57th into the fight, it couldn't have been timelier, as the very next night another successful landing would be made by the Japanese, tripling the size of the existing force.

Throughout the next day, meanwhile, the newly arrived 57th confined its activities to reconnaissance of both terrain and enemy position. Neither side knew, of course, that the situation for both would be vastly different the following morning.

Three or four days before, a Japanese officer involved in an unsuccessful attempt to penetrate the newly established II Corps line some 15 air miles away, near Mt. Samat, was killed. A routine search of his body by a 31st Division officer revealed a mimeographed order that, when translated, told of an enemy plan to reinforce Quinauan Point on the night of February 1. With this information in their possession, an American and Filipino welcoming committee began preparing for the intruders that afternoon.

For starters, the 26th Cavalry was moved from I Corps reserve into positions along the beach at Caibobo Point. Next, the batteries of 75 and 155-mm. guns, in position to support the Quinauan operation, were alerted for possible action off Silaiim and Anaysan the night of February 1. Third, Gen. Weaver, whose tankers were already preparing for movement to Quinauan, promised he would have his tanks available for use in the area by the next afternoon. Last, on the other side of the peninsula, ground crewmen on tiny Bataan Field were getting four of the eight flyable P-40s ready for the role they had been given later that night. Two of the remaining four planes were already scheduled for an evening medical-supply run to Philippine guerrillas in the mountains near Baguio and wouldn't be available for the mission. The other two were being overhauled.

General Harold George, who, like Gen. Pierce, had pinned his first star on just a few days before, briefed his pilots personally for the mission. In anticipation of each plane's making two to three sorties over the target, George called eight eager pilots to the meeting where he explained the situation. As soon as the enemy invasion fleet was spotted, the first four would be off.[35]

This is the site of the main but smallest of the three fighter strips on Bataan. Known as Bataan Field, it, like the Cabcaben and Mariveles strips, has reverted back to what it was before the war—rice paddies.

About the time George concluded his meeting, navy Lt. John Bulkeley was walking down the improvised wooden gangplank of the *Canopus*. Having just eaten his usual evening's fill of homemade ice cream, within moments he was on board PT-32, along with Lt. DeLong and its skipper, Lt. Vince Schumacher, and on his way out of Sisiman. Through an oversight, apparently, the navy's Inshore Patrol had not been alerted to the impending enemy invasion that night. But circumstances would put them there for a chunk of the action anyway.

Around 9:15 P.M., the shaky 32, running on just two engines and held together by a jury-rig of wires and braces, was drawn toward heavy gun flashes about three miles up the coast. Fifteen minutes later, a large ship identified as a cruiser was sighted moving north. For a half hour or more the 32 boat, with converted yacht *Maryanne* behind, silently trailed the enemy ship. At ten o'clock, the Japanese slowed and turned for shore, broadside finally to the 32. Schumacher bored in for an attack.

The 32, as Bulkeley told it, was "closing on her fast . . . when suddenly a huge big searchlight came on, holding us directly in its beam." Nearly blinded, Bulkeley, from a little over two miles away, in sheer desperation fired his first torpedo. It splashed into the water off the starboard side at the exact moment an enemy six-inch gun salvo exploded some 300 yards in front of the rapidly closing PT.

Undaunted by either searchlight or gunfire, Schumacher held course to the much more realistic range of 3,000 yards and then launched his second torpedo. With all four of her .50-calibers blasting away at the still blinding search light, the PT swung starboard amidst more geysering splashes of exploding enemy shells.

"Suddenly," said Bulkeley, "there was a dull boom, and we could see debris and wreckage whaling up through the searchlight beam." Apparently the second torpedo found its mark, but the enemy ship, although somewhat slowed in its pursuit of the PT, continued to track its course with light and gunfire for another 15 minutes.[36]

The ship, which actually turned out to be the Japanese minelayer *Yaeyama*, was, of course, there in support of the enemy landing. Recording just minor damage from the PT boat attack, she once more swung her guns toward the Americans and Filipinos on Quinauan.

Just minutes before, engine noises from the anticipated enemy invasion flotilla were picked up by a listening post just north of Caibobo Point. Word was quickly passed. With observers already in position, both artillery batteries, particularily Battery D of the Scouts 88 Field Artillery, whose last fire mission had resulted in disaster for their fellow Scouts on Silaiim, eagerly awaited the enemy's arrival.

When word of the Japanese approach reached Bataan Field, the four American fighters, armed and loaded with six 100-pound fragmentaries each, had already been wheeled out of their revetments onto the dusty apron at the head of the runway. Fifteen minutes later the lead plane, piloted by Lt. Ben Brown, sped across the downhill runway and out over moonlit Manila Bay.

A few minutes later, the late night silence on Corregidor was broken by the wail of air raid sirens. As the fighters wheeled toward Corregidor's North Channel, the four pilots were momentarily transfixed by the sudden appearance of searchlights that literally blocked their way through the two-and-a-half-mile passage. The error, however, was realized in time, and the lights quickly turned off.

As the planes turned north along Bataan's west coast, the anxious eyes of the pilots began probing the moonlit coastline for signs of the fleet of enemy barges. At the same time down below, troops of the 1st Battalion, 20th Japanese Infantry, crammed into a dozen or so landing craft, alerted by the ominous drone of airplane engines, began their apprehensive search of the same midnight sky.

Brown led his little group down to 200 feet. Seconds later he spotted the Japanese. For the American airmen, it was a field day. For their battered comrades on shore, it was 50-yard-line seats at the most exciting spectacle since the war started. For the helpless enemy, it was hell.

Three times the planes exhausted themselves of bombs and ammunition and, after returning to Bataan Field to reload, came back. On the third and last attack, Gen. George switched pilots, allowing a fresh bunch of combat hungry army air corps second lieutenants to tear into what was left of the enemy force.[37]

It wasn't only from the air that the Japanese were being battered. The minute they came within range, the two batteries of Fil-American heavy guns positioned along the rugged coast fired with vengeance. Before they were through, the single battery of Scout 75s and the battery of 155s of the 301st Philippine Army's Field Artillery Battalion had fired a total of 250 four-gun salvos at the enemy force.

For all appearances, the gradual waning of U.S. small arms fire in the direction of the Japanese force as it fled northward indicated the end of the battle and of the enemy invasion. For Maj. Mitsuo Kimura, however, the repulsion of his attempt to land at Quinauan did not mean that he could simply return with the remnants of his battalion and try again later. Quite the contrary. First of all, there would be no facing his superiors after failing to accomplish his mission. Secondly, there was a chance that no more than half of the few remaining boats would be able to make it back to Olongapo anyway. Both circumstances added up to Kimura ordering his force, around 12:30 that night, to turn about again. The reinforcement of Quinauan was on once more.

By the time the handful of enemy barges passed Canas Point, about a mile and a half above Quinauan, the night had darkened appreciably, leaving the unfriendly coastline almost unrecognizable. Relying more on guesswork than on navigational skill, Kimura directed the remnants of his battalion towards what he thought was the beach below Quinauan Point.

Like the three that had gone before him, Kimura too would scrape bottom on the wrong beach. For his remnant force, however, the mistake had been a fortunate one. Instead of Quinauan, he had come ashore amongst the boats left by the 200 men of his own battalion that had landed on the 27th. He was on Silaiim Point. (See Map 18.)

As ironic as it was for the Japanese to land on the wrong beach all four times, it was similarly ironic for them to make the landings without opposition from the Fil-American defenders. Accordingly, the remaining half of Kimura's 1st Battalion successfully reunited with its advance company in the jungle on Silaiim Point on the morning of February 2.[38]

When the battle to dislodge the enemy was resumed early the next morning, to the Scout attackers unknowingly faced three times the number of enemy troops as they had the day before. This fact was borne out by the reports filed that evening by commanders all along the front.

Meanwhile that same night, February 2, Corregidor made preparations to meet an expected and certainly more welcomed guest. The night

Four American "Battling Bastards of Bataan" sweating out an air raid near Lamao. From left: Capt. S. W. Little, Sgt. John G. Graham, Lt. P. W. Frutiger, and Cpl. R. L. Carter.

before, Brig. Gen. Bradford Chynoweth, commanding officer of the army on the island of Panay, radioed Gen. MacArthur. He announced that the first long-awaited blockade-runner, the 1,000 cargo-ton, interisland vessel *Legaspi*, should be arriving sometime the next night from Capiz Harbor on Panay.

The *Legaspi*, not at all unfamiliar with the waters of Manila Bay, left Corregidor on the night of January 21, carrying some 150 selected military personnel on the first leg of their journey to Australia. Of the four or five possible blockade runners anchored in the waters off Corregidor at the time, the newer and faster *Legaspi* was chosen for the job.

Hiding by day and traveling by night, the little vessel reached its destination of Capiz, a small but well-protected port in northern Panay, at dawn of the 24th. But the welcome given the ship was anything but warm. For three days the ship's co-captains, Lino Conejero and Jose Amoyo, on loan for the trip from one of the smaller interisland vessels, *Bohol II*, were kept waiting by Gen. Chynoweth, who, surprisingly enough, actually doubted their reasons for being there.

A message announcing the *Legaspi*'s departure had been sent from Corregidor several days before. Odd as it may seem, Chynoweth halfway believed the message had been sent by the Japanese. The only possible explanation for this was that he and his close friend, Brig. Gen. Charles

Drake, chief quartermaster for USAFFE on Corregidor, had prearranged to send a special signal everytime a ship left. Apparently Gen. Drake had failed to signal Chynoweth of the *Legaspi's* departure. Thus, the delay.

For three days, the puzzled Filipino merchant officers were left waiting for an audience with Chynoweth. Finally, on the afternoon of January 26, they met and, only after a painstakingly detailed report of their trip, were the supplies released. Even then, as the meeting broke up, the still-skeptical Chynoweth told them that he was going to radio Corregidor to verify their story.

Four days later, loaded up to the gunwales with food, she was ready to go. By midnight of February 1, seven long days since entering the harbor at Capiz, *Legaspi* left again for the Rock.

Returning the same way she came—hiding by day and traveling by night—at 3 A.M. on the morning of the 3d, she answered a welcomed challenge by the PT-boat on duty at the entrance to the mine fields blocking Manila Bay. The starving "Battling Bastards of Bataan," as they would be referred to in rhyme by United Press correspondent Frank Hewlett, would soon be 1,000 tons of precious food richer for the efforts of the little *Legaspi.* With a half-ration, 15-ton per day consumption rate of just rice alone on Bataan, it is easy to imagine why captains Conejero and Amoyo were lauded personally by both MacArthur and Philippine President Manuel Quezon upon their arrival at Corregidor.[39]

Earlier that same night, a routine radio exchange of miscellaneous military information between Corregidor and Gen. Sharp's command in Mindanao carried word that the Japanese had captured Waterous Field on Mindoro. Waterous, one of the few airfields still in friendly hands between Bataan and Cebu, some 300 air miles south, was a vital emergency landing strip for the few American planes traveling back and forth between these two locations.

Early the next morning, Gen. George dispatched four P-40s under the command of Lt. Dave Obert to reconnoiter Waterous. If found to be in enemy hands, the planes, flown by Obert, Ed Woolery, Jack Hall, and Wilson Glover, were loaded with bombs that they were ordered to drop.

The three fighters reached Waterous at dawn. (On the way, Glover became separated from the other three planes and returned to Bataan.) Obert, spotting what appeared to be a row of enemy planes parked at one end of the runway, immediately dove down, releasing his bombs square on the target. The "enemy planes," said the anxious and somewhat embarrassed young second lieutenant, turned out to be "clumps of bushes so arranged that they [were] mistaken for planes in the faint morning light." In fact, a close examination of the strip from the air indicated that the report had been in error. There were no Japanese. So, with nothing better to do, they landed. There to meet them was the same Lt. Ed Bagget that Obert and Woolery had met when they stopped to refuel on their way to Bataan 16 days earlier. After an enjoyable breakfast and a few laughs over Obert's "attack" on the bushes, they took off for Bataan, loaded down with a 100-pound sack of sugar each from the nearby sugar central in San Jose.

Before leaving, Woolery and Hall had made up their minds that since they still had their load of bombs, they would drop them on Japanese positions opposite the II Corps front before returning to base.

Arriving over the eastern Bataan coast at 9:30 A.M., with Obert flying cover against possible intervention by the usually present Japanese Air Force, the two fighters took off after an enemy truck convoy spotted coming down the East Road. Seconds later, according to Obert, who had just glanced up "to look for possible enemy fighters," there was a "large midair explosion below and off to one side." He dove down to investigate, but found no trace of his companions. Thinking that perhaps they had returned to Bataan Field without telling him, Obert turned his Kittyhawk for home. "Lieutenants Woolery and Hall were not there and were never seen again," he said. "Two of the best pilots in the Philippines [who] until their disappearance had above and beyond the call of duty continued to do everything in their power to stop the Japanese advance."[40]

For David Obert, whose story of the incident both saddened and mystified everyone at the field, the day was still not over. General George, around noon, announced that he needed a pilot who was familiar with the route between Bataan and Del Monte Field on Mindanao for an important courier mission. "If you succeed," announced George, "your mission will be of more value than if you shot down 20 enemy bombers." Only two men were qualified, Obert and Lt. Earl Stone, who had flown the route earlier during the campaign. The two men drew cards. Obert picked up the ace and the assignment.

Dawn the next morning found him an hour underway, and after mail stops at Waterous on Mindoro and Cebu, he set down on Del Monte around noon.

General Sharp, it was found, was gone and would not return for a couple of days, during which time Obert was quartered in the plush Del Monte Club, where he "lived royally for the two days. Good food and a soft clean bed, it was wonderful."

When Sharp returned on the February 6, Obert went to see him. Reporting to the general, whose tongue was known at times to match his name, Obert was abruptly asked, "What are you doing here? Did you steal one of the P-40s from Bataan and run away?" Obert, by then "hoping the Japs would come over and give the general in his underground office a good bombing," handed him his orders.

By dawn the next morning, he was back in the air heading for Cebu carrying a sealed pouch containing secret Allied codes that Sharp ordered him to "eat" in case he didn't get through. Touching down at Cebu that afternoon, Obert contacted Col. John Cook of the army's big advance quartermaster depot in Cebu City. Cebu, apparently still very low on the enemy's priority list, had become the main food and medical supply dump in the Philippines. Everything in the crowded warehouses was ticketed for Bataan and Corregidor if the Allies could come up with enough ships and crews, like the *Legaspi,* with the courage to test the enemy blockade.

The next morning, loaded down with the results of his meeting with the generous Col. Cook — candy, cognac and all sorts of other long forgotten treats — Obert in his "heavily overloaded P-40" was off again for Bataan. Little did he suspect at the time that he was opening yet another unusual but colorful chapter to the story of Bataan.[41]

It wasn't until a while later, after the "goodies" had been passed out along with the story of the bulging warehouses on Cebu, that an idea grew among a gathering of several idle pilots. Ever since the battle for Bataan started, a number of nondescript planes of assorted vintages had shown up on Bataan Field. Among them was an eight-year-old Bellanca, owned before the war by William Bradford, general manager and senior pilot of the Philippine Air Transport Company, and a 4-place Beechcraft, the speedster among the group with a 450-horsepower engine and a top speed of 450 mph.

A few days after Obert's trip, Bill Bradford, commissioned a captain after the war started and made engineering officer at Bataan Field, volunteered to fly his Bellanca to Cebu and bring back as much medicine and food as he could carry. When "Old Number Nine," as Bradford called it, returned the next night loaded with quinine, blood plasma and other medicines, food, candy, and cigarettes, the idea of doing this on a regular basis was born, as was the name that would forever be associated with the operation — the Bamboo Fleet.

Captain Harvey Whitfield soon joined in, flying the speedy Beechcraft all the way to Del Monte Field on Mindanao and back — a round trip of more than 1,100 miles.

Before long, along with Bradford and Whitfield, four other pilots — captains Jack Caldwell, Jack Randolph, Roland Barnick, and Bill Strathern — would join the "Fleet," each taking his turn flying south to Cebu or Mindanao with a VIP or two, returning with food, medicine, and a few luxury items. To avoid a run-in with Japanese fighters, all flights would leave and return to Bataan in the early hours of the morning, usually between 2 and 4 A.M.[42]

In the meantime, attacks against the Japanese on Silaiim Point made by the Scouts on February 3 showed little positive result. Facing a much larger enemy force than on the previous day, the Fil-American assault, beefed-up later that morning by the arrival of two platoons of 192d tanks, could gain nothing, nor did it the next day.

The tank and infantry commanders on Silaiim had been trial-and-error fighting their way in a situation almost identical to that taking place simultaneously on neighboring Quinauan. The lessons, although soon learned, were bitter. For example, the day the tanks entered the battle, a tragic incident occurred which probably did much to bring about the necessary improved coordination between tank and infantry. That afternoon, a single tank of the 1st Platoon, Company C of the 192d, as usual too far out in front of its supporting infantry, struck an enemy mine. Attempting to abandon the disabled Stuart, the four-man crew soon found that the Japanese, who had brought machine guns to bear on the escape hatch, were not about to let them out.

By the time friendly infantry, trailing at the usual 100- to 150-yard distance, were able to react to the situation, enemy machine gunners opened up on them too, pinning them down until dark. All efforts to extricate the helpless tankers that night failed. Resuming their attacks at dawn, by mid-morning, Scouts of the 3d Battalion, 57th Infantry had broken through to the crippled vehicle. To their horror, they found that the enemy had almost completely covered it with dirt and had poured gasoline, apparently from its own reserve cans, inside the compartment and set it on fire.

It was this cruel, barbaric incident of first cremating and then burying the helpless crew that sent the rest of the 1st Platoon tankers on a revenge-driven rampage. One of the tank commanders, two days later, was overheard by Associated Press reporter, Clark Lee, to claim that they were "starting to get even with those bastards." Pointing to the commander of the tank parked behind him, he continued, "Joe here shot 25 in one trench alone. They ran around the corner to escape my tank and ran into his fire...." "Two of them took off their shoes and threw them at my tank," said Joe, smiling. "We shouted at them to surrender but they wouldn't give up. We had to run over them."[43]

It is fortunate the tankers didn't get a look at one of Gen. MacArthur's War Department communiqués for that same period. Dated February 2, 1942, message number 88 concluded by drawing attention to fighting on the west coast, saying: "They [the Japanese] resisted with the courage which is characteristic of Japanese troops but at the end were *glad to surrender.*" It is unclear where MacArthur got his information.[44]

As curious perhaps as MacArthur's communiqué was a radio broadcast heard on February 4 over the Japanese-controlled station KZRH in Manila. The regular program of music and enemy propaganda was pre-empted by the voice of an aged Filipino, to whom few of the Americans

To such inhuman deeds ... Roosevelt, the then President of the United States, sent a congratulatory message to General Leonard Wood reading: "I congratulate you and the officers and men of your command upon the brilliant feat of arms wherein you and they so well upheld the honor of the American flag." Can you beat that!! History repeats itself but only to the heedless. Beware of American ... They would be the last to respect the chastity of Filipino women.

Japanese propaganda leaflets aimed at damaging relations between Filipinos and Americans with reminders of the Philippine Insurrection 40 years before.

lucky enough to be near a radio in the middle of the day on Bataan paid any attention. It was obvious that the message was for the Filipinos anyway, and after a few minutes, groups of them clustered around radio sets all over the peninsula.

The speaker was Gen. Amilio Aguinaldo, fiesty leader of the Filipino insurrection against American colonization of the Islands in 1898. For nearly four years he had led a guerrilla army uprising that took over 125,000 U.S. troops to finally quell in 1902. It was 43 years to the day of the opening of that revolution, and once more, he was after his people to resist the Americans—only this time in exchange for a Japanese-controlled government. By the time the old man's speech had ended, few Filipinos were still close enough to their radios to hear it.[45]

Although the entire Philippine Division had been equipped with the army's new semiautomatic Garand M-1 rifle before the war, some of the veteran Philippine Scouts, who had been weaned on the 1903 Springfield, never felt quite comfortable with the new weapon in combat. Consequently, word was soon passed that it was pretty easy to find a Scout who was willing to trade his M-1 for an old reliable '03. With wind of the story, two young naval officers from the Mariveles section base, after getting a first-time look at the M-1, decided they'd hike up to the 57th Infantry bivouac area two or three miles up the West Road in hopes of bartering away a couple of navy-issue Springfields for two of the new rifles.

Warned to avoid the West Road whenever possible because of snipers and isolated Japanese patrols, the two men headed north one morning in early February, armed with Springfields and a couple of grenades apiece. Managing to stay off the road by following a network of newly cut engineer trails, by midmorning they had reached the West Road not far, they hoped, from the 57th's bivouac area. The jungle was extremely heavy on both sides. Faced with having to cross the road for the first time, Ens. Norman Lauchner volunteered to be the first to go. Unbelievably, at the exact moment he broke out of the jungle and started across the road, a Japanese soldier did precisely the same thing from the other side. By the time the two startled men realized what had happened and could stop, they were no more than ten feet from each other. At that point, realizing that discretion was the better part of valor, both just as quickly turned and headed back to where they had come from. Ensign Lauchner, never losing sight of the fact that he had been face to face with the enemy and despite the element of surprise, was able to unclip a grenade from his pack harness and toss it after his fleeing adversary before he dove for cover. In his excitement, however, he had forgotten to pull the pin. At that point, both men decided they could be happy with their navy-issue Springfields after all and quickly headed back for Mariveles.[46]

This wasn't the last time naval personnel had an adventure with infiltrating Japanese. Part of the miscellanea of units that made up Cmdr. Frank Bridget's Naval Battalion on Bataan were grounded airmen from U.S. Navy Patrol Wing Ten. PatWing-10, as it was better known, was originally made up of two Philippine-based squadrons of PBY patrol planes. Like the army air corps in the Philippines, many of its personnel found themselves stuck on the ground on Bataan when the campaign started.

One day in late January, one of PatWing-10's grounded pilots, Ens. Bob Swenson, while driving north on the West Road, picked up three Filipino soldiers, one officer and two enlisted men, who asked to be taken to Philippine Army headquarters. There was something suspicious about them, however. Although dressed in Philippine Army uniforms, they didn't look like Filipinos. Swenson also thought it was unusual that the officer had to ask him for directions to his own headquarters. Pulling into a nearby unit command post to presumably ask for directions, the alert young navy ensign told a sergeant in the headquarters tent that he thought the three men in the jeep were Japanese. Army Intelligence was notified. After a brief questioning by an American corporal carrying a Thompson submachine gun, Swenson's fears were realized when he saw all three suddenly raise their hands in surrender.[47]

Slowly and ever so painfully, the battle for Silaiim, like that for adjacent Quinauan, began to show progress for the Americans and Filipinos. For the tankers and infantrymen, it had been a learn-to-coordinate-or-die situation, which, once achieved, showed remarkable results. Close teamwork between the two brought about a quick end to most of the enemy's tricks. For example, instead of 15 or 20 men trailing 100 or so yards behind the tanks, four or five Scout riflemen were assigned to follow literally within each tank's shadow. This way, the wily Japanese would not be able to sneak up and plant one of their magnetic mines on the side of the tank nor pull one across in front of the tank on a string without being seen. The other popular enemy trick of remaining hidden inside a well-concealed position until the tank had passed before raising up and blasting was also quickly eliminated.[48]

Beginning the second week of the battle of Bataan, it was not uncommon for the Japanese to make propaganda broadcasts at night over a loudspeaker set up on the battlefield. As Carlos Romulo noted after hearing such a broadcast on one of his visits to the front, some of the broadcasters were women. "Out of the night came a woman's voice, sweet and persuasive. ... Songs followed, quavering through the forest. They were selected to arouse nostalgia to the breaking point in a boy facing death and longing for home."

Unknown to most within the U.S. command, during the closing days of the battle for Silaiim and Anyasan points, the same tactic was planned for the Japanese. There were two Japanese-Americans attached to USAFFE Intelligence on Bataan during the battle who could both read and speak Japanese. One evening the two men appeared in a 57th Infantry sector with a soundtruck to try to convince the handful of enemy soldiers hopelessly trapped on the points to surrender.

Because of some bad experiences with Japanese POWs during the battle, as was noted by Maj. Harold K. Johnson of the 57th, "There was no desire on the part of the Scout soldier to take prisoners ... one [of whom] had [already] attempted to blow up himself and a battalion headquarters with a hand grenade." Besides, any Japanese prisoner who voluntarily surrendered would have to be treated according to the rules of the Geneva Convention—something, up to then, the Japanese had ignored. Witness to that was the discovery, on more than one occasion, of the mutilated bodies of Scouts who had unfortunately been captured by the Japanese. Almost all were found with their hands tied behind their backs with telephone wire, and most were bayoneted. The partially decomposed body of one man was found wired up by his thumbs so his toes barely touched the ground.

"A passive resistance to the use of the soundtruck developed," wrote Maj. Johnson, "and there were sufficient delays so that [the loudspeakers]

The farmer in the foreground of this picture, taken of the old Cabcaben airstrip as it looks today, said there was a row of landing lights still buried along one edge of the old runway.

were not used." Besides, said the two interpreters as they climbed back into the soundtruck, they didn't have a script to follow anyway.[49]

By the afternoon of February 6, the situation for the Japanese on Silaiim was fast becoming desperate. For at least one part of the Allied army on Bataan, it had also deteriorated. On the night of the 6th, whose daylight hours had seen Bataan Field bombed heavily in two separate air raids, Gen. George decided to transfer half of his remaining fighters to nearby Cabcaben. A mile and a half south of Bataan, Cabcaben Field up to that time had been used sparingly until the finishing touches had been applied to its revetments.

Beginning at about eight o'clock that night, one by one, four of the remaining eight P-40s from Bataan took off out over the bay, swung back toward Cabcaben, flashed their landing lights, and came in. With the first three pilots already on the ground watching the last plane come down, it happened. Second Lt. Bill Baker misjudged his approach. "Down! Bake, Down!" yelled one of the pilots. "He'll have to make another pass at it," said another. Baker, eyes straining hard to pick out the edge of the dimly lit runway, caught his error in time. But when he pushed the throttle forward to regain his air speed, the engine, still a little cold because of the brief, two-minute run from Bataan, stalled. Seconds of deadly silence were followed by an explosion and a bright orange flash somewhere between the ridges west of the field.

This aerial view of the barrio of Cabcaben, shows the old dock (built in 1942 by the engineers), which although in disrepair and abandoned, is still there. The upper end of the rice valley is the old site of Cabcaben air field.

Baker's fighter hit the ground in the middle of a battery of antiaircraft guns, showering one of them with pieces of the plane that had scattered over 200 yards of jungle. A few minutes later, members of the startled gun crew found Baker staggering about amongst the smoldering remains of his P-40. Although burned and incoherent, he would live. But it was doubtful that the Bataan Air Force would. It was down to just seven flyables.[50]

That same evening on the other side of the peninsula, Associated Press correspondent Clark Lee was interviewing Capt. Arthur Wermuth, who was still recovering from the wound he had received eight days earlier on Longoskawayan. Lee, after leafing through the burly captain's diary, remarked, "I'm going to call you our 'one-man army!'"

He wasn't kidding. Ten days later, under Lee's byline, headlines appeared in most of the papers in the United States: LONE YANK KILLS 116 BATAAN JAPS. The article went on to say that "America's No. 1 one-man army [had] led so many scouting raids [behind Japanese lines] he has lost count." The only thing Wermuth didn't admit modestly was that with "three wounds and still walking around," he'd been "lucky."[51]

For the Japanese high command, the entire west coast operation, by February 6, had become critical. Fate of the 20th Infantry's entire 2d Battalion on Quinauan and Longoskawayan Points was unknown. For the 1st

Battalion on Silaiim, Major Kimura, on the night of the 6th, dispatched a message via one of his beached landing boats to Olongapo. In it he concluded that his battalion, under attack by both tanks and artillery, was "about to die gloriously."

It wasn't until about 6 A.M. the next morning that the barge carrying Kimura's message edged up to the dock at Olongapo. It was taken immediately to 16th Division commander, Gen. Susumu Morioka. Facing the possibility of losing yet another battalion to the points, Morioka ordered as many small boats as could be collected before dark to effect a rescue of what was left of the 1st Battalion.

Unfortunately for Kimura, however, he had no knowledge of the rescue attempt nor, for that matter, did he expect one. It was, in fact, the Filipinos and Americans who had first warning that something was up. A little before midnight, listening posts along the coastline picked up the barely distinguishable sound of small boats moving south. Word was passed immediately down the line to be on the alert for another enemy invasion attempt. A few minutes after midnight, a call came into Bataan Field requesting the air corps also to stand by.

By 3:15 the enemy rescue force was standing off the vicinity of Silaiim Point. Suddenly the coastline erupted with machine gun and artillery fire. On shore, a call went out to "send the planes." Fifteen or so minutes later, homing in on the lines of tracers pouring from the cliffs, two P-40s dove low over the water and unloaded their 100-pound fragmentaries among the disorganized fleet of empty enemy boats.

Three more times the fighters came over and dropped their bombs. There would be no Japanese landing that night. By 4 A.M., what was left of the rescue flotilla was departing for Olongapo. The Japanese had been turned away, but so had Lady Luck for another of the P-40s. On their return to Bataan Field, the pilot of one of them, Lt. Kenneth White, confused by the dimly lit runway, came in wide, caught a wheel and totaled his Kittyhawk. General Harold George's Bataan Air Force was now down to just six fighters. By February 8, just one month and four days since their first action, the air corps had lost its sixth plane. By later World War II standards, that wasn't bad. But on Bataan, it had amounted to the irreplaceable loss of one-half of the entire force.[52]

According to Lt. Tom Garrity, the part of the Japanese rescue force that escaped the air and shore attacks that night didn't get away unharmed. "At dawn there were seven barges about 8,000 yards offshore," Garrity wrote in his diary for February 9, "four being towed by a launch. Our 155s sank the launch and during the day other barges were sunk along the shore. All day long Japs have been found swimming along the coast. A few have surrendered."[53]

If past performance meant anything, then chances were the Japanese rescue force would be back to Silaiim again. They were the very next night, only this time their approach went undetected. Loyal to the cause to the very end, Kimura, however, refused to leave. He did send his wounded back, 34 in all, ordering the boats not to return again.

General Morioka realizing that he was on the verge of losing yet another battalion in the unsuccessful attempt to capture the West Road tried one last time to convince the dedicated Kimura that the best, although least honorable thing to do was to save as many men as possible. To accomplish this, he decided to officially release the 2d Battalion of its original assignment in written orders dropped to them by plane.

The next day, February 9, a Japanese aircraft made several passes over the Silaiim-Anyasan area dropping supplies along with some bamboo tubes containing orders. Unfortunately for the Japanese, several fell inside Fil-American lines. Interpretation of their contents by Gen. Pierce's intelligence section indicated that the Japanese had been released from their original orders and were to save themselves if at all possible. Included were detailed instructions and diagrams on how to build rafts, information on tides and currents, and times of sunrise and sunset for the next ten days. Translations of the enemy's orders into English were printed and passed on to the commanders of various units on beach defense with instructions to be on the lookout the next few nights for escaping enemy soldiers.

On that same day, Maj. Achille Tisdelle, aide to Brig. Gen. Edward P. King, Bataan artillery commander, was at Gen. Pierce's headquarters on the West Road. Prior to returning to Little Baguio, Tisdelle placed a call to King. By mistake, however, the switchboard operator plugged him into a conversation between a signal corps officer and his sergeant. The sergeant, it seems, was in the process of stringing telephone wires in the vicinity of Quinauan Point, and was, at that very moment, talking from atop one of the coconut trees he had selected as a pole. The captain asked him where he was. Frustrated, the sergeant replied: "For Christ's sake, Sir, I don't know. I'm somewhere between asinine and quinine points." From that moment on, for the Americans at least, the battle for Anyasan and Quinauan was over. It would be asinine and quinine until the end.[54]

With the true battle for "quinine" wrapped-up the day before, U.S. action on the 9th opened with an all-out effort by a beefed-up force of Filipinos against Kimura's rapidly deteriorating battalion on Silaiim.

Leading the way that day was the Philippine Constabulary's tough 1st Battalion, the same battalion that had fought so successfully against the Japanese on Quinauan up to its relief on January 27. By early afternoon, after surprising the enemy with a bold headlong charge into their front-line foxholes, a tactic they had used with similar success on Quinauan, they reached the cliffs.

The spirited attack by the 1st Battalion had been triggered by an incident involving its commander, Capt. Jose Tando, earlier that morning. The Japanese had positioned a machine gun on a point of high ground opposite the battalion line the night before, from which they had been keeping the constabulary pinned down since daylight.

Tando arrived in the area sometime around midmorning, when he was briefed on the situation. After a quick reconnoiter of the area, he swung into action. Grabbing a couple of hand grenades, he told the officer in charge of a nearby machine gun platoon to cover him, that he was going after the enemy gun.

Seconds later he began moving forward. Cover was sparse, but steady fire from constabulary machine guns behind him kept Japanese heads down. On open ground within 40 feet of the enemy position, Tando stopped crawling. Rolling over on his back, he pulled the pin on his first grenade and calmly flipped it back over his head toward the gun position. A few seconds later there was a muffled explosion. Suddenly, out of the dust and smoke rose a Japanese officer with samurai sword in hand who made a staggering rush at the startled Filipino captain. The officer on the constabulary machine gun was fortunately still on his toes and shot him dead before he had taken more than three steps toward the shaken but grateful Tando.

The constabulary leader's exploit not only ignited the entire battalion to the attack later that morning, but earned its daring commander the U.S. Army's Distinguished Service Cross as well.[55]

Later that night at his headquarters tent on the West Road, Gen. Pierce, with his foot propped up on a pillow, sat listening to the evening's Voice of Freedom broadcast from Corregidor. Although still in pain from having had a toe shot off by an enemy sniper a few days before, the story being told by Col. Carlos Romulo of the big air battle out over Manila Bay earlier that day, for the moment at least, made him forget his discomfort.

In mid–January, it will be recalled, the Japanese were observed moving a battery of heavy artillery to the southern shore of Manila Bay near Ternate for the purpose of shelling the fortified islands. Despite efforts to destroy them, including aerial and PT-boat reconnaissance, as well as landing men with radio transmitters to direct counter battery fire against them, the enemy guns remained undiscovered.

On the morning of February 6, the Japanese batteries swung into action. Between 8 and 11 A.M. that day, close to 180 rounds were fired against the Manila Bay forts. For Col. Paul Bunker, who had the range and firepower to retaliate, it was an exceedingly frustrating situation. Without knowledge of the exact locations of the enemy guns, buried somewhere in one of the deep, thickly vegetated ravines behind the south shore, Corregidor's giant 12-inch mortars were completely neutralized.

In desperation, Maj. Gen. George F. Moore, commanding officer of the entire Harbor Defense, persuaded Gen. MacArthur to seek help from the air corps on Bataan. General George, when asked if he could help fill the bill, volunteered his entire air force—six P-40s—for the job. To get the good, clear set of reconnaissance photos that Corregidor wanted, George decided to send the old but reliable, open-cockpit Stearman biplane that was hidden with the rest of the Bamboo Fleet in the jungle at the end of the Bataan Field runway. As for a pilot, he had one—Philippine Army Air Corps Capt. Jesus Villamore—a man who, by his courage, had already won the Distinguished Flying Cross for taking on an entire squadron of 27 Japanese bombers on December 10, in his two-gun, open cockpit, 1933 model P-26A fighter. To shoot the pictures, George came up with another PAAC volunteer, veteran Sgt. Juan Albanes.

Taking full advantage of the sun and the enemy air force's penchant for long lunch breaks, the seven planes took off a few minutes after noon. About 12 minutes later, Villamore, under the watchful eyes of his fighter escort flying about 2,000 feet above, crossed the Ternate coast and began his run. With no enemy planes in sight, he crossed and recrossed the area until Albanes had taken 110 exposures.

With the last click of the camera, Villamore waggled his wings to the circling fighters and turned for home. Nearing Corregidor, he fancied "a couple of figure-eights" for a cluster of men watching from Kindley Field and then headed for Bataan. In taking the time to shoot an extra 30 or 40 frames, Villamore had pressed his luck, for unbeknownst to the group as they neared the coast, six Japanese fighters had perched themselves over Mt. Bataan, waiting to jump them as they came in.

Opposite Bataan Field, Villamore, with his P-40 escort strung out behind, turned to land. The fighters, despite the warning they received that enemy planes were near, with throttles back, banked in towards the field at the same time, intent on mothering the unarmed biplane all the way in.

In the meantime, down below on Bataan Field it had become white-knuckle time. Moments before, a message had come in over the radio from an air corps observer on Mt. Samat announcing, "Six enemy pursuits coming in your direction." Receipt of the message sent everyone in the area sprinting toward the edge of the field, including Gen. George and Gen. Richard Marshall, who happened to be there on official business. From where they were standing they could see the flight of P-40s still strung out behind the Stearman as it crossed the edge of the runway. Suddenly, pointing above, George yelled, "There are the Zeros!"

Boring in for a frontal attack from a fairly steep angle at the opposite end of the field, the line of enemy planes unintentionally picked up so much speed that none were able to maneuver quickly enough to draw a bead on any of the slow moving American fighters before they were already past.

"The Japs have overshot them," whooped George. "He's just plain over-shot them. . . . Now give it to 'em kids!" And "give it to 'em" they would.

With throttles all the way forward, Lt. Ben Brown led his group left and by the time they reached the North Channel, had turned and were heading full-bore for the Japanese out over the bay. If a rooting section ever made a difference, then it may have been this time as probably enough friendly troops to fill half the college football stadiums in the United States had been attracted by the crescendo of angry Allison engines.

For the first time since the war in the Pacific started, the Japanese were being met on even terms. No "three-to-one" or "four-to-one" odds this time. And nobody caught on the ground.

Seconds after the planes met over the bay, they paired in deadly one-to-one and man-to-man aerial combat. For the victory-starved spectators watching from Bataan and Corregidor, most of whom doubted up to that moment the existence of more than a single P-40 on the peninsula, it was the Fourth of July, steak and eggs, and New Year's Eve all wrapped into one.

First one then another and then two more Zeros were knocked out of the sky. A fifth was crippled and last seen heading north, smoking and los-ing altitude. At that moment and to the astonishment of all concerned, who should blunder onto the scene but "Photo Joe" himself. It didn't take long, however, for him to realize that he had flown into an American beehive. When last seen, he was heading for home past one of his own faltering comrades.

Meanwhile, the fight involving the sixth American fighter, piloted by Lt. Earl Stone, who was after his fourth kill of the young war, had drifted into the clouds over Mt. Bataan. Both planes were picked up by air corps observers on the ground at Mariveles Field until they disappeared into the mask of gray-white mist covering the heights of the mountain. Then, sud-denly, too suddenly, silence. It was over. A tragic midair collision had ended the life of the ace of Bataan Field, 1st Lt. Earl R. Stone. Days later, a search party sent by Gen. George, reported finding the wreckage of the Japanese plane along with the body of its pilot. But due to the ruggedness of the Mt. Bataan interior, neither Stone nor his plane was ever found.

Despite ending on a tragic note, the day had still been a success. Five enemy planes confirmed lost and one probable, loss against the loss of one American plane and pilot. In fact, a couple of days later, even the probable had become a confirmed kill, but the credit did not belong entirely to the air force.[56]

When last seen by the spectators on Bataan Field, the Zero was smok-ing and fighting to keep altitude as it limped northward. Moments after it passed from view, it was picked-up by U.S. artillery observers on Mt. Orion. A short distance in front of the newly manned positions on the

Lieutenant Earl Stone, killed in a midair crash with a Japanese plane over Mt. Bataan.

Bagac-Orion line was a small, abandoned auxillery fighter strip known as Pilar Field. The complete openness of the field, now sitting squarely in the middle of the no-man's-land that fronted the II Corps sector of the line, had forced the air corps to give it up for use in early January.

It was there that the crippled enemy fighter, unable to make altitude, and to the delight of the artillerymen, decided to set down. Quickly word came down from the observers on Mt. Orion to one of the batteries of 75s concealed in the jungle just below. Coordinates were phoned down followed seconds later by the command to "fire." In one blast, the probable became a confirmed kill.[57] For the air corps and now the artillery, the score for February 9, 1942, was official: Six enemy aircraft destroyed.

That night, an unusually heavy build up of clouds over Mt. Bataan brought rain to the southern tip of the peninsula. On an open, well-exposed hill 100 yards or so behind Hospital No. 1 at Little Baguio sat the gas gangrene ward. Due to the large number of patients suffering from this very contageous disease, a special isolation ward was established well away from the main hospital facility.

As the rain started to fall, quick-thinking Lt. Juanita Redmond hurriedly

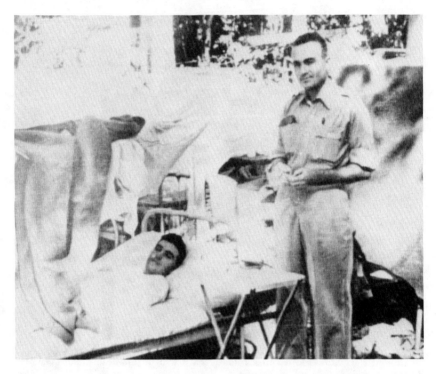

Captain Frank Wilson in the open-air gas gangrene ward, located 100 or so yards above Hospital No. 1. Patients infected with the highly contagious disease had to be isolated in a special ward from other wounded patients.

cleared one end of one of the hospital's tin-roofed sheds being used as a ward and, with the help of a half dozen corpsmen, started bringing the gangrene patients down from the hill. It began raining hard. "We were doing pretty well, carrying the beds themselves rather than transfering the sick men to stretchers," Lieutenant Redmond said, "when suddenly a man in one of the beds sat bolt upright."

"What in hell's going on here?" he yelled as he jumped out of the bed and began running. "Don't run, don't run," she called after him, "Wait, we'll take you in."

"I turned my flashlight on him and recognized him as one of the [hospital] corpsmen." What were you doing in that bed? she asked. The poor fellow explained that he was so exhausted when he got off duty that he fell into the first empty bed he saw. Needless to say, it was the last night that Pvt. William Caston would spend in the Bataan gas gangrene ward.

Ground fighting over the two-mile-wide Silaiim and Anyasan Point sectors by the afternoon of February 10 had reached its mopping-up stage. On the 11th, the wipe-out of a dozen or so of the enemy who had taken

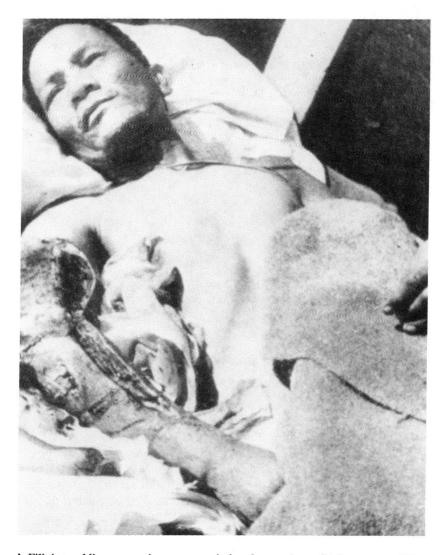

A Filipino soldier, appearing more a victim than patient, displays some of Dr. Adamo's work. Without proper medicine, fresh air proved the lifesaver in the usually fatal gas gangrene cases.

refuge on a small, heavily wooded islet near the mouth of the Anyasan River marked the end of all resistance, or so it appeared.

The unit responsible for securing the sector of the line from the middle of Silaiim Point to the river of the same name on the north side, was the 2d Battalion of the 45th Infantry. Reports had reached Gen. Pierce on February 11, that the points, save the routine mopping-up, had been

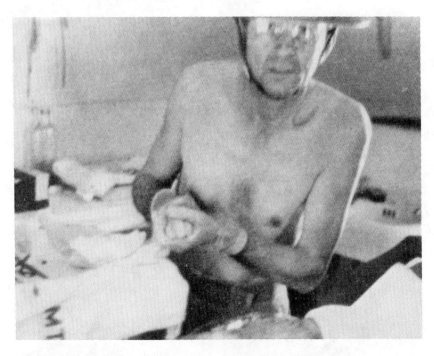

Dr. Tony Adamo washes up after performing one of his life saving operations on a gas gangrene patient.

secured. Neither Pierce nor the commanding officer of the 2d Battalion knew, however, that there was still a densely wooded area about an acre and a half in size near the point that had yet to be cleared.

The outer perimeter of the area had been routinely covered by just two Scout machine guns when, at dawn on the 12th, Maj. Kimura led the remaining 200 or so of his men out of the dense woods against the unsuspecting Filipinos. It was the first time since their landing on Silaiim that the Japanese had assumed the role of attacker. Whether it was an attempt to escape entrapment or an attack launched to kill as many Fil-American defenders as possible in one final, suicidal gesture, can only be speculated.

The two machine gun crews, although surprised and heavily outnumbered, nevertheless fought savagely, taking a high toll on the determined enemy before being overrun and wiped-out. The bodies of 33 Japanese soldiers were found later in front of the Scout position. There was only one survivor from either crew. In the middle of the battle, he had gone to get more ammunition.

The two machine gun nests silenced, Kimura, staying to the trees just off the beach, then moved north toward the mouth of the Silaiim River. As a precaution, a couple of days before, Col. Edmund Lilly, commanding the

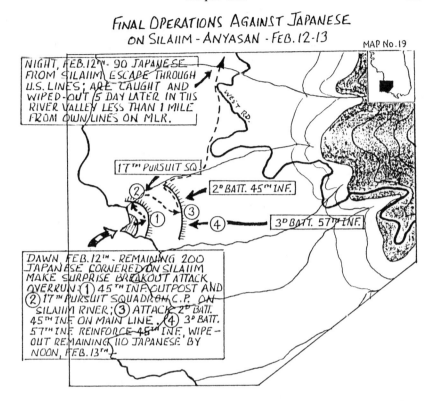

FINAL OPERATIONS AGAINST JAPANESE
ON SILAIIM - ANYASAN - FEB. 12-13

MAP No. 19

NIGHT, FEB. 12 - 90 JAPANESE FROM SILAIIM ESCAPE THROUGH U.S. LINES; ARE CAUGHT AND WIPED-OUT 5 DAY LATER IN THIS RIVER VALLEY LESS THAN 1 MILE FROM OWN LINES ON MLR.

WEST RD.

17TH PURSUIT SQ.

2D BATT. 45TH INF.

3D BATT. 57TH INF.

DAWN, FEB. 12 - REMAINING 200 JAPANESE CORNERED ON SILAIIM MAKE SURPRISE BREAKOUT ATTACK OVERRUN: (1) 45TH INF OUTPOST AND (2) 17TH PURSUIT SQUADRON C.P. ON SILAIIM RIVER; (3) ATTACK 2D BATT. 45TH INF ON MAIN LINE. (4) 3D BATT. 57TH INF REINFORCE 45TH INF, WIPE-OUT REMAINING 110 JAPANESE BY NOON, FEB. 13TH.

operation on Silaiim, moved the 17th Pursuit Squadron to the mouth of the same river to cover the beach approaches below the point.

It was the 17th's command post along with that of F Company of the 45th that Kimura's force ran into when they reached the river. After a brief fire fight, both command posts were overrun within minutes. The 17th, with its commanding officer Capt. Ray Sloan carrying a fatal wound, was sent fleeing up the river. (See Map 19.)

Not wasting a minute, Kimura pressed on, this time cutting diagonally back toward the center of the point. At 10 A.M. he ran into the 2d Battalion of the 45th Infantry, which he promptly attacked. By that time, however, word of the rampaging Japanese force had reached Col. Lilly, who ordered the 3d Battalion of the 57th Infantry, who had just been pulled back from Anyasan, to double-time it for the besieged 2d Battalion area.

For over two hours the Japanese were held at bay while the hastily gathered Filipino defenders organized themselves. By noon the threat was over and the enemy contained. Twenty-four hours later the remnants of Maj. Kimura's counterattackers, less 90 or so who had escaped eastward through the Fil-American position sometime during the night, were forced back for the last time to the shores of the South China Sea. By three o'clock in the afternoon of February 13, the Scouts had the beach secured. For the first time in over three weeks, the entire coast of Bataan, from Longoskawayan to Saysain Points, was free of enemy threat. As grim witness to the fight's being over, for days afterwards the only enemy soldiers found were those whose bodies washed up on the otherwise serene beaches by the tide.

Of the handful of prisoners taken during the three-week battle, almost all were wounded. No doubt it was only because of the severity of their wounds that they were captured in the first place. Some 42 enemy wounded from the points were taken to the special prison ward at Hospital No. 1 for treatment. "[So] exsanguinated, begrimed, with massive wounds covered with dirt and maggots," wrote Capt. Alfred Weinstein of the hospital staff, "most of them were too weak to resist our attempts to clean, feed, and operate on them."

Speaking of hospitals, Lt. Tom Garrity, the air corps liaison officer with Gen. Wainwright, commented in his diary on February 12, that while having supper at Hospital No. 2 that night, they sadly heard that Lt. Ray "Spud" Sloan, 17th Pursuit Squadron commander, shot the day before on Silaiim Point, had just died on the operating table and that his last words had been, "A $10,000 pilot shot to hell in the infantry."[58]

The fate of the Japanese who had "made a run for it" through the Scout lines on the night of the 12th, although insignificant to the outcome of the battle, is nonetheless interesting to follow. For the first three days and nights the Japanese, intent only on reaching their own lines, traveled undetected. Moving principally at night, by the morning of February 16 they were within a mile of their own positions opposite the Bagac-Orion line.

The Philippine Army's 1st Division, after its rugged withdrawal from Mauban in late January, had been reassigned to a position on the new line between the 91st and 11th Philippine Army divisions, some three miles inland from Bagac. It was here, early in the morning of the 16th, that the Japanese force was first discovered. They had stumbled, by accident, into the division motor pool where they were fired on by a Filipino sentry, Cpl. Ramon Velasco. The shots rang through the quiet dawn, bringing troops bivouacked nearby running to the scene. Not wanting to make a fight of it there, the infiltrators quickly withdrew into a nearby jungle thicket, where a heavy volume of return fire from them gave the appearance that they had chosen to make a stand.[59]

Word of the incident went out almost immediately to the 26th Cavalry, which was in corps reserve nearby. Within the hour, the Scout cavalrymen had moved in alongside the 1st Division, and after an hour of only light return fire from the enemy position, they rushed the thicket. It was easily overrun. But all that was found were the bodies of the handful of men left as a covering shell while the main body slipped away. Two of the enemy were still alive.

Questioning of the survivors disclosed that they were indeed part of the 90-man force which had escaped from Silaiim. Their physical condition, considering what they had been through since their landing 16 days earlier, was remarkable. It was obvious that their pilfering of Philippine Army food depots since escaping from Silaiim had gone well. Unable to pick up the trail of what was left of the enemy force, yet still confident that they hadn't seen the last of their prey, the 26th returned to their bivouac.

It wasn't long before their hunch proved correct. At 4 P.M. that same afternoon, a call came in from the 91st Division reporting a "large group of Japanese" in the Tiis River valley behind the division right flank. By dark, the cavalrymen had moved into positions from which they could launch an attack at dawn. But again, for the second time in as many days, results the next morning showed nothing more than a half-dozen dead members of yet another covering force. The main body, now down to less than 70 men, had slipped the noose again.[60]

But this time, their trail was picked up by the anxious Scout cavalrymen who before long had them pinpointed in the 71st Infantry area. The Filipinos did not realize that the Japanese had split themselves into two groups. The smaller of the two had worked its way into a ravine directly in front of 71st lines, almost within hailing distance. While moving forward to attack this group, however, the Scouts were ambushed by a "considerable force hidden in the jungle thickets" just behind 71st positions.

For the ragged survivors of Kimura's command, time had at long last run out. Within just yards of their own wire, the remarkable physical feat which had taken them through more than ten miles of the most difficult jungle on Bataan was halted. In two swift thrusts, troops E and F of the 2d Squadron, under the command of Maj. Don Blanning, cleared both pockets of enemy soldiers. Colonel Lee Vance, commander of the 26th, wrote the following in his diary of the day's action:

> Feb. 17: Troop E and F under Captain Paul Wrinkle locates enemy in front of a battalion of the 71st Infantry, but in rear of our front line wire. Captain Wrinkle sends message to Major Blanning who moves to reinforce Captain Wrinkle. En route Maj. Blanning encounters a party of the enemy, drives them out and joins forces with Capt. Wrinkle. Enemy driven out; Capt. Wrinkle killed in final assault. Ridge shelled by enemy artillery. 2d Squad returned to bivouac at dusk with mission accomplished. Our losses: 1 officer killed, 2 E.M. wounded. Enemy losses: 64.

With the death of the final 64 Japanese soldiers in this action the entire 1st Battalion, 20th Japanese Infantry, to a man, was wiped out.[61]

The book on the battle of the Points could now be officially closed.

Lasting some 25 days, from January 23 to February 18, the Japanese had lost no less than two-thirds of their 20th Infantry Regiment. Two battalions, approximately 2,000 men, had been killed in a futile, piecemeal attempt to take the I Corps from behind.

For the Americans and Filipinos, along with the normal battle-related losses, the mid–February effects of the skimpy Bataan ration had already taken its toll on troops, particularily those involved in the combat zones. As mentioned in Maj. Harold K. Johnson's critique of the Points battles, "It was distinctly natural that the will to fight decreased in direct proportion with the ration. . . . Listlessness grew and it became increasingly difficult to initiate some forward action each day."[62] It was, therefore, a physically as well as an emotionally exhausted American and Filipino soldier who emerged from the hot, humid, death-swollen west coast jungle; men who, in less than one month, had begun their slip toward becoming mere shadows of what they were before Bataan.

CHAPTER THREE

The Battle of the Pockets

"Send platoon to clean out seventeen snipers ..."

On the morning of January 23, the Japanese effected a landing along the Bataan west coast for the purpose of outflanking the I Corps and capturing the West Road. This action, which is referred to as the battle of the Points, was not, however, confined to just that area. The Japanese, unable to fight their way off the coast, made two major attempts to reinforce their positions. One came from the sea (see the battle for Silaiim and Anyasan points in chapter two); the other, unknown as such to the Americans, Filipinos, or even the Japanese cornered on the points, came overland and is called the battle of the Pockets.

About 10 A.M. on the morning of January 21, the 3d Battalion of the 20th Japanese Infantry, after successfully infiltrating the U.S. line above Mauban Ridge, moved in astride the West Road just behind the original I Corps front. The presence of this single battalion, it will be remembered, was responsible for the Fil-American abandonment of the entire line four days later on January 25.

During the time the 3d Battalion was holding off the Americans and Filipinos in their attempts to dislodge it from the road, that same regiment's 2d Battalion made its ill-fated landing attempt on the Bataan west coast.

On January 25, Gen. Homma directed Lt. Gen. Susumu Morioka, commanding officer of the 16th Division, to take over the sagging operations along the Bataan west coast. Morioka believed, after being briefed on the near-disastrous invasion attempt made by the 2d Battalion, that the operation could still be salvaged. Word had already been received of the situation on Quinauan, prompting the new commander, even before he left Manila for his new assignment, to dispatch a single company from the 20th's 1st Battalion to the area. Simultaneously with his arrival at Olongapo on January 27, Morioka received additional orders from Homma supporting his plans to expand the west coast operation even more.

165

Word was immediately passed to the remainder of the 1st Battalion, minus the one company that had already debarked, to prepare to join the 2d on Quinauan. In the meantime, the 20th's 3d Battalion, with less than 24 hours rest since its relief from the Mauban roadblock, had been sent forward to probe Gen. Wainwright's newly established I Corps line south of Bagac. With Morioka's arrival, 3d Battalion efforts picked up. Under the 20th Infantry's commander, Col. Yorimasa Yoshioka, the battalion was directed to infiltrate southward through enemy lines and effect a link-up with the 2d on Quinauan.

Meanwhile, things on the Fil-American side of the strange new line, because of the pressured withdrawal into the new positions on the Bagac-Orion, were also somewhat confused. Anticipating the Japanese to be hot on their heels after the withdrawal from the Mauban-Abucay line, Gen. Richard Sutherland, MacArthur's chief of staff, believed that both corps "needed all available help in order to successfully occupy the new line and at the same time hold the attackers." He also believed that the establish ment of a reserve could wait until "after the withdrawal was accomplished."

All well and good, or so it appeared as the American and Filipino troops settled into their new positions throughout January 25 and 26. The stay for some, however, would be short-lived. Because of the new threat posed by the Japanese landings on the west coast, MacArthur had decided that a strong reserve force would be needed after all. The units chosen for the assignment were those of the Philippine Division: the U.S. 31st and Scout 45 and 57th. According to MacArthur's operations officer, Col. Constant Irwin, these were "the only units that we had upon which we could depend."

In the long run, of course, the move paid off. But in the short term, it proved a near disaster. Two of the three Philippine Division regiments had already taken position on the new line when orders reassigning them were issued. In Wainwright's I Corps area, the 45th, which had been assigned to a mile-and-a-half-wide section of the front some three miles inland from the west coast, began its pull-out on January 26. That afternoon, Lt. Col. Russell Volckmann of the Philippine Army's 11th Division, on line immediately to the right of the 45th, ran into Scouts from that unit "moving to the rear." After learning that they had received orders placing them in corps reserve, he asked them who had taken their place on the line: "To my great surprise, they said no one had relieved them."[1]

The information Col. Volckmann was given was frighteningly correct. The 45th Infantry had left their 2,800-yard-wide sector of the line before their replacements arrived. The move was a costly one, for it would be 48 hours before the replacement unit could take over the partially completed defenses in an area so rugged that some of it had not even been explored by the 45th. To make matters worse, the unit called on to replace the 45th was, for the moment, probably the least qualified on Bataan for the job: the Philippine Army's 1st Regular Division.

Following its exhausting battle and 15-mile withdrawal along the beach from the Mauban Line, the disorganized and equipmentless 1st was promised a much-needed rest by an initial exclusion from assignment to the new line. But, with the decision on January 25 to form a Philippine Division reserve, the wearied, unprepared division staggered back onto the line once again.

Ironically, it was through the middle of this sector that Col. Yoshioka directed his breakthrough on the night of January 28. It was as much, if not because of, the impossible terrain and extremely dense jungle along with the partially completed defenses, however, that facilitated the 3d Battalion's success rather than the ineptness of the Fil-Americans. Few jungled areas on Bataan—save the west coast where the battle for the points was building—were any more forbidding.

The best example of what confronted U.S. troops on that part of the I Corps line came from Col. Russell Volckmann of the nearby 11th Division. Attempting to reconnoiter his sector, he wrote that he had spent hours "cutting and crashing [his] way through the jungle." "It was a wasted effort on my part; the entire front, every yard of it was thick jungle."[2]

Adding to the difficulties presented by the jungle, the area was bisected by several rivers and dense ravines, the most prominent of which were the Cotar and Toul, whose waters junctioned to form the Gogo River near the outer perimeter of the U.S. line. It was up the entangled Gogo valley, in fact, that the 1,000-man strong enemy force came late on the night of January 28.

After a brief fire fight with the 1st Division outpost troops, the Japanese around midnight slipped virtually unchallenged up the Gogo where, at the intersection of the Toul and Cotar Rivers, Col. Yoshioka split his force, the majority moving east along the Toul. The other, less than one company in number, continued southward up the Cotar another 200 yards, leaving it just before dawn to take position on a small, densely wooded knoll to the west.

It was with this small force that contact was first made that day by a patrol from the 1st Battalion, 1st Infantry Regiment, led by Capt. Alfredo Santos. Results of the attack against the unknown number of Japanese, although inconclusive, did result in Santos being able to cordon off the enemy's escape route back to their own lines. Neither force knew that the 1st Battalion's loose, 4,000-square-yard encirclement had also cut off the Japanese access to its parent force to the southeast. The difficulty of Santos' task can best be appreciated by noting that he was recommended and later awarded the Distinguished Service Cross for his accomplishments.[3]

MAP No. 20   BATTLE OF THE POCKETS - JAN. - FEB. 1942

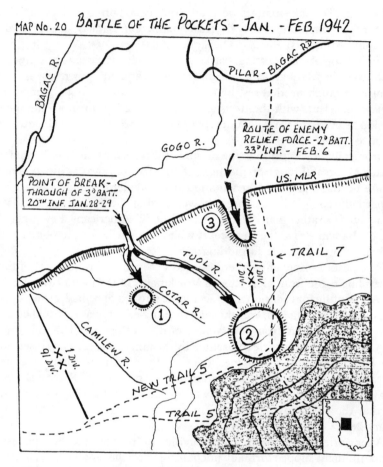

① BATTLE OF LITTLE POCKET - JAN. 29 - FEB. 9

② BATTLE OF BIG POCKET - JAN. 29 - FEB. 13

③ BATTLE OF UPPER POCKET - FEB. 6 - FEB. 17

As soon as Bataan was selected for its role in the defense of the Philippines in late December, army engineers went to work on cutting a network of trails and roads behind the preselected Bagac-Orion line. They cut over 100 miles of roads through impassable jungle and over and around the difficult, ravine-carved landscape. Each "trail," as the army referred to it, was mapped and numbered.

In the I Corps area, near which the Japanese 3d Battalion had penetrated, there were two trails: Trail 7, running perpendicular to the MLR and parallel to the 1st and 11th Division boundary, and what was called New Trail 5, about a mile behind and running parallel to the MLR. It was near the junction of trails 5 and 7 that Col. Yoshioka, with the largest part of his force, found himself at dawn of the 29th. (See Map 20.)

The 11th Division's 11th Infantry, into whose area this enemy force had crept, was unaware of their presence until about 8:30 that morning. At that time, according to its commanding officer, Col. Glen Townsend, "A burst of rifle and machine gun fire was heard very close to headquarters...."

A few minutes before, they had been notified by phone of the arrival momentarily, via Trail 7, of a Filipino medical corps officer in his own car. "The doctor failed to arrive," prompting Townsend to send "some clerks and supply men" to investigate. The car was found less than 200 yards up the trail with the doctor and another Filipino soldier in it, both dead. No sooner had this happened than a sergeant with the group was shot in the head and killed, sending the rest of the group stampeding back to the command post with the story.

Townsend "sent all available personnel from the CP and rear area to the scene," including two companies of infantry, who promptly attacked from the north and northeast. The "no progress" attack results prompted him, about 40 minutes later, to notify the 11th Division commander, Brig. Gen. William E. Brougher, of the incident. Brougher arrived within the hour and, after looking the situation over, "sent back for help" from Gen. Wainwright at I Corps headquarters.[5]

At 12:15 P.M. a dust-covered motorcycle messenger arrived at the 45th Infantry's new bivouac with a note for the 1st Battalion commander, Lt. Col. Leslie Lathrop. The message, penciled on a sheet of yellow-lined tablet paper, read: "Send a platoon immediately to CP, 11th Infantry, at Trails 5 and 7 to clean out seventeen snipers there. J. M. Wainwright."

The response from this message sent the entire battalion, bivouacked near the junction of Trail 9 and the West Road, into the area it had pulled back from just three days before. Ironically, it was to be involved in a battle there that, had its own regimental command acted more prudently at the time, might not have had to be fought in the first place.

The only action taken by the late-arriving 1st Battalion that day, a token effort made at dusk by Company B, was quickly halted as it attempted to move up Trail 7 to the junction of Trail 5.

As darkness settled in, the Japanese, as usual, went to work. Confused by the situation like the Americans and Filipinos, they were unaware of actually where they were, where the enemy was and, finally, where the other group was that had split off at the Cotar-Toul rivers the night before. So the Japanese began to do what they did best: infiltrate and probe.

About 10 P.M. an enemy patrol struck a makeshift battalion of some 70 men from the 51st Division who were dug-in across Trail 5, just a few yards west of Trail 7. Several foxhole positions were attacked by knife-wielding Japanese. The Filipinos, under the command of Capt. Gordon Myers, held their ground, however. At dawn several bodies of those men in some of the more isolated foxholes were found with their throats cut.

Evidence that the enemy force isolated in the small pocket west of the Cotar was also active can best be seen in reading part of a recommendation for a Silver Star. Philippine Army Capt. Simplicio de Castro, a 1936 Olympic boxer from the Philippines, at that time commanding Company B in Capt. Santos' 1st Battalion, 1st Infantry, was killed leading his men in one of the several clashes with the Japanese that took place that night. It read, in part, "In spite of the enemy's patrolling to the rear and the newly established position being unfamiliar to the troops, de Castro led his platoon in overcoming enemy centers of resistance in numerous clashes."[5]

Due to the dense jungle and the "position being unfamiliar to the troops," the entire area for several nights following the initial breakthrough remained alive with infiltrating enemy troops, ambushing, sniping, and cutting communications.

By nightfall of January 30, results of five separate, company-size attacks on that day alone by the 1st Battalion of the 45th against the Japanese near Trail 7, showed, according to Maj. Adrianas Van Oosten of the same battalion, that "the enemy was extremely well dug-in and camouflaged. No sand from his foxholes was observed, [and] he [had] utilized the fallen trees for his protection and concealment in their natural fallen locations." Losing, on the average, three men per attack, which, on all five occasions had included a BAR (automatic weapon) man, little was accomplished other than getting a fix on the Japanese position. This was penciled in on U.S. maps as a rather large, 500-by-500 yard area, whose southeasternmost corner overlapped onto the junction of New Trail 5 and Trail 7.[6]

The "Big Pocket," as it was called from that day on, was reconnoitered the same day by Gen. Wainwright himself, who, for the second time in the campaign, narrowly missed being shot by a sniper just a few steps outside the 1st Battalion command post. Lt. Col. Edgar Wright of Wainwright's staff, walking behind him, was nicked in the forehead by the shot, prompting a quick but thorough raking of the surrounding trees by Scout machine gun fire. Moments later, a completely green-clad—including face and gloves—sniper fell dead at the end of the short rope with which he had tied himself into the nearby tree.

Little during the next few days could be accomplished against the well dug-in Japanese, who by then had further improved their defenses with a series of interconnecting tunnels. On February 2, Wainwright was back again in the vicinity of the Big Pocket, this time bringing four tanks of the 192d Tank Battalion with him. In three days, 13 separate attacks had been launched by the tough 1st Battalion with little or nothing to show for it. Perhaps with the aid of the tanks, control over vital Trail 7 could at last be wrested from the enemy.

At three o'clock that afternoon, with Sgt. Leroy Anderson's Stuart in the lead, the tankers made a successful reconnaissance run, without infantry support, through the enemy controlled section of the road. With the information gathered on the run, plans were laid that night for a major attempt at clearing the trail the next morning. Because of the dense, unnavigatable jungle, the tanks would be confined, for the most part, to the road. The narrowness of Trail 7 was also a factor, and it was planned to have them, supported in between by riflemen, fight their way single file through the enemy controlled sector, blasting and wiping out enemy strong points as they went.

That night at the final briefing, Lt. Bob Roberts voluntarily attached his unit, Company B, then in battalion reserve, to be part of the accompanying infantry for the operation. At the same time, another lieutenant, Bill Bianchi, from uninvolved Company D, attached himself to Roberts' company so he too could "be in on the action."

The next morning, as the tanks began their single-file penetration of Trail 7, both Roberts and Bianchi moved out behind the lead tank. It wasn't long before the Fil-Americans, especially those on foot, were pinned to the ground by intense enemy rifle and machine gun fire from the west side of the road. To do anything but crawl invited disaster or sudden death.

Within a few seconds Bianchi traced the heaviest volume of enemy fire to the base of a large banyan tree on his left. Attempting to get within grenade range, he edged forward. The enemy machine gun clattered. Bianchi felt something strike his left hand. He was hit, but couldn't stop. Discarding his now-useless rifle, whose stock had also been shattered by the machine gun fire, he continued on toward the enemy gun. As soon as he was close enough, he slipped a grenade out of his shirt pocket, painfully pulled and twisted the pin out with the index finger of his left hand and lobbed it at the base of the tree. A second one followed. The resulting explosions silenced the enemy gun.

Meanwhile, Sgt. Anderson, in the lead tank a few feet ahead, had turned toward the same position and was trying unsuccessfully to fire his 37-mm. gun into the enemy hole. Bianchi, seeing that he couldn't make it, jumped up on the back of the tank, grabbed the unmanned .30-caliber machine gun on top of the turret, and began firing. But the American was too large a target to miss, and the Japanese didn't miss, as the young

Lieutenant Willibald "Bill" Bianchi, third Medal of Honor recipient on Bataan.

lieutenant was staggered for the second time with a bullet in the shoulder. Still somehow conscious and past the point of worrying about his fate, once more Bianchi pulled himself up behind the gun and opened fire. Suddenly the engine of Anderson's tank sputtered, stopped, and then exploded, knocking the stunned and bleeding lieutenant onto the ground. A second muffled explosion inside brought the crew, with hair singed and burning, clambering out of the turret and into the bushes.[7]

Anderson's tank was now out of it, but the three remaining Stuarts continued slugging it out with position after position of enemy snipers as they went along. Before long, however, the lead tank hung itself up on a tree stump that protruded partway out onto the trail. At that point, Lt. Archie McMasters of Company C hand-signaled two of his men to go after the enemy machine gun that had the tank's crew pinned inside. The two men, one an American lieutenant named Edward Stewart, crawled forward with grenades to do the job. The Scout accompanying Stewart threw three grenades into the Japanese gun position, but all three were pitched back out to explode harmlessly nearby. Stewart and the Scout each lobbed one at the same time. A few seconds of silence followed by a pair of muffled explosions indicated the end at last of the enemy gunner.[8]

That afternoon, among the American and Filipino wounded that were loaded into trucks for evacuation to the hospital was Lt. Bill Bianchi. Unbeknownst to the courageous American, who would be back with his unit in less than a month, his actions had just earned him the third Medal of Honor to be awarded for heroism on Bataan since the battle opened.

The next day, February 4, another attack, the fifteenth, was launched up Trail 7. Little, however, could be accomplished, other than successfully extricating the tank that had been hung up on the stump the day before.

For six consecutive days, attacks by the Americans and Filipinos against the enemy pockets had been frustrated. On the evening of February 4, word was passed to Gen. Brougher of the 11th Division, Brig. Gen. Fidel Segundo of the 1st Division, and Gen. Albert Jones, former 51st Division commander, to report at 10 A.M. the next morning to the 1st Division command post for a meeting with the corps commander.

General Wainwright opened the meeting by acknowledging the fact that one of the problems with the operation thus far had probably been that of command, because there had been little coordination in use of available forces. To simplify the situation, Wainwright placed the senior American officer among the three, Gen. Albert Jones, in command of the entire operation. Jones, already in command of the Left Sector of the MLR, which included the 1st Division area, had a plan in mind.

Both pockets would be completely isolated from one another, something evidence showed had not been accomplished. Once this was done, Jones ordered the attacks on the Big Pocket held up until the Little Pocket could be closed off. Jones gave the tactical responsibility for the Big and Little Pockets to Lt. Col. Les Lathrop of the 45th and Col. Kearie Berry of the 1st Infantry, respectively. H-hour was set for 9 A.M. the next morning.

On the other side of the line, the Japanese command had just seen its third battalion swallowed up by the Bataan jungle in less than two weeks of fighting. The entire 20th Infantry Regiment, for all practical purposes, was now isolated inside Fil-American lines with little hope of extrication. On February 6, Gen. Morioka decided to make a stab at either reinforcing or, if necessary, rescuing his beleaguered 3d Battalion. Stragglers from that unit who had slipped the Fil-American cordon had, in the meantime, pinpointed Yoshioka's position on their maps, prompting the Japanese commander to order an air attack on what was thought to be the U.S. perimeter, followed by an air drop of supplies to his own men.

In both cases, their judgment was off. Filipino units on the west side of the Big Pocket reported that every bomb dropped by the enemy planes fell on enemy positions. Of the dozen or so supply parachutes dropped on the eastern side, 11 drifted into the hands of 11th Division troops. The only one on the Japanese side of the line could be seen hanging high up in the inaccessible limbs of a giant banyan tree.

Later that night, Morioka sent the 2d Battalion of the 33d Infantry down Trail 7 in an attempt to get through to the besieged Yoshoika. Shortly after midnight lead troops of the 1,000-man enemy force successfully infiltrated the frontline positions of Company F of the 11th Infantry. By the time the large Japanese force was discovered, it was too late. Only 11 of the 29 men deployed from Company F escaped death. The effectiveness of the enemy's cunning coupled with the element of surprise, was demonstrated by the discovery of 18 dead men in their fox holes that morning.

This kind of infiltration by the Japanese was responsible for over one-third of all frontline-related casualties that occurred on Bataan. As seen here, the tactics employed against green, unseasoned troops who had spent little or no time in frontline foxholes was devastating.

Veteran frontline units quickly learned that to survive required both discipline and courage, for like all creatures of the jungle, as the Americans and Filipinos considered their adversaries, the Japanese were most adept at seeking their prey at night, every night. Discipline was needed once it became dark, for to do anything more than crouch in the bottom of your foxhole and quietly breathe and listen could attract an uninvited guest. Empty ration cans were provided for men to urinate in. Men suffering from dysentery were automatically excused, for once you climbed into your foxhole, you dare not move until dawn.

Adept as they were, two things the Japanese had to do gave them away—crawl and breathe, for more often than not the infiltrator was less aware he was nearing a foxhole than the man crouching inside was. It was not uncommon, in fact, for the enemy to blunder right in on top of a crouching defender.

Courage was needed when the man in the foxhole knew he had to kill the intruder with his bare hands, knife or bayonet, because with a gun you could miss or give your position away. Even when daylight came the danger wasn't over, as an infiltrator by night might have become a sniper during the daytime. Men stayed hidden in their foxholes until the area was secured by troops who, some mornings, had to fight their way up to relieve them. Rare was the morning when the first order of business wasn't to bury the bodies of dead Japanese infiltrators or their victims of the night before.

Word that the Japanese had overrun Company F reached its battalion commander, Maj. Helmert Duisterhof, shortly after 1 A.M. First Infantry units on the other side of the breakthrough, along with Gen. Brougher, were quickly alerted, after which, with a handful of headquarters personnel and a few stragglers, Duisterhof headed west. This quick thinking and quick action paid off. The Japanese were stalemated at the eastern periphery of their newly created opening in the U.S. line.[9] (See Map 21.)

The leading edge of the enemy force, after penetrating southward approximately 700 yards, slowed down with the coming of daylight about a mile short of the Big Pocket. General Brougher, after being notified of the breakthrough, pulled Company A of the 92d Infantry and a platoon of 192d tanks from the Big Pocket attack force and threw them in front of the enemy advance. There Company A dug in for what was to be 11 days, according to commander Maj. Beverly Skardon, of "the most bloody and bitter [fighting] of the campaign...."[10]

General Morioka, to insure that this force would not suffer the same fate as Yoshioka's battalion, ordered the opening near the junction to Trail 7 and the MLR held at all costs. One platoon from overrun Company F of the 11th Infantry found itself trapped in the middle of the 200-yard-wide enemy salient. With no food, little ammunition, and no entrenching tools, but under the inspiring leadership of Philippine Army Lt. Juan Duyan, the dogged force beat off no less than five Banzai attacks until it was rescued and able to slip out two days later.[11]

Had the Japanese attack achieved its goal, the timing could not have been better. General Jones had ordered his coordinated offensives against the two enemy pockets to begin at 9 A.M. that same morning. But the Big Pocket attack force, weakened by Gen. Brougher's "unauthorized" transfer of Company A of the 92d, was held on its line of departure by an irritated Jones until it could be reorganized.

The assault against the Little Pocket, under the direct command of Col. Berry, nevertheless opened as scheduled at 9 A.M. For his 1st Division troops, fighting without armor, artillery, or mortars, the latter two proving ineffective because of the high percentage of tree bursts and duds, the toughest part of its assignment was the linking-up of the units into a solid ring around the Japanese.

The difficulties encountered with both enemy and jungle in the ensuing action are perhaps best described on the Philippine Army Gold Cross citation of 1st Battalion commander, Capt. Alfredo Santos, whose unit spearheaded the drive to close off the Little Pocket. It reads, in part, "After great difficulty due to the terrain, vegetation, and stubborn enemy resistance, the Pocket was finally surrounded, but the enemy, employing cover to great advantage and using [automatic weapons] held their ground." During the vicious fighting that took place on February 7, "on one of the enemy's Banzai charges, three [of four] machine guns were put out of action while the other was captured [along with its crew]."[12]

By 10 A.M. the next morning, however, Santos' battalion was standing

ACTION AND REDUCTION OF POCKETS - FEB. '42

MAP NO. 21

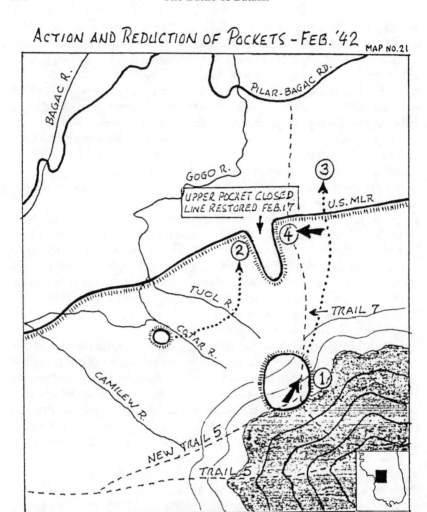

① FEB. 2 - LT. WILLIBALD BIANCHI WINS MEDAL OF
   HONOR IN BATTLE ALONG TRAIL 7.

② ESCAPE ROUTE AND SITE OF ANNIHILATION OF
   REMNANTS OF JAPANESE LITTLE POCKET TROOPS.

③ ESCAPE RT. OF REMAINING 377 OF ORIGINAL 1000 JAP.-
   ANESE TROOPS FROM BIG AND LITTLE POCKETS.

④ LOCATION OF IGOROT TROOP ACTION AGAINST
   LITTLE POCKET

on the high ground in the center of the pocket. The final push was surprisingly easy. After checking the state of decomposition of enemy dead within the perimeter, it was surmised that 30 or so of the estimated 200 Japanese soldiers caught in the Little Pocket had slipped out through a gap in the Filipino encirclement sometime during the night.

The surmise was correct. Working northeast toward their own lines, by dawn of the same day the 30 or so enemy troops were within 100 yards of their own lines. They had, however, worked their way into a corner from which, this time, there would be no escape. (See Map 21.)

The morning the Japanese 2d Battalion, 33d Infantry pushed its salient, now being referred to on U.S. maps as the "Upper Pocket," up Trail 7, units of the 1st and 11th Divisions on either side of the gap fought successfully in keeping the Japanese flanks from moving forward. The unit at the horseshoe-shaped corner of the MLR and the westernmost edge of the Upper Pocket into which the escaping Japanese had stumbled was I Company of the 1st Infantry. The small enemy force was soon detected and quickly surrounded. The Filipinos offered the enemy a chance to surrender. The Japanese reply was a volley of rifle fire, at which time the Filipinos went to work. An hour later, the Japanese had been granted their final wish—they were all dead.

Following the closing off of the Little Pocket, Col. Berry, officer in charge of the operation, was ordered to report to 1st Division headquarters. Two days earlier, a major change in command within the division had taken place. Brig. Gen. Fidel Segundo, its commander since before the war, had been relieved. The change, occurring at the height of the pocket battles, had come, apparently, because of them. Someone had to be blamed for allowing the circumstances to exist under which the enemy had successfully penetrated the 1st Division line. Unfairly perhaps, it had been Gen. Segundo.

Berry, when he reported, was given the division, but, interestingly, it was not Segundo he would replace. For two days the command had belonged to Col. Albert Dumas, at the time considered senior among the American officers with the division. Further investigation, however, showed Col. Berry, then busy leading the fight against the Little Pocket, with more time-in-grade and, as of February 10, 1942, in command of the 1st Regular Division, Philippine Army.[13]

Anticipating the consolidation of the Little Pocket, Gen. Jones, by February 10, was ready to go to work on the big one. The American commander didn't know that Col. Yoshioka had been ordered to give up the fight in the Big Pocket and withdraw back to his own lines.

Following a February 8 staff meeting at San Fernando, the Japanese

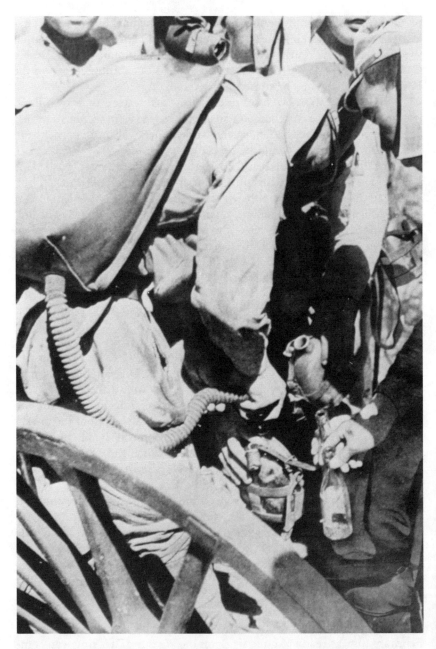

A Japanese "Gunga Din" supplies water to thirsty troops. The intense heat and humidity of the Philippine dry season of 1942 drove thirst-crazed men on both sides to drink from stagnant pools and ponds when fresh water wasn't available, regardless of the risk to health.

Japanese mounted troops pause on their way to the front to let their horses drink. The difficult terrain and lack of roads on Bataan forced the Japanese to resort to using horses and mules to transport troops, supplies, and light artillery to some of their more remote positions.

decided that they'd had enough for the time being. Every effort to crack the U.S. Bagac-Orion position had failed. With part of the 20th Infantry already lost and the remainder trapped on Anyasan and Silaiim and cut off behind U.S. lines, Gen. Homma agreed that the remaining forces lacked enough power to continue the fight aggressively. In anticipation of reinforcements, orders to disengage went out that night.

On February 10, two important gains against the Big Pocket were made by the Americans and Filipinos, signifying that the end would not be long in coming. The 92d Infantry, as a result of their attacks that day on the west side of the pocket, gained control over the Toul River, the enemy's principle source of water. The 45th, fighting from the southeast side, meanwhile regained control over most of Trail 7. In 12 days of close-quarter, nose-to-nose fighting, the Scouts of the 1st Battalion had advanced only 150 yards. According to Van Oosten, "Approximately 100 enemy dead were counted . . . the odor of [them] was strong and there were many bluebottle flies."[14]

The next day, February 11, the provisional battalion of 51st Division troops, tagged then as the 51st Combat Team (C.T.), with help from the 45th, cleared New Trail 5 up to the junction with Trail 7. The 92d also had continued to gain, enough for Jones' chief of staff, Col. Stuart Mac-Donald, to write that "it was quite obvious the end was in sight."

The bodies of two Japanese soldiers killed during the battle of the Pockets.

The end was in sight, but Gen. Jones wouldn't be there to see it. Suffering from an attack of acute dysentery, the fiery general was reluctantly transported back to Hospital No. 1 for treatment. Reference to this, plus the fact that the battle for the Big Pocket was concluded the next day, was recorded routinely by Lt. Col. Leslie Lathrop, tactical commander of the operation, in his diary: "February 12 Gen. Jones duty to Hosp. Pocket closed about 3 P.M. 200 enemy dead—450 graves."

As the Scouts moved through the abandoned enemy command post, a more detailed scene was recorded. In an adjoining draw, they found the decaying carcasses of a dozen or so horses, possibly some of those lost by the 26th Cavalry near Moron on January 15, which the Japanese had been eating. "Nearby," noted Van Oosten, "were three neatly laid-out graves with wooden headboards and surrounded by a border of cigarettes."

A couple of days later, 25 more horses and mules were found alive, but in horrible, neglected condition, which prompted putting them out of their misery. The effects of inadequate rations on the Filipino troops during this time may be best understood when Maj. Van Oosten described the scene that followed: "the PA [Philippine Army] men were so hungry, they [began] eating the uncooked flesh of the dead horses."[15]

One common item continuously found among the overrun enemy positions were unexploded U.S. three-inch mortar rounds. The World War

I–vintage ammunition, typically, on one recorded occasion registered only 11 effectives out of 72 fired, and only 14 out of 70 on another. "No wonder," wrote Col. Glen Townsend of the 11th Infantry, "the Japs once set up a captured Stokes mortar between the lines and scoffingly draped it with flowers."[16]

The rather sudden, feeble end to enemy resistance in the Big Pocket plus the discovery of either the remains or graves of only 450 men indicated that quite a large number of Japanese had somehow slipped the Fil-American noose.

Colonel Yoshioka, in reaction to Gen. Homma's order to withdraw, which he received on February 9, began to probe for a weak link in the northern perimeter of the U.S. line. He found it in the northeast corner in an area of extremely dense jungle whose impenetrability kept the right flank of the 45th and the left flank of the 11th Infantry from physically joining.

After a very difficult four-day journey, 378 men of Yoshioka's original command of 1,000, a hundred of whom were wounded, reached their own lines. Avoiding "many enemy positions" along the way, the starved, haggard remnants of the 20th Infantry represented one-half of the living survivors of the entire regiment.

The day the remainder of Yoshioka's reduced battalion reached their own lines, February 15, the battle to close off the salient of Japanese who had been sent to rescue him eight days earlier was within 24 hours of being over.

It will be recalled that in order to contain the enemy in what was quickly named the "Upper Pocket," Gen. Brougher, early on the morning of February 7, had shoved Company A of the 92d Infantry into a critical, 100-yard-wide blocking position directly in front of the advancing Japanese. The 30 or so hours this single company held off the Japanese before being relieved by the 2d Battalion of the 2d Philippine Constabulary tell a story that could fit into those of a dozen other units involved in the pocket fights. According to its company commander, Capt. Beverly Skardon, it was first "necessary for the men to be placed not over six feet apart to prevent the infiltration of the enemy ... nevertheless, the matted bamboo [and] fallen trees presented such concealment that men crawling forward sometimes found themselves dropping in on top of a Jap and vice versa." Because of the Japanese adeptness at infiltrating after dark, "all movement at night was prohibited." Anything that moved automatically drew fire.

The chore of feeding the men was also found to be a "laborious and extremely dangerous process." Fed twice daily, at dawn and just before nightfall, their ration of a cup of rice and a spoonful of salmon gravy traveled in the same canteen cup "the entire length of the company line, being passed from foxhole to foxhole to the sheltered position of chow carriers and back again."[17]

By the time the constabulary effected the relief of Company A, who still remained on-line after moving to a less critical position, the entire Upper Pocket was pretty well surrounded. It wasn't until February 11, three days later, however, that the tough constabulary men were able to gain, and then only 50 yards.

The Filipinos didn't know that by then the worst was over. Relative to the enemy's orders of February 9 to pull back to their own lines, the 2d Battalion, 33d Infantry, fighting in the Upper Pocket, had been instructed to make one last attempt to break through to the Big Pocket. After blunting two days of enemy efforts, the precious 50 yards gained on the 11th by the Constabulary 2d Battalion was the indication that the withdrawal was under way in the Upper Pocket too.

Despite orders to concede their positions, the Japanese remained determined to make it difficult for the Filipinos. With the focal point of the action remaining with the constabulary, despite the addition of three 192d tanks, the next day, February 12, gains of only 50 or so yards were registered.

On February 14, the addition of, among others, the 1st Battalion of the 45th and the 51st Combat Team to the Upper Pocket perimeter brought Gen. Brougher to order an all-out push the next morning. It paid off. By sunset, troops of the 45th dug in some 200 yards closer to the original MLR than they were that morning.

Efforts, in the meantime, were being made to pinch off the upper part of the salient near the MLR, but the going was tough. Even on the east side where tanks had been brought in, gains were slight and the battle fierce.

The effect of the tanks, because of the prevailing problems of difficult terrain, dense jungle, fallen trees, and entangling undergrowth, was at first minimal. But help in an unexpected way was soon to come from members of Maj. Helmert Duisterhoff's 2d Battalion, 11th Infantry, who had held and were now attacking this vital corner since the initial enemy breakthrough.

Members of the Philippine Army's 11th Division had been conscripted entirely from northern Luzon, many from what was known as the Mountain Provinces. Included with the men from this area were members of a one-time savage tribe known as Igorots. The Igorots, befriending civilization in the early 1920s, although found to be "kindly, appreciative, truthful and . . . faithful," remained nonetheless, wild, tough, and fearless. Most of Dutch Maj. Duisterhoff's battalion were Igorot.[18]

The tankers, frustrated by their lack of success in the impenetrable jungle, were reinforced by Duisterhoff's 2d Battalion—only not in the usual way. The Igorots, who were fascinated by the noisy steel "monsters," took it upon themselves to leap up on top of the tanks and, acting as eyes for the all-but-blind driver, direct him toward the enemy. By pounding on top of the tank with rifle butts or bolos, they could guide and direct him to turn, speed up, or slow down. Whenever one of the tanks stalled or got hung up on a rock or tree stump, they jumped to the ground and quickly hacked them loose.

News of the Igorots' piggybacking exploits swept through the command. In part of Gen. MacArthur's official communiqué number 119 of February 22, 1942, he commented, "Bataan has seen many wild mornings, but nothing to equal this. No quarter was asked and none was given. . . . Always above the din of battle rose the fierce shouts of the Igorots as they rode the tanks. . . . No gun, no thicket, only death itself could stop that mad rush. Of all the bloody spots on the peninsula, that proved to be the bloodiest." He was later heard to comment that "for sheer breathtaking and heart-stopping desperation, I have never known the equal of those Igorots riding the tanks."[19]

By nightfall of February 15, Fil-American success against what was left of the Upper Pocket had progressed to the stage where, because of the pocket's small size, firing during simultaneous attacks from opposite sides had become just as dangerous to the Fil-Americans as it was to the enemy.

On the morning of February 16, Gen. Wainwright asked his aide, Maj. John Pugh, to take a first-hand look at the mop-up operation that was taking place against the Big Pocket. United Press correspondent Frank Hewlett, who overheard the conversation, got permission to go along, as did Maj. Joseph Chabot. When the three men returned later that day, Hewlett sat down and wrote the following story under his usual byline, "With General MacArthur's Army in the Philippines":

> Death in the form of bullets from the rifle of a green-painted Japanese sniper whizzed past my head today, and I'm shaking yet.
>
> My experience with the sniper came when I accompanied Major Joseph Chabot and Major John Pugh to investigate a sector where a small group of Japanese had been cut off.
>
> We were in sight of our destination when we stopped to talk with a Tank Corps lieutenant.
>
> "Any snipers around?" asked Major Pugh.
>
> "I haven't heard of one on the trail," the lieutenant said. Just then a bullet kicked up the dust a foot from where we were grouped. Another whined past my ear, and then two more shots whizzed past.
>
> Before the third and fourth shots came, however, the four of us had dived into the brush. We started squirming through the jungle floor flat on our bellies. It isn't pleasant to burrow through that stuff, but you're glad when there's an enemy waiting to pick you off if you show yourself. When we were out of range we got to our feet again and compared notes. No one could agree where the shots came from.
>
> Walking down these Bataan Peninsula trails where enemy snipers are lurking is like a boy walking past a graveyard on a dark night. Only you don't dare whistle. You don't dare run, either. Better crawl and jump from

tree to tree. You'll live longer, as three American Army officers and I discovered.

The snipers—nicknamed "the rattlesnakes of Bataan"—take particular pains to pick off officers. The one who shot at us was killed later. When we saw him we understood why we hadn't even been able to determine where he was firing from.

He wore a green uniform that blended perfectly with the foliage of the high tree he had climbed. His face was painted green. His hands were green and he wore green shoes. He wore linesman's climbers to aid in scaling the trees and his ammunition was smokeless.

Our sniper is still up that tree. He had tied himself to a limb and when an American rifleman picked him off his body remained high in the branches.

Hewlett's story, which hit papers in the United States three days later, had the fitting headline: JAP SNIPERS IN BATAAN HIDE BEHIND OWN PAINT.[20]

Sunrise of February 17 was the last one the remaining 200 or so enemy soldiers in the salient, which by then had been reduced to less than football field size, would see. The fight for the last few yards of ground was surprisingly ferocious. Surprising because many of the Japanese, whose commanders had already conceded defeat and who still held a 50-yard-wide escape route through to their own lines, refused to save themselves. To the contrary, the bitter, four-hour fight for the remaining handful of yards of the salient would be for most of the enemy to the death.

On line for the final thrust was the constabulary's 2d Battalion, who had taken over the day before for the 45th and 51st CT. The dawn assault was prefaced by a heavy mortar and artillery barrage whose concentration into such a small area, within seconds, had the battlefield totally obliterated from view. When the fire lifted and smoke cleared, revealing a grotesque, barren, rock strewn patch of earth completely denuded of vegetation and hopefully of live Japanese, the anxious constabularymen attacked.

But the Japanese, as they would do under similar circumstances throughout the entire war, literally rose up out of the rubble to take on the Filipinos. Hand-to-hand, bayonet-to-bayonet, a yard-by-yard struggle began with the constabulary, under the leadership of Maj. Deogracias Tenazas, slowly pushing their adversaries back across the broken ground.

By 10 A.M. the begrimed Filipinos reached the trenches that marked the original U.S. MLR. At long last, the battle was over. Behind them, across the scarred, denuded battlefield, reeking with the smell of gunpowder and blood, lay the bodies of close to 200 enemy soldiers along with a miscellaneous assortment of weapons and equipment. Included among the five artillery pieces and 27 machine guns found were several flame throwers that had been used for the first time in the battle by the Japanese against the American tanks.[21]

So ended the battle that, relative to terrain, jungle, and enemy tenacity, was equal to that which had just been concluded on the points. The Americans and Filipinos had fought, many without relief and on meager rations, for 19 days. They had persevered with little or no artillery, completely unreliable mortar support, unsatisfactory "Casey Cookie" hand grenades and inadequate signal corps equipment. On February 10, their twelfth day on the line against the enemy in the Big Pocket, Maj. Van Oosten, of the 45th's 1st Battalion, noted that "progress was being made by inches, from foxhole to foxhole."[22] Captain Beverly Skardon of the 92d Infantry commented regarding his company's action against the Upper Pocket that "the men [had] lived in foxholes for approximately 11 days. If killed, the man was covered in his hole. Malnutrition had so sapped the strength of the Filipino soldier that even the evacuation of wounded turned out to be a problem of physical strength." Before long, "even men counted as effectives could not do much more than walk about."[23]

Back at Bataan's two general hospitals, the story of the battles of both the Pockets and Points was also being told, only without words. The troops, wrote Dr. Alfred Weinstein, "showed the strain of their ordeal when they [reached] the hospital. Haggard, hungry, dehydrated, bled out, they had lain in their foxholes and first-aid stations for days until carried by hand litter or mule pack over mountains and through swamps to where ambulances could navigate. Their wounds stank to high heaven and crawled with fat maggots."

Near Disaster in the II Corps

"You're not going to take those goddamn troops out of the line."

Prior to its being called to action at Abucay in mid–January, the American 31st Infantry Regiment was bivouacked on the extreme eastern edge (referred to by the Americans as the Pandan position) of what would before long become the second and final MLR—the Bagac-Orion line. The Pandan, during the 31st's brief six-day stay there, had thoroughly prepared it for the role it would eventually play. It was back to this area that the regiment was ordered following its withdrawal from Abucay when orders reassigning it into II Corps reserve at Limay were issued.

In anticipation of the occupation of the new Bagac-Orion MLR, Gen. Parker, II Corps commander, earlier had divided his eight-and-a-half-mile-wide half of the peninsula into four sectors. Covering the bulk of a nearly two-and-a-half-mile-wide area near the center, known officially as Sector C, was the Philippine Army's 31st Division along with a remnant unit from the 51st Division, both under the command of Gen. Clifford Bluemel.

Top: "Preceding the general attack, all troops, horses, vehicles, and guns start moving up to the front" read the caption under this *Philippine Expeditionary Force* photo. *Bottom:* Japanese 65th Brigade commander Gen. Akira Nara reading the orders that would send his troops against the final U.S. line near Mt. Samat.

The view from Mt. Samat overlooking the site of Japanese positions behind the Orion-Bagac Line. Had the Japanese air force allowed U.S. artillery the freedom to fire during daylight hours, it is easy to see how enemy troop and supply movements could have been held up or destroyed.

When the decision was made to form a Philippine Division reserve on January 25, Parker, like Wainwright, found himself with a dilemma. Wainwright was losing only one regiment off the line, the 45th. Parker was losing two, the U.S. 31st and the Scout 57th Infantry, which was being reassigned to USAFFE reserve near Mariveles. In desperation, Parker grabbed the closest Philippine Army division, the 31st, which was bivouacked at nearby Orion. Although already committed to Sector C, the II Corps commander ordered its 33d Infantry, minus one battalion, to the 57th's spot in adjacent Sector D, and its 31st Infantry into the American-prepared Pandan position. Of these changes, however, Parker failed to notify either the 31st Division's commander or the sector commander—both positions held by Gen. Clifford Bluemel.

There was, needless to say, a series of emotional outbursts on the morning of the 26th upon Bluemel's discovery of what had happened, and they reverberated throughout the entire II Corps.

The first one came when Bluemel ran into a column of Filipinos from his 31st Infantry being led away from the front line. "Where the hell are you going?" he queried the officer in charge. The American 1st Battalion commander leading the group, taken somewhat aback, said that they had been ordered by corps to report to Sector A on the east coast. "You're not going

This aerial view of the northeast corner of Mt. Samat, is where Trail 4 (located along the lower slopes of the mountain but no longer visible) and the Pilar River junctioned. Most of Bataan has been denuded of its once-lush jungle by logging companies in search of the peninsula's great abundance of hardwoods.

to take those goddamn troops out of the line," Bluemel retorted. "You're under my command." Instructing them to remain in their positions until relieved by his "personal orders," he sent the 1st Battalion and its cowed commander back from where they had come.[24]

Thirty minutes later upon reaching what was supposed to be the 33d Infantry area, Bluemel was jolted again, this time by empty foxholes. The 33d too, had pulled out and, in doing so, had left a vital avenue of approach down Trail 2 wide open to an opportunistic enemy. Bluemel was now beside himself. How could anyone at Corps Headquarters be so imbecilic? The next six hours were spent scouring the local countryside for troops to help plug the gap. By sunset the frustrated general had somehow enough men back on line across the abandoned corridor to at least consider it reconnected.

But the coming of darkness did not signal the end of his troubles. At six o'clock, a dust-covered messenger arrived from Gen. Parker with written orders for the immediate release of the 1st Battalion of the 31st Infantry, who he had ordered back into the line early that morning, to Sector A on the east coast. To replace it and the other 31st Division units he had tapped, Parker was sending him two battalions of 41st Infantry troops from Sector D on Bluemel's left, who would arrive "late" the next day.

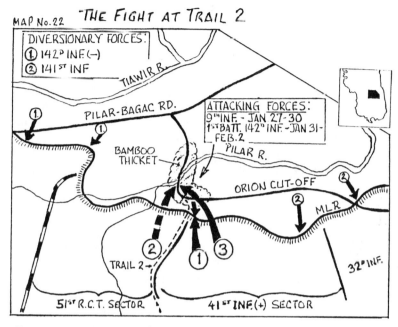

MAP No.22 THE FIGHT AT TRAIL 2

① 41ˢᵀ INF. AMBUSH INITIAL 9ᵀᴴ INF. ATTACK - NITE JAN. 28

② HEAVIEST AND MOST EFFECTIVE P.A. ARTILLERY BARRAGE OF BATTLE OF BATAAN BREAKS UP 1ˢᵀ BATT., 142ᴰ INF. ATTACK - NITE JAN. 31ˢᵀ

③ 41ˢᵀ INF. CLEAR THICKET - FEB. 2-3; POSITION RESTORED

Faced for the third time in a single day with having to fill the positions he was assigned to command with troops he didn't have, Bluemel reluctantly decided to bring the reserve battalion over from the 32d Infantry, whose regiment was on line on the sector right. It wasn't until just before midnight that the part of the line which, for all practical purposes, had been unmanned for some 15 hours, was again considered connected. Only, instead of an entire division, it was now bandaged together by little more than a single, and needless to say, unprepared and thinly spread regiment.

General Homma, at the same time he ordered an attack against the I Corps with the last of the ill-fated 20th Infantry on January 25, ordered Gen. Akira Nara to mount the same against the II Corps.

Earlier in Manila, the Japanese reportedly found a secret map of Bataan, outlining the next main U.S. battle line as extending westward across the peninsula from Limay. The Bagac-Orion positions, which were just lightly defined, were incorrectly interpreted as the outpost line. (A map showing the same "Limay Line" as the "Last Line of Defense," was published in the February 9, 1942, issue of *Life* from an article by that magazine's correspondent to the Philippines, Melville Jacoby.) Reacting to their "secret map," Homma ordered Nara to move out against the "lightly defended outpost line" on the 27th. For his attack, Nara ordered no less than three infantry regiments to positions within half a mile of his chosen focal point, which, ironically, would be none other than Trail 2.

Fortunately for the newly arrived and unorganized Americans and Filipinos, the enemy attack started late in the day on the 27th. The assault, scheduled to begin on the heels of a preliminary artillery bombardment in which all the north-south roads in the area were hit, failed to get underway before dark, resulting in the diminishing of enemy efforts by nightfall.

Meanwhile, the two battalions of 41st Infantry promised by Gen. Parker had moved out of their positions west of Mt. Samat and had begun arriving in Sector C. As they arrived, Gen. Bluemel directed them into positions on the east side of Trail 2 adjacent to the 51st CT, with frontline responsibility for close to three-quarters of a mile.

The enemy attack the next day, again scheduled for late afternoon, was prefaced this time by an hour-long barrage against the mile-wide section of the line opposite and to the west of Trail 2. Less than 500 yards in front of the U.S. line and directly in line with Trail 2, the cut-off road leading to Orion junctioned with the Pilar-Bagac road. In fact, less than 100 yards from the MLR at the point where it turned 90 degrees east toward Orion, Trail 2 began as an almost north-south extension.

One of the three Japanese regiments involved in the attack, none other than Col. Susumu Takechi's 9th Infantry "Abucay encircling unit," was positioned in the huge L-shaped bamboo thicket within which Trail 2 and the Orion cut-off road joined. (See Map 22.)

As the barrage lifted, Takechi attacked. What he assumed would be a tokenly defended outpost line was, of course, the main U.S. line. This he soon found out as the Filipinos, using a tactic learned from their adversaries, bayonet-charged the unsuspecting Japanese as they were negotiating the MLR barbed wire. The efficient 41st Infantrymen, who had already been decorated with a Presidential Unit Citation for their actions on the Abucay line, made quick work of the stunned Japanese. The 9th fell back. With the first grey light of dawn, the bodies of a dozen or so enemy soldiers could be seen hanging on the wire and on the ground were close to 90 more.

All of the enemy attacks against the mile-wide sector of US II Corps line had, in fact, been similarily frustrated. The 9th along with the 141st and 142d Regiments, all having been in the thick of the battle continuously for close to 20 days, were beginning to wilt. According to Gen. Nara, "battle strength [had] rapidly declined and the difficulties of officers and men became more extreme."

The story of the next two days was the same. Each Japanese attack against the U.S. "outpost line" was easily frustrated by the defenders. On the afternoon of the 31st, Nara made his biggest effort at cracking the line.

It began late in the afternoon with a 5 P.M. dive-bomber attack against II Corps artillery positions near Mt. Orion. Then, at six o'clock, the first shells from what was to be a 90-minute enemy artillery barrage struck Filipino positions all along Trail 2. "Bataan," according to the Japanese commander, "shook with the thunderous din of guns," as the focal point of the enemy fire mission, Trail 2, was systematically raked with gunfire.

The enemy's thoroughness, however, had forced him to tip his hand. As troops of the 1st Battalion, 142d Infantry, who had replaced most of Takechi's regiment, were moving up to their line of departure at the edge of the bamboo thicket, Bataan "shook" again with what was recorded as the opening rounds of the "heaviest artillery barrage ever fired by U.S. II Corps guns." Over two dozen 75s of the Philippine Army's 301st Field Artillery, frustrated constantly from daylight fire missions by the planes of the ever present Japanese Air Force, ripped the area opposite the trail. Their devastating interdiction in a short time had shattered Nara's attack plans for that night, while at the same time spreading great joy among the long-suppressed Philippine Army artillerymen.

Unbeknownst to the Fil-Americans, the back of the planned Japanese assault against Trail 2 had been broken. When the Filipinos moved in to mop up in the thicket two days later, on February 2, they ran up against only a single battalion of 9th Infantry troops who were themselves in the final stages of withdrawing from the area. After successfully halting the U.S. advance, sometime during the night the last remnant of the Japanese 9th Infantry pulled out, leaving only empty foxholes and a sapper trench full of rotting corpses. The battle for Trail 2 was over.

Although focused on Trail 2 for diversionary purposes, the enemy attacks had been launched across the entire II Corps front. As a result, U.S. positions west of Trail 2 on the northwest slopes of Mt. Samat, manned by the bulk of Gen. Vincente Lim's 41st Division and Gen. Mateo Capinpin's 21st Division, had been in a steady tug-of-war struggle with the Japanese over control of the Fil-American outpost lines during the same eight-day period. On February 3, the same day Trail 2 was being secured, the 42d and 43d Infantry Regiments were involved in a nine-hour long battle with the enemy's 142d Infantry. By five o'clock that afternoon, however, the Filipinos had successfully dislodged the Japanese from their threatening position less than 100 yards from the MLR.

After the area had been secured, Gen. Lim's intelligence officer, Capt. Isegami Campo, who had earned himself a U.S. Silver Star for behind-the-

Top: More than 100 white crosses mark the graves of Americans and Filipinos in this temporary battlefield cemetery at the eastern end of Mariveles air field. *Bottom:* This Japanese photograph of Mt. Samat (left) and the Mariveles Mountains, was taken during the artillery barrage prior to the final Japanese offensive against the U.S. Bagac–Orion MLR.

lines reconnaissance action earlier that day, and three other officers came across the ravaged bodies of two young Filipinos in a partially covered Japanese foxhole. Both had been raped by their captors and then murdered. Pinned on the tattered clothing of one of the girls was a photograph. It was an undelivered picture of her to her boyfriend or husband, across which was written "With love forever to my dearest darling," signed, "Erlinda."[25]

Incidents of Japanese atrocities on Bataan had, of course, been reported before. The tortured remains of men captured on patrol or cut-off behind enemy lines had been found by friendly troops several times since the battle began. In most cases they had been tied to trees or hung-up by their thumbs and used for bayonet practice. In his official communiqué of January 24, Gen. MacArthur made specific mention of a "flagrant instance" where the body of a Philippine Scout, Pvt. Fernando Tan, was found in a stream. "His hands had been bound behind his back and he had been bayoneted several times before being thrown in a stream to die." Just two days earlier, a lone "left for dead" survivor from an overrun 11th Division outpost in the I Corps, returned with numerous bayonet wounds and the story of the torture, stabbing, and eventual murder of 18 fellow Filipinos of his unit.[26]

The story of the ravage of Erlinda and her friend, repeated over the Voice of Freedom radio broadcast several nights later by Carlos Romulo, enraged Filipinos throughout the command, while at the same time prompting several unauthorized "Remember Erlinda" revenge raids across enemy lines. From then on, few Japanese unlucky enough to be captured by the Filipinos would know a painless end to their lives.

The Japanese Break Off the Fight

"See You in Manila in 80 Days."

In reaction to the discovery of the "secret" U.S. map of Bataan by the Japanese, it will be remembered that Gen. Homma, on January 25, ordered his army to carry the battle forward, without pause, to the newly established Fil-American line at Limay.

The results of his eagerness, compounded, of course, by the miscalculation of the whereabouts of the U.S. line, were nearly fatal to his command. On January 26, Lt. Gen. Susumu Morioka dispatched 1,000 men of the 3d Battalion, 20th Infantry, against the United States MLR near Bagac, resulting in the battle for the Pockets and the loss of close to 825 men in the process. On the same day, Gen. Akira Nara moved the three regiments under his command forward against the U.S. II Corps positions east of Mt. Samat, resulting in the battle for Trail 2 and the estimated loss of close to 200 more.

Lt. Gen. Masaharu Homma, commander of the Japanese 14th Army in the Philippines.

On January 27, Gen. Morioka, with Homma's blessings, sent the only remaining battalion of 20th Infantry troops to reinforce their beachhead at Quinauan Point. For all practical purposes, there were no survivors from this operation. In the earlier battles of Longoskawayan and Quinauan Points, the Japanese came just 43 men short of losing their third battalion of 20th Infantry soldiers.

On February 8, the day the Americans and Filipinos concluded their mop-up operation on Quinauan Point, Gen. Homma called a staff meeting in his headquarters in hot, muggy San Fernando, 40 miles north of the U.S. main line on Bataan.

The meeting, held to decide the immediate future of Japanese operations on the peninsula, was already somewhat after the fact. The harbinger had come six days earlier with Homma's order to abandon the offensive against the II Corps at Trail 2. The "loss without a trace" of the 2d Battalion, 20th Infantry on Longoskawayan and Quinauan had also been acknowledged by then. The fate of the remaining two battalions of the regiment, one on Silaiim-Anyasan and the other in the Pockets, looked, for the most part, to be out of their hands as well. The casualty rate in the 65th Brigade, the only unit of divisional size at that moment not committed, yet active nearly continuously since the 11th of January, had reached a whopping 65 percent. It alone was incapable of carrying the offensive. Lastly, Bataan's deadly combination of tropical diseases had not been at all kind

Altar of Courage Memorial, Mt. Samat, Bataan. Built by the Philippine National Shrines Commission, this beautiful Italian marble structure dedicated to Filipino and American soldiers who fought on Bataan sits majestically on the heights of Mt. Samat. Fronting the marble balcony that surrounds the structure are several bas relief sculpture scenes depicting significant battles and incidents that occurred during the campaign. Alternately placed between the scenes are large brass insignias of the military units that fought in the battle.

to Homma's army either. At that moment, over 10,000 Imperial Army soldiers were down with malaria and dysentery.

The question, therefore, became one of what strategy to follow: to tighten the naval blockade and starve the U.S. command into submission, or to send for reinforcements. Either decision would cause the Japanese commander to lose face, for both would represent the only real failure the Japanese Imperial Army had known in the Pacific since the war started. It would also mean breaking off the fight and withdrawing a safe distance away from U.S. lines — something else no Japanese army had yet done.

Of the two, Homma made the most honorable choice: reinforcements. With this decision, the Americans and Filipinos on Bataan were granted the opportunity to enter the history books as an army that went down fighting. Orders for the general withdrawal went out that night, followed a few days later by a message from Homma to Japanese Southern Army Headquarters in Saigon, stating, in part, that "at present strength, the attack [on Bataan] could not be continued."

Encouraged by their successes against the Japanese all across the Bagac-Orion front and along the west coast as well, it wasn't long before the Fil-American troops on Bataan recognized just what they had accomplished. Wrote the assistant supply officer on Bataan, Lt. Col. Nicoll Galbraith, "the morale of our front line troops appears very high and they want to take the offensive." In a radio message to the War Department in Washington, Gen. MacArthur noted that the enemy had "definitely recoiled. He has refused [bent back] his flank in front of my right [II Corps] six to ten kilometers. ... His attitude is so passive as to discount any immediate threat of attack."[27]

A 31st Division patrol from Sector C near Mt. Samat reported that it had successfully probed as far north as the original line at Abucay, prompting a request from their bellicose commander, Gen. Clifford Bluemel, to investigate the possibility of reoccupying the former positions. Galbraith wrote that he wouldn't have been surprised to hear that "they were in San Fernando next." Another incident came along about this time that also helped raise morale. A rumor, later proved to be false, had come through from several intelligence sources in Manila that Gen. Homma had committed suicide in Gen. MacArthur's old top-floor suite at the Manila Hotel. As stated in USAFFE communiqué number 139 of March 8, the suicide had been "motivated by the fact that his numerically superior forces had been unable to destroy the American and Filipino defenders of Bataan and Corregidor." In addition, it was reported that his replacement was to be none other than Gen. Tomoyuko Yamashita, vaunted Tiger of Malaya and hero of Singapore.[28]

News of the enemy withdrawal and suicide prompted the *International News Summary* newspaper, distributed from the USAFFE Press Relations Office on Corregidor, to enter a small caption on the bottom line: "SEE YOU IN MANILA IN 80 DAYS." This in turn started "See You in Manila" betting among the Filipinos as to on what date it would actually take place.[29]

General MacArthur, of course, would have none of it. Despite the fact that, as Gen. Homma put it, the American and Filipino army could have gone straight to Manila "without encountering much resistance on [the Japanese] part," the overall strategic picture would have remained the same: the Philippines were isolated. There would be no pot of gold at the end of a successful offensive, just the increased need for food, ammunition, transportation, gasoline, and medical supplies, plus an increase in the overall area to be defended. Although the static, defensive battle being fought on Bataan wasn't a winning one, it wasn't a losing one either ... but it was the one the Bataan Army was stuck with.

CHAPTER FOUR

The Lull Begins

"We spit on our hands and waited."

USAFFE Communiqué No. 101, February 11, 1942, read "fighting in Bataan, as well as enemy air activity has appreciably lessened...." USAFFE Communiqué No. 119, February 22, 1942, read "Enemy action in Bataan was largely confined to frequent air raids...," while USAFFE Communiqué No. 132, March 3, 1942, noted "practically no ground or air activity in Bataan." USAFFE Communiqué No. 140, March 9, 1942, said "no fighting in Bataan during the past 24 hours."[1]

And so it happened: Through February just a cautious hope; by March a reality. The Japanese, for the first time since the war started, had been turned back. On February 12, Lt. Henry G. Lee of Headquarters Company, Philippine Division, wrote a letter home that typified the feelings of many on Bataan. "I am proud," he said, "to be a part of the fight that is being made here; and would not, even if it were possible, leave here until it is over and we have won, as we inevitably will." In the letter, which did not reach the United States until March 30, he went on to qualify his words by saying that "Bataan may fall, but the eventual outcome of the war is foreordained."

Doubtlessly, most Americans and probably many Filipinos felt as Lee did, that Bataan, despite what had happened, would probably "fall." All knew the Japanese would be back. All knew that a single defeat to a conquering army was just a momentary setback, a lull in the fight. General Wainwright probably put it best: "We [just] spit on our hands and waited for the enemy to come again."

Despite the recognized lull in ground fighting, the Japanese Air Force continued to keep everyone's heads down. On the afternoon of Friday, February 13, an unfortunate tragedy occurred near the junction of the Mariveles and East Roads near Cabcaben. It happened at the very moment air corps Capt. Harold "Lefty" Eads was returning from Mariveles to Bataan Field. Just before reaching the turn marking the junction of the two roads,

Despite the fact that the compound at Hospital No. 1 was clearly marked with giant red crosses (note galvanized metal sheets on ground at right painted with a red cross), the Japanese deliberately bombed it twice during the last 14 days of the battle.

he spotted three enemy dive-bombers coming in low over the bay heading straight for him. He quickly pulled over, jumped from his still-rolling car, and flattened out against a nearby road bank.[2]

Seconds later the Japanese released their bombs. Instead of hitting the road, which at the time was crowded with traffic that had slowed to make the turn, the bombs landed in the barrio of Cabcaben on one side, missed the road, then went on to fall on one of the crowded refugee camps on the Real River. Cabcaben became a burning shambles, with over 48 people dead and wounded. As far as the refugee camp, it was much worse, the final count of dead reaching 75.

On Tuesday, February 17, Capt. Allison Ind of the air corps wrote that four separate bombings of Bataan and Cabcaben Fields had taken place that day. "Bombs for breakfast. Bombs where lunch should have been— but hasn't since December 25th. Bombs for afternoon tea. And bombs for dinner."

On February 23, Capt. Al Poweleit, surgeon with the Provisional Tank Group, after surviving an attack by Japanese planes while on a routine visit to one of the tank companies, described the persistence of the enemy air force: "We hit a slightly open stretch [of the road] just when a number of Japanese strafers came over," he wrote in his diary. "Several soldiers were killed and wounded. While [we] were dressing the wounded, [the] planes returned . . . killing more. We tried to move all the wounded along the side of the road. Again the bastards bombed and strafed [us]. . . . They continued strafing back and forth for almost an hour."[3]

Colonel Russell Volckmann wrote that he and Brig. Gen. William Brougher of the 11th Division needed "hours" to travel across the open 10 mile Orion-Bagac Road, which in normal times would take 30 minutes. "Japanese planes overhead harassed us all the way; we would no more than get on the road when the 'California National Guard' [so nicknamed because the round red insignia on their wings looked like California oranges] would swoop in and force us to take cover."[4]

Among the units assigned to beach defense along the edge of Manila Bay near the two fighter strips was a group of half-tracks from the 194th Tank Battalion. The constant threat of air attack, primarily against the air fields, coupled with a need to break the monotony, as Col. Ernest Miller wrote, brought the crews to "work out a system of baiting the Jap planes." With enemy planes overhead and several .50-caliber-toting half-tracks camouflaged in readiness nearby, one member of the crew would pull his vehicle out in the middle of the road and begin waving a large white bed-sheet. "It was somewhat like a bullfight," said Miller. "In quite a number of instances, [the Japanese plane] would immediately dive and strafe the 'toreadors' with a deluge of bullets and sometimes, bombs," at which time the until then well-camouflaged half-tracks would cut loose with everything they had at the unsuspecting Japanese pilot. It wasn't long before this little trick stopped working, however. The enemy planes just wouldn't come down any more.

When the war broke out, the Philippines were loaded with well-known and widely read newspaper correspondents. Five of them, on the eve of the Japanese arrival in Manila, escaped to Corregidor. They were Frank Hewlett of the United Press; Clark Lee of the Associated Press; Melville and Annalee Jacoby of *Life* and *Time* respectively; Nat Floyd of the *New York Times;* and Curtis Hindson of the British Reuter's news agency. (Ten correspondents who decided to stay in Manila were captured and interned by the Japanese.)

Of the correspondents who worked Bataan, AP's Clark Lee and UP's Frank Hewlett, along with Mel Jacoby, were the most active. Lee and Hewlett in typical newspaper reporter fashion vigorously competed with one another for news. Hewlett's favorite source was Gen. Jonathan Wain-wright, with whom he spent a great deal of time. More than once, in fact, both narrowly missed death when the vehicle in which they were riding was strafed by low-flying Japanese planes.

On one of those occasions, before Wainwright traded in his Packard for a jeep, the two men were chased from his car by an approaching enemy plane. The doors of the car flew open and the occupants scrambled out. "The driver hit the ditch on the opposite side of the road," leaving Wainwright, Hewlett, and the General's orderly, Sgt. Hubert "Tex" Carrol, staring at two small ditches on the other side. Carrol dove into one of them while Wainwright and Hewlett made for the other. Hewlett, a few years quicker, got there first, with Wainwright landing squarely "on [Hewlett's] back [just] as the Zero's wing guns opened up." It was close, the enemy's bullets ripping through the roof of the Packard, less than 15 feet away. Wainwright quickly picked himself up off Hewlett's back, "feeling foolish." "Hate to be such a groundhog, Frank," said the somewhat embarrassed but still alive I Corps commander.

Although Clark Lee's source of information offered a little less excitement, it was a bit broader in scope than Hewlett's. Lee, pretty much digging up news where he could find it, prided himself on datelines like "With the Anti-Aircraft in Bataan," "With the 31st U.S. Infantry at the Bataan Front," or "With the Artillery in Bataan." He traveled to the Abucay front, went on patrols with Bulkeley's PT-boats, and interviewed some of the heroes of the campaign, such as Capt. Arthur Wermuth, Lt. John Bulkeley, and Cmdr. Frank Bridget.

In the middle of the fight at Abucay, Gen. Max Lough, commanding officer of the Philippine Division, made a comment that, for correspondents, was really what it was all about. On seeing Lee, he said, "I knew you AP reporters got around, but I never expected to meet one here."[5]

After Lee's first patrol with Bulkeley, the two men stayed in contact with one another. One day in mid–February Bulkeley told Lee of a plan for escape he and his men had worked out. "I liked the idea," said Lee, "and included myself in." Anticipating that the end was near for the Inshore Patrol with fuel and torpedoes almost exhausted, Bulkeley "suggested that we fill up our boats with the gas that's left and go out and raid Jap shipping along the China coast." "After firing all our torpedoes," he continued, "we'll land along the coast, destroy the boats, and hike overland to Chungking."

Bulkeley had served in China in the thirties. He knew the coast and could get by with the language. Although a 550-mile trip over the open seas would first be necessary, when the plan proposed to Adm. Rockwell, it came back stamped APPROVED.

Lee's role, having spent time in China as a correspondent, was to coordinate the plan with the Chinese Army, who, it was suggested, should have a small raiding party fight its way through to the coast and link-up with the PT force. Lee's contact was with an officer in the Chinese Army, Lt. Col. Chih Wang, who was sent to the Philippines as an observer before the war.

Wang, a West Point graduate, at that moment assigned to Philippine Army Headquarters on Bataan, wired Chungking for approval. In a few days it came—the plan for the "Frank Merriwell" escape of the fighting arm of the Bataan Navy to China was on. The only question left was "when?"[6]

On the night of February 17, things began to happen with the navy that indicated the escape might not be long in coming.

As the Inshore Patrol left Sisiman that night, 16 days had passed since the PTs had been able to stir up any activity along the west coast. In the interim, Bulkeley was given orders not to go back inside Subic Bay. Intelligence had it that "the Japs had the bay's rim lined with guns and it would be suicide."

Ignoring orders, by eleven o'clock the two boats, Ens. Anthony Akers' 35 with Bulkeley on board and Lt. Bob Kelly's 34 were sitting off the entrance to the bay. According to army intelligence, there were two or three destroyers in Subic. Bulkeley's plan was to enter the bay and raise enough ruckus to "coax them outside," so Kelly could "lam a couple of torpedoes into the engine room as they came by."

Bulkeley ordered Akers in. After a few tense but quiet minutes they spotted what appeared to be an enemy trawler moored near Grande Island, at which they launched their first torpedo. But there was no explosion. It was guessed that it had passed underneath the shallow drafted ship and settled quietly on the bottom of the bay.

Still undiscovered, the 35 crept on. Well within the bay, Bulkeley saw "the outline of a big ship tied up to Olongapo dock." At 500 yards, they loosed their second torpedo, kicked the 35 into a hard-right rudder, and headed out with engines roaring and all guns blazing at the shoreline. But again, nothing happened—no explosion and no destroyers in hot pursuit for Kelly to "lam a couple" into either.

"They were [the] last torpedoes fired in defense of Bataan," said Bulkeley. "On the way back I realized that we had fired our last torpedoes, except those we would need to fill our tubes for the run to China." That morning when the two little boats tied up at Sisiman, Bulkeley learned that the navy was abandoning the Section Base at Mariveles and moving to Corregidor. Suddenly the China trip appeared near.[7] (See Map 23.)

At about the same time the two PT boats were clearing Sisiman that night, the little interisland ship *Legaspi* was being led out through the mine field. Her predawn arrival the night before marked the second time in 12 days that she had cracked the Japanese blockade. It was also only the second time since the battle opened that a ship had delivered supplies to Bataan.

After unloading her 1,000 tons of cargo, a mere four days' rations for

P.T. Boat Action Around Bataan
Jan. 18 – Feb. 17

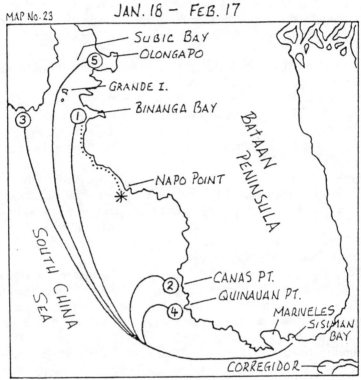

MAP No. 23

① BINANGA BAY   NITE JAN. 18/19   PT. 34 & 31
   ATTACK 5.000 TON MERCHANT SHIP
 ✳ CREW OF LOST PT. 31 RESCUED BY 91ˢᵗ DIVISION

② OFF CANAS POINT NITE JAN. 22/23 PT. 34
   SINK TWO ENEMY LANDING BARGES

③ SAMPOLOC BAY   NITE JAN 24/25 PT. 41
   ATTACK 6.000 TON TRANSPORT

④ OFF QUINAUAN POINT NITE FEB. 1   PT. 32
   ATTACK ENEMY MINELAYER SUPPORTING LANDING

⑤ IN SUBIC BAY   NITE FEB. 17   PT. 35
   FIRED TORPEDOES AT TWO UNIDENTIFIED
   SHIPS; STRAFED BEACH ON WAY OUT

the 100,000-plus soldiers and civilians on Bataan, she was on her way again. Before leaving, Gen. MacArthur sent both her captains, Conejero and Amoyo, Distinguished Service Crosses and her crew Silver Stars in recognition of their blockade-running achievements.

As the *Legaspi* pulled away from Corregidor's North Dock that night, she had on board, along with a select group of U.S. Navy VIPs, a remnant force of Philippine Army Air Corps pilots.

After being badly mauled fighting as infantrymen in the battle for Quinauan Point, it was decided that this handful of trained pursuit pilots could best serve where there were planes to fly. Thus, they were ordered to Australia.

No sooner had Conejero cleared the *Legaspi* of the minefield than he received orders to return. Enemy warships, it seems, had been reported east of Lubang Island, smack in the middle of the ship's path. So it was back to Corregidor.

To the surprise of her crew when they awoke the next morning, a second interisland blockade-runner, the *Princesa de Cebu,* had come in that night and moored nearby. Her 700 tons of foodstuffs, unfortunately, would provide little more than two days' rations for the starving Bataan garrison.

The arrival of the *Princesa,* to a few select personnel in headquarters lateral on Corregidor as well as at the Army Quartermaster Depot at Cebu, had a very special meaning. A week earlier, Maj. Cornelius Byrd of the Army Transportation Service was ordered to Cebu by Gen. MacArthur. With him went the responsibility of rounding up and hiring blockade-runners for the 350-mile trip from Cebu to Corregidor.

The weight of the major's assignment, which was to get food to the army on Bataan before it starved to death, was somewhat lifted by the arrival of the *Princesa* in Manila Bay that night—the first ship he had sent into the blockade had made it.

However, on February 21, the ship *Cia de Filipinas,* carrying 300 tons of corn and rice was sunk off Mindoro. But spirits rose again five days later when the *Elcano,* with 1,100 tons of rations and ammunition edged into Corregidor's North Dock, having made it all the way from Mindanao.[8] Maybe the "mile-long convoy" everyone on Bataan was talking about would make it after all.

Just how much did the Americans and Filipinos believe that there would be such a convoy? Lieutenant Juanita Redmond noted that every day at Hospital No. 1, "the doctors, nurses, corpsmen, and patients made bets with each other as to how many hours, days, [or] weeks it would be before our boats reached us...." "[Men] and nurses too," she wrote, "would [even] climb to the top branches of a tall tree on the hospital grounds, from which we could look out over the bay. If there were ships coming ... we would see them from there."

At the fighter strip at Cabcaben one morning word was passed that a "big convoy" had reached Corregidor. Everyone took off running for the top of a nearby ridge for a look. "There was a general mass movement from the camp area up the hillside," wrote Lt. Edgar Whitcomb. "Many men with more enthusiasm than strength fell by the wayside." Word soon came down from the top that it was true. "They're American ships," said one man, "I saw them myself."[9]

What the men at Cabcaben probably saw was the *Legaspi* and *Princesa*, prompting Whitcomb to write later that the "letdown that followed . . . left us lower than we had ever been before."

He wasn't alone. Correspondent Clark Lee had the displeasure of informing Capt. Arthur Wermuth that the *Legaspi* and *Princesa* were not part of the convoy. Wermuth "got mad as hell at me," wrote Lee, "when I told him the truth—that [the] group of small ships which had suddenly appeared in the bay was not [the] convoy. . . . I thought [he] should know the truth and could stand knowing it. But he didn't want to hear it."[10]

Despite Wermuth's disappointment, since Maj. Byrd's assignment to Cebu, three ships, carrying over 2,700 tons of desperately needed supplies had cracked the enemy blockade of Manila Bay. But the high-water mark had, unfortunately, been reached. On February 28, two days after the *Elcano* arrived at Corregidor, the Japanese hit the jackpot, sinking no fewer than four of Byrd's blockade-runners. The next day, March 1, *Legaspi*, returning to Corregidor for the third time, was run aground by captains Amoyo and Conejero and set on fire in the face of an approaching enemy minesweeper. Later that day, 1,300 more tons of cargo destined for the empty stomachs of the Bataan Army went under, victim of the same enemy ship.

Six days later, March 7, the last two blockade-runners were caught and sunk by the Japanese. The "last two" because on the following day, reacting to the loss of eight ships in eight days and the sharp increase in Japanese naval activity in southern waters, Gen. Sutherland ordered all blockade-running attempts halted until further notice. Bataan, as of February 26, for all practical purposes had had its last "helping hand" from the outside world.[11]

With the lull, and soldier's minds, for the time being, off war and fighting, it was natural for their concerns to turn to the other main threat to their well-being: starvation. Any Bataan soldier, whether an American with a signal unit near Mariveles, or a Philippine Army private on the MLR, if asked what he did with his off duty time, would have answered, "look for something to eat." There were no exceptions—officers and men, Americans and Filipinos—everyone was starving. All were hungry. All had lost weight. Most, by the end of March, including those lucky enough to have avoided malaria and dysentery, had dropped to at least 25 percent below their normal weight.

How hungry were they? On February 15, Capt. Allison Ind, with air corps headquarters on Bataan, wrote, "The rice was moldy today. Pretty hungry. But couldn't keep it down." Moldy or not, he still ate it, and so did everybody else. Eating with the pilots, Capt. Ed Dyess commented that "at some meals we had only rice. At others there was a thin salmon soup. Salmon gravy had been unheard of since our flour supply had given out." With, as poet Lt. Henry G. Lee wrote, "one small salmon can for every 15 men," men were constantly searching for ways to supplement their often-cussed Bataan ration.

How hungry were they? Major Eugene Conrad of the U.S. 31st Infantry wrote that "most of our time was taken up in searching for that ever-elusive item called food." With the daily ration reduced to "8 ounces of moldy rice per man per day and one-fourteenth of a can of fish," it is no surprise that even the Americans had turned to "roots, snail, and snakes."[12] Ambrosio Peña, with a Philippine Army artillery unit near Mt. Orion, witnessed a starving American airman "sucking the juice out of a tiny green pineapple while completely ignoring the fact that his face and tongue had broken out in a rash from the stickers."[13]

How hungry were they? The nasty but necessary business of sending patrols behind enemy lines during a period of stalemate between battles had never been looked forward to by officers or men. Not so on Bataan. Many men eagerly volunteered for these patrols, which gave them a chance to forage for or, in some cases, actually buy food from some native food stand in an unguarded barrio. One of the favorite stopping off points for II Corps patrols was a molasses tank near Pilar where, wrote Lt. Sheldon Mendelson of the Provisional Air Corps Regiment, "men would drink a pint or more of the craved food."[14] At the coastal barrio of Camachile, about two miles north of Orion, a few brave Filipino civilians set up a little black-market food operation, bringing food in across the bay by banca. This lasted until mid–March, when the smugglers were intercepted and killed coming ashore one morning by a Japanese patrol. The few American C-rations available to the command were reserved as either emergency or, in some cases, patrol rations. To use them otherwise was a court-martial offense. In units where there were no C-rations for use as patrol-rations, Lt. Mendelson wrote that "units furnished their patrols with one sandwich per man for 36 hours."[15]

A "full stomach" was necessary to sustain not only the physical condition of the troops, but the mental as well. On March 26, air corps Lt. Tom Garrity wrote in his diary, "Had a special treat last night—canned figs, two slices of bread, and some real coffee. I felt so good afterwards I couldn't sleep. I felt like whipping the whole Jap army."[16]

In some of the on-line Philippine Army units, men on food patrol were actually decorated. Captain Jose Razon, supply officer of the 41st Division, was awarded the Philippine Army's Gold Cross—equal to the U.S. Army's Bronze Star—for, as is stated on his citation, reconnoitering an area "in close proximity to hostile troops and arranging for the procurement and shipment of supplies."[17]

In one case, an American on "food patrol" well within friendly lines probably should have been decorated. Private Kai Martin, attached to the 724th Army Air Corps Ordnance Company near Little Baguio, had hiked down to his favorite waterhole along the Real River one afternoon in early March. There he had bathed, washed his clothes, been strafed by a passing enemy plane, and then routinely "went out looking for something to eat." Fortunately for Martin, he had run into an off-duty medical corpsman from nearby Hospital No. 2 while at the river, and the two men took off together.

A hundred or so yards down river, not far from one of the civilian refugee camps, they were approached by a pregnant woman who through sign language and gestures indicated that she was in labor. Martin and the corpsman looked at each other. There was nobody else around. So "we somehow delivered the baby," said Martin, who an hour later was "out scrounging for something to eat again."[18]

On March 18 an incident over the ration occurred that, had the men the strength, might have caused a food riot.

Early in the campaign, as mentioned earlier, Corregidor released two antiaircraft and one searchlight battery to the Bataan defense, where they were to remain throughout the fight. It was prearranged at that time that these units would continue to be fed from their own mess on Corregidor, which, as the troops on Bataan were assured, issued half-ration quantities and food of similar quality as their own.

Three or four times a week throughout the campaign, Corregidor rations were sent by boat and then by truck to these units. On March 18, the truck delivering the food was spot-checked at a Bataan military police checkpoint.

Upon examination of the waybill, it was found, to the astonishment of the MPs, to contain no less than one case of ham, a case of bacon, 24 cans of sausage, 60 cans of vegetables, a half-dozen cans of potatoes, 24 cans of peaches, and 600 pounds of rice. To top it off, over 50 cartons of by far the most sought-after luxury item on the peninsula—cigarettes— were also included.

The crowning blow came when it was discovered that on top of all of this, these same three batteries had been drawing Bataan rations too.

Word of the incident, of course, spread like prairie fire through the starving command, causing the Bataan troops to resent even more the troops on Corregidor. And who could blame those who that same evening would be sitting down to their four ounces of moldy rice and single spoon-ful of salmon gravy?

Some men sought fresh fish as a supplement to their meager diets, only not in the conventional way and not without risk. It was popularly called "grenade fishing." Captain Al Poweleit, Group Surgeon of the Provisional Tank Group, recorded such a trip that he and his sergeant took on March 8. "[We] took a few Japanese hand grenades down . . . and tossed them into the sea," he wrote in his diary. "To our surprise, many fish came to the sur-face. . . . As we were recovering the last ones, Japanese planes came down and strafed us. We got to shore and dashed up the bank." To top it off, Poweleit thought he'd had a heart attack halfway up the hill. He didn't, and although the fish were recovered, the captain's diary showed this as his last fishing trip.[19]

On the night of March 27 several men from a small quartermaster detachment near Cabcaben were called out on a burial detail. Burying the dead was one of the jobs of the quartermaster, but this call was a little different. Judging from the size of the detail, the men thought that they must be going to bury a whole army.

On the morning of March 26 Japanese bombers in one of the six air raids made on Corregidor that day knocked out one of the freezer units in the Rock's cold-storage plant. The Bataan ration, it will be remembered, was by then being distributed entirely out of Corregidor. Twenty-four thousand pounds of carabao—nearly one day's meat allotment for Bataan—was threatened by spoilage with the shutdown of the freezer unit unless it could be transported across the Channel and issued. But the beefed-up Japanese Air Force, which by then had begun its round-the-clock bombing of Bataan, Corregidor, and anything afloat in the North Channel, delayed the loading until dark. By dawn the next day, the lighter carrying the meat was tied up at the dock at Cabcaben. But again, because of the ever-present Japanese planes, it couldn't be unloaded.

That night, as Quartermaster supply trucks pulled down to the dock to unload the meat, some 32 hours after it had been removed from the refrigeration unit on Corregidor, there was no need to tell anyone that it was too late. The gentle onshore breeze, carrying the undeniable odor of spoiled meat, met the nostrils of the detail when they reached the dock.

The meat was loaded onto trucks and driven to one of the slaughter-houses where it was buried. The quartermaster detail wasn't burying an army after all, but if things like this continued to happen to the starving Bataan soldier, it wouldn't be long.

To take their minds off of their empty stomachs during this time, many of the men, particularly in the rear areas, turned to cards. It helped pass

the time and it didn't take any energy. An incident occurred at the U.S. 31st
Infantry's Rear Command Post that dampened interest in the gambling,
however. A Filipino Scout orderly who had won several thousand pesos in
a game was later robbed and murdered. The culprit was never found. It was
thought unusual that at a time when food was by far the most valuable and
sought-after commodity on Bataan anyone would be murdered for
anything else.[20]

On the morning of February 22, AP correspondent Clark Lee ran into
Life's Mel Jacoby near the west entrance to Malinta Tunnel on Corregidor.
Jacoby told Lee that he and his wife, Annalee, were planning to leave that
night on the *Princesa* and that Lee had "better come along."

Lee hesitated. "I'm supposed to go [to China] with Bulkeley," he said.

"Better check up on it," Jacoby told him. "I hear there is a possibility
his trip may be called off."

A few minutes later Lee got a similar answer after talking to Adm.
Rockwell's chief of staff, Capt. James Ray. The boats, he was told, "may
be required for some other purpose."

Convinced, Lee and Jacoby made an appointment to see Gen. MacArthur early that afternoon to secure permission. Unbeknownst to the two
men, the General had been ordered to Australia by Washington the day
before, an order that he was considering disregarding.

"Do you want to go?" asked MacArthur. "Depends on whether we
could do more good by staying than by going," they said. "Do more good
by staying. . . ?" was a question that, no doubt, the General had been asking
himself ever since February 4, when Chief of Staff Gen. George C. Marshall, queried him on that very possibility should his forces on Bataan no
longer be able to "sustain themselves."

MacArthur talked to Lee and Jacoby for over an hour about the situation in the Philippines, the Pacific, and the world in general. When he was
finished, the two men had made up their minds. They would go. It is indeed
possible that in his "stirring" and very influential talk with the two correspondents, MacArthur had helped convince himself that, in reality, he
too "could do more good . . . by going."[21]

Two days later, February 24, after further pushing by his staff as well
as a direct order from President Roosevelt, MacArthur decided to go. In
his response to the president, he pleaded for permission to select the "right
moment for so delicate an operation" himself, or a "sudden collapse" of
the entire command might otherwise occur. March 15 was targeted as the
probable date.

On the morning of March 1, Lt. John Bulkeley received an order to
report to Gen. MacArthur's headquarters lateral on Corregidor. There

the General told him that he had been ordered to leave the Philippines and that it was possible that he would be needing the services of all four of Bulkeley's PTs for part of the trip.

After Bulkeley left, an order was sent to Air Corps Headquarters near Bataan Field for four P-40s to supply cover for 30 minutes that evening over Corregidor's North Channel. No other explanation was given.

On his return to Sisiman, Bulkeley told Lt. Bob Kelly to get his 34 boat ready for an early evening run back to the Rock. Kelly received no further explanation either.

There was less than an hour of daylight left when Kelly and Bulkeley tied up at the easternmost of Corregidor's North Docks. Moments later, MacArthur, his aide, Lt. Col. Sidney Huff, and, to their surprise, Mrs. MacArthur, arrived and were helped aboard the 34. (The General wanted his wife to get the feel of riding in one of the little plywood boats before making his final decision.)

Just as Kelly pulled away from the dock, four P-40s from Bataan Field cleared Real Point and banked west over the North Channel.

As the trip got underway, Kelly got more confused. "We felt honored, but I just couldn't understand why the General would choose a time like this for a pleasure trip," he said. "Suppose something had come up which might upset our dash to China?"

Everything seemed explained when they returned, however, at which time the General presented Bulkeley with the Distinguished Service Cross he had won back in January. He then personally congratulated each member of the 34's crew for "the fine work they had done, and handed each a package of cigarettes."

Later that night at their revamped goat slaughterhouse headquarters at Sisiman, Bulkeley let Kelly in on the secret. His suspicions about the China trip had been proved correct: the chance was "gone forever." "Now the MTBs [would be] like the rest here in the islands — the expendables who fight on without hope to the end."

Three of the four PT boats were ordered to stand-down for overhaul, while at the same time Bulkeley was to report daily to the General for the possible green light.[22]

Though Bulkeley didn't know it, his boats had been, and still were, part of an alternate plan of escape. Back on the 26th of February, MacArthur had forwarded his concurrence with Gen. Marshall's plan of evacuating himself and his party by submarine. Two days later, the sub, SS *Permit*, left Australian waters for Corregidor, due to arrive sometime on March 14.

On the morning of March 1, Capt. Ed Dyess was summoned by Gen. George to air corps headquarters behind Bataan Field. "What's up, General?" Dyess asked with anticipation in his voice.

"I think we ought to have a party," he said.

Taken by surprise, Dyess asked, "With whom and with what?"

"The nurses from Hospital No. 2 and with whatever we can scare up. If this war is going to be fought by our boys and girls," he said, "they might as well have what little good times they can."

The party was held in one of the thatched huts the pilots used as a clubhouse. There was a piano someone had salvaged from a bombed-out village, and canvas was laid on the floor for dancing. One of the walls of the room was decorated with an array of Japanese souvenirs: helmets, rifles, swords. On another hung the squadron scoreboard, complete with the record of each pilot: missions, number of planes downed, citations. Outside, hanging over the door was a sign that read

THE DYSENTERY CROSS
Awarded to the Quartermaster by
THE MEN OF BATAAN FIELD

The nurses, of course, were just as eager for a party as the pilots, already having been the guests of several other units on similar occasions. "What was left of our cosmetics was hoarded like a miser's gold," said one of the guests, "to be used only on the rare occasion when we went to a party."

"[The girls] wore civilian dresses," said Dyess, "and we were in our best, handwashed, unironed uniforms, without ties."

Despite their efforts, however, there was no escaping the realities of the world around them. "It had been so long since we had seen a white woman," lamented Dyess, "we were shy and awkward ... until almost time for them to start home. There was no jitterbugging either. We were too tired and [besides] the shack couldn't have taken it."

Another pilot, Capt. Dick Fellows, provided his observations of the party. "Having access to a battered sedan, I carried a load of nurses to and from the event. It was a blast! Our flight surgeon obtained some, what we called "torpedo juice," from the Navy and mixed a punch. I saw no shy or awkward dances after the half-starved assembly had a few drinks of this potent concoction. As a designated driver I had to keep in mind the winding, narrow, bombarded road I had to navigate—in the blackout. Therefore, I can report on the party authentically. The boy-girl relationships remained on a brother–sister–comrade-in-arms level. Starving men and women lust for food, not for each other, believe me. One and all had only this to say: 'Boy, what a party! Best time I had since the war started!' "[23]

On the evening of March 3, with the sun about 40 minutes behind its South China Sea horizon, the air raid siren on Corregidor wailed at the approach of unidentified planes. Searchlight and antiaircraft positions were manned, and steel helmets were donned. Fifteen minutes later the all-clear sounded; it was a false alarm. It didn't take MacArthur's chief of staff, Gen. Richard Sutherland, long to trace the planes picked up on Corregidor's radar to the Bataan Air Force.

Upset, he called Gen. George, who was at that moment at his advanced headquarters behind Bataan Field. For the second time in six weeks, he bellowed, the air corps had failed to notify Corregidor of pending night operations. And for the second time in six weeks, they had avoided being blasted by Rock guns by the mere skin of their teeth.

Surprise registered on George's face. During the entire battle for Bataan, there couldn't have been a less appropriate time for a chewing out. Sutherland didn't know that George's boys had just blasted a Japanese convoy up in Subic Bay, a feat that was probably unmatched by anything the entire United States Air Corps had done against them since the war started.

George told him that the air raid alarm incident was caused by his planes returning from their last raid on the Japanese convoy in the bay.

Sutherland, who earlier that morning had been the one that tipped the air corps to the entrance of the "good-size enemy convoy into Subic," asked, "What were your losses?"

Four planes and one pilot, George answered, quickly adding that one of the planes could probably be salvaged.

"What'd we do to them?"

To George, this moment was worth all the chewing out he'd ever had. Now he could tell him, and tell him he did.

After Sutherland's tip, which came just before noon, George contacted Capt. Ed Dyess, leader of the 21st Pursuit Squadron and senior pilot of those currently on flying status. Ironically, just the day before, the ground crew, under the guidance of Warrant Officer Jack Day, had put the finishing touches on a homemade 500-pound bomb rack on Dyess' fighter, made from cannabalized parts of automobiles and wrecked planes.

"Do you think that your homemade rig for releasing the heavy egg is ready for a practice test?" asked George.

"There was never a better day, General," answered the tall, slender Texan. He'd be "ready in an hour."

After Dyess left, George contacted Capt. Joe Moore, CO of the 20th Pursuit Squadron at Mariveles and told him to have his two fighters standby for a run on Subic.

A few minutes later, 2d Lt. John Posten, loaded with a half-dozen 30-pound fragmentaries, took off from Bataan Field for the bay. He found it full of ships and the docks at Olongapo crammed with newly arrived supplies. Knowing his 30-pounders were useless against big ships, he chose the docks, but couldn't stay around long enough to find out the results.

It was now Dyess' turn. At 12:30, he and 2d Lt. Donald "Shorty" Crosland took off from Bataan followed by Lt. John Burns from nearby Cabcaben.

As the three reached the mouth of Subic, the following scene unfolded before their eyes: There were four transports already in the bay, two of them unloading on the north side of Grande Island. A fifth, just arriving, was at that moment passing between Grande and the western shore. Farther inside, there looked to be two cruisers and two destroyers along with several smaller vessels scattered about. Dyess noted at least a dozen ships of various sizes alone unloading at Grande Island.

Dyess picked the late-arriving transport as his target. He began his run from 10,000 feet. At 5,000, all hell broke loose when the previously alerted Japanese antiaircraft batteries around the bay began to fire. At 2,000 feet he released his bomb, but overshot the target by 40 feet. Angered, he turned to strafe, raking the ship "three times, from stern to bow, bow to stern, and from stern to bow again. ... The transport stopped dead and didn't move again that day."

Next he ripped a row of warehouses on Grande Island with his six .50s, and then jumped a 100-ton motor vessel near the damaged transport that was departing for shore.

"The Japs aboard her were putting on quite an act," said Dyess. "Those astern were running forward and those forward were rushing astern. ... They met amidship where my bullets were striking."

A second pass started her sinking and after a final "short burst at her sister ship," Dyess signaled to Burns and Crosland, and the three Kittyhawks turned for home.

While these pilots were on their return leg, Capt. Joe Moore launched his two Mariveles fighters, flown by 2d Lt. Erwin Crellin and Kenneth White. Loaded with 30-pound fragmentary bombs, White, with Crellin close behind, dove on the docks at Olongapo. Antiaircraft fire was heavy when White dropped his bombs and pulled up. But Crellin, apparently hit, had disappeared. He was never seen again.

While Dyess and Crosland were being rearmed, 2d Lt. Sam Grashio took off from Cabcaben loaded with a half-dozen fragmentaries for a run on a string of enemy barges that were reported in the bay.

Finding his assigned targets right where he had been told they would be, Grashio lined up his Kittyhawk and headed in. A few seconds after releasing his bombs he glanced back over his shoulder to see the results. But there were none; no explosions could be seen.

Angered by the thought that he had badly missed his target, he headed back for Cabcaben.

Unbeknownst to the young second lieutenant, he had not seen his bombs explode because they had never been dropped. This wasn't realized until

Lt. Ozzie Lunde, in the Cabcaben tower, screamed at him over the radio transmitter as he was approaching to land, "Don't land, your bombs are still on your wings. Bail out!"

The last thing Grashio wanted to do was bail out. Too many bad things could happen, not the least of which would be the loss of the precious P-40. The choices left to him raced through his mind. Of the three landing fields he had to choose from, Mariveles was the biggest, offering more margin for error. The space would be needed, for he would have to stretch out his landing to avoid the usual bouncy, three-point touchdown, which could jar one of his bombs loose.

Meanwhile, back at air corps headquarters behind Bataan Field, Gen. George and Capt. Allison Ind, who had been listening to the radio, heard someone announce, "That plane over Bataan seems to be having trouble," and that Grashio's bombs were still on his wings but he had decided to try to land at Mariveles.

Off in the distance they could hear his engine. Then there was silence—no explosion anyway. Then, on the radio they heard, "Landed OK . . . Palafox." (Palafox was the call sign for Mariveles.) He had made it.

By the time Grashio had touched down, Dyess and Crosland were returning from their successful second run. During this run, making the same approach as they had the first time, they dove on one of the two transports unloading at the north side of Grande Island.

This time Crosland led off, but missed with his six fragmentaries. Then Dyess went in. But he too overshot with his 500-pounder, only instead of landing in the sea as Crosland's had, it "exploded among the ships." "They went up in a glorious cloud of smoke, water, and debris," Dyess said. He felt better.

The explosion, in the meantime, had sent the Japanese who were unloading the ships "stampeding along the dock toward shore," so Dyess whipped the plane he'd named Kibosh around and "cleaned off the dock with [his] machine guns."

Then one more pass at the four already riddled warehouses, another pass at the second 100-ton motor vessel, which sank, and then home.

As Dyess brought Kibosh to a stop at the head of Bataan Field, the excited ground crew rushed out to hear the news of the second attack. But the squadron leader was out of the cockpit and gone before they got there. Apparently he had been "fighting on two fronts that day—against the Japs and against diarrhea."

It was now after four o'clock. Shadows covered the entire length of the runway and the wind was picking up off the bay. Was there time enough for one more strike? Dyess contacted Gen. George and asked.

"He eventually granted permission," said Dyess. "If he hadn't, I'd have missed the best shooting of the day."

Thirty minutes later—and for the third time that day—Dyess gunned old Kibosh down Bataan Field's red-dust runway, crossed over the East Road, and then began an arching 180-degree turn that would take him over the North Channel and up the west coast into Subic.

Over Grande Island at 10,000 feet, he noticed that the two large enemy freighters that had been unloading on the island had "shoved out from the dock and were running around like mad." He therefore decided to go after the huge mass of supplies and equipment, unloaded from the two ships, that was literally covering the entire northern end of the island.

Waiting a little longer this time, he released the 500 pounder at 1,800 feet. Seconds later a tremendous blast shook the island—a direct hit. Soon huge fires erupted, intermittently punctuated by small explosions.

By now the sun had dropped down behind the horizon. It was almost too dark to see anything, and besides, it was becoming dangerous to be in the air. "Cruisers, destroyers, and shore batteries had all cut loose. They really were filling the sky."

The day, at last, appeared over. A few seconds later Dyess received a message that said observers from Signal Hill on Mt. Mariveles had picked up a large transport trying to slip out of the bay just south of Grande Island.

Dyess banked Kibosh northeast across the bay until he saw the ship's silhouette against the horizon. He then turned and headed in, all guns blazing. A second pass had "fires started all over the bow and in the well deck," Dyess said. "Then she blew up."

"The glow in the west now served me well for a second time," Dyess continued. "Silhouetted against it was [yet another] fairly large ship that had been reported variously as a cruiser, destroyer, tanker, and transport." Dyess felt that the unusually heavy amount of antiaircraft fire it put up, however, pretty well eliminated it as either of the latter two.

Dyess first "struck from the southwest, raking it from bow to stern." Two more passes had all antiaircraft guns "silenced and small fires . . . blazing up on both bow and stern."

Although Dyess was unable to "make it blow up as the other ship had," the Japanese were forced to beach it, and it "burned all night . . . and was still burning the next day."

It was dark when Dyess and Burns, who had scored hits too, headed back to Bataan. In the meantime, as ordered, Capt. Joe Moore had put up his two Mariveles fighters to, as Gen. George put it, "cover the landing" of the two planes, whose expended ammunition would render them defenseless against pursuing enemy fighters. The Japanese Air Force, strangely absent in the skies over Subic during all of the attacks, did not give chase.

As Dyess began his over-water approach to Bataan Field, he sensed the presence of one of nature's obstacles to making an uphill landing on a short dirt runway, "a terrific tail wind." He was able to set old Kibosh down safely, however, even though it was "a pretty bum landing."

In the meantime, just over the ridge at Cabcaben, John Burns, fighting a losing battle with the same wind conditions, had come in too fast. In order to save himself and the plane, he ground-looped his P-40 at the end of the runway. The crash caused the inadvertent firing of his guns, sending "a stream of tracers going up against the mountain," and making Dyess think for a minute that they had drawn some "flies" (Japanese planes) after all.

Things with the two Mariveles planes, meanwhile, had also gone poorly. Second Lt. Bill Fossey brought his Kittyhawk in first. In the radio shack behind Bataan Field, Gen. George and Capt. Ind had just finished sweating out Burns' crash when word came in from Mariveles that Fossey was in "heavy tail wind. He overshot and cracked up at far end. They don't know how he is."

Minutes later, word on the second plane, flown by 2d Lt. Lloyd Stinson, came over the radio. He too "overshot because of heavy tail wind. He cracked up at far end."

The pilots? "Both OK!" So was Burns.

The day was at last over. Captain Allison Ind, who had sweat it out sitting next to the radio, probably summarized the results as well as anyone. "At least the death of our little air force," he wrote, "was one of unmitigated glory. It delivered a gigantic blow out of all proportion to its size — then literally collapsed."

"Out of all proportion" was right. At the cost of one pilot, Lt. Crellin, and four overworked P-40s, the Japanese lost no less than one 12,000-ton transport sunk; one 6,000-ton ship beached and gutted by fire; two 100-ton motor vessels sunk; several barges and lighters destroyed; an unknown but vast amount of supplies and equipment blown up and burned on both Grande Island and Olongapo docks; and a large but undeterminable number of the enemy killed or missing. (See Map 24.)

The next night in response to the attack, Tokyo Radio announced that "[54] heavy bombers, mostly four engined," had attacked their shipping in Subic Bay, with "[some] tonnage sunk." Four U.S. bombers were reported to have been shot down.

The following night came an announcement of a retaliation raid on the "secret" U.S. air base that had launched the bombers. Thirty-seven American planes were claimed to have been destroyed.

Although nine different pilots actually took part in the day's activities, the bulk of the credit, of course, goes to Ed Dyess. In tribute to the hero, Lt. Ben Brown, who was his back-up that day, said "He made three trips. I was his relief pilot but he wouldn't let me fly."

As for old Kibosh, Dyess had brought it back a virtual sieve. "You

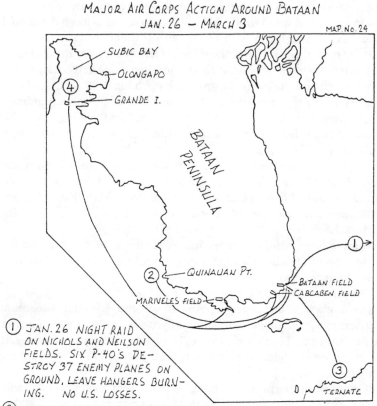

MAJOR AIR CORPS ACTION AROUND BATAAN
JAN. 26 – MARCH 3

MAP. No. 24

SUBIC BAY
OLONGAPO
④
GRANDE I.

BATAAN PENINSULA

①

QUINAUAN PT.
②
BATAAN FIELD
CABCABEN FIELD
MARIVELES FIELD

③
TERNATE

① JAN. 26 NIGHT RAID ON NICHOLS AND NEILSON FIELDS. SIX P-40's DESTROY 37 ENEMY PLANES ON GROUND, LEAVE HANGERS BURNING. NO U.S. LOSSES.

② FEB. 1-2 NIGHT ATTACK ON JAPANESE QUINAUAN PT. INVASION FORCE. FOUR P-40's IN THREE SUCCESSIVE RAIDS; BREAK-UP AND SCATTER ENEMY SHIPS.   NO U.S. LOSSES.

③ FEB. 6 SIX P-40's ESCORT RECONNAISSANCE PLANE OVER TERNATE ARE ATTACKED BY SIX JAPANESE PLANES ON RETURN; SHOOT DOWN ALL SIX.   U.S. LOSSES: 1 PLANE AND PILOT.

④ MARCH 3 FIVE P-40's ATTACK JAPANESE CONVOY IN SUBIC BAY. SINK 22,000+TONS OF ENEMY SHIPPING; DESTROY TONS OF SUPPLIES ON DOCKS.   U.S. LOSSES: 4 PLANES, 1 PILOT.

could hardly see [it] for the patches," he said. "The plane was olive drab and the external patches were bright blue. There were 60 or 70 of them."

As for the future of the one plane Bataan Air Force, by March 5, under the watchful eye of Lt. Leo Boelens, the ground crew managed to piece together a second fighter from parts cannabalized from other wrecked P-40s. A couple of days later, two P-35s flew in from Mindanao, bringing the number of operational fighters in the Bataan Air Force back to four.[24]

Things, in the meantime, were happening in waters around the Philippines that would help settle Gen. MacArthur's transportation decision. On March 8, Gen. Sutherland, because of the noted increase in Japanese naval activity in the south—eight blockade-runners, it will be recalled, had been sunk over the eight-day period of February 28 to March 7 –stopped all ships from blockade-running until further notice. By March 10, no fewer than ten more were reported to have suffered similar fates.

The increase in Japanese naval activity was not confined to southern waters, however. Reports on the 7th, 8th, and 9th of March indicated that enemy ships, from patrol vessels to destroyers, from north and south, were discovered to be converging on Manila Bay. This news caused MacArthur to decide not to wait for the sub that, it was anticipated, could not be ready to reembark until sometime on the 15th. It would be the alternate plan, PT boats, and it would be the next night, March 11.

"Bulkeley went over early in the morning [of March 11] and returned to us at noon...," said Kelly, "and for the first time showed [us] copies of our secret orders."

1. Motor Torpedo Boat Squadron Three is to be used for the transportation of a party of 21 passengers to a southern port which will be designated later...
2. The party will embark ... March 11, in time to rendezvous at Turning Buoy at 8:00 P.M. Proceed to sea ... and arrive Tagauayan Island about 7:30 A.M. March 12....

Later that day while the crews were busily preparing their boats for the trip, Nat Floyd, correspondent of the *New York Times*, dropped by. "Exactly the last guy in the world we wanted to see," said Kelly. Floyd, who had been included in the China trip plans with Clark Lee, had dropped in to see "if we had any news." "Then he kind of glanced around. What were those planks on the deck for? And all that gasoline on the wharf?" Kelly tried "every way in the world to get rid of him before Bulkeley got back, but it was no use; he stuck like glue."

Afraid that after they had gone, Floyd, by putting two and two together, could easily guess what had happened and then let the story out, Bulkeley and Kelly made a decision. Suppose Nat "should happen to stow away in the lazaret, and we didn't find him until we were out to sea...?" Add one more to the passenger list: Nat Floyd, correspondent, *New York Times;* stowaway.

With the possibility of running into Japanese ships increasing, Gen. Sutherland ordered Gen. George to send a P-40 patrol south to scout the Mindoro Strait before leaving on one of the PT boats himself that night. It paid off. The two pilots brought back news that they had seen two Japanese

The PT-32 in this prewar photograph is the same boat skippered by Lt. Vince Schumacher on Bataan as well as on MacArthur's escape from Corregidor to Mindanao.

destroyers in the passage operating close to the western shoreline of Mindoro Island. Mindoro Strait at its narrowest point was 50-miles across. If Bulkeley kept his course free of eastern landfall, chances were they could slip through unmolested.

Bulkeley was given one final chore before leaving. To keep all Inshore Patrol activities around Bataan appearing status quo, he ordered Philippine Q-boat commander, Capt. Alberto Navarette, to conduct a diversionary raid against known enemy shore installations that night near the entrance to Subic Bay. Since the Q-boats would be taking over the responsibility of patroling the Bataan west coast from the departing PTs, what better time to start?

So at dusk, the two Q-boats, *Luzon* and *Abra,* slipped out of Sisiman Bay for the west coast—a direction unfamiliar to their crews who, up to then, had only patrolled the Manila Bay side of the peninsula.

The Q-boats were followed out shortly by the first of the four PT boats, PT-32. Lieutenant Vince Schumacher, again to keep things from appearing suspicious, was to pick up his passengers at Quarantine Dock in Mariveles. Bulkeley in the 41 boat would make his pick-up at Corregidor.

General MacArthur and his chief of staff, Gen. Richard Sutherland, take a stroll on Corregidor during the battle. "In case of my death," MacArthur recommended that Sutherland, who had "the most comprehensive grasp of the situation," take over for him.

Kelly in the 34 and Akers in 35 would have their parties brought into Sisiman by launch.

By eight o'clock, as planned, the four history-making PTs, strung out in single file behind the 41 boat, left Turning Buoy and Bataan for the last time. On board were seven generals: MacArthur, Sutherland, George, Akin, Casey, and Marquat; an admiral, Rockwell; two women,

Lieutenant General Jonathan Wainwright

Mrs. MacArthur and the MacArthurs' Cantonese nurse, Ah Cheu; and a four-year-old boy, the General's son, Arthur—a greater array of VIPs than MTB Squadron 3, or any other torpedo boat squadron in history, would ever see again.[25]

Change in the Command

"Boat ... Mariveles ... noon."

With the General's leaving, of course, came change. Some was ordered, some was anticipated, and some was not.

The "ordered" changes that occurred, of course, were those of command. Of those, the biggest and, unfortunately, most confusing as it affected Bataan, was that involving the replacement for MacArthur.

Senior among the officers left in the command was Jonathan Wainwright. And the command went to Wainwright. No surprise there, unless

The gutted remains of the old Quarantine Station at Mariveles. The Quarantine dock is on the eastern edge of the bay, some 100 yads in front of the old building, just out of camera range.

you were Wainwright himself, who was not even let in on what was transpiring until the afternoon of March 10. Late the night before, Gen. Sutherland, MacArthur's chief of staff, called the exhausted Wainwright, telling him that the General wanted to see him. "Too tired to ask why," the sleepy-eyed I Corps commander scribbled on his pad, "boat ... Mariveles ... noon," hung-up and went back to sleep.

It was early the next afternoon when Wainwright entered Malinta Tunnel and headed for the headquarters lateral. There he was met by Sutherland. General MacArthur was "up at the house" some 400 yards east of the tunnel, so Sutherland filled him in while they walked. "General MacArthur is going to leave here and go to Australia," he said. "He's going to divide his Philippine forces into four subcommands, himself retaining overall command while in Australia."

"You will be placed in command of all troops on Luzon," Sutherland told him. "All troops on Luzon" for all practical purposes meant those on Bataan only, as "General Moore [would] remain in command of the harbor defenses and fortified islands [Corregidor] in the bay."

MacArthur met Wainwright on the porch of the cottage, where the two men talked for a half hour or so before saying goodbye. Shaking hands, MacArthur said, "When I get back, if you're still on Bataan, I'll make you a lieutenant general."

"I'll be on Bataan if I'm still alive," Wainwright retorted, then turned and walked away.

The man MacArthur picked to take Wainwright's I Corps job was Brig. Gen. Albert Jones, who, along with all the general officers of his old command, was informed of the changes on March 12 at Corps headquarters near Bagac.

Wainwright, as Bataan's first commander, told them that MacArthur "had been forced, by order of the commander in chief to leave." "I watched their faces as I spoke," he said, "but . . . soon saw that they understood. . . . They realized as well as I what the score was."

Later in the day as Wainwright began moving his "creaking [command] trailer" down the tortuous West Road to his new headquarters at Little Baguio, word was already racing through his new command of MacArthur's departure. Reaction was, of course, mixed. To most of the Americans, particularily at the enlisted-man's level, it was "abandonment." To the Filipinos, it was to bring help. Yet, despite the numerous, sarcastic jokes and poems about "Dugout Doug" that swept the peninsula, even the most outward of doubters still secretly believed that help would still arrive. Young Pvt. James Wall with an air corps ordnance unit at Little Baguio probably reflected fairly accurately how most men felt. "Even after MacArthur left," he said, "we couldn't believe that the United States, with all its power and resources, wouldn't come to our rescue."[26] An air corps officer, Lt. Edgar Whitcomb, commented that "Despite the fact that rumor after rumor . . . was proving false day after day, we had faith and hope so strong that we embraced each new rumor as if it were the first we had ever heard."[27] Colonel Ernest Miller of the 194th Tank Battalion, added that he "never gave up hoping." "Faith in Uncle Sam," he said, "kept the spark alive."

Captain Dick Fellows, commander of the Philippine Air Depot located near Bataan Field, had become convinced before the war started that reinforcements were coming. A few weeks before Pearl Harbor, his depot received a shipment of 40 A-24 propellers. No way, he thought, would they have sent that many propellers unless the planes were to follow.[28] As late as mid–March, he was still convinced of this. Lieutenant Tom Garrity, air corps officer with Gen. Wainwright, wrote in his diary on February 3 that he had missed his guess about help arriving by February 1, but that he was "willing to compromise and make it March 1." "I don't know how long we can hold out here because the frontline troops need rest. At any rate, I continue to hope for the best—for that old photo finish."[29] Colonel Richard Mallonee, with the PA's 21st Field Artillery, wrote in his diary that" we continued to hope and have faith in our leaders, in our ability to hold out, and in our government's efforts to send a relief expedition that would arrive in storybook fashion." In his estimate of the situation, he wrote, "there was one favorable fact: sooner or later the relief expedition would have to arrive."[30]

There was no doubt that this feeling carried the men through the long, dreary days of March. It certainly wasn't the Bataan ration; a memo from Brig. Gen. Arnold Funk, Wainwright's chief of staff on Bataan, indicated that on March 25, less than 20 ounces—less than one-fourth normal peacetime allowances, of which over half was rice—had been issued at chow that day. It was estimated that a man expended upwards of 3,500 calories per day in performing his duties on Bataan. His daily intake during March was barely 1,000 calories. A few days earlier, Capt. Al Poweleit of the Provisional Tank Group, had noted that "the average man [in his unit] had lost about 30 to 40 pounds."[41] Indications that men were already on their last legs came from the commanding officer of Battery B of the 92d Coast Artillery Regiment. Of the hundred or so Scouts in Capt. Robert Lawler's battery, only four were strong enough to lift the 98-pound shells up to the breeches of their 155s.

Colonel Richard Mallonee, with the P.A.'s 21st Field Artillery, wrote of the condition of the Filipino's under his command, "Our men are . . . actually weak to the point of staggering when they walk after any . . . burst of energy." "Shortages of equipment . . . have been aggravated by the rigors of the campaign. Clothing is worn, torn, and ragged. Personal equipment is supplemented by makeshifts. Men are cooking what little rice they can get in bamboo tubes. Many are eating off [banana] leaves. Bamboo tubes substitute for canteens. Nipa leaves serve for hats. Bare feet are more common than shoes."[32]

On March 12, Gen. Wainwright, and three days later Gen. Parker, both estimated that the combat efficiency within the two corps was near 25 percent. This wasn't all due to the starvation diet and accompanying malnutrition. Major Everett Mead's comment about the malaria and dysentery and the U.S. 31st Infantry troops pretty well summarized the effects of the two most common diseases on Bataan units during this period. "Approximately 50 percent of the regiment," he wrote, "was down with malaria or dysentery at all times. Those who were up and around were either just recovering or coming down with one or the other of the diseases."[33]

Of the two, by early March malaria had become the more uncontrollable. For this there were two basic reasons. First, there was exposure. Ninety-five percent of the troops manning front line positions across the peninsula were Philippine Army. Few, if any, had mosquito bars or netting for protection. The location of the MLR was probably the main contributor, however. Aside from the fact that Bataan, for its size, was one of the most malaria infested areas in the world, the U.S. main line at this time paralleled a low, swamp-filled valley that, by far, was the heaviest breeding grounds for mosquitos on the peninsula. The second reason was, of course, the lack of quinine. Its use as a prophylactic was generally discontinued throughout the command during the first week in March due to the scarcity of the drug. Within ten days, close to 500 men with the disease were qualifying daily for admission to the hospital. By the end of the month, this figure had doubled—nearly 1,000 men per day during the last week of March were reporting to morning sick-call throughout the command with malaria so acute as to render them unfit for duty.

Efforts to supplement the nearly exhausted supply of quinine were made as often as possible by planes of the little Bamboo Fleet. On March 30 it was reported that they had flown in close to 800,000 tablets—a mere fraction, however, of the estimated minimum of 3 million needed to quell the spread of the disease.[34]

One final attempt to help solve the quinine shortage began with a request for a volunteer from Bataan's Bamboo Fleet to fly a special mission to Mindanao and back. Captain Bill Bradford, a prewar commercial air lines pilot in the Islands, took it. Just before dark on the night of March 31, he flew his Bellanca over to Kindley Field on Corregidor where he picked up Lt. Col. Arthur Fischer. After clearing "Old Number Nine" from Kindley, he asked his passenger about the reason for the trip.

Colonel Fischer, it seems, had knowledge of an experimental cinchona plantation on the island of Mindanao. Cinchona, if extracted in time from the bark of the tree, could furnish enough quinine to save the command.

Unbeknownst to Bradford, the plantation, which was over 16,000 acres in size, had actually been started more than 15 years before by Fischer himself. Back in the early twenties he had smuggled cinchona seeds into Mindanao in order to help break a Dutch monopoly on the drug. The Dutch in the nearby East Indies had cornered the market on quinine, mainly because of their huge productive plantations in Java. Because of this monopoly, they had been able to charge outrageous prices for the drug. Fischer's plantation had helped make it available throughout the Philippines at a price people could pay.

After a brush with Japanese fighters on the way to Del Monte Field, resulting in an abrupt ground-loop finish to the landing, the two men were met by Fischer's old friend, Father Edward Haggerty—soon to become known as the legendary "Guerrilla Padre" for his work with the underground on Mindanao against the occupying Japanese.

By noon they had the Bellanca loaded with every available gallon of precious quinine that could be crammed into the plane's empty cabin. Bradford, leaving Fischer behind to carry on with what he called his "Operation Malaria," made it back to Corregidor safely. Tragically, no more of the drug reached Bataan in time to be used.[35]

As the load on the two field hospitals on Bataan increased in early

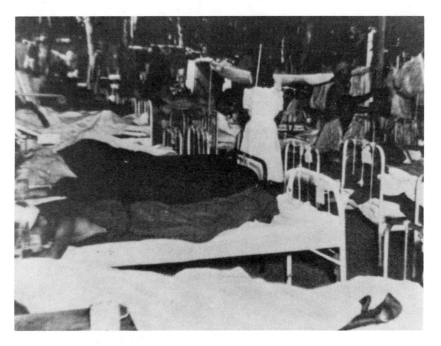

An open ward in Hospital No. 1 before heavy casualties forced the installation of double- and triple-decker beds.

March proportionately to the high frequency of malaria and dysentery cases, it was decided to seek a site for yet a third hospital on the peninsula.

One day around the 6th of March, the commanding officer of Hospital No. 2, Col. Carlton Vanderboget, along with two fellow medical officers, went to look over a possible site on a ridge above the Sisiman River, not far from Hospital No. 1. While there, a bomb from a Japanese plane landed in the midst of the three men, killing the two officers and putting Col. Vanderboget in the hospital for the rest of the battle.

Although foundations were laid and lumber delivered to the site to begin construction, the loss of Vanderboget meant that Hospital No. 3 would never be completed.[36]

The Light Dims

"No gleam of victory."

As the month of March drew to a close, the Japanese military build-up continued in proportion to their attempts to break American and Filipino morale.

Men gather around one of the few radio sets on Bataan as part of their nightly routine, to listen to the "Voice of Freedom," shortwave station KGEI's "Freedom for the Philippines" broadcast, Tokyo Radio and occasionally, station KZRH in Manila. The man on the left of the picture with rifle and helmet is William Seckinger.

The Filipinos, considered the possible weak link in the U.S. position on Bataan, were hit the hardest during this time. Everything from anti–American propaganda pamphlets to "Ticket to Happiness" surrender handbills to battlefield loudspeakers were used, all to no avail.

American morale, interestingly enough, was damaged more by well-meaning, friendly radio broadcasts than by anything of enemy design. Aside from the Voice of Freedom, the program Freedom for the Philippines, broadcast nightly from station KGEI in San Francisco, left many dispirited and homesick. Lieutenant Edgar Whitcomb with the army air corps communications at Cabcaben Field noted that after a few weeks of KGEI, "only a handful of hollow-eyed, ragged soldiers hung on, trying to glean a word of hope. . . . It was heart rending to see them turn away evening after evening and walk back to their areas without a word."[37] Captain Allison Ind wrote of its effects: "Heard Jack Benny's hour tonite—KGEI. The first since before this crazy upside-down world became a real one. Finally shut it off. Does funny things."

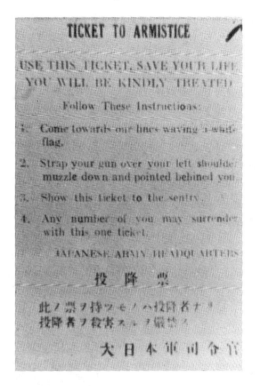

A Japanese "Ticket to Armistice" pamphlet instructing Filipinos how to walk away from their predicament on Bataan and go home.

Around this time, UP's Frank Hewlett, the only U.S. correspondent still working on Bataan, wrote a poem that appeared in the *International News Summary*. It mirrored, as effectively as anything ever said or written, the feelings Americans on Bataan by then had for themselves and their predicament. The poem, whose first line would label them for posterity, went

> We're the battling bastards of Bataan;
> No mama, no papa, no Uncle Sam;
> No aunts, no uncles, no cousins, no nieces;
> No pills, no planes, no artillery pieces.
> . . . And nobody gives a damn

Although it appeared by now that most Americans on Bataan believed nobody on the outside world really gave a "damn," not all Americans believed this. Major Eugene Conrad noted that "when the full impact of the situation hit [the U.S. 31st Infantry troops] it seemed to help their morale. They became more determined."[38]

Top: Four Japanese infantrymen hit the ground as a U.S. mortar scores a near miss. This picture is especially rare as over 80 percent of U.S. mortar ammunition were duds. *Bottom:* A Japanese loudspeaker set up opposite the Bagac-Orion Line. The broadcasts, usually made at night and occasionally by a woman, appealed to the Filipinos to give up the fight, saying that Bataan was America's fight, not theirs. The appeals were usually followed by music, according to Col. Carlos Romulo.

Colonel Richard Mallonee, senior instructor with the 21st Field Artillery, upon hearing through the grapevine from Gen. MacArthur in Australia that Bataan's food reserve period could be extended to last "with safety" to July 1, commented in his diary that "morale increased. We could stand on our heads until July 1."[39]

The concerns of a group of those lucky enough to be given the opportunity to mix with the opposite sex during this time, however, had found it impossible to get their minds off the war.

It was after the party held for the nurses by the pilots at Bataan Field that Ed Dyess complained that it had been "ruined by a beautiful full moon.... [On] Bataan [this] meant only that if the Japs had [planned] a landing before moonrise, they would be attacking soon." "We thought more about the Japs," he said, "than about our pretty dancing partners."

Bataan poet Lt. Henry G. Lee of the Philippine Division headquarters on Bataan, like Hewlett, reflected the feelings of the Americans. Calling it "Fighting On," Lee wrote:

> I see no gleam of victory alluring
> No chance of splendid booty or of gain
> If I endure—I must go on enduring
> And my reward for bearing pain is pain
> Yet, though the thrill, the zest, the hope are gone
> Something within me keeps me fighting on.

Both Sides Make Some Changes

"They confined themselves to the bottom of ravines."

Upon Gen. Wainwright's assignment as Bataan commander on March 10, the immediate "problem staring [him] in the face," became, as he looked at it, the food situation. This prompted a trip to Corregidor five days later to see if he could get USAFFE supply officer Brig. Gen. Lewis Beebe to increase his Bataan ration allowances from Rock stockpiles.

Finding that he "had no control over [their issue], which irked [him] a bit," the old cavalryman returned to Bataan "with heart made heavier" by the knowledge that he would have to trim his meager issue "by another third in order . . . to exist until April 10."

Unbeknownst to the Bataan commander, things within the next six days were to happen that would give him not only the authority to increase the Bataan rations himself, but much more. When Gen. MacArthur left on March 11, overall command of the Philippines went with him to Australia. Wainwright, as senior ranking officer in the command, was given

Bataan. Several assumptions were made in Washington, however, that would soon change all that. Because of MacArthur's failure to notify the War Department of his reorganization, Gen. Marshall and President Roosevelt both assumed that command of the entire Philippines had gone to Wainwright.

On March 17, with the unknowing Wainwright back on Bataan, Gen. Beebe, who had been assigned the position of MacArthur's deputy chief of staff, received a message dispatched to the "Commanding General, USAFFE." It read, in part,

> General MacArthur had arrived in Australia and has been assigned to supreme command. The President and the War Department felt justified in agreeing to his new assignment because of confidence in your leadership and the demonstrated fighting morale of your army.

It concluded by stating that the Philippines were still under Gen. MacArthur's supervisory control, but "because of the isolation of your command, you are instructed to maintain direct communication with the War Department and submit daily reports."

Although obviously meant for Wainwright, Beebe forwarded it on to MacArthur, accompanied with a plea to the General to please notify Washington of the new command alignment. MacArthur apparently did nothing.

Two days later, March 19, confusion mounted. It was started by a message from President Roosevelt, the contents of which told of the USAFFE commander's nomination to lieutenant general. Before the day was over, two more messages came in, both from Gen. Marshall, both recognizing Wainwright as the new commanding general. Beebe was left no choice other than to recognize Wainwright, which he did the next night.

Wainwright, busy on Bataan, had, of course, remained completely oblivious to what was transpiring until receiving a call from the distraught Beebe on the night of March 20.

Over a very bad phone connection, causing Beebe to literally yell the news to Wainwright, the surprised Bataan commander was barely able to hear about the two most important promotions of his life: one to lieutenant general and the other to commanding general of all the United States Forces in the Philippines, known officially from then on as USFIP.[40]

At 10:00 sharp the next morning, brand new Lt. Gen. Jonathan Wainwright, who "did not sleep much that night," was standing on Quarantine Dock waiting for transportation to his new assignment; a job, that according to Washington, he had already been working at for ten days.

To take his place on Bataan, Wainwright picked an old artilleryman, Maj. Gen. Edward P. King, senior American officer remaining on the

A prewar photo of Maj. Gen. Edward P. King, the Bataan commander who was ordered not to surrender.

peninsula. Before he left, Wainwright presented King with his old command trailer. "It was not much of a gift," he said, "nor was his role an enviable one."

On the enemy side, the position of commanding general had, since the latter part of January, not been an enviable one either. The Japanese timetable of conquest of the Philippines was, of course, long overdue. General Homma was the only theater commander who had thus far been stopped.

Following the general withdrawal of Japanese troops from their assault positions on the Bagac-Orion line in early February, Japanese Imperial Army Headquarters in Tokyo rushed a team of high-ranking generals to Bataan to find out what had gone wrong.

After a thorough inspection tour, the headquarters observers had to agree with Gen. Homma's conclusion—"Bataan could be subdued only if additional troops were [sent]."

One key change was also recommended and made in Homma's 14th Army staff. Lt. Gen. Masami Maeda, Homma's chief of staff up to that time, was relieved for spending too much time "attending to military administration in Manila rather than to the vital military operations in the field."

He was replaced by Lt. Gen. Takeji Wachi, who, after a quick inspection tour of Bataan positions in early March, reported that "The morale of the troops [was] completely broken down and they confined themselves to the bottom of ravines ... in the face of too many defeats, their morale could not be sustained.... [T]he Japanese army," he concluded, "[had been] severely beaten."[41]

The decision made, beginning in mid–February Japanese troops were beckoned from all over occupied Southeast Asia, a beckoning that revealed just how damaging the Fil-American stand on Bataan had been to Japanese overall war strategy. Of the 50,000 troops involved in the final assault, 80 percent had to be withdrawn from newly occupied or still active theaters.

The round-up of troops included the following: from China, the only complete division to be sent, the 4th, consisting of 11,000 men; diverted while actually en route to assignment in Indo-China, the 4,000-man strong 62d Infantry Regiment (called the Nagano Detachment after its CO, Maj. Gen. Kameichero Nagano), which included a battalion of artillery and a company of engineers; from Hong Kong, to fill what was recognized as the biggest void in earlier Japanese operations on Bataan—artillery—the bulk of the artillery and mortar units, amounting to close to five regiments in strength; from Japan, the 10th Independent Garrison, under the command of Col. Torao Ikuta, made up of five independent battalions of infantry without organic support. Additionally, both existing units on Bataan, the 16th Division and 65th Brigade, were each bolstered by 3,500 replacements from the home islands.

For the air phase, two heavy bomber units of 30 planes each were transfered in mid–March from Malaya to Clark Field. The Japanese Navy also contributed 27 of its planes, 18 of which were bombers, bringing the overall number of Japanese combat aircraft available for Bataan operations to close to 100.

The Japanese Prepare to Move Up

"Yamashita may be regrouping his forces for a long-delayed offensive."

On the morning of March 23, Gen. Homma, not Yamashita as was indicated in the USFIP communiqué of March 21, called a meeting of all his subordinate commanders in his headquarters at San Fernando, where plans for D-day were unveiled and the date, April 3, announced. Much of the Japanese strategy for the final assault, according to Gen. Wachi, was based on an official USAFFE map found in Manila showing "the disposition of the defending forces along the Pilar-Bagac Line." The map pinpointed the layout of U.S. positions on the MLR "as they were committed in late February." (The final, major change of the MLR by the U.S. command, it will be recalled, had taken place well before the time the map was discovered.)[42]

The luck was not all with the Japanese when it came to finding important documents, however. On the night of March 24 a set of orders that directed a patrol to probe the area around Samat for accessible river crossings, tank routes, and U.S. artillery positions were discovered on the body of a Japanese officer killed in a patrol skirmish near Mt. Samat. They also revealed what turned out to be the general plan of attack that was to be used against Fil-American positions on Mt. Samat, as well as a date, March 26, anytime after which the attack could start.

The discovery of the above information along with a marked increase in enemy patrol and air activity sent Gen. Wainwright hurrying to Bataan for a staff meeting the next day. The seriousness of the situation can probably be best explained by taking note of those in attendance. Along with Bataan commander Gen. King, and both corps commanders, Parker and Jones, every division commander on Bataan was there, from Brougher of the 11th to Stevens of the 71st-91st; from Francisco of the constabulary to Pierce of the west coast; 11 brigadier generals in all, the biggest gathering of the brass since the war started.

The topic for discussion was, obviously, the impending Japanese offensive. That the II Corps would be the focal point was assumed by all. United States I Corps positions, whose best defense was provided by nature—a thick jungle and nearly impassable terrain—precluded a major enemy effort against it. General Brougher of the I Corps 11th Division wrote that artillery as well as "enemy air control was almost completely neutralized in the I Corps sector, the thick jungle and big trees making it impossible to see anything from the air."

The II Corps positions along the MLR were weak for the same reasons I Corps positions were strong—jungle. For II Corps, there was none. II Corps frontline units, wrote Brougher, "were located in exposed areas along the Pilar-Bagac Road where there were no large trees to conceal them from air and ground observation." This allowed the Japanese "to build up a strong offensive concentration within artillery and mortar range."[43]

Because of II Corps' vulnerability to enemy attack a great deal more effort was put into preparation of its defenses than those of I Corps. Although manned by fewer men—28,000 to 32,600—there were no less than twice the number of interconnecting roads and trails in the II Corps Section, facilitating rapid movement of reinforcements to areas under attack, and Mt. Samat, the dominating Fil-American high-ground strong point, would have to be reckoned with before a major Japanese assault on Bataan could succeed.

United States' money went on the probability of the main enemy thrust coming up the wide Pantingan River valley and then wheeling east

Japanese troop columns marching south toward Bagac past the junction of the Pilar-Bagac and West roads.

behind Mt. Samat to the coast. This move, which would isolate and therefore neutralize Mt. Samat's strength, however, was looked at differently from the other side of the line.

General Homma, too, recognized the difficulty presented by both terrain and jungle should he strike out against the I Corps. But because of the dominance of the 2,000-foot Samat, a major effort across the open terrain fronting II Corps, a move no doubt being anticipated by the U.S. command, could be just as difficult.

Homma pondered a third choice. Why not a direct assault on Samat itself? Of the choices available to the Japanese, this would probably be the one least expected by the American and Filipinos. Also, if successful, the toughest part of the fight would be over. The heights of Mt. Samat could be used by artillery observers to assure maximum support in the fight down the east coast. The plan was adopted without argument, and the following details worked out:

1. *Diversionary action against the I Corps:* Action against the U.S. I Corps was planned in order to occupy and thus keep it contained west of the Pantingan River. Assigned to this task was the reoutfitted, Bataan-hardened 16th Division and four battalions from the Ikuta Detachment. The 16th was to remain only lightly engaged, however, so that somewhere around the 4th of April, it could move east into reserve position behind the

Several well-concealed batteries of Japanese heavy artillery, located somewhere near Balanga, fire against U.S. II Corps positions on Mt. Samat.

main attacking forces opposite the II Corps, a point from which it could be used accordingly.

2. *Main assault against the II Corps:* Action against the II Corps would be in the form of a three-pronged attack. The western prong would act as a wedge, driving south along the eastern bank of the Pantingan River, whereby it would wall off the important central column from interference by the I Corps. This force would be made up of the 65th Brigade and led by its veteran Bataan commander, Gen. Akira Nara. To the middle or center column would go the main responsibility of capturing Mt. Samat itself. This column, made up mostly of Japanese 4th Division troops, was subdivided into two parts or wings. The right wing (westernmost) was to attack up the Catmon River valley, then pivot east toward the heights of Mt. Samat. The left wing's job was to assault the mountain over Trail 4, which skirted its eastern slope.

The 4,000-man strong 62d Infantry Regiment Nagano detachment, as the easternmost prong of the Japanese II Corps assault forces, had a two-fold mission. First, it was to protect the 4th Division's east flank, while at the same time causing a diversion from Manila Bay by feinting a seaborne landing between Orion and Limay. Once Samat had been secured, the regiment was to lead the main assault down the East Road.[44]

The East Road looking south towards Mt. Samat. The main Japanese offensive was launched down this road. Men making the Bataan Death March also traveled up the road on their way to San Fernando, some 40 miles of hell to the north.

Almost 2000-foot-high Mt. Samat as it looked from Japanese positions on the Bagac-Orion Line. Despite acknowledging it as the strong point of the U.S. II Corps line, Gen. Homma chose it as the focal point of his final offensive, smashing the starved Fil-American defenders from its slopes in just two days.

CHAPTER FIVE

Overtures to the End

"Our positions on Bataan were heavily bombed."

By the third week in March, it had become obvious to the command that the Japanese had initiated their preoffensive softening-up and probing operations.

Official USFIP communiqués, originally concealing or watering down the true situation on Bataan, began, for the first time, delivering more candid pictures of what was happening. On March 24, for example, communiqué no. 158 noted that "our positions in Bataan were heavily bombed this morning by 54 Japanese heavy bombers of a new type." It went on to mention that "several sharp encounters occurred . . . between hostile ground forces."

Again on the 27th, a communiqué noted "a number of sharp clashes between patrols." Also that there were "troop and truck movements behind enemy lines which indicated that increased activity may be expected. . . . Japanese dive-bombers [also] attacked our rear areas."[1]

Suspecting U.S. artillery positions were the prime targets for air attacks, Col. Richard Mallonee, senior instructor with the Philippine Army's 21st Field Artillery, wrote during this time that "every few minutes one plane would drop down, lift up the tree branches, and lay one or two eggs. Every vehicle that tried to move, every wire-laying detail, infantry patrol, every individual moving in the open was subject to these spot bombings."[2]

Also noted was a marked increase in the volume and accuracy of enemy artillery fire. Indications came that the Japanese were not just preregistering their guns for the offensive, but had brought up heavier caliber pieces as well after the installation of an observation balloon on the upper slopes of the Abucay plantation.

Its effects can be best understood, perhaps, by reading two entries made in the "Bataan Diary" of Maj. Achille Tisdelle, an aide to Gen. King. On Monday, March 16, after writing of the "routine bombing and shelling"

Top: This Japanese photograph shows a dummy U.S. artillery or antiaircraft position somewhere on Bataan. Although the sandbags were real, the gun was made of bamboo. *Bottom:* This Japanese artillery observation balloon, floating leisurely over Balanga, was effective enough to cause American Maj. Achille Tisdelle, after being shelled by the Japanese, to write in his diary "If we could only get that damn balloon."

that day, Tisdelle noted that "the Japs now have an observation balloon just out of range of our 155s." Little did he speculate that 15 days later he would discouragingly write that the "Nip artillery [was] raising hell. If we could only get that damned balloon."[3]

Despite the increased blasting by air and artillery, little important physical damage was reported. In one isolated case, however, physical damage done to a Filipino officer had a psychological effect on everyone around him.

The officer, with the Philippine Army's 41st Field Artillery, had had the unenviable experience of being wounded on three different occasions during either air or artillery bombardments. Upon his return to duty after the third time, his comrades, feeling that his luck was far overextended, all refused to share either shelter or foxhole with him. When he "jumped in," they just as quickly "jumped out."[4]

Enemy activity was not confined only to air and ground during this time, however. Intelligence observers had noted a marked increase in the number of small boats at Cavite and along the north shore of Manila Bay, heightening the possibility of an invasion of the east coast.

In fact, sometime during the night of March 25, three American river-gunboats, *Oahu, Luzon,* and *Mindanao,* on their nightly patrol inside the bay ambushed a string of Japanese boats and barges making a crossing from Cavite to Bataan's eastern shore. The old China Station gunboats, under Lt. Cmdr. Alan Macracken, although not fully aware of the outcome until later, sunk at least six of the enemy craft and scattered the rest before being chased off by fire from Japanese shore batteries in eastern Bataan.[5]

Back in mid–February, it will be remembered, an old Bellanca and a Beechcraft biplane, making up what was called the Bamboo Fleet, began making medical, supply and VIP runs back and forth from Bataan Field to Mindanao. On March 24, a third plane and two more pilots would join the fleet.

On the second or third day of the war, in December 1941, three U.S. Navy J2F4 Grumman "Duck" amphibians were caught on the water by the Japanese and sunk in Mariveles Harbor. One day in early March, air corps Capt. Joe Moore, commander of the remaining two planes left of the 20th Pursuit Squadron at nearby Mariveles Field, decided to try to salvage one of the Ducks. He went after the one that was setting closest to shore, where its engine and most of the fuselage had remained out of the water. Ground crew and pilots alike joined in the project.

Pulling the plane out of the water with block and tackle, the hull was patched, and it was re-floated and towed across the harbor up onto the field and into an unused revetment. Using parts salvaged from the other two planes, within a week Moore's ground crew got the engine running.

On March 23, Moore took off from Mariveles to test the old Duck. Everything went smoothly, and the engine, though vibrating and sounding like a coffee grinder next to a P-40 Allison, performed flawlessly.

Happy with its performance, Moore decided to join the Bamboo Fleet. At 4 A.M. the next morning he, along with another pilot, Capt. Bill Cummings, took off on the first leg of the flight to Mindanao. Lumbering along at barely 120 mph, three hours later the Duck was on the ground at Cebu. Spending the rest of the day resting and taking advantage of the generous supply of food at the army's quartermaster depot on the island, Moore and Cummings took off early the next morning, reaching Del Monte Field just after daylight.

Loaded down for his return flight with medical supplies and radio parts, Moore headed back alone for Bataan via Cebu, leaving Cummings at Del Monte to make the next return flight.

And so a third plane, the old Grumman Duck, soon better known as the "Candy Clipper" because of the supply of candy and goodies brought back by Moore, Cummings, and later, a third pilot, Jack Caldwell, joined the "Fleet."

In all, between the Duck, Bradford's Bellanca, and the Beechcraft, over 30 trips were made to Mindanao or Cebu and back, with a total of close to 20 tons of badly needed medical supplies and food flown in to aid the desperate situation on Bataan. The 90 or so VIPs flown out of Bataan on the southern leg of the flights, considering what was in store for those who stayed, were no doubt just as thankful as those who benefitted from the food and medicine.[6]

With the arrival of 60 twin-engined Japanese bombers from Malaya in mid–March, as previously noted, the preliminary air assault on Bataan was in full swing by the end of the month. In fact, from about March 22 on, as reflected in Maj. Tisdelle's diary, there were "heavy bombings in front [and] in rear areas." Also, "night bombing raids [were] initiated on our front." His entry for Monday the 30th began the same way as his previous entries: "Enemy bombers exceptionally active." But there the similarity ended, as the next line astonishingly reads: "Bombed Hospital No. 1 today, reported killing 7 and wounding 11."[7]

The story of the bombing raced through southern Bataan.

"Bombed Hospital No. 1?" "Wasn't it marked?" Yes, it was, with big red crosses liberally painted on roofs of buildings and on white sheets spread on the open ground.

"Must have been a stray bomb that was meant for the nearby Quartermaster Supply Dump." No, it was more than one bomb dropped by more than one plane. It was deliberate.

About 7:30 that morning, navy nurse Ens. Ann Bernatitus, "on loan" to the army medical corps, was on her way to the surgical tent when a

Army nurse Lt. Juanita Redmond

Japanese plane suddenly appeared bearing down over the tree tops. Bernatitus dove for the nearest foxhole just in time to hear and feel the "crump, crump, crump" of enemy bombs as they strung out through the hospital compound. The concussion was tremendous, the noise, earsplitting.

When it stopped, Bernatitus peeked over the edge of her foxhole, expecting to see nothing but total devastation. Surprisingly, things didn't look too bad. The wards and operating rooms had not been hit, but several other buildings and a few vehicles were on fire. And somewhere men were screaming.[8]

Asleep nearby in the right wing of the officers' nipa hut quarters was an exhausted Capt. Alfred Weinstein. After operating almost continuously for the previous 24 hours, it would take nothing less than a bomb to wake him. And a bomb did, as "panic stricken," he sat up to "the roar of exploding bombs and [the] pungent odor of smoke."

The adjoining left wing of the officers quarters had taken a direct hit. (Interestingly, the only American officer in the entire left wing, confined there with malaria, had the good fortune to be out walking when the attack came.) Weinstein, meanwhile, "confused by the blast, stumbled out" to the second stick of enemy bombs that "sent their burning, sputtering contents in all directions."

Bataan nurses, left to right, Lt. Josephine Nesbitt, Capt. M. C. Davison, and Lt. Helen Hennessey, outside nurses quarters tent at Hospital No. 2.

Weinstein quickly flattened himself in a nearby drainage ditch, "chest heaving with terror," waiting "for the ear-shattering explosions to subside." Then he, as Nurse Bernatitus had done in between explosions, made a mad dash for the operating rooms.

Tending patients in one of the wards when the first bombs hit was army nurse Lt. Juanita Redmond. The first one "sounded closer than any I had heard before," she wrote later, but the next one, "threw me on the floor, [along with] several of the patients." "It seemed," she said, that "the explosions went on forever."

After they stopped and she was able to struggle to her feet, she could see "flames shooting in every direction." Everyone outside was "working wildly, throwing buckets of dirt on the fires, and litter-bearers [were] hurrying off into the jungle after casualties."

Nurse Bernatitus, meanwhile, had reached the side of navy surgeon Lt. Cmdr. Smith in one of the operating rooms when the second wave of enemy planes came over. Again the hospital grounds shook. Lamps flickered and the heavy operating table bounced and slid, bringing Smith, in the middle of an operation, to comment that if they killed him, it would have to be "while I'm working." Neither he nor Nurse Bernatitus left the operating table.[9]

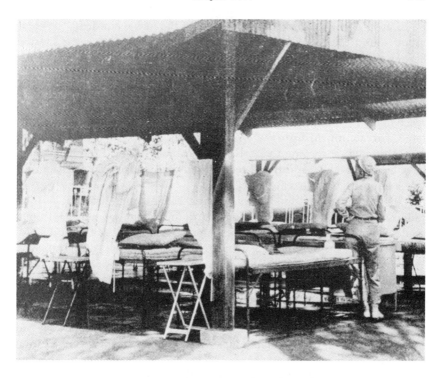

An army nurse dressed in khakis glances down the row of empty beds under her tin-roofed, makeshift ward at Hospital No. 1. The only permanent buildings inherited by the medical corps at No. 1 were former motor pool sheds.

In the kitchen area the first bomb sent the Filipino mess attendants into a nearby slit-trench. An American PFC, finding no room in the trench for himself when he arrived seconds later, threw himself into a nearby drainage ditch. "In the blinding crash that followed," wrote Weinstein, "the Filipinos were all crushed to death." "Legs, arms, heads, bodies were strewn all over the area, some parts suspended from tree limbs," added Capt. Al Poweleit, who had been assigned to the hospital just 16 days earlier.

Outside, after the last planes departed, Capt. Weinstein "counted the silent bodies of 14 . . . native hospital bed-makers." Nearby, "a truck loaded with dead, charred bodies lay on its side in the road." Medical Corpsman Fred Lang was found dead "with a hole through his heart," and Sgt. Speilhoffer had his foot torn off.

In the other surgery ward, Capt. Poweleit, at the shriek of falling bombs "dropped immediately to the floor," spilling Lysol all over himself in the process. "I thought at first [it] was blood,"he said, relieved to find out otherwise.[10]

Later, after she finished "taking care of the new wounded," Lt. Redmond found the courage to look around outside. "There were sheeted figures on the ground," she said, "most of them hospital personnel, men we'd been working with a long time; men we knew and liked."

Aside from the direct hit on the left wing of the officers quarters, damage to the hospital had been remarkably minor. Both surgery and receiving wards had received near-misses, and a couple others got splattered with shrapnel.

Although, according to Lt. Redmond, most believed the raid "must have been a mistake, additional red crosses were strewn over the grounds, and a siren [rigged] in a [nearby] tree."

That night, over Manila radio station KZRH, men listening to their radios on Bataan and Corregidor heard the Japanese make a formal apology for, as Weinstein put it, "the unfortunate bombing of Hospital No. 1. It was a mistake." Disagreeing with Lt. Redmond and the KZRH apology, Weinstein felt "it was deliberate." Later events would prove him to be correct.

Another of the "exceptionally active" bombings noted by Tisdelle that day led to yet another interesting, although far less tragic, incident.

As was indicated, the Japanese Air Force, since about March 24, had been swarming all over Bataan attacking everything on the ground and in the water.

Around ten o'clock that morning a flight of three enemy dive-bombers began working over two of the river gunboats moored in Sisiman bay. The two American ships, the *Oahu* and *Mindanao,* quickly got under way, heading east out of Sisiman toward the bay.

What had now become a running air-sea battle as it moved through the North Channel, was picked up by an antiaircraft observer on Corregidor, who promptly ordered one of his batteries to come to the aid of the besieged gunboats. The intense fire from the ack-ack guns very quickly "balanced the odds" with a direct hit on one of the Japanese planes, causing the other two to break off the attack and run for home.

That night, a dozen warm, homemade mince pies were delivered to the surprised crews of the antiaircraft battery from the appreciative cook and crew of the *Mindanao.*[11]

From March 29 through April 2, everyone throughout Bataan was aware of the increase in enemy pressure, particularly against Sectors C and D, opposite Mt. Samat. Every one of the entries in Maj. Tisdelle's diary for those five days referred to Japanese troop buildup opposite the two sectors.[12]

Of the many men who remembered and recorded their feelings during that period, perhaps Gen. Wainwright's statement best portended what was in store for his command. Noting that Gen. Parker's II Corps had been hit hard by Japanese patrols on the night of March 31–April 1, he wrote that they "came with bared bayonets and were met by the bayonets of malarial men with not enough food in their bellies to sustain a dog." Although slowing down the enemy assault, "the handwriting was vivid on the wall."

The Final Attack Begins

"The most devastating concentration of [enemy] fire seen."

The official launching of what was to be the final Japanese offensive on Bataan began on March 31 with the opening of the diversionary action against the I Corps. On the heels of what was to Col. Glen Townsend of the 11th Infantry "the heaviest concentrations [of artillery and bombing] we had experienced," elements of Gen. Sasumu Morioka's 16th Division, supported by four battalions of infantry of the Ikuta Detachment, simultaneously struck the outpost lines across the entire I Corps front. (See Map 25.)

H-hour for the main enemy thrust against Mt. Samat and the II Corps was scheduled for 3 P.M. Friday — Good Friday — April 3. The attack would be prefaced by no less than a five-hour-long preparatory air and artillery bombardment.

Both Thursday and early morning Friday remained ominously quiet of both air and artillery bombardment in the II Corps. Then at ten o'clock began an hour of steady registration fire, close to 150 Japanese field artillery weapons firing the first rounds of what would amount to nearly five hours of continuous bombardment against the eastern-half of the U.S. line. The entire II Corps shuddered. All of Bataan shook. Windows 30 miles away in Manila rattled for five hours.

The largest concentration of enemy guns was near Balanga. There the Japanese had arranged a solid square-mile of field pieces, spaced at one gun every 30 yards, all booming at Mt. Samat.

Recorded effects of the bombardment were consistent throughout the command. Captain Carlos Quirino of the Philippine Constabulary's 2d Division remembered it as "the most devastating concentration of [enemy] fire seen during the Philippine campaign."[13] Had he known, he could have added "and entire Pacific war to come."

Old timers with the Americans paralleled the experience with those they had lived through on the Western Front in France during World War I.

Not to be overlooked were the effects of the Japanese Air Force that

MAP No. 25

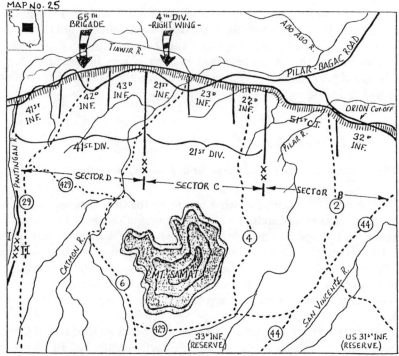

U.S. II CORPS POSITIONS - MT. SAMAT AREA
- AND DESIGNATED FOCAL POINTS OF JAPANESE ATTACK APR. 3 -

day. The entry in Maj. Tisdelle's diary that day said that the "sky was black with planes," no fewer than 150 sorties were flown by the Japanese who dropped close to 70 tons of explosives and incendiaries.[14]

Although it may have seemed to those men along the II Corps front as through the entire line was being blasted simultaneously, the Japanese were actually directing the bulk of their air and artillery bombardments toward one point in particular.

Sector D, westernmost portion of the II Corps' area of responsibility and widest of the four sectors, stretched some three miles across the lower slopes of Mt. Samat. Divided roughly in half, defense of the sector was shared by two Philippine Army divisions: Gen. Mateo Capinpin's 21st Division on the east and Gen. Vincente Lim's 41st Division on the west. Both generals had assigned all three of their regiments to the line. General Lim had his in numerical order from left to right, the 41st, 42d, and 43d regiments. (See Map 25.)

It was the 41st Division, and more specifically, the 1,000-yard wide corridor defended by the 42d Infantry, at which the main Japanese assault was aimed on April 3.

A Japanese light tank leaves the trail near the slopes of Mt. Samat. The extremely dense jungle did much to neutralize the effect of Japanese armor—and American tanks as well—on Bataan until the final offensive.

If the combination of enemy air and artillery bombardments was devastating to those along the II Corps front, there may not be a word left in the dictionary to adequately describe what happened in the 42d Infantry sector.

Despite the initial pounding of 42d frontline positions by the Japanese artillery and air force, the Filipino soldiers of perhaps the toughest of Philippine Army divisions on Bataan didn't budge.

After riding out over two hours of steady bombardment, little attention was paid at first to the next squadron of enemy bombers that came over until the usual "freight-train" roar of falling high explosive bombs didn't occur.

As the Filipino soldiers cautiously looked up from their holes to see what was happening, they saw what looked like hundreds of sticklike objects falling from the sky. When they hit, they burst into flame. They were firebombs, incendiaries.

It was the tail end of the Philippine dry season. Situated where it was—in the flat, open, lower slopes of Mt. Samat, an area devoid of lush tropical jungle but overgrown by brush and tinder-dry clumps of bamboo

Top: A converted, open-sided commercial bus used as an ambulance parked near the entrance to the Hospital No. 1 compound. *Bottom:* Four Filipino leg-wound cases at a forward clearing station awaiting transportation to Hospital No. 1 or 2 for treatment. It was not uncommon for wounded men to spend 24 to 36 hours en route to the hospitals.

and uncut sugar cane—it wasn't long before the hundreds of small fires started by the incendiaries along the line, fanned now by an afternoon breeze, united to prairie fire dimension.

Gradually as the heat grew in intensity, men were flushed out of their frontline positions back across what had become a churned-up, cratered, lunarlike landscape towards their regimental reserve line. Although it was possible to outrun the fire, continued heavy interdiction of the 42d's corridor by Japanese artillery forced the Filipino soldiers to seek refuge in shell holes or abandoned foxholes along the way.[15]

Soon, perhaps as with horses when the barn is burning, no matter where men went there appeared no escape. Panic stricken, those who tried to outrun the fire were killed by enemy artillery. And just as many of those who stayed to avoid the artillery burned to death.

At three o'clock, the line, masked in smoke, already racked by steel and fire, was hit again. Only this time by men and more steel—men from Gen. Nara's 65th Brigade and steel from accompanying tanks.

The rout of the panicked 42d, acting like a rampaging river at flood-tide, overflowed onto the bulk of the 43d Infantry on its right, carrying most of it with it. General Nara, who, at best had expected to get only as far as the MLR that day, surprisingly found a 1,600 yard-wide corridor completely abandoned to him when he arrived later that afternoon. To the Japanese soldiers, as they pushed unchallenged up the smoke-filled gap in the U.S. line, permeated with the smell of burning flesh, it appeared as though only darkness could stop them from reaching the Limay line.

By sunset the Japanese had forced no less than a two-square-mile salient into the U.S. line on the southwest slope of Mt. Samat; two square miles of ground that by far surpassed the most optimistic hopes of Gen. Homma.

The price of the Japanese gain was, of course, the 41st Division. As an organized fighting outfit, it was through. Of the division's three regiments, only the 41st, on the extreme left of Sector D, which had escaped the brunt of the Japanese assault, remained intact. Due to the deterioration of the 42d on its right, however, the regiment had pulled back in good order some distance past its own reserve line when it halted that evening. (See Map 26.)

It wasn't until about five o'clock that afternoon that Gen. Parker, at II Corps headquarters, was able to assimilate the pile of fragmentary reports that had been pouring in throughout the afternoon into a true picture of what had happened. His first act was to release the only "immediate reserve" unit in II Corps, the Philippine Army's 33d Infantry Regiment, less one battalion, to Sector D commander Gen. Max Lough. Lough, with the addition of the 33d, was far from acting the defeated commander.

Centered, at the time, on the southwestern slopes of Mt. Samat, an

MAP No. 26

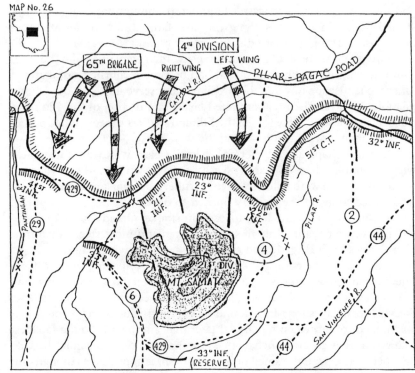

EXTENT OF JAPANESE GAINS - MT. SAMAT AREA BY APRIL 4

area bisected by two south to north flowing rivers—Pantingan and Catmon—the fighting was confined pretty much to the trails cut through the area by U.S. engineers. (See Map 27.)

One, Trail 29, led directly south up the center of a ridge dividing the Pantingan and Catmon rivers. The other, Trail 6, generally followed the steep eastern bank of the Catmon for about a mile and a half. At that point it split southeast from the river, following the lower contours of Mt. Samat for another mile, where it was intersected by Trail 429. Running predominantly east-west, 429 linked Trail 6 with Trails 4 and 2 on the east, and 29 on the west, some three-quarters of a mile behind the MLR.

To halt the Japanese drive, Gen. Lough, with the addition of the 33d, hoped to have the semblance of three infantry regiments in position on the 41st Division reserve line by dawn of the 4th. So it was north, back up Trail 29 to their own reserve line, that Lough ordered the reasonably intact 41st Infantry that night. Next he sent the 33d Infantry, with only 600 men, to establish a position on Trail 6, where it could block the enemy from use of both the trail and Catmon River valley. For his third regiment, Lough sent Col. Malcom Fortier, senior American instructor with the 41st Divi-

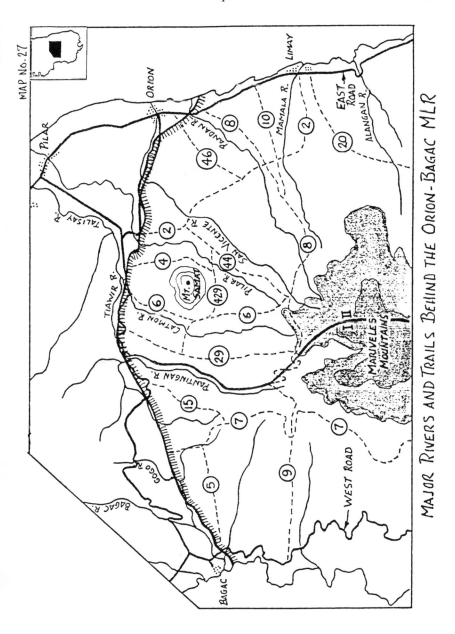

MAP No. 27

MAJOR RIVERS AND TRAILS BEHIND THE ORION-BAGAC MLR

In this general area below Mt. Samat's west slope junctioned the very important trails 6, 429, and 29. The valley nearest the foot of the mountain is the Catmon River valley. Initial Japanese success against II Corps positions on Mt. Samat on April 3 and 4 was through this valley.

sion, to round up as many 42d and 43d Infantry stragglers as possible and use them to fill the gap between the 41st and 33d.

With much difficulty, 400 or 500 Filipinos from the two shattered regiments were rounded up and, by various means, persuaded to move north back down Trail 6. Daylight found them just 200 yards north of the 6-429 junction, however, and a mile and a half short of their assigned position.

At dawn the next morning, April 4, the Japanese offensive resumed with the same preattack air and artillery intensity of the day before. Pressing their advantage in the 41st Division salient, Japanese artillery went to work immediately on the 42d-43d Infantry. It didn't take much to flush the jittery, shellshocked Filipinos from their positions, only this time, according to Col. Fortier, we "could do nothing to stop them." With one-third of Gen. Lough's defending forces "stampeded" from their positions even before the Japanese infantry had jumped off, the epitaph of the western half of Sector D, for all practical purposes, was written.

Sharing the responsibility of defending Sector D with the 41st, was Gen. Mateo Capinpin's 21st Division. The area assigned to them placed them squarely on the front slopes of Mt. Samat. And it was squarely at the 21st on Mt. Samat that the Japanese would make their heaviest assaults that day.

With enemy tanks coming on the heels of the morning's air and artillery bombardments, it wasn't long before the obvious happened against the unprotected western flank of the 21st. Hit by armor from the 7th Tank Regiment, and again before the Japanese infantry had moved out, the 21st Infantry—one-third of the entire 21st Division—gave way.

Almost simultaneously with the disintegration of both the 42d-43d and 21st Infantries that morning, without an assault made nor a shot fired by Japanese ground troops, came the collapse of yet a third Filipino regiment under similar circumstances—the 23d Infantry.

As 21st Infantry troops on the 23d's left flank began falling back, and Japanese left wing forces began to mass at its front, the 23d fell back with little more than a fire fight to show for its efforts. Then at eleven o'clock, still 60 minutes from the enemy's scheduled H-hour, the only remaining regiment on the U.S. MLR in Sector D, the 22d Infantry, also quietly gave up its positions and joined the 21st and 23d on the division reserve line across the base of Mt. Samat.

On Saturday, April 4, from noon on, little if any action took place. In fact, the entire day, beginning with the abandonment of the remainder of the MLR in Sector D by U.S. forces, remained void of ground fighting. Japanese infantry, which had moved out from their lines of departure around noon, met absolutely no opposition in attaining, in less than 36 hours, objectives originally estimated to take at least twice that long.

By now, of course, the panic button had been pushed on the U.S. side. General King, for all practical purposes, committed the entire Philippine Division plus the Provisional Tank Group to II Corps' use. For II Corps' use, Parker ordered the already alerted U.S. 31st Infantry to standby at the junctions of trails 10 and 2 near Mt. Orion. From its bivouac in the I Corps, the 45th Infantry, less one battalion, was ordered over the northern slopes of the Mariveles Mountains to the junction of trails 29 and 8. There, supported by a company of tanks, it was to attack north down Trail 29 to the old 41st Infantry reserve line. The 57th Infantry was ordered to move up from its bivouac near Mariveles to II Corps reserve near Lamao.

And so, the Philippine Division, the Fil-Americans' last and only hope, moved out to stem the tide. But could it? The answer was obvious even before they got started. Major Eugene Conrad of the 31st Infantry's 2d Battalion, wrote that "before we could move, we had to first eliminate all men who were unable to march. About 20 men per company (30 percent) were so sick with malaria and dysentery, that they were unable to even start."[16] Major Everett Mead of the same regiment added that "some men who could hardly walk, moved out with their battalions; they had left sick beds to join their outfits, not wanting to be left behind."[17] Colonel Ernest Miller of the 194th Tank Battalion noted that members of the 31st were in "very poor physical condition [so] they could march for only about ten minutes and then had to rest." There was little doubt, as the division moved forward into the darkness of the night of April 4, 1942, that the handwriting for the entire command was already "vivid on the wall."

As they had done on April 3 and 4 on the western slopes of Mt. Samat, trails on the eastern side were to play key roles in the last few days of the fight there. As on the west, there were also two key north-south trails on the east. Westernmost and the highest up on Mt. Samat was Trail 4, which, like Trail 6 on the opposite side, junctioned with Trail 429 on the backside of the mountain. About a mile further east the other military road, Trail 2, was found. It, like Trail 29 on the western slope, followed a ridge back from the MLR for about two and a half miles before veering southeast across the San Vicente River and then moving on to Limay. About a mile before the San Vicente, Trail 44 passed through, linking 2 with the junction of 4-429, about three-quarters of a mile to the southwest. From there, 44 continued south, eventually linking with Trail 3, some three miles away. (See Map 27.)

The Japanese, finding themselves already a full day and a half ahead of schedule on April 5, were forced to use Easter Sunday as a day to allow their lagging supply trains to catch up, while at the same time, to make preparations for their assault on the 6th. Although minor in scale, some important action did take place that day, the highlight being the capture of the heights of Mt. Samat. Equally important, since the fight had and would remain essentially a battle for the trails and trail junctions, enemy right and left wing forces also pincered the 21st Division at the important junction of trails 4 and 429 on the southeast corner of Samat, giving them control over this key linkage by late that evening.

Although little had gone well for the Fil-Americans in the first 72 hours, these were not days without heroes or heroic action.

One of the most effective and courageous acts of the fight took place around the 41st Division Field Artillery, in position high on the upper slopes of Mt. Samat.

The 41st Field Artillery, under Capt. Alfonso Arellano, from the 3d until midday on the 5th, had periodically blasted advancing enemy troops from both Trail 4 and 6, until, being overrun, were forced to "push their guns over the cliffs" and flee on the afternoon of the third day. In fact, Arellano, even at the warnings of Gen. Lim, as noted on his Philippine Army Distinguished Conduct Star citation, "to leave the observation post as there were many enemy snipers scattered around . . . insisted on remaining at his post to direct artillery fire against the enemy."[18]

To write of the heroes of the 41st Division is not to leave out its commander, Gen. Vincente Lim. Lim, a West Point graduate who had honed his troops into probably the best Philippine Army Division on Bataan, was seen by Capt. Carlos Romulo around April 4.

Smoking a crudely made cigar "of rolled guava leaves tied together with a piece of string," Romulo and Lim shook hands. "He was haggard and his eyes were sunken," remembered Romulo, "and his hair, once so black, had turned gray." Holding his battered division together with little more than was holding his cigar, "his scarecrow body outlined against the sunset of that terrible day seemed," to his old friend, "the embodiment of the Philippine Army on Bataan: ragged, starved, sick to death, beaten back hour after hour—but invincible."

About that same time, Capt. Ferdinand Marcos, then Combat Intelligence Officer of the 21st division, set out to effect the rescue of another Filipino general, Mateo Capinpin, whose division command post had been overrun by the Japanese. Although unsuccessful, Marcos disregarded a shrapnel wound in the stomach and was able to rally a disorganized remnant force of 21st Division troops on Trail 4 to make a stand against the hard pushing enemy. The ensuing fire fight against the left wing's 8th Infantry was later recalled by Japanese officers as the "fiercest . . . fought in the second Bataan campaign."[19]

On that same Easter Sunday afternoon, Gen. Wainwright, after a visit to Gen. King at Little Baguio for an "overall picture of what was happening on Bataan," headed north to get the details of Gen. Parker's counterattack plans.

Captain Tom Dooley, the general's aide, driving "like a wild man, [as] time was indeed precious," skidded the jeep to a stop under a clump of trees near Parker's II Corps headquarters behind Limay. As the dust-covered Wainwright, wearing goggles to keep the dirt out of his eyes, entered the tent, he was met by Col. Harrison Browne, chief of staff of the Philippine Division. Browne, on loan to II Corps headquarters to help Gen. Parker who had been down for several days with malaria, was just leaving. Wainwright briefly mentioned a plan to relieve the pressure on the II Corps by launching a counterattack with the still intact I Corps. Browne concurred. Probably the "best solution" he said.

Wainwright proceeded to meet with the gaunt, fevered II Corps commander, whose look of despair reflected the hopelessness of the situation. Lines on Parker's maps indicating the extent of Japanese gains looked like a red-colored lasso dropped over the shoulders of Mt. Samat. With "misgivings as to the outcome," Wainwright approved Parker's plan "which he hoped would restore the ground the 41st had lost and reestablish the position of ... [the] battered 21st Division."

On their way back to Cabcaben, Dooley, who had had his share of close calls with the Japanese Air Force while driving the general, "drove so hard that he broke an axle."

The few minutes' delay in securing new transportation gave Wainwright pause to watch a small convoy of troops as they passed on the way to the front. It was a sad sight. The men were all terribly thin. Mere shadows of what they once were. Their heads were down, bouncing and rolling with the bumps in the road. The sight was still with him later that evening on Corregidor when he phoned his chief quartermaster, Brig. Gen. Charles Drake. Wainwright asked Drake if there was anything at all that could be done to increase the rations on Bataan. Drake told him there was plenty of rice and a little flour, and that there were 45,000 C-rations being held for emergency.

Double the rice and flour issue and hand out all the C-rations except enough for 5,000, he told Drake. Send anything that can be spared.[20]

During the next 24 hours on the peninsula, unit mess sergeants were made to feel like Santa Claus. Portions were doubled. Bakeries were back at work baking bread. There was salmon again, and tomatoes, and even cigarettes. The 2d Battalion of the U.S. 31st Infantry got their food drop on the evening of April 6. "We received about 12 cans of ... C-rations per man, also cigarettes," remembered Maj. Eugene Conrad of that unit.[21] "We were told they came from Corregidor." Captain John Gulick noted that his Scout coast artillery unit even got "a few cans of abalone ... and wonders of wonders, some cigarettes."[22] At a Philippine Army artillery unit behind Mt. Orion, an additional reaction to the surprise issue of rice and salmon was recorded. "We thought," remembered 3d Lt. Ambrosio Peña, "it meant that the mile-long convoy had finally arrived."[23] Unbeknownst to the Filipinos and to probably most of the Americans, when these rations were gone, there would be no more. The troops on Bataan were having their last supper.

Despite the fact that the total collapse of Bataan was inevitable, efforts from the outside were still being made to save it. On April 1, Corregidor received a message from Col. John Cook at the army's quartermaster supply depot on Cebu, advising that eight small transport ships would be loaded and ready to leave for Bataan on April 8. A request was made to fly three Bataan pilots to Del Monte Field on Mindanao, where, along with another pilot, they would pick up four P-40s and fly cover for the eight blockade-runners. If all went well, they would arrive sometime on April 10.

The first pilot to go was Lt. Andy Krieger, who left on April 3. On the night of April 5, Capt. Jack Randolph left Del Monte Field for Bataan in an old Waco four-seater to pick up the other two pilots. He arrived at Bataan Field at 2 A.M. One hour later, Capt. Dick Fellows, with lieutenants Dave Obert and John Posten, gunned the little biplane back down the dusty, blacked-out runway for Mindanao, landing 3½ hours later at Cebu. There his old friend, John Cook, treated the three to "ham and eggs, bacon, fruit ... and even ice cream." "If one wasn't so hungry," commented Fellows, "there was even beer and booze." Cook told the three men that he had some 40,000 tons of food just waiting for ships to get it to Bataan.

Later that afternoon Fellows flew the Waco to Del Monte and dropped off his passengers. When he started back for Bataan the next night loaded down with medical supplies, the big six-foot four-inch captain had officially become a member of the Bamboo Fleet. Two days later Dick Fellows would pilot the last flight the Bamboo Fleet would ever make.[24]

In general, Parker's counterattack plan for April 6 called for the U.S. 31st Infantry to advance north down Trail 4 to regain control of the 21st Division reserve line. On the west side of Samat, spearheaded by the tank-supported 45th, U.S. forces were assigned to recapture and regain control of trails 29 and 6 up to the 41st Division's reserve line.

In contrast, the focal point of Gen. Homma's attack that same day, with Sector D already his, was to go to work on the exposed but still intact left flank of Sector C.

On paper, it would be a match of strength against strength, a showdown—the American 31st Infantry against the main Japanese left and right wing forces. In reality, of course, it would be no contest. A single American infantry regiment, depleted of nearly 50 percent of its effectives by malaria, dysentery, and malnutrition, was up against the bulk of the powerful, barely tested Japanese 4th Division.

Prelude to the important confrontation began, interestingly enough, on a note far from that of "the Americans to the rescue."

General Harold George standing next to one of the shacks built in the jungle behind Bataan Field to be used by pilots of Bataan's diminutive air force.

The specific objective of the U.S. 31st that day was to move from the junction of trails 2 and 44 in Sector C, southwest down 44 to 429. H-hour for the attack north on Trail 4 was 6 A.M.

The regiment, as scheduled, moved by truck from its bivouac near trails 2-10 to 2-44, arriving there at nine o'clock on the night of the 5th. Routinely, upon arrival, the regimental Service Company was ordered to establish its bivouac at a previously selected spot at the junction of trails 8 and 10, some six and a half miles south.

Assuming Trail 44 still to be in U.S. hands, the Service Company trucks started off. No more than five minutes under way, word came back that they had been ambushed by the enemy less than 50 yards down the trail. Upon investigation, it was found that an ambulance moving north on 44 with 21st Division wounded had become stalled and abandoned by its driver when fired on by infiltrating Japanese.

"Mess sergeants, cooks, and drivers of the kitchen trucks," according to Maj. Clarence Bess of the 31st's Service Company, "took up the fire fight while one of the drivers got the ambulance started." The driver, who had "jumped off and taken cover," was found, "put back in his ambulance and [sent] off to the clearing station."[25]

To 31st commander Lt. Col. Jasper Brady, discovery of Japanese troops so far north on Trail 44 portended only one thing: the infiltration of

260 The Battle of Bataan

Sector C from behind. This indicated that not only was the regimental departure line at 4-429, a mile and a half away, in jeopardy, but possibly 44-429, as well. Brady ordered the leading 2d Battalion, after securing the trail of enemy infiltrators, to pick up the pace.

Of course, part of what Brady feared had happened. Japanese 4th Division left and right wing forces, it will be remembered, had secured 4-429 earlier that night. In fact, indications of enemy success were already evident. As early as eight o'clock that night on Trail 2, about a mile below the junction of 2-44, the regiment found the road ominously "blocked," according to Maj. Eugene Conrad, "by wounded, sick, barefoot, disorganized Philippine Army soldiers."[26] Around midnight, the 2d Battalion ran into stiff enemy resistance on 429 just a few hundred yards west of the 44-429 junction. During this time, heavy firing was heard coming from the west, as the Japanese put the finishing touches to the 21st Division.

Any doubt remaining in the Americans' minds was cleared up around 4:30 that morning, when things suddenly quieted in the 21st area. Also around that time, Col. Uhrig, an American observer with the 21st, and two Philippine Army colonels wandered into the 31st CP. Uhrig informed Brady that his division along with the 31st's jump-off point at 4-429 had been completely overrun by strong Japanese forces.

With fewer than 800 effectives left in the entire regiment and most of them unfit by normal standards, it was obvious that the American objective could not be reached. Brady contacted Gen. Lough at Sector D headquarters and was instructed to break-off the attack in lieu of establishing defensive positions around 44-429, which he was told to hold "at all costs."

Brady, knowingly having placed Sector C's left flank in serious jeopardy, also contacted its commander, Gen. Clifford Bluemel.

Bluemel, meanwhile, had been having his troubles too. With, for all practical purposes, the disintegration of Sector D the day before, twice he had requested Gen. Parker to allow him to pull the sector line back to the far bank of the San Vicente River. Actually a line along the San Vicente, a river running diagonally across the middle of the II Corps area, offered the Fil-Americans perhaps the best chance to stem the on-rushing Japanese.

Parker, in anticipation of the already ordered counterattack to restore the eastern half of Sector D by the U.S. 31st the next morning, had refused Bluemel both times.

At the time Brady's call was made to Bluemel, because of communication difficulties, Bluemel had not yet received confirmation from Lough canceling his counterattack plans. Regardless of this, since his action would also affect the situation in Sector C, Brady needed acknowledgment from its commander as well.

He didn't get it. In fact, the fiery Bluemel, who had reluctantly left his sector left-flank in jeopardy in lieu of Brady's counterattack, was furious.

"Not by a damn sight" would he confirm Brady's action. In fact, if he refused to attack as ordered, Bluemel threatened to "report [his] actions to the Sector commander."

Brady told him that he hadn't been able to get through to Lough yet, prompting Bluemel, before slamming the phone down in his ear, to tell him to report his "failure to counterattack to General Parker," then.[27]

It wasn't Brady, interestingly enough, who contacted Parker of his failure to launch the counterattack. It was Bluemel later that morning who, upon Brady's action, again requested permission to pull back to the San Vicente.

The II Corps commander, hoping the 31st could hold the junction at 44-429, was reluctant to give up the still intact Trail 2 without a fight. He therefore, for the third time, refused Bluemel's request, in turn ordering him to dig-in on the steep west bank of the Pilar River.

But Parker's "hope" for the 31st to hold, was short lived, as by one o'clock that afternoon Japanese left wing forces had successfully flanked the southernmost battalion of Americans at 44-429. In fact, when men of this, the 2d Battalion, began their withdrawal, according to Maj. Eugene Conrad, they found "all trails ... denied," forcing them, after "successive delaying actions," to get to the San Vicente "across country," where they arrived around three o'clock.[28] (See Map 28.)

The turning of the 31st's left flank had, at last, brought the granting of Gen. Bluemel's request to pull back to the San Vicente. But not, of course, under the circumstances he had hoped for.

"What remained of the [31st] reached the river," remembered Maj. Conrad, "badly disorganized and exhausted." So exhausted, in fact, that "many of their machine guns were destroyed and abandoned as they were [too weak] to carry them."[29]

Bluemel's easternmost flanking unit, the 51st Combat Team, had had a rough go too. About the time the 31st Infantry found its flank giving way, the Japanese 37th Infantry troops were in the process of overrunning still another American position, having routed the 51st from the west bank of the Pilar River back across Trail 2 toward the San Vicente.

From that afternoon until late that night, an all-out effort was made by the American command, or, more specifically, an American commander—Gen. Clifford Bluemel—to organize the shattered Fil-American army on the south bank of the San Vicente.

Few unit histories, including those of the 26th Cavalry, 57th Infantry, and the Provisional Air Corps Regiment from Sector A, who joined those already on line on the San Vicente, fail to mention the personal efforts of Bluemel during this period.

As men straggled across the river throughout the afternoon, many were met by Bluemel, who "pesonally attempted to organize the resistance."

With rifle in hand, he and several other officers by late that night had prodded, talked, threatened, but in most cases, forced a semblance of a line along the south bank.[27] Bluemel did not know that what he had been working so hard at throughout the afternoon, since 4:00 P.M. had been his responsibility anyway, as at that time Gen. Parker had turned command of the entire San Vicente River line over to him.

U.S. Counterattack on the West Slope of Mt. Samat

"In a state of intense confusion."

On the morning of April 4, it will be remembered, Sector D commander Gen. Lough, in hopes of halting the Japanese advance along Trail 6, had ordered his reserve—the 33d Infantry—to establish a line across it. As ordered, the 33d, under the command of an American major named Holmes, dug in at a zigzag in the trail about a mile north of the junction of 6-429.

Behind the 33d on Trail 6, it will also be recalled, was a remnant force of 42d-43d Infantry troops, who were unlucky enough to have dug in at a key artillery interdiction point for the Japanese preattack bombardment that morning.

Whereas the 42d-43d were literally stampeded back from their positions, the 33d not only received little artillery fire but went unchallenged by enemy ground forces throughout the day as well. In fact, not only did the Japanese unknowingly go over and around them on the 4th, but on the 5th too.

For the counterattack on the 6th, the untouched 33d was given the assignment of securing Trail 6 up to the old 41st Division reserve line. Ironically, assigned to its support were about 400 Filipinos from the same remnant force of 42d-43d Infantry troops that had twice before been routed from their positions in Sector D.

Before dawn on the morning of the 6th, as the 42d-43d neared the spot on Trail 6 from which they had been blasted just two days before, incredibly, they were struck again, only this time by a force of 65th Brigade troops. Again, as before, the jumpy Filipinos broke, and, as before, they couldn't be stopped.

The 33d, in the meantime, unaware of the 42d-43d's plight, stood fast in anticipation of their arrival. Around noon it began taking mortar and artillery fire. By midafternoon, with the failure of a patrol sent down Trail 6 to contact the 42d-43d, Maj. Holmes knew his time was up. Although, for all practical purposes, the 33d had been surrounded for three days, all now knew that at long last the Japanese had discovered it too. (See Map 28.)

MAP No. 28

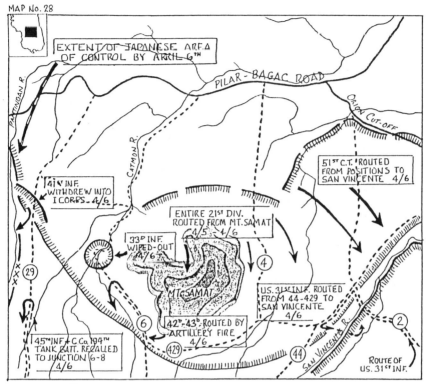

DISINTEGRATION OF U.S. MT. SAMAT DEFENSES - APRIL 6

So the U.S. counterattack down Trail 6 on April 6, with the simple routing of the 42d-43d and discovery of the 33d by the Japanese, was stopped before it even got started. But what of the other half of the objective—Trail 29?

As on Trail 6, the U.S. objective on Trail 29 was to restore and then reestablish Sector D up to the old 41st Division reserve line. To execute the attack, Gen. Lough had selected what was left of the 41st Infantry (about 300 men), two battalions of 45th Infantry troops, and Company C of the 194th Tank Battalion.

The 41st, for the third time in four days, was asked to reestablish itself in its old reserve line positions. It had done it successfully on April 3, but in accord with the collapse of the 42d on its immediate right, it too had fallen back, although orderly. General Lough's plan to reestablish the 41st Division sector up to its reserve line on the 4th, however, sent the regiment back again to its positions astride Trail 29, where it arrived 12 hours later. Enemy pressure from the air and ground on the morning of the 4th, though, coupled with the threat of being outflanked, forced the regiment to drop back about a half a mile to the southwest, where it established its perimeter along the edge of the Pantingan River.

So, for the second time, the game 41st was ordered to counterattack back across the now familiar ground to its old positions. And, for the second time, it was reasonably successful.

Around 2 A.M. on the 6th, acting as lead element of the assault to recapture Trail 29, a regimental patrol ran into a small encampment of unsuspecting Japanese 65th Brigade troops. Bayonets of the men of the 41st, who were already holders of a Presidential Unit Citation, made quick work of the surprised enemy soldiers and then moved on.

At dawn the Filipinos ran into another unit of 65th Brigade soldiers, only this one, about a battalion in strength, was not asleep. By noon, the exhausted but tough 41st had withdrawn to a tenable position along the edge of the Pantingan, in wait, like the 33d on Trail 6, for help from the north.

Help for the 41st would come from the tank-supported 45th Infantry. Two battalions of that regiment's Scouts, in anticipation of the counterattack, arrived at the junction of trails 8-29 from their reserve position in the I Corps on the morning of April 5. Its tank support, under the command of Col. Ernest Miller, arrived there under the most arduous of circumstances, whose detail exemplified the confusion found throughout the II Corps. The following excerpts from Miller's narrative bear witness to what was happening.

After almost taking himself "into enemy occupied territory" trying to find Philippine Division Headquarters on the night of April 4, he luckily "stumbled into the 31st Infantry." He got little help from the newly arrived Americans, however, as things throughout the entire II Corps "were in a state of flux. Positions were being shifted . . . constantly to meet the ever-changing situation."

After traveling "up and down trails" all the rest of the night, Miller finally found the headquarters at six o'clock that morning.

It wasn't until two that afternoon, however, after "much consultation, pulling plans apart and putting them back together again," that it was decided that the 194th would accompany the 45th north on Trail 29 the next morning.

Following the meeting at Division Headquarters, Miller drove across to the 45th Infantry bivouac at 29-8, where he and 45th commander Col. Tom Doyle formalized their plans for the next day. Then it was east again all the way back to where he had left his company at the junction of 10 and 2.

Miller briefed his company on the upcoming operation and then around midnight started back. The return was hell. By now, everything was "in a state of intense confusion." The trails, if they had been difficult to negotiate before, were nearly impossible now, as the stream of "vehicles containing wounded going to the rear," continually impeded progress.

No wonder the five-mile journey had "seemed like years" to Miller, for he had "coaxed, cussed, and hauled" his company over the tortuous trail at the pitiful rate of less than one mile per hour, arriving at his rendezvous point with the 45th at "6:10 A.M.—ten minutes late."

Turning single file down Trail 29, the line of lumbering C Company Stuart's caught up with the 45th around eight o'clock. Except for his tankers, Miller soon realized it was going to be the same old story: the "dense jungle loom[ing] on each side" would make it impossible for the 45th to take advantage of their presence.

First contact with the enemy came at nine o'clock, but the Scouts, with the tanks waiting helplessly on the narrow trail, easily pushed aside an advance patrol of 65th Brigade troops and then continued on.

Under sporadic mortar fire for the next six hours, progress was reduced to less than half a mile an hour. Finally, at 3:30, having covered only a mile and a half since 9 A.M., Miller and Doyle "went into a huddle."

Doyle's primary concern was the repeated failure to make contact with friendly troops on either side of them. He was particularily disturbed with the possibility of having Trail 29 behind him severed, thus closing off his only escape route back to safety.

Throughout the day, patrols had been sent out in both directions, but none ever returned. Despite this, wrote Col. Miller, "witnessing the mettle of [the] Scouts, as each succeeding group was called up to receive . . . orders for patrol duty, every last man took his . . . with no trace of reluctance or fear whatever." Even with the knowledge that death "awaited them, the last patrol went just as eagerly as the first."

At about 4:15, the advance was halted by probably the same force of Japanese 65th Brigade troops that had pushed the 41st off the trail earlier that morning.

The situation warranted the use of mortars. Coming up with only ten rounds, it was decided to fire five—half of the regiment's entire allotment—in an attempt to open up the road, so, as Miller put it, "the tanks could follow up and put the Nips on the run."

At five o'clock the Scouts opened up and, at last, recorded Miller, "the enemy received a taste of the medicine they had been dishing out all day" "The five pathetic shells were exploded with miraculous results," routing the enemy from their positions. The Scouts, quick to seize the initiative, pounced on the remaining few enemy soldiers "on either side of the breach . . . before the tanks could even make their way up the trail!"

Their deftness, it was discovered later, no doubt saved Miller some losses, as, in anticipation of the use of tanks, "the Japs had placed their vicious pie-pan mines" all over the area.

With the onset of darkness it was decided to consolidate the newly won positions on Trail 29, with hopes of continuing the attack in the morning. A little less than a mile farther on, ever alert for the expected sounds of American tanks coming from the south, the 41st Infantry, like the 33d a mile or so east on Trail 6, prepared to sweat out the night in isolation.

Meanwhile, things had happened further south on Trail 6 that weakened the 33d's and 41st's chances of being rescued. Back at the junction of trails 6 and 8, the situation had changed drastically. It was no longer in friendly hands.

Around noon, the same elements of Japanese 65th Brigade troops that had earlier routed the 42d-43d from Trail 6 overran the trail junction, while at the same time forcing Gen. Lough to move his sector CP east from 6-8 to 8-29. (See Map 27.)

Lough's move had been in the wrong direction, however, as he, along with the 45th and 41st, were now cut off from the entire western two-thirds of the II Corps. In reaction to this situation, Gen. Parker ordered the 57th Infantry, already in the process of moving into Sector D over Trail 8, to attack the enemy holding the 6-8 junction from the west.

Word of what had happened reached the dog-tired 45th and C Company tankers just as they were settling into their new positons on Trail 29. They were ordered to retrace the day's footsteps back to their original line of departure at 8-29. From there, they would move so they could strike out against the vital 6-8 crossroads from the east.

By the time the 45th reached the junction of 8-29, it was close to 1 A.M. Disappointingly, they had given up in less than three hours what had taken them 20 hours to gain. Despite this, Miller remembered not hearing "one word of complaint" from the Scouts, "only extreme attention to duty."

Fearing a possible enemy trap on Trail 8, it was decided to detach a small force to act as a reconnaissance for the bulk of the waiting regiment and tanks. If the enemy was found there in force, Lough reasoned that little probably could be done and the patrol would break off the action and return.

Some of the details of the events that followed were recorded by Col. Miller, who accompanied the patrol. A reconnaissance force of two tanks and the 2d Battalion of the 45th, with Miller "riding in a jeep directly behind the second tank," left the junction of 8-29 around 1 A.M. Two hours later the column halted, as it had routinely done on the hour, to allow the exhausted Filipinos to "take ten." The tanks, forming the point of the patrol, had stopped just past a bend in the trail when someone yelled "Japs." "Almost simultaneously," recorded Miller, "a shot was fired from an [enemy] antitank gun located at the junction." The shell "went directly through the turret of the first tank," knocking it out and stunning its commander, Lt. Frank Riley.

Japanese artillerymen stockpiling heavy artillery shells in preparation for the final offensive on April 3. The deadly combination of Japanese preattack air and artillery bombardments broke the back of U.S. defenses in less than six days, almost singlehandedly bringing about the total collapse of the II Corps by April 7.

Suddenly the entire enemy roadblock erupted with heavy antitank and machine gun fire. With the crew of the quickly abandoned lead tank clinging desperately to the tank behind, it began slowly backing around the bend in the trail to safety. To cover the withdrawal, the Scouts hurriedly "formed a line to our rear and fired blindly in the direction of the Japs." "Their actions," said Miller, "would have been a credit to the best trained and bravest soldiers in the world."

Determining that the enemy was there in force, the column, still under covering fire from the Scouts, turned and headed back for 8-29. It wasn't until eight o'clock that morning that the exhausted patrol reached the road junction again. They returned after a grueling, disappointing seven hours to find the situation drastically changed there also. The 45th Infantry had left.

With news of the failure of the reconnaissance force to break the enemy hold on 6-8, Gen. King ordered the 45th, along with the 41st Infantry, back across the Pantingan River to the temporary sanctuary of the I Corps. The 41st, still over two miles inside enemy controlled territory, was able to slip free of its noose early that morning and later join the 45th west of the Pantingan.

The only remaining unit still in the north, the Philippine Army's 33d Infantry, still dug-in on the zigzag over on Trail 6, was not so lucky. Surrounded but still holding, at dawn on April 6, they were struck by the Japanese. Time and time again the remarkable 33rd beat off the enemy assaults. But at noon, after over six hours of continual pounding, the regiment at last gave way.

The attack scheduled to be made by the 45th against the Japanese roadblock at 6-8, it will be remembered, was to be the western half of a two-pronged pincer of that junction. The eastern half, assigned to the 1st and 2d battalions of the 57th Infantry that night, never eventuated.

To understand this and the subsequent collapse of the San Vicente River line, it is perhaps best to examine a trail map of the area in question. It showed east-west running Trail 8 as the southernmost road in that part of the II Corps. Junctioning with it at the point of the 6-8 intersection was the San Vicente River, along which the II Corps was forming to make its next stand. (See maps 27 and 28.)

Had the 45th and 57th been successful in recapturing the 6-8 junction, it was planned to extend the new line west across 8 to 29 and the Pantingan River. Failure of the 45th and subsequently the 57th to link up, portended, therefore, the collapse of the entire San Vicente River line.

The area south of the 6-8 junction was hilly and densely wooded, making it physically impossible to extend U.S. lines in that direction. For the Japanese, recognized masters of infiltration, the situation proved ideal.

The 57th, finding the going as tough as the 45th had on the west, was unable to penetrate the enemy perimeter around the 6-8 roadblock from the east. The Japanese, in turn, taking immediate advantage of the difficult terrain, began working their way around the unprotected southern end on the U.S. line.

Back on April 4, with Gen. King's release of the Philippine Division to Gen. Parker at II Corps, three battalions of engineers, the U.S. 803d and

Philippine Army's 201st and 202d, were divested of all engineer activities, ordered to prepare for combat, and placed in II Corps reserve.

At the time the 57th Infantry was ordered to attack the roadblock at 6-8 on the afternoon of the 6th, a gap of nearly two miles existed between it and the southernmost unit on the San Vicente line.

It was into this gap that the 201st and 202d Engineers were ordered from corps reserve that afternoon. But the opportunistic Japanese, before the Filipinos could reach the river, had already crossed to its eastern bank. Ambushed several hundred yards short of their objective, the engineers hastily retreated back over the rugged, unfamiliar terrain, all the way to their debarkation points on Trail 46.

Facing a double-envelopment, the 57th commander, Col. Edmund Lilly, broke off the fight and withdrew east over Trail 8 towards Limay. With this move, by midday of the 7th, II Corps trails 29, 6, 4, 44, and 429 had been irretrievably lost to the Japanese—and the day was far from over.

As opportunistic and successful as the Japanese Army was during the first five days of their offensive, much of the credit for its success must go to its air force. So intense were enemy efforts to keep the reeling army on Bataan on the run, that even attacks on Corregidor were suspended. After launching its 120th air raid against the island on April 5, all attacks for the next few days were ordered against Bataan only. Averaging 150 sorties and 90 tons of bombs each day, Japanese planes saturated roads, bivouacs, command posts, troops moving forward, troops withdrawing—everything. The bombing caught the 201st Engineers moving up on the 6th, causing its commander, Maj. Harry Fischer to comment that flying "300 or 400 feet off the ground," where they couldn't be seen through the thick jungle, they "had a field day."

Major Clarence Bess recorded the two-hour long bombing of the 31st Infantry Service Company that same day as the "worst it had experienced on Bataan." After one flight of dive-bombers "had released their bombs, one plane would remain and strafe the area until another flight appeared."

Colonel Ernest Miller wrote that "Japanese bombers and strafers pounded [him] unmercifully [sic]" on April 7th. "They came in veritable clouds—wave after wave. At times the sky was almost black with them."

It was under that same "sky . . . black with [enemy bombers]" on the morning of the 7th, that Hospital No. 1 was deliberately bombed for the second time.

Around ten o'clock that morning, a two-and-a-half ton truck loaded with artillery ammunition had unwisely ventured out onto the Mariveles Road from one of the nearby ordnance depots. As it was passing the entrance to the hospital, it was pounced on by a Japanese dive-bomber. The well-aimed single bomb made a direct hit on the truck, blowing up it and its two occupants. The men standing guard at the hospital gate dove into

Three unchallenged Japanese "Sonia" dive-bombers prepare to peel off over Bataan.

a nearby slit-trench at the sight of the diving enemy plane, only to be buried alive by dirt and debris from the ensuing blast.

The "screech of Nip dive-bombers" sent Capt. Alfred Weinstein and hospital Chaplain William Cummings, at that moment crossing the middle of the hospital compound, diving for cover. Concussion from the exploding truck momentarily knocked both men unconscious. Not knowing how long they were out, "bleeding from nose and ears, drums shattered [and] concussed," the two men got up and "stumbled on towards the wards."

The tremendous explosion knocked almost everyone in the hospital compound down. Patients were bounced off their beds onto the floor. In the orthopedic ward, where arms and legs were suspended in traction, men who had been tossed to the floor only to be left dangling by their tied-up extremities, screamed to be cut down. Other men in the ward, knowing they couldn't be moved to a safe place, began to sob.

Father Cummings and Capt. Weinstein, in the meantime, half stumbling and half running, made it safely across the center of the compound. Cummings, attracted by the screams of the orthopedic patients, entered the ward. Weinstein, from the surgery ward nearby, witnessed Cummings' first few moments with the men.

"OK, boys, OK," he said. "It's all over. Calm down. The planes have gone." Climbing to the top of a small metal table in the middle of the ward, he said, "OK, men. Let's say a prayer together." Arms outstretched, he began, "Our Father who art in Heaven." The screaming stopped. Men quieted. Some joined in. The work of the nurses and corpsmen became easier. But the raid wasn't over. In fact, it really hadn't begun. Lieutenant Juanita Redmond, on duty in one of the open-sided, tinroofed, converted motor pool sheds, known as a general medical ward, heard some one outside yell, "They're coming back!" Bearing down on the mess hall and the doctors' and nurses' quarters, the Japanese scored direct hits on both. Again the concussion knocked people down. Again patients bounced like rubber balls off their beds onto the hard cement floors.

Miraculously Father Cummings was able somehow to ride out the blasts on top of his makeshift pulpit in the middle of the orthopedic ward. Standing there, arms still outstretched, paying little attention to what was happening, he no doubt instilled the helpless patients with courage. The ward remained calm. Listening to Father Cummings made everyone realize that their fate was indeed in someone else's hands.

With sights centered on a giant red cross atop one of the buildings, the Japanese dove again, laying their last stick of bombs among the row of wards. According to Lt. Redmond, who was in one of the wards hit, the "thousand-pound bomb pulverized the . . . sheds, smashed tin roofs into flying pieces . . . and broke [wooden beds] jaggedly like paper matches."

The blast left only one end of her ward standing. A big hunk of its galvanized roofing was "blown into the jungle." Mangled bodies, many impossible to identify, lay partially buried by debris. Arms and legs had been "ripped off and flung among the rubbish."

In the untouched surgery ward, meanwhile, doctors worked frantically to save some of the "unrecognizable masses of human wreckage still pulsating with life." Of these, Capt. Weinstein recognized at least one of the faces of those littered in. It was Father Cummings, "face gray, eyes open, lips moving."

After an anxious check-up of the courageous priest, his relieved friend leaned over and said, "Not bad, Father. Not bad. Your left forearm is torn up a little, but everything else is OK."

But few things were "OK" elsewhere in the compound. Amid the screams of those newly wounded and those dying, a hospital corpsman was climbing up a tree to cut down the mangled body of one of the patients who had been blown there by the bomb blast. "Shaking and sick at [their] stomachs," nurses and attendants feverishly pulled at wreckage, under which men might still be alive. The upper limbs of the tall pine tree in front of the surgical ward would remain draped with blankets, pajamas, linen, sheets, shattered arms, legs, and tin roofing metal for days afterwards.

With the suffering and pain, came also sympathy and concern. An American soldier named Freeman, "our boy with no legs" remembered Lt. Redmond, was knocked out of his bed and buried under debris. When found, the first thing he wanted to know was if "Miss Redmond [was] alive." Not far away in the next ward, Nurse Willa Hook was knocked down by a falling bunk bed. "You all right, you all right, Miss Hook?" she heard. Dazed but okay, she raised her head and looked into the concerned face of a young Filipino soldier who, ironically, was another "boy with no legs."

A survey of the casualties showed 73 had been killed outright in the raid and 117 more injured or wounded. Of those, 16 would die later, some from shock. The cost in hospital personnel was light: No one killed; along with Father Cummings, three nurses and two medical corpsmen wounded.

Remarkable was one aspect of the damage done to the beds in the hospital. Of the 1,600 or so estimated to be available for use before the raid, only 65 were left standing afterward.

Physical damage to the hospital was extensive. One of the general medical wards was a total loss. The pharmacy had also been hit, leading to the loss of most of what was left of the drugs. A crater 40-feet across and 16-feet deep was left in the middle of the compound.

While clean-up crews worked to salvage as much as possible, patients were being transferred to Hospital No. 2. Doctors, like Weinstein, were standing over the operating tables working on a steady flow of new-wounded that would keep them there for 24 hours. Nurses and corpsmen, too, worked long into the night, as did burial details. And sleep, if it came at all, would come in a foxhole.

The San Vicente Line Collapses

"Every man for himself."

Meanwhile, back on the vital northern end of the San Vicente River line things were already happening to indicate that despite Gen. Bluemel's heroic efforts to get it ready, it could never hold. Men who were sick, starving shadows of what they once were, could give no more.

By the time Japanese planes had emptied their bellies of bombs on Hospital No. 1 that morning, other planes of its air force, paired with the devastating artillery bombardment that had preceded every enemy attack since April 3, had broken the back of the northern half of the San Vicente River line. (See Map 28.)

After acting the invader from the bay for the first four nights, some 4,000 Japanese troops of the eager Nagano Detachment were first into the fight that morning. Striking near the northwest corner of the U.S. line, by nine o'clock they had driven a wedge between the sole possessor of Sector B, the American Provisional Air Corps Regiment, and the only remaining regiment still left in position in Sector C, the Philippine Army's 32d Infantry.

Facing heavy frontal attacks, with no antitank weapons and enemy armor "running well behind [his] line with Jap infantrymen," Capt. John Coleman began withdrawing his airmen from their threatened position around 10 A.M.

The withdrawal of the Provisional Air Corps triggered a domino-effect collapse of the entire line as, not long after that, reacting solely to the impact of the air-artillery bombardment, the 32d Infantry and 51st Combat Team to the air corps' left followed suit. "Whenever a stand of any kind was [attempted]," according to 51st commander Col. Young, they were hit by "low flying airplanes [that] bombed or fired on the troops."

Next to go were the two battalions of Philippine Army 31st Infantry troops on the left of the 51st. Their flight, at the mere sight of advancing Japanese soldiers, left Trail 2 across the San Vicente wide open to enemy use.

The U.S. 31st Infantry, in position just south of the Trail 2 crossing, could do little more than last through the three-hour bombing and shelling before withdrawing back to Trail 46 around noon. Alone and in danger of being pincered by advancing Japanese forces on both sides, the last remaining Fil-American unit on the San Vicente, the 3d Battalion, 57th Infantry, gave up its untested position on the river around 12:30.

Along with the U.S. 31st, the 57th was ordered to reestablish along Trail 46 in the vicinity of Trail 2, a little over a mile to the southeast. Denied use of either Trail 2 or 44, both units, however, were forced to make their way cross-country. All semblance of organization was soon lost. The men, many sick, some wounded, and all dog tired and hungry, were no match for the difficult terrain. It became, according to Maj. Eugene Conrad of the 31st, who went through it, "every man for himself. Units became separated, the men straggled and it was extremely hard to keep any contact at all."[28] Troops of the two regiments, beginning their trek as organized units, ended it as stragglers. Because of this unfortunate break-up, they would never again fight as anything more than a remnant force.

Meanwhile, Gen. Bluemel's almost personal fight to keep his reeling command intact had continued throughout the morning. As on the day before, many a soldiers' path was blocked by the rifle-carrying general as they fled the broken San Vicente line. But, unlike the day before, many, including Americans, were now ignoring him.

Major Clarence Bess of the U.S. 31st Infantry, witnessed Bluemel that afternoon, "rifle in hand, trying to collect units streaming to the rear and form them along a delaying position." "This," said Bess, "he was unable to do."[29]

Around one o'clock, however, the exhausted, disheartened general got an unexpected lift. Rifle still in hand, "moving slowly and reluctantly southward" along Trail 2, he was somewhat surprised at the sight of a lone

American officer actually moving forward. He was again surprised and even "cheered up a bit," to find that the officer, Maj. William Chandler, had been sent north to find him. Help in the form of the 26th Cavalry, he was told, had arrived.[30]

Bluemel had not known that the 26th had been assigned to him from I Corps reserve the night before, but didn't actually arrive at their ordered destination at trails 2-10 until late that morning. By that time Gen. Parker had conceded all chances of holding on the San Vicente and ordered Bluemel to try again from the south bank of the Mamala River, the next most defensible position—a position identified on Japanese maps as the Limay Line.

To gain time for Bluemel to reestablish on the Mamala, the relatively fresh 26th was dispersed across Trail 2 and told to "execute a delaying action, with which [they] had become so familiar."

With the sound of enemy "small arms fire about a kilometer to the north," Col. Lee Vance, 26th commander, split his two squadrons, sending one, the 2d, north to 2-46, and the other, the 1st Squadron, about a mile to its rear near 2-10.

Around three o'clock that afternoon, "close on the heels of the [last of the retreating] 31st Infantry," Japanese 8th Infantry troops ran into the 2d Squadron line. The 26th, veterans at the delaying action, stopped the 8th cold. The ensuing "lively battle" was a short one, however, "as the squadron was soon outflanked on both sides" and forced to withdraw back through the 1st's position at 2-10.

There, for the first time, the cavalrymen were hit by the combination of air and artillery bombardments that had been ravaging the II Corps since April 3. Major Chandler taking note upon the 26th's arrival of how "open and . . . sparsely covered," and therefore subject to "hostile artillery fire and bombing" the II Corps appeared, was to more than realize his fears. The attacks, "more severe than anything the regiment had ever been through before," broke the Scouts' hold on the trail. The 1st Squadron, catching the "brunt of the fire . . . was forced to pass the junction on either side by short rushes in small groups." Casualties were "high, and a much reduced Troop A and [only] a portion of Troop B . . . reached the Mamala River."[31]

Later that afternoon, as Gen. Bluemel pessimistically surveyed his chances on the Mamala, some interesting things were happening at the command level on both sides. (See Map 29.)

In anticipation of meeting much stiffer opposition from the Fil-Americans on the phantom "Limay line," Gen. Homma ordered his commanders to prepare to slow down and consolidate positions before moving on. Although things had gone well for the Japanese, they were only two days ahead of schedule when they reached the north bank of the Mamala. It had been anticipated that another two weeks of hard fighting would be needed

MAP No. 29

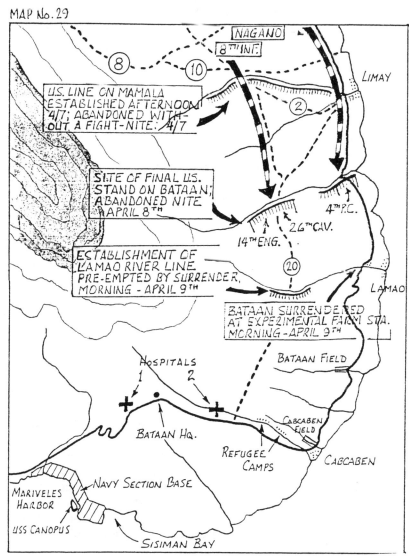

NAGANO
8ᵀᴴ INF.

⑧   ⑩

LIMAY

U.S. LINE ON MAMALA
ESTABLISHED AFTERNOON
4/7; ABANDONED WITH-
OUT A FIGHT-NITE: 4/7

②

SITE OF FINAL U.S.
STAND ON BATAAN;
ABANDONED NITE
APRIL 8ᵀᴴ

4ᵀᴴ P.C.

26ᵀᴴ CAV.

14ᵀᴴ ENG.

ESTABLISHMENT OF
LAMAO RIVER LINE
PRE-EMPTED BY SURRENDER,
MORNING - APRIL 9ᵀᴴ

⑳

LAMAO

BATAAN SURRENDERED
AT EXPERIMENTAL FARM STA.
MORNING - APRIL 9ᵀᴴ

BATAAN FIELD

HOSPITALS
1   2

CABCABEN
FIELD

BATAAN HQ.

REFUGEE
CAMPS

CABCABEN

NAVY SECTION BASE

MARIVELES
HARBOR

USS CANOPUS

SISIMAN BAY

FINAL COLLAPSE OF II CORPS - APRIL 7,8,9

to crack the Limay line, and nothing thus far had occurred to portend anything different.

In contrast, the realities of the situation had prompted Gen. King at Bataan Headquarters in Little Baguio to send his chief of staff, Gen. Arnold Funk, to see Gen. Wainwright on Corregidor.

"His face was a map of the hopelessness of the Bataan situation," reflected Wainwright upon seeing Funk. And Wainwright knew why. Earlier that day, he had ordered King to launch a counterattack east out of the I Corps against the western edge of the enemy's II Corps salient.

General Beebe, calling for Wainwright, told King that the 11th Division was to attack east in a general line with Trail 8 and link up with the II Corps troops on the Mamala River.

King, with his aide, Capt. Achille Tisdelle witnessing the conversation on another line, told Beebe that he couldn't attack. "The troops are so exhausted that they could not move a hundred yards out of their foxholes before collapsing."

"Nevertheless, those are your orders," said Beebe.

"Very well," answered King and then hung up.[32]

Ironically, if it could be accomplished, there would be a real Limay line for the Japanese to assault after all.

General Funk, however, had come not only to explain to Wainwright that it couldn't be done, but to tell him that things were deteriorating so rapidly on the peninsula, that Gen. King "might [even] have to surrender."

Unbeknownst to Funk, the Philippine commander was hamstrung. "Under no conditions" could he allow Bataan to be surrendered. On April 4 he had received orders from Gen. MacArthur, endorsed by Gen. Marshall in Washington, stating emphatically that "Under no conditions should [Bataan] be surrendered...; ... any action," he continued, "[was] preferable to capitulation." Bataan was ordered, in so many words, to fight to the death; the troops, as MacArthur more tactfully put it, were to "give a good account of themselves."

Interestingly enough, the details of MacArthur's ill-founded plan, which included a "feint" by the I Corps followed by "a sudden surprise attack ... by the II Corps," astoundingly directed that it should not be launched until all "food or ammunition failed." In other words, although the Japanese had steamrollered more than over 30 square miles of Bataan real estate in less than five days, and although 70 percent of the command had malaria and dysentery, and over 90 percent were suffering from near-acute malnutrition, things weren't quite bad enough to initiate MacArthur's plan.[33]

Wainwright paused, looked up at Funk, "a picture of weariness," and said, "go back and tell General King that he will not surrender. Tell him he will attack. Those are my orders."

Disbelievingly, tears filling his eyes, Funk reminded Wainwright of just how bad "the situation [was] over there. You know what the outcome will be."

"I do," replied the heartsick Wainwright, unable to speak more.

Crestfallen, Funk left the headquarters lateral and headed back to

Top: This flat, wide field of rice paddies is the site of the old Mariveles fighter strip. Although infrequently used by the air force on Bataan, at the urging of Gen. MacArthur engineers continued to lengthen it throughout the campaign so it could handle the promised squadrons of army bombers—which of course, never came. This was also the main marshalling point for American prisoners on April 9 and 10—the real "starting point" of the Bataan Death March. *Bottom:* Deep in thought, Gen. Douglas MacArthur contemplates the chances of his army on Bataan.

Bataan with the news. By the time he reached Little Baguio, however, something had happened that brought some relief to the situation.

It started with King receiving a call from his I Corps commander, just promoted to major general, Albert Jones. The fiery Jones, who had been informed of the counterattack in person by King's operational officer, Col. James Collier, was dumbfounded. He told Collier that the attack, scheduled for four o'clock that afternoon, couldn't possibly be mounted before 4 A.M. the next morning. Furthermore, 11th Division troops were too weak to even make the precipitious Pantingan gorge, let alone drag their artillery with them.

With Jones' report, King got both Jones and Gen. Wainwright on a 3-way telephone hook-up. After several minutes of deliberation, Wainwright gave in. The decision to attack was left to King.

The Bataan commander wasted no time in ordering Gen. Jones to stand down. "I'm taking the responsibility myself and order you not to attack," he said. In fact, it was agreed by both men to pull the still intact but highly exposed I Corps right flank back about four miles parallel with the Mamala River line. By the afternoon of the 8th, if all went well, the Bataan front would again appear as a straight line across the peninsula.

After the II Corps' withdrawal from the San Vicente to the Mamala River had been acknowledged on the afternoon of the 7th, Gen. King pulled out all stops in making an attempt to hold the Japanese there. In addition to the Scout 14th and American 803d Engineers, whom he had given to Bluemel earlier as infantry, King ordered men of the 4th Philippine Constabulary Regiment out of their beach defense positions along the bay and into the line.

Despite this, a stand on the Mamala wouldn't be realized. General Bluemel hadn't liked the chances the south bank of the river had presented him the moment he saw it. The higher, much steeper north bank would give the Japanese complete command of the line, making it virtually untenable even before the fight began. Additionally, the resulting break-up of the 57th and 31st Infantries during their strenuous cross-country trek from the San Vicente that afternoon had rendered them impotent as organized fighting units. It was much the same for the American Provisional Air Corps Regiment, as well as units of the Philippine Army's 31st Division. Another unit, the 201st Engineer Battalion, had been overrun and captured even before it reached the Mamala. Wrote its commander, Maj. Harry Fischer, whose men were "practically dead ... from fatigue, hunger and dysentery [anyway], we were so tired that the idea that the Japs finally had us didn't bother us a bit."[34]

Around nine o'clock that night, Bluemel ordered the Mamala abandoned in order to gain a few hours to rest and reorganize what was left of his army—one more time.

Two and a half miles to the south lay another river—the Alangan, whose prominent southern bank would, if nothing else, make it much more defensible at the outset than the Mamala. And so, slowly, painfully, men who had seemingly expended the last bit of energy they possessed digging in on the Mamala, arose to move south once more. (See Map 29.)

Leaving the 26th Cavalry to cover the withdrawal, men moved out across pitch dark roads and trails, many hanging on to one another to keep from becoming separated or lost, many who were sick with fever or weak with wounds dropping out along the way.

An American with the 31st suffering from dysentery had to stop five different times that night to relieve himself, each time finding it more and more difficult to catch up. Finally, after the fifth time, he gave up, sat down, and waited for the Japanese. Fortunately, he was picked up by the 26th Cavalry, who, covering the withdrawal, were the last ones out.

As Americans and Filipinos prepared to make what would be their "last stand" that night, some 300 miles to the south a tiny Waco biplane flown by Capt. Dick Fellows was preparing to take off from Santa Barbara Field at Iloilo on Panay Island. Fellows, it will be remembered, had left Mindanao earlier that night with a load of medicine for Bataan, landing at Iloilo at nine to refuel. By 11:30 he was in the air again, on his way to making what would be the last landing of an American plane on Bataan. That "last landing" would be far from routine, however.

Two and a half hours later as Fellows, in his own words, "prepared to grease the Waco onto Bataan Field," a red light from the field appeared. "In happier times a red light meant 'do not land'." Now it meant "enemy airplanes in the vicinity. With no place to hide or time to do it, I made a good, short, no-light landing. As I turned off the strip . . . I saw a ground crewman . . . jumping up and down madly and pointing at the sky. I got the message and made a record leap from the cockpit to the good earth. [Fortunately] the half-dozen bombs did no damage to my rear end nor, more importantly, to the Waco."

The anxious captain, who, with his Waco, had at last joined the Bamboo Fleet, suddenly realized after seeing "the glum faces of two of [his] friends, Jack Caldwell and Bill Kennard, [that] Bataan's end was at hand." By 4 A.M., two hours later, Fellows was in the air again heading for Iloilo. With him were Caldwell and lieutenants Bill Rowe and Gus Williams. Although ordered to continue flying in and out of Bataan each night, he would not be back. No one would be back. In less than 24 hours Bataan would be in enemy hands.[35]

Although Dick Fellows' Waco was the last plane to land on Bataan, the last American fighter to land had come in about 12 hours earlier. It was flown by Lt. Sam Grashio, who had flown a reconnaissance mission as far south as fuel would allow, scouting the waters for Japanese ships. It seems the command on Corregidor wanted to be kept up to date on the safest escape routes for anyone lucky enough to find a boat that could possibly slip the Japanese cordon around Manila Bay.

Outside of having to overcome the strong temptation to keep going south, Grashio's flight was pleasantly routine, up to the time he was preparing to land back at Cabcaben. "The tower observer radioed me that the field was under attack . . . which was precisely what I had prayed would not happen. . . . I was almost out of fuel." Just after making the decision to land at Mariveles instead, the anxious young lieutenant got the all-clear from Cabcaben, but "just as I touched down a new . . . attack began." Hitting the ground running, Grashio dashed for a nearby slit-trench. He made it, but, tripping over a tent stake and tumbling into it like a sack of potatoes wasn't quite the finish to the day's activities he would have preferred. Unlike Dick Fellows, Sam Grashio would not be lucky enough to escape Bataan's fate.[36]

Later that night, Gen. Wainwright, upon hearing of the withdrawal, penciled a message on his yellow-lined note pad for Washington, which read, in part,

> Continued heavy enemy pressure, constant bombing, strafing, and shelling of frontline units forced all elements of the right half of our line in Bataan to fall back. A new defensive position is forming on the high ground south of the Alangan River.

But the "new defensive position" referred to by Wainwright, on the morning of April 8, offered a pathetic sight. The II Corps, listing 26,000 effectives on April 3 — not including the U.S. 31st and 57th — could muster only 1,600 men on the Alangan — including the 31st and 57th — for what would be its last stand. The Americans alone, entering the fight just three nights earlier with 800 men, were down to just 120 riflemen.

Depleted as it was, the handful of Americans and Filipinos who were still standing on the new U.S. line (standing they had to remain, according to one American, "to stay awake"), by dawn of April 8, had been hurriedly dispersed up and down the Alangan.

The bulk of the II Corps withdrawal had been accomplished over two routes: the East Road and Trail 20, some two miles inland along the base of the Mariveles Mountains. For the sake of control, Gen. Parker had decided to split his command at this point, giving the eastern half to Col. John Irwin. Having no more than 1,200 men to work with, Irwin's main charge was, of course, to hold the important East Road. General Bluemel, in command of the rest of the II Corps, spread them across the remaining mile and a half of river bank from Trail 20 east. Although on paper his strength was shown at eleven battalions, in reality, it was closer to just two — 1,360 men.

As it arrived, Bluemel assigned his exhausted army to its positions on the new line. For the third time within the past 48 hours, the battered remnants of the II Corps found themselves hurried into a strange, unprepared, and unreconnoitered position.

It was little wonder that men who had not eaten or slept in nearly four days got confused or were unable to respond, for only two of the five units actually ended up in their assigned positions. They were the 14th Engineers and the 26th Cavalry—both Philippine Scouts—who were assigned to the left and right sides of Trail 20, respectively. From the right of the 26th all the way to Col. Irwin's sector, the U.S. line appeared a sieve, as unknowingly or perhaps unavoidably, the American 31st had left a 1,000-yard gap between themselves and the 26th on their left, and 500 yards between them and the 57th on their right. Worse, the American 803d Aviation Engineer Battalion, assigned as the connecting link between the 57th and Irwin's left flank, unable to make contact with troops on either side when it reached its position, had continued south.

When informed that a gap of a half-mile existed between the two forces, Bluemel phoned Gen. Parker for reinforcements. He was told that troops couldn't possibly be there before dark.

That was over 12 hours away. "That'll be too late," Bluemel said. Unless the gap was filled immediately, they could be "damned sure" the enemy would have it by then.

You'll have to hold with what you've got until then, he was told.

Bluemel slammed the phone down and angrily went out to assess his chances.

Japanese foot soldiers, in the meantime, having acted cautiously in first crossing the phantom Limay Line on the Mamala River, were still some two hours away. But the air force wasn't. Around ten o'clock, enemy reconnaissance planes discovered the Americans and Filipinos digging in along the south bank of the Alangan. An hour later, the Japanese fighters and light bombers struck. The focal point of their attack on the eastern end was the remnants of the 31st Division, which had been assigned to the left of Irwin's 1,000-yard wide sector.

Japanese planes hit the 31st area three times within the two hours, each time sending the Filipinos fleeing to the rear. But each time they were stopped, rounded up, and sent back.

In Bluemel's sector, it was a fight of a different kind. There, Japanese incendiaries had set fire to the tall, dry grass and clumps of bamboo throughout which the U.S. 31st and 57th were digging their foxholes. Exhausted men were forced to beat out fires and clear areas around their foxholes just to avoid being burned out of their positions.

Around noon, leading elements of the Nagano Detachment hit the 4th Philippine Constabulary's roadblock across the East Road. By one o'clock, enemy air and ground pressure had forced the withdrawal of units on both sides of the constabulary, leaving them, along with a small band of American Provisional Air Corps men, to go it alone. And go it alone they would—for a while.

Under the inspiring leadership of its commander, Col. Rafael Jalandoni, Col. Frank Lloyd, senior American advisor with the regiment, and Lt. Col. Vincente Torres, committing everything they had, from cooks to truck drivers to medics, the constabulary held.

Torres, commanding officer of the Constabulary Engineers, in particular, was courageous in his personal direction of the defense of the vital East Road throughout the entire afternoon.[37]

At the same time, a couple of miles to the west, another officer was busy "personally directing" his men, as well. It was Gen. Clifford Bluemel, by then nearing a "complete state of physical exhaustion, but," according to Maj. William Chandler of the 26th Cavalry, "[still] refusing to spare himself."[38] The General was supervising the preparations of the roadblock of Trail 20 for the inevitable stand to be made by the 26th and 14th Scout Engineers sometime that afternoon.

Despite the threat of eventual encirclement, both Bluemel and Irwin continued their hold on the only two roads south throughout the afternoon.

While waiting the arrival of the Japanese, an example of the futility of the situation within the crumbling II Corps occurred.

Around 2 P.M. four 75-mm.–carrying half-tracks, under the command of Lt. Col. Joseph Ganahl, arrived to help support the Trail 20 roadblock. The battery was promptly placed in position to cover the high ground north of the river. "With artillery support for the first time in the war," commented Maj. Chandler, "we began to feel that the forthcoming struggle might not be so one-sided after all."

But that "feeling" was short lived, however, as moments later "enemy tanks were reported on the East Road and Ganahl's guns were ordered [there] ... just 30 minutes before the Japs hit [our roadblock]. ... It is doubtful," lamented Chandler, "if the guns ever reached the East Road and [besides] the [enemy] tanks ... turned out to be ours anyway."

But the tanks that appeared "about 4:00 P.M." at the Trail 20 roadblock, "were decidedly not friendly." But again: futility—for although the Japanese tanks were unable to either penetrate the roadblock or back up along the narrow trail, neither did the Scouts have the necessary weapons to knock them out. Enemy infantrymen quickly arrived "by the truckload, and were soon swarming [all] over the terrain to the front."[39]

Meanwhile, another Colonel Irwin, Col. Constant Irwin of Gen. Wainwright's staff, along with his G-2, Col. Nicoll Galbraith, had come over from Corregidor to Gen. King's headquarters at Little Baguio with some special orders.

One order had originated some two months earlier, on February 3, when Gen. MacArthur told Gen. George F. Moore that if Bataan's fall ever appeared imminent, he wanted the entire Philippine Division brought to Corregidor. To Wainwright, the "imminent" time had arrived. But two of the three regiments, the 31st and Scout 57th, were too heavily engaged on the Alangan to be pulled out. That left the 45th, which, from its reserve position in the still-quiet I Corps, alone was selected. After securing transportation for his regiment, 45th commander John Doyle and his staff headed for Mariveles by car.

The second order was for the evacuation of all the nurses and a few of the doctors from hospitals 1 and 2. Transportation to the docks was arranged for that evening along with boats to take them to Corregidor.

Arrangements were also made for two more groups—the last Corregidor would take—to come across. They were the few remaining navy men at the Mariveles Section Base and the three coast artillery units "on loan" to Bataan from Corregidor since January.

In the meantime, back on the Alangan, despite the gallant and stubborn fight made throughout the afternoon by the Scouts and Constabularymen, the inevitable had occurred: the Japanese had discovered the gaps in the line. Withdrawal of the remnant U.S. 31st and subsequently the 57th from the river earlier had precluded all chances of holding. Around 6 P.M., both the 4th Philippine Constabulary and Provisional Air Corps at the East Road and the 14th Engineers and 26th Cavalry at Trail 20, with flanks turned and facing possible encirclement, began to fall back.

To constabulary colonel Vincente Torres, whose afternoon work would earn him three Purple Hearts and a Legion of Merit from the U.S. Army as well as the Distinguished Conduct Star from his own army, it was a bitter blow. Under his inspiring leadership, the Philippine Constabulary had repulsed everything the Japanese had thrown at them from the East Road. Now they had to walk away from it.[40]

Although it was never known, it is very probable that the breakup of the Alangan River line that evening was the turning point in Gen. King's decision to surrender some nine hours later. In retrospect, from that time on, events were recorded that leave little doubt of it. These events began at 7 P.M.

With news that the Alangan had been abandoned an hour earlier, the Bataan commander, completely exhausted of reserves, ordered members of the 200th and 515th Antiaircraft units to report, as infantrymen, to the ridge immediately to the south of Cabcaben air field.

About four miles up the road, the last pathetic remains of the II Corps were trying to form along a ridge too. This one overlooked the Lamao

River. But, as had happened after each successive withdrawal, there were fewer men to work with. Of the 1,000 or so who were there, it is safe to surmise that less than 20 percent were fit for duty. (See Map 29.)

To help slow the enemy down, King had his chief of staff Gen. Arnold Funk call Corregidor's Seaward Defense commander, Col. Paul Bunker, to see if he could bring any of his big guns to bear on the East Road above the Lamao River. Bunker told him that he could reach as far north as Limay. Fifteen minutes later batteries Smith and Hearn opened up. Off and on for the rest of the night, the big 12-inchers would be heard whistling northward into the teeth of the advancing Japanese army.[41]

Bataan's Last Hours

"It's an impossible situation."

Halfway between the two lines being hastily formed at Cabcaben and the Lamao River, a beat-up Ford command car skidded to a stop near the edge of Bataan Field. Out of it stepped Capt. Ed Dyess, who, since Gen. George's departure in mid–March, had been in command of the squadron at the field.

A half hour earlier, while sitting down to what would be his last meal on Bataan, Dyess received a phone call alerting him that the Japanese had broken through at the Alangan River and were now less than two miles away. With what was left of his air force in jeopardy should that be true, he "grabbed Lt. Jack Donaldson . . . and told him to take off in old Kibosh [Dyess' old Kittyhawk] . . . and to bomb and strafe the approaching Japs."

More importantly, he told him if this is a false alarm, "come in and land. [But] if the Japs are as close as they tell us, rock your wings and keep going for Cebu."

Fifteen minutes later Donaldson was back, "bomb racks empty. . . . He rocked the plane like hell and kept going."

Dyess relayed the information over the phone to air force headquarters at Little Baguio, where he was told to begin evacuating the remaining pilots in the planes that were left.

Meanwhile, in the event the Japanese broke through, Dyess got the two P-35s out onto the field "with their motors running." First out was Capt. "Ozzie" Lund. Lieutenant Randy Keator, who had happily stuffed himself into the baggage compartment, went with him.

Next Dyess called captains Ben Brown and Hank Thorne at the headquarters shack above Bataan Field and told them that a P-35 was waiting for them. "They both refused to go," wrote Dyess, "but as the field commanding officer, I sent them off."

With Brown and another pilot, Lt. Larry McDaniel, crammed in the baggage compartment, along with a half dozen 30 pound fragmentaries to "drop on the advancing Japs," Thorne somehow cleared the field.

Word came down that Capt. Joe Moore, in the meantime, had taken off from Cabcaben in the last P-40. That left only one plane, the old Grumman Duck. But things didn't look too good for it to even leave the ground.

Ironically, it was Moore who had last flown the old "Candy Clipper" on April 6. Returning from Cebu with a load of medical supplies, the Duck blew a cylinder about 80 miles south of Bataan. Moore, a skilled veteran pilot, was able to nurse it back to Cabcaben for what he thought would be the last time. But it wasn't the "last time."

At four o'clock that afternoon, Col. Carlos Romulo was ordered to report to Gen. Wainwright. The little Filipino, known for his Voice of Freedom broadcasts, still made three times each day from Corregidor, entered the hot, stuffy headquarters lateral. Wainwright, sitting behind his desk at the far end of the tunnel, stood up when he saw Romulo.

Knowing of the price—dead or alive—the Japanese had placed on Romulo's head for what they called the "propaganda of lies being conducted" as the voice of freedom, Wainwright said that he was ordering him out of Corregidor.

"What do you mean, Sir?"

"Bataan is hopeless," he said, handing Romulo his orders.

"At seven tonight, take the little launch to Bataan. Go to the Bataan air field. From there you will take off for Mindanao."

Formalities over, Wainwright stepped around his desk and grabbed Romulo's hand. "God bless you, my boy," he said, shaking it warmly. "Tell President Quezon and General MacArthur I will do my best to the end."

Three hours later, "pockets . . . bursting" with letters from friends to be mailed home, Romulo climbed into a waiting jeep outside Malinta Tunnel for the short ride to the dock. As they drove down the hill, looking at Bataan, he wondered "what was taking place across that three-mile stretch of water."

At that very moment on the other side of that "three-mile stretch of water" a few select people had been having the same thoughts about Corregidor. They were the nurses and three doctors from hospitals 1 and 2, who had just been notified that boats were waiting to take them there.

"Be ready to leave in 15 minutes," someone yelled. "Take only what you can carry."

"What's happening," wondered Lt. Juanita Redmond. Why were we being ordered out?

All the doctors and corpsmen had come to see them off. It hurt to say goodbye. "Farewells were hasty and tearful," remembered Capt. Alfred Weinstein, "kisses sweet and salty."

Captain (later Col.) Carlos P. Romulo, the "Voice of Freedom" throughout the battle, and author of the Pulitzer Prize–winning _I Saw the Fall of the Philippines_.

As the two _Pambusco_ buses carrying the nurses from Hospital No. 1 turned right out of the compound for Mariveles, Capt. Nelson, in the lead bus, turned and said, "Girls, there are going to be a lot of trucks, soldiers, and civilians on the road. There'll be a great deal of confusion." In a voice turned somber, he said, "Bataan has fallen!"

"It shocked us into silence," Lt. Redmond recalled. Slowly, however, all began to realize "how [they] had been hiding from the thought [of it], refusing to believe it would happen." but now that it had come, few were surprised.

What about the girls at Hospital No. 2, someone asked.

"They've been ordered out, also," Nelson answered.

Yes, they had. But since No. 2 was closer to the dock at Cabcaben, they had been directed there instead.

With the exception of the handful of Provisional Air Corps troops covering the bridges between Lamao and Cabcaben on East Road, and Troop G of the 26th Cavalry rear-guarding Trail 20, by 9:30 P.M., April 8, 1942, for all practical purposes, the Fil-American army on Bataan had fired its last shot.

It was 9:30 when Gen. Bluemel reported to II Corps headquarters that without some help getting his men organized behind the Lamao River, trying to halt the Japanese there "was not possible." II Corps' answer was that they couldn't spare anyone for that purpose.

"We can't hold ... here," Bluemel retorted. "It's an impossible situation."[43]

Interestingly, most of those in the rear area, by then, didn't have to be told about the tactical end of it to know that it was an "impossible situation." Signs of the collapse had grown steadily throughout the day.

Lieutenant Edgar Whitcomb at Cabcaben Field, as the day wore on, witnessed "more and more men ... straggling through [his] camp." All had the same story. "Each had been separated from his unit during the attack in which most of his outfit had been wiped out."

"Oh, God, it was terrible," said one man. "They bombed and shelled us all day along the road."[43]

Colonel Richard Mallonee, on his way to contact Col. John Erwin on the Alangan that afternoon, commented when he reached the East Road that "bombers were working the road again and it was a shambles, choked with refugees, military and civilian. Hardly a hundred yards was without its ditches lined with dead. One bomb hit near a running soldier, and when the smoke settled only the torso was in the center of the road."[44]

Just before dark, it took Ed Dyess almost an hour to drive two and a half miles from his headquarters to Bataan Field, "the road was [so] choked with Filipino troops in wild retreat!"

Around 8:30, the launch carrying Col. Carlos Romulo to Bataan, after a harrowing trip across the North Channel, pulled up and unloaded its passengers at what was left of the Cabcaben dock. A few minutes later, standing on the edge of the East Road waiting for his transportation to Bataan Field, Romulo remembered thinking it funny that all the traffic was coming his way. He "didn't dream it was retreat."

Moments later, his mind was jolted into reality however when the driver of the car commandeered for his ride north told him that it would be impossible to get through to the airfield. Nevertheless, orders from Wainwright directed them to try.

The old Quarantine Dock at Mariveles, as it looks today. The nurses from both Hospital No. 1 and No. 2 left for Corregidor from this dock April 9. The boat carrying the women from Hospital No. 2 was the last one to reach Corregidor from Bataan.

Less than a hundred yards up the semblance of what once was a paved two-lane highway, Romulo realized what his driver was talking about. "Such a melange of vehicles swarming together was surely never seen before in the world," he wrote later. "Truck loads of soldiers jammed together so that they could not slump with the weariness that was written on their haggard faces . . . ambulances crammed with men, and command cars filled with haggard-faced officers . . . all . . . headed for the bay, for the shoreline that was the end of the world."

For a few lucky ones, the shoreline wasn't quite "the end of the world," however. For the nurses and doctors from Hospital No. 1, who had arrived at the Quarantine Dock in Mariveles around 9:30, it would be a two and a half hour wait for the boat to Corregidor, a wait that few would forget, but all would live through.

Bombers "came over while we waited," remembered Lt. Redmond, "but as we didn't know where [the foxholes] were, we stayed on the dock."

Not far away on the other side of the bay, the navy had begun destroying its Section Base facilities. The old Dewey Drydock, which for so long had fooled the Japanese Air Force into believing it was sunk while actually being used to full capacity at night, met its end with the detonation of six well-placed 155-mm. shells inside the hull.

The "blue and red flares, shrapnel, tracers, gasoline exploding," remembered one of the nurses, "[were] like a hundred Fourth of Julys and Christmases all at once. But we were too frightened to be impressed."

Despite his own orders to destroy Bataan's naval facilities earlier that day to avoid their capture, despite nurses' evacuation for the same reason, and despite sending the 45th Infantry to Corregidor and telling Carlos Romulo that Bataan was "hopeless" before ordering him out, by 11:30 P.M., Gen. Wainwright had still not issued the order for Bataan's surrender.

On his desk, staring him in the face, were the April 4 orders from Gen. MacArthur not to surrender, but to attack.

The timing of MacArthur's counterattack plan, which, as mentioned earlier, was not to be launched until either food or ammunition ran out, was perfect. Bataan's food supply, with the issuance of the last 45,000 C-rations earlier, was now exhausted.

At 11:30, Wainwright had the Corregidor switchboard connect him with Gen. King on Bataan. Doubtlessly knowing that this exercise in futility couldn't be carried out, he told King that the pressure had to be taken off the II Corps before it was too late.

King told him that it was already too late.

Nevertheless, Wainwright ordered him to reinforce the "suppressed II Corps" with units of Gen. Jones' I Corps, and then attack "northward toward Olongapo" with the rest.

Stunned yet still answerable should he fail to notify I Corps of the plan, King called Gen. Jones.

Jones, as outspoken as Gen. Bluemel, particularily concerning "asinine" command decisions, told King that MacArthur's plan was "ridiculous." His men had just completed a tortuous four-mile withdrawal to the banks of the Binuangan River in compliance with his order of the night before. They had nothing left.

King did not press it. He would not order an attack that was doomed to failure even before it started. There would be no counterattack by the I Corps.

King looked at his watch. Both hands were at 12. It was Thursday, April 9, 1942—the beginning of what would be recorded as Bataan's last day.

The weary Bataan commander called Gen. Funk and his operations officer, Col. James Collier, in for a conference. Together they reflected on the meeting they had had two days before with frontline commanders. When questioned about what percent of their units were still considered "effectives" (defined by King as a soldier who could walk 100 yards without staggering and still have the strength to shoot), they unanimously agreed it was no more than 15 percent. Together they retraced the old lines on the map of Bataan; they looked like the rungs of a ladder leading to the firepits of hell itself: the San Vicente, the Mamala, the Alangan, the Lamao, and, before long, the Cabcaben. Was there a chance? Could the Japanese be stopped before reaching the high ground above Mariveles?

The entrance to the abandoned U.S. Navy Section Base at Mariveles as it looked after the surrender on April 9 or 10.

They looked at the words "Provisional Coast Artillery Brigade" (200th and 515th Antiaircraft Battalions), penciled-in as the defense of the Cabcaben line. The Japanese would be in Mariveles no matter what happened by tomorrow night.

"II Corps as a tactical unit no longer existed," reflected Collier. Just behind Cabcaben were the refugee camps and the hospitals with over 13,000 defenseless patients already "within range of enemy light artillery"—no place to fight a battle.

"I've decided to surrender," Gen. King said. But, knowing the position Wainwright was in with MacArthur's "no surrender" orders, he decided to put his own two stars on the line and not notify the commanding general until he had already contacted the Japanese. "I don't want [Wainwright] to be compelled to assume any part of the responsibility," he said.

Like the notification of the death of someone who had been terminally ill for some time, to everyone in the room, it was no surprise. Yet, remembered Col. Collier, it hit us "with an awful bang and a terrible wallop." By the time Gen. King left for his trailer to begin outlining his surrender terms for the Japanese, "there wasn't a dry eye present."

Slowly the agonizing wheels of capitulation began to turn. Word went out at 2 A.M. to the large engineer and ordnance depots above Little Baguio to destroy everything. Motor pools were told to destroy all vehicles. Artillery and antiaircraft guns were ordered spiked. Of the remaining 50,000 gallons of precious gasoline 40,000 were ordered dumped. The quartermaster was ordered to hold back 10,000 gallons to be used, hopefully, to transport the defeated garrison to POW camps. Unit commanders were told to bury their records and then have their troops report to Mariveles at dawn to surrender.

For many, however, official word that Bataan was through wouldn't be necessary. A handful of such people had gathered in a small cave at the end of Cabcaben Field while frantic preparations to get the old navy Duck in flying condition went on. Under the supervision of Lt. Leo Boelens, crews had been working for two days at installing a cylinder reclaimed from another Duck that had been resting on the bottom of Mariveles Harbor since sinking on December 10.

Captain Joe Moore had just taken off in the last remaining P-40 when Ed Dyess drove up to see how things were coming. The three pilots who were assigned to go if they could get it running, lieutenants Stewart Robb, "Shorty" Crosland, and Bill Coleman, came out of the tunnel to meet him. Dyess told them to keep their eyes open for another passenger, a Col. Romulo "sent over by General Wainwright from Corregidor."

Boelens and Capt. Roland Barnick, the pilot, working nearby on the engine, overheard Dyess. They looked at each other. That'll make six; four more than she had seats for, they thought.

"What about you, Captain," one of the pilots asked Dyess. "When are you going to leave?"

"[I still] have some men to take care of," he said, avoiding the question. Unbeknownst to the three men as they watched him drive off into the horrible night, one of them was there because Dyess, although ordered out, had refused to leave.

Not too far away, the sixth man, Col. Carlos Romulo, was sure he had missed his plane. Around ten o'clock he had seen Hank Thorne's P-35 head out from Bataan Field and turn toward Corregidor. "There goes my plane, [he] thought sickly."

For over two hours, he and his driver had been literally fighting their way against a "swarming, out going tide" of vehicles and men fleeing south. At least half a dozen times he had jumped out and pleaded for help. None came.

He remembered seeing boys "of seventeen or eighteen . . . dragging their guns and stumbling in the dust. Some walked with spraddled knees, like old men, falling and rising and staggering on."

They reached Bataan Field only to find it abandoned, but fortunately they ran into an officer with orders for Romulo from Corregidor.

"Word had been left . . . that I was to go to Cabcaben and ask for Lt. Barnick," said Romulo. There was a plane there.

Meanwhile, work on the old Grumman Duck at Cabcaben had been progressing. They were just ready to test the motor, when someone yelled, "Lieutenant Barnick?"

"Is that Colonel Romulo?"

"Yes!" exclaimed the relieved little Filipino in a voice that "could have been heard in Tokyo."

But after seeing the old Duck, which he thought "looked like something reclaimed from a city dump," the "sickly" feeling that he had had earlier when he thought he had missed his flight returned.

"Let's test the motor," said Barnick.

Romulo "crossed [his] fingers and prayed while the boys spun the propeller." Miracle of miracles, it started. At last, they were off. Or were they?

Barnick told them to turn off the engine and then calmly stretched out on the field with his head on his musette bag. "Had to wait for the moon," he said. Finally, at "eighteen minutes past one," remembered Romulo, Barnick sat up, looked around and said, "let's go!"

The six men crawled into the old plane. It was pitch-black inside. Aside from the two in the cockpit, there were no seats.

Barnick started the engine. It kicked right over and then began to vibrate. "Quit shaking the plane," Barnick shouted to the four men huddled on the floor in the back.

They weren't. But something sure was—at that very moment Bataan was being rocked by a heavy earthquake.

"If this thing flies, I'm a genius," Romulo remembered Barnick saying earlier. Little did he or the other passengers know that part of what he meant was due to the fact that he had never flown a Duck before.

Barnick related later in a letter to Romulo his version of the next few seconds. In words here rearranged somewhat, he wrote,

> There was no light in the cockpit, so I was forced to use a flashlight. On take off, I discovered that the propeller would not change pitch—the equivalent of starting an automobile in high gear. [I] succeeded in taking off Cabcaben Field by bouncing the plane [and then] retracting the landing gear . . . as we cleared the end of the field, we settled to within a few inches of the water. Our load was too great, [but I] managed to maintain altitude by running the motor [wide-open].

Unable to gain any more altitude, Barnick handed a hastily scribbled note back to the passengers: *Throw out all extra weight! Hurry!* it said.

Everything went, baggage, tin helmets, parachutes, radio equipment, sidearms, even a chunk of the floorboard. That "seemed to give the old Duck a new lease on life," said Romulo. "She roared upward—50 feet."

The plane, with Barnick "swearing so loudly that we could hear down below," continued to climb and was heading for Iloilo, Panay, at 125 feet when it passed by Corregidor over the South Channel.

The earthquake that had rocked the old Duck before it took off, and which was severe enough to make the skipper of an approaching American submarine think he had run aground, was only slightly remembered or felt on Bataan. Amid exploding 12-inch shells from Corregidor batteries Hearn and Smith on the Japanese advancing along the East Road, and amid the explosions of 500-pound bombs being set off by army air corps ordnance at various bomb dumps, few could differentiate between the vibrations.

At 2 A.M., however, two back-to-back explosions occurred that everyone felt—Bataan's death knell.

Behind Little Baguio on a hill known as Cemetery Ridge, men had been preparing for over an hour to blow-up Bataan's main Engineer Supply Depot.

The oil had already been drained "from what cars and trucks remained in our motor pool," wrote Corp. Robert Levering of the engineers. "Then we set their engines racing—wide open."

At 2 A.M., "our cache of 500,000 pounds of dynamite was touched off," Levering continued. "Seemed as if the old volcano [Mt. Bataan] had come back to life." Seconds later, with dirt and debris "still falling around us ... magazines of the [nearby] 75th Ordnance Depot let go. The sky boomed with explosions of heavy shells and all kinds of small arms ammunition."[45]

About the same distance away on the other side of the ordnance depot, Sgt. Jerome Leek heard the explosions but misinterpreted their meaning.

A few days earlier, Leek, a coast artillerymen on Corregidor, volunteered for duty on Bataan.

"How come you are going to Bataan?" asked the skipper of the launch taking him across. "Get shanghaied?"

"No, I asked for it," said Leek.

"Asked for it? My God, wasn't it bad enough on Corregidor?"

Leek had taken an assignment driving a ration truck back and forth to the front and was less than a mile away on the Mariveles Road on the morning of April 9, when the two explosions, so close together as to be interpreted as one, occurred.

"Must have been the largest ammunition dump in the Philippine Islands," he thought.

He continued on another quarter mile and then pulled off at a familiar supply dump. In a nearby tent, he aroused a sleepy second lieutenant and said, "Sir, our big ammunition dump just went up. It looks like the end ... if we don't try to save it."

"Save it hell," answered the young officer. "Our own engineers blew it up. Bataan has fallen, you know."

"Bataan has fallen?"

"Yeh, Bataan has fallen. You are on your own."[46]

Not too far away, several others had the feeling that they were on their own, too. They were the nurses from Hospital No. 2 who earlier had headed toward the dock at Cabcaben where the boat scheduled to take them to Corregidor was waiting. But the trip to the dock, against the endless stream of vehicles and men, had made them late. The boat, if there ever had been one, was gone.

Carlos Romulo saw them on the Cabcaben cut-off road, "fleeing toward the waterline, where there might or might not be a boat to carry them to Corregidor." It was a sight he would never forget.

But there was still a chance . . . if they could reach Mariveles.

By the time they got back onto the road, it didn't seem to make any difference which way they were going. Traffic would crawl along, then stop, move a few feet, and then stop again. They had driven over and through wreckage, bypassed shell holes, and even had to wait for a body to be removed from in front of them before continuing. From the back end of their foul smelling garbage trucks, they were living Bataan's death.

Around 1:30 A.M., they slowly drove past the road leading to their hospital, from which they had started some five hours before.

A half hour later, not far from the turn off to Hospital No. 1, they were held up. "They're going to blow up the ammunition dumps," someone said.

A few hundred yards away, in his foxhole inside the Hospital No. 1 compound, Dr. Alfred Weinstein was waiting for the same blast. "At the appointed hour," he wrote, "the skyline behind the hospital was illuminated with an eye-searing glare . . . the earth trembled as if shaken by a giant fist . . . [and] the air was filled with the roar of released energy. Blast followed blast," he said, "until it seemed as if . . . my already ruptured eardrums would be ripped from their moorings."

By 3 A.M., for the most part, it was over, and Weinstein climbed out of his foxhole and went back to work "putting the camp to rest."

Back on the Mariveles Road traffic again began to move. Along with everyone else, two strangers who had hitched a ride on one of the nurses' trucks back at the Cabcaben turn-off were happy to be moving again.

The two, air corps officers from Cabcaben, had received orders to report to Kilometer Post 184, north of Mariveles. Had they known that by the time they would reach their destination they would be directed to surrender to the Japanese, they wouldn't have been quite so pleased to be getting under way.

But maybe it wouldn't be such a surprise after all, considering what they had witnessed earlier near Cabcabcn. It happened when one of the officers, Lt. Edgar Whitcomb, leading a group of 20 men over a jungle trail, reached the East Road. "There we were greeted by a sight that made our blood turn cold," he remembered. "The entire road was packed with vehicles of all kinds, each one overflowing with combat-weary soldiers. Both sides of the road were choked with soldiers unable to find a place on a vehicle. I was so surprised and stunned by the sight," he said, "that I was unable to speak for a few moments."[47]

As the long column of vehicles resumed its slow crawl toward Mariveles, the wheels of a mission important to the lives of thousands on Bataan were also turning.

Following his decision earlier that morning to surrender Bataan, Gen. King's primary task was to somehow communicate with the Japanese beforehand as to those desires. Col. Everett Williams and Maj. Marshall Hurt, two bachelors on the General's staff, were selected to make the initial contact at dawn.

King handed Williams an official two-page "memo of instruction," to be used as a guideline in arranging a formal surrender meeting with Gen. Homma later that morning.

To cover the possibility that the Japanese should decline his offer, the memo instructed Williams to "ask him terms under which he [would] accept the surrender of the Luzon Force on Bataan."

Listed also were several points of "consideration" toward which King wanted Japanese attention drawn, points such as the dangerous proximity of the two hospitals to the current battle zone; to the fact that, because of the unusually poor physical condition of his command, it would take quite some time to organize and deliver them as prisoners of war; and that he had already "issued orders" to have them delivered "by motor transportation ... to places as might be directed." Lastly, hoping for their immediate release, he directed attention to "the vast number of civilians present ... in Bataan," who had remained "in no way connected with the American or Philippine Forces."

It was decided that in order for Hurt and Williams to reach the Japanese lines by dawn, they should leave Little Baguio around 3:30 A.M.. At 2 A.M. the two men were sitting in one of the headquarters shacks, when the II Corps ammunition and dynamite stores went up less than 800 yards away.

Hurt had just finished addressing what he feared might be his last letter home and was talking on the telephone, when "a terrific explosion occurred ... followed by a second." He started for the door. Just then another blast rocked the "whole earth," and the shack began to break up. This was followed by a fourth explosion. "The window [fell] on my head," he dimly remembered, "and lumber [fell] all around," as did rocks, tree stumps, and chunks of concrete.

Shaken and dazed, Hurt heard Williams calling. "I [rushed] back. [He was] OK. Just wanted me to turn off the lights."

Williams helped his benumbed comrade up the hill to the safety of Gen. King's dugout. Although wobbly, Hurt was still "determined to go."[48]

Major Achille Tisdelle, who lived through the experience with Hurt and Williams, recorded the two explosions in his diary as the most terrific he "had ever heard. . . . [I]n the morning, our overhead cover [tops of the trees] was gone and there were empty shell cases all over the camp. It is miraculous we came through this."[49]

A few minutes after the explosions, the light from Gen. Wainwright's extension began flashing on the Corregidor switchboard. It was Gen. Lewis Beebe, his chief of staff, asking to be patched through to Gen. King's headquarters. Wainwright, who had not heard from King since ordering him to counterattack at 11:30, was wondering how it was progressing.

The explosions, however, had momentarily disarranged the telephone communication system on the peninsula, and instead of getting King, Gen. Bluemel answered. He was still up on the Lamao River trying to organize the pitiful handful of men from his disintegrated II Corps into some kind of a fighting force. It was impossible.

Bluemel told Beebe that very thing. Beebe, relaying instructions from Wainwright, told him that he was on his own, that the commanding general would approve "whatever action he deemed best."

After hanging up, Beebe tried to ring through to Gen. King's headquarters again. "That line is still out, Sir," he was told by the operator. They had to wait.

While Beebe and Wainwright waited, three miles away near the eastern edge of Mariveles Harbor the sentimental pride of the Bataan Navy, the USS *Canopus,* had started on her last voyage. It would be a short one from its mooring next to the rock quarry to the deep water of Lilimbon Cove—less than 400 yards. There she would be scuttled. But even her death would be a purposeful one. Lilimbon would remain forever blocked to enemy use.[50]

As desperate as things were on Bataan at that moment, few of the officers, men, nurses, and PT boat skippers who had partaken of her generous supply of long-forgotten favors during the battle would not have paused in salute to her memory.

Back at Corregidor, anxious as ever about news of his counterattack, yet still unable to reach Bataan Headquarters, Gen. Wainwright rung Gen. Jones at I Corps. General Beebe was still talking for the commanding general, whose slight deafness made it almost impossible for him to hear anything because of the existing poor conditions.

Beebe asked how Jones' plans for the attack were progressing.

Orders for the attack had not yet been given, Jones answered.

Beebe told him to "stand by," that he would probably be receiving them any minute from Gen. King, and then hung up.

The fact that Jones still had received no orders at that late hour drew no reaction from Wainwright, strongly indicating that the Philippine commander hadn't expected it anyway.

Further evidence along those lines surfaced a few minutes later, at 3 A.M., when Gen. King, after hearing of Beebe's conversation with Jones, phoned across to Wainwright.

Beebe picked up the receiver.

"I want a definite answer as to whether or not General Jones will be left in my command regardless of what action I may take," King said.

Beebe relayed the question to Wainwright. Wainwright nodded his head, yes. "General Wainwright says you're still in command of all forces on Bataan," Beebe answered.

The subject of why King, after three and a half hours, still hadn't informed his commanders of the counterattack wasn't even broached by Wainwright. Nor did King mention that in less than 30 minutes he would be sending two men forward with white flags to implement the surrender he had ordered three hours earlier.

About that same time, not too far away from Gen. Wainwright's headquarters in Malinta, a small boat was being tied up to the island's North Dock. Minutes later, a group of weary army nurses and three doctors from Hospital No. 1 were seen trudging their way up the dock toward waiting trucks.

They had left the Quarantine Dock in Mariveles at midnight for what was usually a 45-minute trip across. Three nightmarish hours later, they thankfully stepped ashore on Corregidor.

Over at Little Baguio on Bataan, explosions were still being felt and debris was still falling as engineers and ordnance crews continued to destroy their depots.

In a blacked-out dugout at nearby Bataan Headquarters, a man looked at the green, luminous dial of his watch. It was 3:15, time to get started for the front.

Colonel Williams and Maj. Hurt, the officers selected to carry word to the Japanese of Gen. King's desire to surrender, left the dugout and headed for the Mariveles Road.

After a quick stop at Hurt's tent for a piece of bed sheet that could be used for a white flag, they "commandeer[ed] a reconnaissance car and a motorcycle escort and [were] off."

Latest word put the front north of Lamao at somewhere around Kilometer Post 152, a little more than 15 miles away.

The two men started but, of course, found the traffic impossible. They decided to abandon the car. Hurt remembered that Williams looked at his watch, then grabbed the white flag, "[climbed] on the rear of a passing motorcycle and [took] off."

Left to follow the best he could, Hurt began working his way through the "maze of traffic; worming through crouching, demoralized, beaten foot soldiers." It was 4 A.M. He remembered what was written on the copy of instructions in his pocket: "You will proceed . . . in time to arrive at our front lines by daylight." Bataan was down to its last two hours.[51]

Back at Mariveles, an explosion on the eastern shoreline momentarily illuminated the side of the old *Canopus*, slowly settling into her watery, 12-fathom grave. The first of the four navy tunnels were being dynamited closed.

Forty minutes later, all tasks completed, a small fleet of motor boats filled with the last of the Naval Section Base personnel shoved off for Corregidor. As the last three boats, loaded mostly with exhausted *Canopus* crewmen, cast off, a tremendous explosion erupted from the northernmost of the four tunnels.

Commander Earl Sackett, skipper on the *Canopus*, witnessed what followed from one of the boats:

> The whole hillside seemed to erupt in an orange burst of flame, hurling huge boulders half a mile out into the bay. . . . Evidently, gasoline drums stored in the tunnel had broken open when the entrance was dynamited, and fumes in the corked-up passage had built up a gigantic explosive charge. Our three boats were squarely in the path of that deluge of destruction. Two of them were struck with massive boulders, one of them sinking instantly under an impact which sheared off the whole stern, leaving the three occupants struggling in the water. The other damaged boat did not sink, but boulders crashing down through its canopy killed an officer and three men.

Nine men were hurt, some seriously, by the "rain of heavy rocks," but two of the three boats were still able to make it across to Corregidor.[52]

By 5 A.M., Major Hurt, after "saying a few prayers . . . bumming a few rides, and [doing] a lot of walking," was within about three-quarters of a mile of Lamao. He had been virtually all alone on the road for the last half hour. There, in the faint, early morning light, sitting in a jeep parked next to Kilometer Post 155, Hurt recognized Col. Williams and his driver.

Williams had discovered that the front, or more accurately, the covering force of the II Corps, was less than a mile and a half to the north, around Kilometer Post 151.8.

The night Bataan fell, the entrance to this old navy tunnel at Mariveles was dynamited closed. A few minutes later, a second explosion occurred from deep within the tunnel, blowing the boulders and rocks blocking the entrance out into the bay with such force that they sunk one of three boats loaded with *Canopus* crewmen who had just shoved off for Corregidor. Four men were killed and nine wounded from the explosion. The tunnel is still there.

Hurt climbed into the back of the jeep and the three men started forward. It was still quiet, "except for the far away explosions of the dumps and the chattering teeth of our driver," he wrote.

After crossing the bridge over the Lamao River, they ran into Lt. Col. Joe Ganahl, who, with a few tanks and half-tracks and a handful of troops, represented the entire covering shell. Colonel Williams told Ganahl that it was all over, that he and Maj. Hurt had come forward to meet the Japanese and surrender Bataan.

Leaving the three men alone to wait for the enemy, at 5:30 A.M. Ganahl turned his tiny armored column around and disappeared into the night.

An hour later they were still sitting. There were still no Japanese, and it was now broad daylight. Interestingly, Bataan had folded up so fast within the last six hours, that the Japanese army had found it tough to keep up.

Since "nothing has happened, we start slowly forward to make contact," said Hurt. "After a mile, everything is [still] deserted and quiet. We see and hear nothing."

They crossed the bridge over the Alangan River and started up the hill on the other side. Unlike the Lamao River they had just passed, judging from the wreckage and debris, it appeared that somebody had put up a pretty good fight at the Alangan. Just then, a large group of Japanese soldiers came onto the road. "We stop the car, raise our hands and wave the white flag," wrote Hurt later. Yelling, they "rush at us with their bayonets flashing. Is the end here?"[53]

Ironically, less than an hour earlier, a "yell" of a different kind was heard over the same question.

At 6 A.M., when Gen. King was confident Hurt and Williams either had or would soon be in contact with the Japanese, he phoned Gen. Wainwright to tell him what he had done.

Lt. Col. Jesse Traywick, who took the call, rushed to the commanding general with the news.

Wainwright was shocked. "Go back and tell him not to do it," he yelled.

The night duty officer hurried back to the phone. It was too late, he was told. Contact with the Japanese had already been made.

"I had my orders from MacArthur not to surrender on Bataan," wrote Wainwright later, "and therefore . . . could not authorize King to do it." But he was quick to show that he had "no criticism" of the Bataan commander for doing what he had done. "It was a decision which required great courage and mental fortitude."

Wainwright's next thought was how to tell Gen. MacArthur. Sitting at his desk contemplating just how he would explain it, he began writing:

> At six o'clock this morning, General King, commanding Luzon Force, without my knowledge or approval, sent a flag of truce to the Japanese commander. The minute I heard of it I disapproved of his action and directed that there would be no surrender. I was informed too late to make any change, that the action had already been taken. Enemy on east had enveloped both flanks . . . of what was left of the II Corps, and was firing . . . into the hospital area, which undoubtedly prompted King's action. . . . I had ordered the I Corps to attack north . . . but the attack did not get off. Physical exhaustion and sickness due to a long period of insufficient food is the real cause of the terrible disaster. When I get word terms have been arranged, I will advise.

Over on Bataan, meanwhile, the men who would carry that word were, at about that moment, not at all sure they would live.

Colonel Williams and Maj. Hurt, were being rushed by a platoon of

A group of Philippine Army troops surrendering to the Japanese on April 9, 1942.

bayonet-wielding Japanese soldiers. A minute or so later, a noncommissioned officer appeared and ordered the soldiers, who had already begun ransacking the jeep, to put everything back. "We heave a sigh of relief," wrote Hurt.

Williams pulled out Gen. King's surrender instructions and showed them to the sergeant. Seeming to understand, he climbed into the jeep and motioned them to drive on. They soon passed more enemy soldiers who "stare at us and do a lot of talking." Before long, they were turned over to an officer who, in turn, "relayed us further to the rear."

"We pass several [exhausted] 31st Infantry soldiers being herded along by the Japs," wrote Hurt. "A rope is tied around the wrist of each, but they ... tell us they are not being treated badly."

At Kilometer Post 146 they stopped and got out of the jeep. Seated at a small rickety table nearby was Maj. Kameichiro Nagano, whose detachment had been assigned to capture the East Road. Hurt and Col. Williams, carrying their white flag, entered the clearing and were introduced to Nagano. No one saluted. Nagano did not stand up.

The interpreter read Williams' surrender instructions. The two Americans answered several questions which, among other things, included challenges to their authority to surrender Corregidor. Nagano, at Williams' suggestion, agreed to set up a meeting with Gen. King at the Bataan Agricultural Experimental Farm Station back near the Lamao River bridge.

Colonel Williams was left behind while Hurt, escorted by four Japanese tanks as far as the Lamao River, was sent on alone to bring back Gen. King.

"How long?" his escort asks.

"Two to four hours depending on traffic," he told him.

"Speedo," the Japanese said as Hurt pulled away," "Speedo!"[54]

CHAPTER SIX

The Surrender

"Bataan has fallen."

As Maj. Hurt began his difficult journey to pick up Gen. King at Little Baguio, back at Mariveles dawn had offered no more than an extension of the dreadful night before.

The line of garbage trucks carrying the nurses from Hospital No. 2 had filed slowly through the smashed remains of what was once the pleasant barrio of Mariveles. The only thing left standing, remembered one nurse, was the statue of a saintly lady pointing off toward the rising sun.

The trucks passed the turn-off leading up the West Road, rumbling on toward the old Quarantine Station and the docks in front. In the last truck, the two army air corps officers who had hitched a ride from Cabcaben earlier that morning, jumped off.

"Better come along to Corregidor with us," one of the nurses shouted.

"Sure like to," answered one, "but we have to go up to meet the rest of our outfit north of Mariveles."

"Good luck to you, then."[1]

As the trucks continued on through the maze of abandoned vehicles toward the waterfront, one of the nurses stood up to take a look. "There's no boat!" she cried. "No boat!"

They'd been bouncing about on the back end of stinking garbage trucks for close to ten hours; had missed one boat at Cabcaben; been held up for over an hour by the explosions of the engineer and ordnance depots; stalled; been pushed by a half-track; had one truck break down, forcing its occupants to make it on foot, and now, no boat.

Exhaustion, by then, had anesthetized the fears and anger of most. Seemingly no longer caring about the boat, within a few minutes, practically all were sound asleep in roadside ditches or shelters near the dock.[2]

Like the nurses, many men had hopes of making Corregidor when they reached Mariveles that morning. Few did.

"The most unforgettable sight of all," remembered Lt. Cmdr. John

"The statue of a saintly lady pointing off toward the rising sun," was remembered by one of the nurses as almost the only thing left standing in Mariveles on the morning of April 9. (It is actually a statue of Philippine hero Jose Rizal.)

Morrill, skipper of the minesweeper *Quail* watching from Corregidor, "was the groups of men standing on the south Bataan shore in the early half-light of the morning, beckoning and signaling with flashlights for help. . . . How many were ferried across . . . we never knew."[3]

One man, Sgt. Jerome Leek, along with two Filipino nurses, made it with the aid of a simple bamboo pole. Leek, after hearing of the surrender, destroyed his truck and headed for Cabcaben to "commandeer a native banca," for his escape to Corregidor. Cabcaben, of course, had already been well stripped of boats by the time Leek arrived. Not long afterward he met the two nurses who, with the same thought in mind, suggested they "get a bamboo pole and ride it over."

At one of the nurses' direction, Leek went out and cut down three of the fattest bamboo poles he could find.

With each of them laying "full length on the pole . . . weight [distributed] even on each side," they began what would end a remarkable three-hour paddle to safety.[4]

In the meantine, several hundred men, mostly Americans from the units stationed in southern Bataan, had gathered just off the West Road in a huge open field adjacent to Kilometer Post 184.

Those who had started out for there that night were told that they

A happy group of Japanese soldiers pose in front of two captured American 155s. The guns have been spiked, making them useless except for scrap.

were going to organize for a last-ditch stand against the Japanese. By daylight, however, the picture had changed.

The two officers who had hitchhiked over from Cabcaben on the back of one of the nurses' trucks were headed to Kilometer Post 184. They had picked up a ride on a truck moving south just outside Mariveles. Many of the vehicles heading toward them, they noticed, were displaying white rags and sheets as they passed. But it wasn't until they reached their destination and were told that Bataan had surrendered that they realized that the sheets were really white flags.

Many others, by then, had heard the news of the surrender. Reactions varied. Some men cried. Most swore. A few, like Sgt. Leek, tried for Corregidor. Some contemplated escaping into the hills.

Because of the anticipated reactions of the Americans to the surrender orders, a few air corps officers were dispatched to the area around Mariveles to round-up stragglers as they filtered in from the roads and jungle trails. Everyone by this time was looking for a way to get to Corregidor. Under the guise of leading them to an isolated spot on the beach where they would be met by a boat that would take them to the Rock, it was announced instead that they were to discard their weapons and wait for capture by the Japanese. It is a wonder, under such circumstances, that the bearer of such news was not shot by one of his own men.

Top: A Japanese road gang rebuilds one of the many bridges destroyed by U.S. engineers on Bataan. It is safe to say that the enemy inherited few if any standing bridges on the peninsula. *Bottom:* Japanese guard a large group of American prisoners near Mariveles, Bataan. The guards ordered everyone to keep their hands visible at all times.

Engineers at the main supply dump on Cemetery Ridge had just finished destroying their equipment when word of the surrender reached them. Their reactions, recorded by Corp. Robert Levering of that unit, reflect the feelings and response of most soldiers.

"Some men," wrote Levering, "didn't want to surrender."

Down at Mariveles, they had heard "men were abandoning the peninsula like rats leaving a sinking ship . . . bancas and leaky boats were selling to the highest bidder."

"Several . . . wanted me to join them in an escape party up the mountain," he remembered. But we "gave up the idea when we considered that we had no foods or medicine to ward off starvation and disease in the . . . jungle."

Finally, with the attitude of "not caring very much about what might happen . . . we started for Mariveles airfield, where all troops were ordered to assemble."[5]

Over on Corregidor, they knew too. As soon as it became light enough, binoculars were broken out for a look at what was happening. Although it wasn't much, they could tell one thing for sure: "If King did surrender, some [of the] Japs don't know about it," said one man, alluding to the enemy planes seen still bombing and strafing.

He was right. Until Gen. King could make his surrender official, the Japanese Air Force had been instructed to continue their attacks on Bataan.

Of that order, King himself need not have been told, for no sooner had his surrender party left Little Baguio than they were strafed off the road by a Japanese fighter.

Major Achille Tisdelle, carrying a white flag in Gen. King's jeep, wrote in his diary that they were bombed and strafed by "three fleets of dive bombers . . . all the way, repeatedly." Colonel James Collier, carrying the flag in the lead jeep with Maj. Hurt, was a little more specific, stating that they were attacked no less than once every 200 yards, forcing everyone to dive into ditches or behind trees each time.

"Colonel Collier . . . and I . . . ran out of the ditch and waved the white flags hoping the Japs would see them," continued Tisdelle. "If they did," he said, "they paid no attention."[6]

It was now ten o'clock. The surrender party had been on the road for an hour and had only progressed a mile and a half. If the next mile was as tough, chances were they wouldn't make the Japanese lines alive, and there would be no formal surrender of Bataan.

About that time in the Press Relations Office back on Corregidor, Philippine Army major Salvador Lopez wasn't sure he could do what he had to, either. Word had come from Gen. Beebe, Wainwright's chief of

General King, center, initiates surrender proceedings with Col. Motoo Nakayama at the Bataan Experimental Farm Station near Lamao. The other Americans present include Col. Everett C. Williams, on the far left, and majors Wade Cothran and Achille Tisdelle, on the right.

staff, that although nothing official had been heard from Gen. King's headquarters, they should begin preparing the announcement of the fall of Bataan.

Lopez, one of the principal writers of the Voice of Freedom scripts since the beginning, was given the job. He looked up at his companions, Lt. Francisco Isidoro, who would translate what he wrote into Tagalog, the native language, and Lt. Norman Reyes, who would read it in both languages over the Voice of Freedom. "I don't think I can do it," he said.

"Mechanically," he remembered, "I placed a sheet of paper on the typewriter and began writing."

> Bataan has fallen. The Philippine-American troops on this war-ravaged and blood-stained peninsula have laid down their arms. With heads bloody but unbowed, they have yielded to the superior force and numbers of the enemy.

In all, Lopez would write 282 words of "the epic struggle that the Filipino and American soldier put up" on Bataan—a 282-word epitaph filled with praise befitting the "intrepid fighters [who had] done all that human endurance could bear."

In these two pictures, the American surrender party on Bataan, made up of Gen. Edward King, Col. Everett Williams, and majors Achille Tisdelle and Wade Cothran, apprehensively await the arrival of Gen. Homma's representative, Col. Nakayama, at the Bataan Agricultural Experimental Farm Station near Lamao.

"The flesh must yield at last," he wrote in moving conclusion, "endurance melts away, and the end of the battle must come.

"Bataan has fallen, but the spirit that made it stand—a beacon to all liberty-loving peoples of the world—cannot fail!"[7]

Yes, Bataan had fallen, but still not officially. The American half of the surrender party, about the time Lopez had finished writing his announcement, had been received by Maj. Nagano at the Agricultural Experimental Farm Station near Lamao. They had been two hours traveling the three miles from Little Baguio. They had been harassed and strafed continuously by the Japanese Air Force for the first half of their journey, until an enemy reconnaissance plane acknowledged their white flags just outside Cabcaben. (See Map 29.)

Through an interpreter, Nagano told the frazzled Americans as they sat down that he was not authorized to make the arrangements himself, but that a member of Gen. Homma's 14th Army staff was on his way.

A few minutes later, a 1940 Cadillac, still shining through its coat of red Bataan dust, arrived and out stepped Col. Motoo Nakayama, Homma's senior operations officer. As Major Tisdelle remembered: "General King and all the rest of us [including Col. Williams who they found waiting for them at the Farm Station], stand up when he strides in. No one salute[d] on either side and no one [shook] hands."

"We arrange ourselves around the table," Tisdelle continued. "I cross my legs but a Jap officer knocks my feet down. I light a cigarette, but he knocks it down too."

Tisdelle glanced over at King, braced stiffly in his chair in front of Nakayama. "I never saw him look more a soldier than in this hour of defeat," he remembered.

General King, reflecting back on his history at that moment, remembered that almost to the minute, 77 years before, April 9, 1865, Gen. Robert E. Lee was meeting with Gen U. S. Grant at Appomattox. Like Lee, King lamented that he, too, "would rather die a thousand deaths" than do what he was about to do.

Nakayama's interpreter opened the conversation. "You are General Wainwright?" he asked.

King identified himself as the commander of the army on Bataan.

"Where is General Wainwright? We want to see General Wainwright."

King told them that he had "no means of getting in touch with Wainwright," and that he was only representing his command in the negotiations.

"Japanese cannot accept surrender without [Wainwright]," emphasized the interpreter.

Again King patiently explained that he had no authority to speak for Wainwright or to surrender Corregidor either, as he had also been asked.

"Finally the Japs appear to be convinced," Tisdelle observed, "so the aide blurts: 'You will surrender unconditionally'."

King explained that his forces "were no longer fighting units," and that he wished an armistice period so he could prepare his "army for deliverance as prisoners of war." He also requested that the air bombardment be lifted.

The Japanese Air Force was ordered to bomb until noon, he was told. "You will surrender unconditionally!"

"I desire to surrender with these four conditions," King went on, listing the points he wished the Japanese to honor. Would his men be treated as prisoners of war under the provisions of the Geneva Convention?

"You will surrender unconditionally!" was again the rsponse. It was absolutely impossible, continued the interpreter, for Col. Nakayama to negotiate for the surrender of Bataan only. If the forces on the peninsula wished to give up, it would have to be done "voluntarily and unconditionally . . . [by] each individual or each unit."

"How will the prisoners be treated?" King asked again. Would they be protected by the rules of the Geneva Convention?

"Of course," came the reply, "we are not barbarians. Will you surrender unconditionally?"

At that moment, a flight of Japanese planes roared over the trees heading south. Realizing that each minute of debate meant death to more and more of his shattered command, the Bataan commander nodded in agreement.

Nakayama then asked him for his sword.

"I have none," King replied, rather shocked.

The Japanese appeared even more surprised. "They jabber some more," wrote Tisdelle, "but finally decide that the crazy Americans can surrender without sabers."[8]

At 12:30, Maj. Hurt and Col. Collier, who were standing some distance from the surrender scene, saw the four Americans stand up, take out their pistols, and lay them on the table in front of the Japanese.

With terms apparently agreed upon, Gen. King called Collier and Hurt over and instructed them to take a jeep south. "Move all American and Filipino troops south of Cabcaben. They are to be assembled by unit for surrender," he told them.

The two Americans, with two Japanese lieutenants, started down the East Road. At ten o'clock, after covering about a mile, they reached a group of Philippine army troops.

Haggard and barefoot, barely looking like soldiers, Hurt told them to keep moving south to Cabcaben, but was overruled by one of the Japanese lieutenants, who ordered them to stay put. "Japanese troops will find them," he said.[9]

Back on Corregidor, meanwhile, a message had been phoned into the headquarters lateral from the western end of the island that, by the sounds of the large caliber guns they'd been hearing, there appeared to be a naval battle taking place in the direction of Fortune Island, some 20 miles to the south. Although too late to help Bataan, maybe the "mile-long convoy" was coming after all. Forty minutes later, some ships did arrive. Only they were not part of the "convoy."

Earlier that morning, headquarters had ordered the two remaining Philippine Navy Q-boats and the launches *Maryanne* and *Fisheries II* to Corregidor. Around eight o'clock they were seen coming out of Sisiman Bay, but instead of continuing for the Rock, they rounded Gorda Point and headed west toward the entrance to Manila Bay. Spotters on Corregidor watched with bated breath as they somehow passed safely through the minefield. Colonel Paul Bunker, Seaward Defense commander, when notified of what had happened, was furious. As far as he was concerned they were deserting, and he ordered Battery Smith to fire a few rounds across their bows in effort to convince them to return. It was in vain.

About 12 miles down the coast they ran into an enemy destroyer who opened up on them, forcing them to turn around and head back to Corregidor. Having been "excited" earlier by what appeared to be "heavy cannonading at sea toward Fortune Island," wrote Col. Bunker in his diary that night, "[we] were deflated to learn that it was caused by a Jap destroyer firing at our deserting Q-boat, which came back into our harbor. Hope they shot the skipper." The second Q-boat, not far behind, also returned, prompting Bunker to conclude the paragraph in his diary with one word, "Skunks."[10]

About that time at Bataan Headquarters in Little Baguio, Brig. Gen. Arnold Funk, Gen. King's chief of staff, who had been nervously waiting for official word of the surrender, got a phone call. It was from Corregidor. It was news he had been waiting for, but it was not about the surrender.

Around eight o'clock that morning, calling as to the whereabouts of his nurses who had supposedly left Bataan for Corregidor sometime during the night, he was astonished to hear that the girls from Hospital No. 2 were missing. They'd missed their boat at Cabcaben, he was told, and were not at Mariveles either.

Funk told them to send a boat back to find them.

They weren't sure they had one to send, came back the reply.

Only through a lot of "vim, vigor, and swearing," to put it mildly, did he finally get them to promise to send a boat back to look for them.

At dawn, when the nurses from Hospital No. 2 arrived at the empty Quarantine Dock, nurse Dorthea Daley Engel (she had married a soldier on Bataan on February 14), like everyone else, succumbed to the demands of physical exhaustion and fell asleep.

The next thing she remembered was being aroused by the noise of people cheering. Raising up out of the drainage ditch where she had been sleeping, she soon saw why. It was a boat, the *Mitchell*, from Corregidor.

To avoid becoming a sitting duck for the ever-present Japanese Air Force, the skipper pulled in, hurriedly took on a dozen nurses, and then pulled out into the bay. At that moment, a Japanese plane dove down and dropped its bombs some distance behind the dock. Despite the big explosion, none of the nurses was hurt. Once more the rescue craft came in, took on a few passengers, and then pulled out. After the third time the dock was empty.

Three hours later, as the little engineer launch edged up to Corregidor's North Dock, a runner was dispatched to the communications lateral in Malinta Tunnel. Notify Gen. Funk that his nurses from Hospital No. 2 have arrived, he was told.[11]

After giving the switchboard the message, the courier paused for a moment to listen to the noon broadcast of the Voice of Freedom, coming in over one of the many civilian radio sets in the tunnel. The voice was an unfamiliar one. The man, identifying himself as Lt. Norman Reyes, began, "Bataan has fallen. The Philippine-American troops on this war-ravaged and blood-stained peninsula have laid down their arms."

Three hundred miles away, on the edge of a dusty little auxiliary fighter strip on the east coast of the island of Panay, a half-dozen men gathered around a radio carrying the same message. They were lieutenants Barnick, Robb, Boelens, Crosland, and Coleman. The sixth man was Col. Carlos Romulo, the "last man off Bataan," as Lt. Barnick had called him, and except for the old Grumman Duck, the man who would be back on Corregidor reading the very same message they were listening to.

Romulo didn't think he could stand hearing Reyes message read through. "I turned...," he said, "with some crazy idea of running somewhere. Barnick's big arm reached out to [steady me]. He was crying too—the husky soldier from North Dakota, the wisecracking flier, the tough guy. We stood there on that airfield at Iloilo, an American flier and a Filipino soldier ... tears running unashamedly down our cheeks. And we didn't give a damn who saw us."

The End: Honorable but Not Easy

"Put white flags all along your line."

Bataan had fallen. But the many unusual circumstances, increased because of the chaotic state of affairs within the shattered command, promised that the actual surrender would be a touchy one. Lack of communication, of course, was the greatest contributor to the confusion on both sides. By and large, troops in the II Corps, who had borne the brunt of the fighting since April 3, didn't have to be told that it was over. By the morning of the 9th, they were through. Officially or unofficially, it made no difference. Yet there were a few diehards who still had to be convinced.

One of the first confrontations with the Japanese over the surrender occurred just north of Cabcaben on the East Road. Only the fortunate arrival on the scene of Maj. Hurt and Col. Collier saved it from becoming serious. The two Americans, heading south from Lamao with two Japanese officers, arrived just in time for Collier to jump from his jeep and step in between a Japanese tank commander and a feisty Philippine Constabulary major, seconds away from blowing the Japanese "in two" with his drawn and cocked .45.

"Colonel, this SOB demands my surrender," said the major, voice shaking, "and I am not going to . . . and if he makes a move to give a command, I'm going to shoot him in two."

Collier calmly explained that Bataan had been surrendered to the Japanese less than an hour before. The major, shaking his head, disgruntedly turned his pistol over to Collier and walked back to tell his troops, who were dug in some 150 yards away.[12]

At 11 A.M. over on Trail 20, remnants from Gen. Bluemel's Lamao River force, withdrawing south toward Cabcaben, ran into a regiment-size enemy force that had worked its way in behind it and was blocking the trail. A fire fight had erupted between the Japanese and the 26th Cavalry's 1st Squadron, Bluemel's advance guard, when the General arrived. Having hoped to avoid contact with the Japanese frontline troops in case they may not have received news of the surrender, Bluemel, despite the protests of several American officers, was not about to stop the fight. Before going much further, however, word was sent back that white flags had already been uncased across the U.S. front. The fiery general, according to Maj. William Chandler of the 26th, "reluctantly decided to send forward a white flag in hopes that the hostile unit had heard of Gen. King's surrender. Whether or not they had was never determined, but they did accept [it]."

Meanwhile, in the jungle a mile or so to the west, G Troop of the 26th Cavalry, who had split off from Bluemel's force, had run into two American military policemen, who informed them of the surrender. The officer in charge, Maj. Don Blanning, decided to make for Signal Hill on the southwestern slope of Mt. Bataan, where it was rumored a last stand was being organized. After an hour or so of unsuccessfully trying to locate the trail leading across the foot of the mountain, however, Blanning gave up. Calling his gallant little band of Scouts together for the last time, he gave them the opportunity to either surrender or escape. Wisely, wrote Major Chandler, they "elected to trust the jungles rather than the Japs."[13]

About that time in a remote area near Little Baguio, a scene quite contradictory to what was happening throughout most of southern Bataan was unfolding. It was, of all things and of all times, a poker game, involving the men of the 194th Tank Battalion, who had been ordered to pull back to that area the night before. They were informed of the surrender early that morning.

At 7 A.M., the battalion commander, Col. Ernest Miller, was handed a message with one word: "Blast." Miller wrote, "Black Thursday had arrived," as it was the signal to "destroy all vehicles, guns, and ammunition."

Miller ordered his tanks and half-tracks spread out over the area. Fuel valves inside the tanks were then broken off, so as to flood them with gasoline, and then set fire. "The armor plate on the tanks was subjected to such intense heat that it was made useless except for scrap iron," noted Miller. "We also fired 37-mm. armor-piercing shells into the tank and truck motors. Gasoline was dumped into the cabs and bodies of trucks." Weapons were stripped and parts thrown into the blazing vehicles, stocks were smashed, gun barrels heated and bent around trees.

Miller then ordered a detail of men to go to a nearby Quartermaster Ration Distribution Point in hopes of getting some food. Despite the acknowledged fact that Bataan had already surrendered, the officer in charge refused to issue either food or rations without proper authority. Captain Clinton Quinlen, in charge of the tankers, according to Miller, "used his initiative," and took what he wanted, "even while being threatened with court-martial."

"We had more to eat that day than we [had] had ... since the start of the war," remembered the battalion commander. With stomachs full for the first time in months, men relaxed to wait for the Japanese. Some slept, some actually played poker or shot craps. "I never participated in a game of chance," remembered Miller, "which meant so little as that one."

The Japanese, although close by, did not move in to take the 194th until the next day, April 10.

Not too far away from the 194th's bivouac, close to 2,000 men within the Hospital No. 1 compound would not be so lucky as to realize the same 24-hour grace period. Surrender or not, it was business as usual for the doctors and hospital staff until the Japanese arrived. Surrender or not, 1,800 patients would still need tending.

Earlier that morning, Col. James Duckworth, commanding officer of the hospital, after notifying his staff that the fight was over, ordered Red Cross flags taken down and white bed sheets raised in their place.

Not long afterward, a column of Japanese tanks were seen coming down the Mariveles Road. Colonel Duckworth and two fellow officers went to meet them at the hospital gate. With guns from the lead tank trained on the three Americans, a Japanese general and his interpreter climbed out and jumped to the ground.

Duckworth saluted and said that he was surrendering the hospital.

You have Japanese wounded . . . in your custody?" the interpreter asked.

"Yes, forty-two," Duckworth replied.

"Send them here immediately."

A few minutes later, 30 or so Japanese walking wounded filed out of the prison ward and lined up in front of the general. "There was much bowing, scraping, saluting, and questioning," observed Capt. Alfred Weinstein. Before long the general turned to Colonel Duckworth. "These soldiers say you have treated them well. . . . How many have you killed?"

"None," answered Duckworth, "although there are many who are still seriously ill. . . . Some of these may die."

"Show them to me," he ordered.

"Of all the wards," continued Weinstein, "fate had destined that the Nip ward was to suffer least from the [recent] bombings. . . . Showers were functioning; latrines were working; the roof was intact. The slopeheads, wearing clean pajamas, were lying on surgical beds covered with clean linen. Candy and cigarettes were on their side tables."

The general was pleased with what he saw and asked to be taken on a tour of the rest of the grounds. Near the center of the compound, he paused and pointed at the huge unfilled bomb crater in the middle of the grounds.

"A Japanese bomb," explained Colonel Duckworth. One-hundred patients had been killed and the ward completely destroyed.

"Too bad," the general said with apparent concern. "That is unfortunate."

Then, turning to Duckworth, he repeated again that his wounded had been treated very well, and that he had decided to use the hospital for the next few days as headquarters and bivouac for his tanks. "I shall instruct my men to refrain from interfering with you or your duties," he said. "Carry on with your work."

Duckworth and his staff would be allowed to "carry on" for a month and a half at Hospital No. 1. before leaving for their prison camps.

Under the tall trees of the same Little Baguio forest some two miles to the east, the staff of Hospital No. 2, unfortunately, would find "carrying on" much more difficult.

Both staff and patients of the hospital, with its quarter-square mile of open wards, had spent most of the night and morning in slit-trenches, many dug conveniently underneath their beds, dodging Japanese bombs, and stray bullets.

Around 3 P.M., with word that the surrender had taken place, Col. James Gillespie, hospital C.O., ordered white bedsheets displayed next to his Red Cross flags. For the next five hours, and for the first time in days, doctors and medical corpsmen went about tending their over 7,500 patients without the roar of heavy guns or rattle of small arms fire. The quiet seemed strange, almost out of place.

It wasn't until eight o'clock that evening that the first Japanese officers and a handful of soldiers arrived. Calling the staff together, the officer in charge, an arrogant major named Hisashi Sekiguchi, announced that he was taking over the operations of the hospital, firmly stating that everyone was a prisoner of war and could be shot for disobedience.

After listening to the major's speech, Col. Gillespie asked him if there was a chance of increasing the size of the rations of the patients.

If your own army didn't feed you enough, he retorted, then he didn't see why he should "feed [them] any more than [they'd] been receiving."

"That night," according to Col. W. H. Waterous, a member of the staff at No. 2, "Japanese soldiers roamed at will through the hospital area, relieving everyone of watches and any other item they wanted."

Few of those who were allowed to sleep after that went to bed without the ominous feeling that the presence of Maj. Sekiguchi portended trouble.

Their instincts proved correct, as at dawn they were told that sometime during the night, the American woman refugee (married to a Filipino naval officer) convalescing in the officers' ward with her baby of two months, had been gang-raped by the Japanese in the presence of everyone there. Later, while most of the staff was sitting down at their meager breakfast of steamed red rice, an American medical corpsman ran up with the news that the Filipino patients were all leaving.

Chief surgeon Col. Jack Schwartz led the line of doctors out of the mess hall toward the open wards. Schwartz stopped one of the patients. "Where are you going?" he asked.

The Japanese had freed all the Filipinos. They were going home, he was told.

Word of this started when some Japanese soldiers, without authorization, even from Maj. Sekiguchi, ordered the staff of a small Philippine Scout medical detachment camped on the edge of the hospital area to join the line of men marching north out of Bataan. At the sight of the Scouts moving out, rumor spread that the Filipinos were being freed to return home.

Schwartz and his fellow doctors went from ward to ward and soldier to soldier trying vainly to convince them that they were in no condition to leave, that the whole thing was a trick. Struck with mass hysteria, few listened and almost none remained. Amputees, using tree limbs for crutches, joined the pathetic procession. A row of blind patients formed a human chain behind one of the walking wounded and headed for the road. Men holding their hands over fresh stomach wounds to keep them from breaking open, staggered out—most to become just another one of the hundreds of corpses that, within a few days, would line the roads leading out of Bataan.

Colonel Waterous, whose clinic was near the lower end of the hospital, "could see the never-ending column of men from the upper wards moving down the road towards Cabcaben ... all moving like cattle on their last mile. ... This went on," he remembered, "for 48 hours."

There had been over 5,000 Filipino soldiers in beds under the trees of Hospital No. 2 before the incident. Fewer than 600 remained.

Later that same day, several batteries of Japanese field artillery positioned themselves in a circle around the hospital. Anticipating return fire from Corregidor as soon as the Japanese opened up, Col. Gillespie asked Maj. Sekiguchi if the hospital could be evacuated or at least, relocated.

Nobody, said the major, would leave until Corregidor had fallen.[14]

He was right. It wasn't until six days after Corregidor surrendered, that the Hospital No. 2 site was abandoned and the staff and patients attached to Hospital No. 1.

The situation surrounding the surrender of the I Corps on the rugged, western half of the peninsula, of course, was much different from that of the II Corps. I Corps units had gone virtually unchallenged except during the opening hours of the enemy's April 3 offensive. And the only withdrawal had been as a strategic necessity brought about by the rapid collapse of the II Corps.

Word that Bataan was going to be surrendered came to I Corps commander Gen. Albert Jones around 2 A.M. on the morning of the 9th. Jones had been prompted to call Gen. King at Little Baguio about that time, following the detonation of the engineer and ordnance depots above Mariveles.

"What's going on?" he asked King.

Explaining that the II Corps ammunition dumps had just been blown, King told him that he was surrendering at 6 A.M. "Put white flags all along your line ... destroy your artillery and machine guns and standby for further orders."

Jones agreed to spike his artillery, but said he'd hold off destroying his small arms until the last minute.

"Use your own judgment," said the despondent Bataan commander, and then hung up.

As opposed to the situation in the II Corps, the absence of fighting or, in some cases, even contact with the Japanese on the west coast, offered I Corps no hint of how bad things really were throughout the command. Where II Corps units didn't have to be told that Bataan was through on the night of April 8, men scattered throughout the quiet I Corps, even when told, still didn't believe it. If there was a chance for an incident, it would be here and here it happened.

On April 8, Gen. Wainwright, it will be remembered, had issued orders to withdraw the Philippine Division (31st, 45th, and 57th infantries) to Corregidor. The only regiment able to free itself was the 45th, which started south that night from its positions in the I Corps. (Despite this, the 45th was unable to make it to Mariveles in time to be picked up, and met its fate on Bataan with the rest of the division.)

With surrender still unanticipated in the I Corps, the 1st Battalion of the 1st Infantry Regiment of the Philippine Army's 1st Division, was ordered to relieve the 45th from their positions near the junction of Trail 8 and the Pantingan River.

The next morning, April 9, the battalion fired on a column of Japanese 65th Brigade troops as they attempted to cross the Pantingan. A good-sized fire fight ensued. But before long, the outnumbered Filipinos began withdrawing westward over Trail 8, in hopes of receiving help from the 11th Division, into whose area they were being pushed.

The frustrated 1st Battalion commander did not know, however, that the 11th, which had received orders to surrender, had already abandoned its frontline positions and had begun to stack arms about a mile to the southwest.

Late that afternoon, word was received by 1st Division commander Col. Kearie Berry that a battalion from his 1st Infantry Regiment was in the middle of a big fight with a large Japanese force near the junction of trails 8 and 9. He was stunned. Why hadn't they surrendered? he wondered.

By the time Berry could react, the game but outnumbered 1st Battalion had been pushed back over Trail 9 into the 1st Division area. The only thing standing between it and total annihilation was the impenetrable jungle that had continuously held the Japanese to the confines of the trail.

Grabbing what units he could to help, the worried division commander moved forward with the hope that the Japanese would still accept his surrender after what had happened.

Upon reaching Trail 9, Berry placed the two battalions he brought with him astride the trail behind the battered 1st, and then went forward to find out why it hadn't surrendered. The startled battalion commander's answer was simple—he hadn't been informed that he was supposed to.

It was twilight on the morning of April 10 when Berry and two Filipino officers, vigorously waving a large white flag, cautiously moved across Trail 9

Top: Lines of American prisoners going through an equipment shakedown at the edge of Mariveles Field on April 9, 1942. Note the line of vehicles in the background, some still displaying white flags. *Bottom:* "Upon the faces of the defeated are smiles with no mirth," was the caption under this picture of American POWs in the Japanese propaganda book, *Philippine Expeditionary Force.* American prisoners were the favorite subject of Japanese photographers.

toward Japanese lines. After 50 or so agonizing yards, several Japanese soldiers appeared. One of them was the regimental commander, who, with no apparent disdain over what had happened, accepted the surrender. Although over, it wouldn't be forgotten, however, nor go without repercussion.[15]

The first repercussion came that night. Eleventh Division troops, upon receiving the order to surrender that afternoon, according to their commander, Gen. William Brougher, were waiting for their captors "with large bonfires built in all directions and white flags displayed." Unaware of the altercation between the 1st Division and elements of the Japanese 65th Brigade, which was still unresolved at the time, "the Japanese came in with machine guns blazing and shot into our soldiers disarmed and huddled in their bivouacs. The men were terrified and took off down Trail 7 toward Mariveles Road," leaving guns and even food behind. "In my C.P.," Brougher continued, "we debated ... the merits of sticking it out or following the men to the rear ... with machine gun bullets whistling [all] around. ... We decided to follow [them] ... and took off."

By ten o'clock the next morning, Brougher, with help from his staff, had rounded up most of his division and was ready to try again. Once more, white flags were displayed. This time, however, the Japanese honored them and peacefully accepted the surrender.

The disappointment registered among the proud, confident Filipinos of Brougher's 11th Division when the surrender was announced was noted by its commanding officer: "Strong men wept like children," he said. "Those that had been willing and heroic in [the] desperate conflict, were the ones who were most completely overcome with emotional collapse [on] having to surrender."

No one had been more confident or was more let down than Brougher himself, who wrote afterwards, "We had worked unstintingly for two months building an impregnable defense in our subsector front and felt that we could hold the Japs indefinitely."[16]

The last thing anyone wanted was to provoke their wary conquerors into suspecting that they were resisting surrender. The efforts of one I Corps officer on the evening of April 9 bears witness to this.

While preparing the troops of his regiment for surrender to the Japanese, who were expected momentarily, Col. Virgil N. Cordero, of the 72d Infantry, heard an outburst of small arms fire coming from the vicinity of one of his frontline units. He quickly dashed through a patch of jungle and into the clearing from where the noise was coming. There he discovered the source. A truck loaded with .30-caliber rifle ammunition had caught fire and bullets were exploding in all directions.

Fearing the Japanese might mistake the shots for an ambush, Cordero ran up to the truck and began throwing dirt onto the flames, while at the same time yanking hot, yet-unexploded ammunition boxes out onto the ground. Within a few minutes, he had the fire out. For his courage, partially in saving the truck and the ammunition, and partially for risking his life while doing it, but mainly for avoiding a possible incident with his captors, Col. Cordero received a Silver Star from the United States Army.[17]

The surrender of various I Corps units continued throughout the entire day and into the night of April 10. The corps commander, Gen. Albert Jones, interestingly enough, might have been the last man on the peninsula to surrender. Although I Corps headquarters was captured on the evening of the 10th, the Japanese officer in charge waited until the next morning before officially accepting Jones' capitulation.

Up on Signal Hill, a prominent observation point about three-fourths of the way up the western slope of Mt. Bataan, several hundred Americans and Philippine Scouts had been gathering since the night of April 8.

Exactly why men were ordered to Signal Hill is not clear. Many heard it was to organize for a counterattack. General Max Lough, commander of the Philippine Division, relayed an order from Gen. Parker to his division command post that it had been established there "to set up a defensive position and fire on the Japanese only if they attacked."

Nevertheless, it wasn't until late in the afternoon of the 10th that the American troops were ordered down off the hill by the Japanese. At dusk, wrote Lt. Henry G. Lee of the U.S. 31st, "our column moved out down the Signal Hill road, which was crowded with our Scour comrades whom we were now forced to leave behind. Many had already gone into the brush, refusing to surrender."

"At the foot of the [road]," Lee continued, "columns were stopped and thoroughly looted by a body of Japanese infantry. Finally we were allowed to proceed to [Kilometer Post] 181, where we were again . . . searched and herded into a prisoner of war enclosure. We were never again together as a unit."[18]

The access road the Americans took from Signal Hill to K.P. 181 on the West Road was actually part of Trail 7. It was the only north-south trail, other than the West Road, on the western half of the peninsula. About six miles north of the Signal Hill turn-off up Trail 7, it junctioned with trails 8 and 9. About five winding miles east over Trail 8 was the junction of Trail 29. On the morning of April 11, Lt. Reynaldo Perez of the Philippine Army's 41st Division, along with a handful of other men from miscellaneous units, arrived on foot at that junction, to find "hundreds of [Filipino soldiers] seated on the ground on the south side of the trail," guarded by Japanese soldiers.

The day before, upon receiving notification of the surrender, Perez had been discharged from the 11th Clearing Station. Still shaky from his bout with malaria, he was able to hitch a ride on a truck that, as ordered

Abandoned U.S. trucks and commercial buses, many still displaying white flags, parked on the edge of Mariveles Harbor following the surrender. The prewar commercial owners' name, Pantranco, can still be seen on the one at left, as can its motor-pool designation on Bataan—II Corps.

Japanese troops moving through the completely leveled barrio of Mariveles sometime after the surrender.

by the Japanese, was to proceed on its own toward Balanga on the east coast.

Unable to reach their destination that night because of a large tree across the road, they spent the night sleeping in the truck and, at dawn, removed the obstacle and continued on. Less than a quarter-mile from the junction of trails 8 and 29, a column of Japanese soldiers commandeered their vehicle and, after thoroughly searching everyone, sent them on foot.

Upon sight of Perez and the men with him, the Japanese ordered them to sit down with the rest of the prisoners. About noon, a high-ranking Japanese officer, identified as Lt. Gen. Akira Nara, commander of the 65th Brigade, drove up. Upon seeing the large number of Filipino prisoners sitting beside the road, he stopped and beckoned the Japanese officer in charge over to his car. After a brief conversation with him, Nara drove away. Although no one at the time knew what was said, many would soon find out.

Japanese guards immediately began separating the officers and ranking noncommissioned officers from the enlisted men. Once this was done, the Filipino enlisted men were herded out onto Trail 8 and marched off toward Limay.

"A few minutes later," remembered Perez, "a Jap officer called our attention. In fluent English, he asked for the ranking officers. Among this officer group were two majors," whom he ordered to "form the group into a company, three platoons and a column of fours." As the company formed out on the road, Perez, for the first time, got a look at how many men there were. "I estimated that we numbered 300 officers, more or less," he said.

Soon, several Japanese soldiers appeared carrying reels of telephone wire. Guards with fixed bayonets were increased. Perez was the second man in line. "[The] Japs commenced tying my file leader. His hands were tied behind him . . . [and] with the same telephone wire, my hands were likewise tied. All the officers in each file were tied in tandem."

The Japanese, as soon as everyone except the leaders of each platoon and the ranking officers were tied, started the columns down Trail 8 toward the Pilar-Bagac Road. "Our gait was very slow," recalled Perez, "for we kept pulling [and] dragging each other."

A few hundred yards down the trail, Perez spotted several army trucks. He was relieved. "I thought [they] would take us to a concentration camp," he remembered thinking, "[but] when I saw that the leading units were not getting on . . . my fears were confirmed. It was going to be a massacre."

Before long the columns were led off the south side of the trail into the jungle, file after file disappearing into the dense growth. They were halted on the edge of a steep, 100-foot-high bluff overlooking one of the tributaries to the Pantingan River and told to sit down. Because of the jungle, none of the other groups, although only a few yards away, could be seen.

"There was a foreboding silence around us," said Perez. "I never prayed so much in my life." Then it came. The explanation of what was about to take place. Over 300 Filipino officers and noncoms had been selected to pay the price for the mistake the battalion of 1st Infantry Regiment troops of the 1st Division had made. Uninformed of the surrender, it will be remembered, they had engaged a regiment of Geneal Nara's 65th Brigade on the morning of April 9, in a fight that lasted over 20 hours. "Had you surrendered earlier," said the Japanese interpreter in Tagalog, "you would not have met this tragedy. ... Many of our soldiers died fighting against you."

Cries and pleas for mercy arose from the now-doomed Filipinos, but fell on deaf ears. Even requests to be killed by machine gun or rifle fire were denied. And then cries of another kind began. They were "of my comrades," remembered Perez, "coupled with the beastly shouts of the butchering Japanese. My hair stood on end. I wondered what the Japs were doing to them."

Before long, he and the men in his column were to find out. Soon a Japanese officer, "brandishing a saber dripping with blood," led a dozen or so soldiers in behind the file of terror-stricken Filipinos. "Their bayonets red with blood," they readied for their grisly task.

And then it began ... bayoneting and beheading. Now and then a shot. And with each thrust of sword or knife, an inhuman cry of pain. When his turn came, Lt. Perez, with his back to his assassins, felt like he was hit in the back with a "big club. I was knocked out momentarily," he said. "When I came to, I felt an excruciating pain on my back." He had taken a single thrust from the 16-inch Japanese bayonet that went all the way through his body, making an exit wound in his stomach. But he was not dead, nor even unconscious; "My God," he thought to himself, "this is it. I did not [dare] move. I played dead."

His ordeal was far from over, however, as the officer next to him, the next man to be bayoneted, was pushed over on top of Perez. "He was lying on my right arm," he said, "then I felt the pain of the bayonet [that had gone through him] slowly piercing my arm. [Again] I dared not move for fear the Jap might give me the works again."

The "cold-blooded murderers moved on," he continued, and "after a while there was quiet, except for the groans of the dying." Before long the Japanese came back to doublecheck the bodies to make sure everyone was dead. "A Jap soldier grabbed me in the face and turned me upwards," said Perez. "I held my breath and kept my eyes closed. I was expecting another bayonet thrust. Thank God it never came."

About ten feet away, another Filipino officer, Maj. Pedro Felix, of the 71st Division, had also been able to fool his executioners. Felix had miraculously survived not one but four bayonet thrusts from the Japanese and, like Perez, remained conscious through the entire ordeal. Fortunately for the husky Philippine Army major, unmoving, lying face down in the bloodstained dirt, the officer next to him had tossed his legs over his head and shoulders at the first thrust of the enemy's bayonet into his body, and then died. Concealed from the eyes of his killers, Felix was able to breathe freely and, after the Japanese moved on, actually open his eyes and look around.

It was dark before both men felt it was safe enough to try to free themselves. Both were weak from the loss of blood. Both were in terrible pain. Felix had actually tried to end it all by smothering himself, but failed.

"I had a big problem before me," Perez said. "Freeing myself was impossible. Then the unexpected happened. My file leader [Felix], was not dead after all. I whispered to him to get nearer to me. After some difficulty we managed to get near each other. I gnawed at his bonds and set him free. After resting a while, he untied me also."

It is, of course, impossible to know exactly how many men lived through this experience, or escaped to tell the tale. Three of the survivors came out with Maj. Felix, while Perez, after spending two days and three nights along a tributary of the Pantingan River, also made his way safely out of Bataan.[19]

Although certainly the worst, this was not the first nor the only incident of Japanese treachery. The brutality continued as the Japanese prepared their vanquished adversaries for movement out of Bataan.

It was at dusty Mariveles air field, which, for the most part, had become the main assembly point of the Bataan troops, where another incident occurred to portend what lay ahead.

The foremost concern among Japanese soldiers over prisoners on Bataan became looting. It can be said with relative certainty that most of the more than 70,000 American and Filipino prisoners would be searched no less than half a dozen times before reaching the prison camps.

The first thing air corps Capt. Ed Dyess heard as he and his men reached Mariveles Field to turn themselves in on the morning of April 10 was, "Get rid of your Jap stuff." ("Jap stuff," of course, meant souveniers—a hobby most Americans had acquired during the three-month-long battle.) "We did so ... and just in time," he recalled, as Japanese soldiers soon ordered packs and duffle bags opened and their contents spread out.

As the Japanese guards began searching, things started getting rough. "I saw men shoved, cuffed, and boxed," Dyess said. "[We were] mystified. It was uncalled for. We were not resisting." Before long, the puzzling attitude of their captors was explained, when a few ranks away, a Japanese guard held up a small shaving mirror. "Nippon?" he asked the American

A diminutive Japanese soldier indulging himself in one of the favorite pastimes of the conquering enemy army—searching American prisoners. Some men were searched as many as ten times before reaching their POW camps.

from whom he had taken it. The soldier nodded. Yes, it was "Made in Japan."

"The Jap stepped back," witnessed Dyess, "then lunged, driving his rifle butt into the American's face . . . and then lunged again. The Yank went down. The raging Jap stood over him, driving crushing blows to the face until [he] lay insensible."

A few minutes later, it happened again. "A Jap was smashing his fist into the face of another American soldier, who went to his knees," only to receive a kick in the groin. "He too, it seemed, had been caught with some Japanese trifle."

On another part of the now hot, dusty, and crowded fighter strip, a scene of horror was unfolding that would bring even the strongest of prisoners to retch with abhorrence for their captors.

As had been occurring with the men in Capt. Dyess' group, an American air force captain was being frisked by a Japanese private. A

An American officer, incorrectly identified by the Japanese as "General Ives," being interrogated by an enemy intelligence officer following the surrender of Bataan.

routine search of one of his shirt pockets turned up some Japanese yen notes. An eyewitness later told Dyess that a big Japanese officer was shown the money. "Without a word he grabbed the captain by the shoulder and shoved him to his knees. He [quickly] pulled [his] sword out of [its] scabbard and raised it high over his head, holding it with both hands."

"There was a swishing and kind of a chopping thud," he told Dyess. "The captain's head seemed to jump off his shoulders ... [hitting] the ground in front of him ... rolling crazily ... between lines of [horror-struck] prisoners."[20]

Little did the men dream that this and similar scenes of murder and brutality lay before them. As recorded in the last four lines of Henry G. Lee's poem, "Prisoner's March," these scenes would become so commonplace as to

> ...anesthetize the mind.
> I cannot mourn you now. I lift my load
> The suffering column moves. I leave behind
> Only another corpse, beside the road.

To complete the humiliation of defeat, one of the first groups of prisoners, as they left the airstrip at Mariveles on their march, were halted

beside a small building. In front was a flagpole still flying an American flag.
"Face the flag," they were told. The men turned around and looked up to
see the Stars and Stripes being lowered to the ground and the Rising Sun
hoisted in its place. The Bataan poet, Henry G. Lee, who was somewhere
among the vast throng of prisoners on the field, probably summed up the
feelings each American had at that moment better than anyone. For of this
generation of young men standing there in the scorching Philippine sun
that morning in April 1942, Americans back home before the war had said,

> . . . (We) were weak, (we) were aimless
> . . . said (we) were lost past reclaim —
> (We) had "left the faith of their fathers"
> [and] were "blots on America's name."
>
> We were "soft and useless and drifters"
> And the last youth's census reveals
> We were "parasite growth of the nation"
> We had "sacrificed muscle for wheels."
>
> Weak? And drifters? And aimless?
> Go where the steel was sowed
> Ask the nameless fox graves
> That dot the Hacienda Road
>
> And ask at Limay and Balanga
> Where outposts burrowed like moles
> And the sky-trained flying soldiers
> Died in their infantry holes.
>
> And ask of the bamboo thickets
> Deadly green and hot
> And the bloody Pilar River
> And the forward slopes of Samat.
>
> And, last seek the silent jungle
> Where the unburied remnants lie
> Asleep by their rusting rifles
> The men who learned to die.
>
> Who led the Scouts at Quinauan
> Who plugged the break at Moran
> Who but your parasite youngsters
> The desperate men of Bataan . . .

And what of the Filipinos? The beloved Scouts who

> Polished and trained since nineteen-four
> To be expended in four months war.

Part of the Altar of Courage Memorial, this 300-foot-tall cross stands on the very top of Mt. Samat, about 100 feet behind and above the main building. Serviced by an elevator that takes you to the windowed crossbeam where you are greeted by a panoramic view of Bataan and Manila Bay, the cross when lit up at night can be seen from Manila, some 30 miles away.

This marker, typical of several placed at appropriate battle sites throughout Bataan by the Philippine National Shrines Commission, marks the general location of the Battle of the Pockets.

And of their countrymen, the Philippine Army which had

> Obsolete rifle without a sling
> And bolo tied with a piece of string

The men who had carried the fight? Monuments would someday be erected on Bataan to what they had done there, and its bloodstained fields consecrated by those who had done it.

And so, as the men of Bataan began their march to prison camp, the last chapter in this "epic struggle," as Gen. MacArthur described it, came to a close. What lay before them was 65 miles of hell. Sixty-five miles of brutal sun and heat—but of little or no food or water. Sixty-five miles of barbarity and inhumanity as no army in the history of the civilized world had ever known. So the Battling Bastards of Bataan, who had fought the good fight and earned the right to be treated with the respect due both victor and vanquished alike, before it was through would provide history with yet another story and title like no other ever written. It would be called "The Bataan Death March."

APPENDIX A

Special Philippine Defense Units

USAFFE: On July 26, 1941, in anticipation of the coming conflict in the Pacific, a new command, designated as the United States Army in the Far East (*USAFFE*), was established. Appointed its commander that same day was 62-year-old Gen. Douglas MacArthur, recalled to duty after three and a half years of retirement from the U.S. Army. Induction of the Philippine Army into the Army of the United States also took place on that date.

USFIP: On March 20, 1942, following Gen. MacArthur's departure from the Philippines to Australia, the United States Forces in the Philippines (*USFIP*) command was created and Lt. Gen. Jonathan M. Wainwright placed in command.

APPENDIX B

192d and 194th Tank Battalions

By late November 1941, the arrival of 108 General Stuart light tanks in two fully equipped battalions in the Islands was more than welcome. The Stuart tank was the same one that had been used with such great success by the British against the Italians in the Libyan Desert earlier in 1941. The troops were so pleased that they affectionately nicknamed each tank "Honey," in honor of their responsiveness and reliability in open desert warfare.

The role of the two tank battalions prior to Bataan was active as well as vital. Suffering under the same limitations and handicaps of the hasty December withdrawal as the friendly army around them, it is little wonder that only half of the original 108 were able to make it safely to Bataan.[1]

Since the tank, up to this time, had remained untried in jungle warfare and perhaps thought impractical—as the British had mistakenly anticipated theirs would be in the Malayan jungle—the command on Bataan remained somewhat skeptical and often reluctant to release it throughout much of the campaign. What was eventually learned the hard way on Bataan about the capabilities and limitations of the tank in close jungle combat, however, would go a long way in promoting its use throughout the remaining war in the Pacific.

Bataan Artillery and Antiaircraft

Caught in a state of only partial preparedness, as with all of what was thrown together as the army on Bataan, the artillery was no exception in finding its role a large and difficult one. An early boost to its defensive capabilities came with the September 1941 arrival of the 200th and 515th New Mexico National Guard Anti-Aircraft Regiments, along with 50 versatile armored half-tracks carrying 75-mm. guns (also known as SPMs, self-propelled mounts). Unfortunately, like the tanks, nearly one-half of the half-tracks were lost while making the December withdrawal into Bataan.

Important big gun support on Bataan came from 30-odd 155-mm., tractor-drawn World War I GPFs, Grand-Prix Filloux. (Filloux was the designer of this French made gun.) The long-range effect of the 155 "Long Tom's," as the Americans called them, whose fire missions could be accurately plotted off any of the many prewar selected registration points on Bataan, was anticipated to be great. Regrettably, however, a shortage of ammunition for these and other long-range guns, along with the ever-present Japanese Air Force, forced artillery units to abandon "target of opportunity" shooting beginning in late January.

A few weeks before the war started, six 8-inch railroad guns were shipped into the Philippines from Hawaii. After the withdrawal was ordered on December 23, four of them were sent by rail from Manila to San Fernando in hopes of somehow getting them into Bataan. Unfortunately, two of the guns were lost en route as a result of Japanese air attacks. The job of moving the two remaining 17-ton giants into the peninsula fell on the shoulders of the 803d Aviation Engineers, who, despite the lack of proper heavy equipment, were somehow able to manhandle them onto waiting flatbed trailers. After the difficult transfer was accomplished, the small convoy headed south into Bataan. Just outside the barrio of Luhao, however, Japanese fighters caught the two slow-moving truck-driven trailers, shooting out several of their irreplaceable heavy-duty tires. A day later, two replacement trailers arrived and men of the dauntless 803d were put to the task of switching the 33,000-pound tubes from one carrier to another for the third time in as many days. Again the ingenious engineers were successful, and the guns were towed without incident to Pilar on the East Road. From there, with much difficulty, which included having to reinforce several bridges, they were taken over the Pilar-Bagac Road, crawling into Bagac itself around midnight of January 4. With its 14-mile range, one of the 8-inchers was later set up on Saysian Point, in position to defend against a possible enemy invasion of Bagac Bay.

For direct support, aside from the two Scout artillery regiments of the Philippine Division, seven of the nine Philippine Army divisions had their own artillery. Unfortunately, like their own infantry regiments, they too were undertrained and undermanned. On loan from Corregidor Harbor Defense was one battery (Globe) of the 60th U.S. Coast Artillery Regiment (antiaircraft), one battery (Cebu) of the 91st P.S. C.A. Regiment, and Battery B of the Scout 92d C.A. Regiment. Battery Erie, a four-light searchlight unit, was also assigned duty on the peninsula.

Most hampering of all to the artillery throughout the campaign was the constant menace of the virtually unchallenged Japanese Air Force. Daylight fire missions had to be held up until dark for fear of being spotted by the ever-present "Photo Joe" reconnaissance plane or an unnoticed enemy bomber or fighter. Lt. Col. Alexander Quintard of the P.A.'s 301st Field

Artillery Regiment, summed up the situation that existed between the
Japanese air force and the artillery units on Bataan: "Mr. Moto is over us
here in his observation plane just about from sun-up to sundown. When
we have to fire he spots our positions and radios back to his own guns. Then
we catch hell. The dive-bombers were on us for three hours yesterday. So
we try to fire mostly at night, or when [his] back is turned." Antiaircraft
protection around the airfields and rear area installations did much,
however, to neutralize the effects of the complete aerial superiority enjoyed
by the enemy over most of Bataan.

A shortage of original as well as replacement parts for some guns, including the sighting device for the half-track's 75s, continually plagued the
artillerymen. Also, certain batches of ammunition, usually that of World
War I vintage, had high misfire rates, which kept ordnance crews busy taking preventive or corrective measures. Other faulty ammunition problems
came from the old World War I Stokes mortar, used as an infantry support
weapon. On the average, only 30 percent of its rounds detonated upon contact. The rest, disappointingly, became mere battlefield litter. Even worse,
ammunition for the newer 60-mm. mortars, supplied to the heavy weapons
companies of the Philippine Division, failed to reach the Islands in time to
be used.

Despite the problems created by faulty ammunition, the lack of parts,
and the enemy air force, Bataan's artillery remained, by far, the most feared
weapon used against the Japanese.

Bataan Engineers and Quartermaster

Between the Bataan Engineers and Quartermaster Corps is where the
real miracle of the story of Bataan's survival lies. No American fighting
army, either before or since, has had to rely so heavily upon the pure in-
genuity of these two service units as on Bataan.

The Bataan Engineers

The role of the Army Engineers on Bataan began several months
before the war. To aid an understrength 14th Engineer Regiment in their
efforts to improve the existing military roads and installations on Bataan,
the army was forced to obtain help from private construction firms. In late
1941, the 1,500-man 803d Engineer-Aviation Battalion arrived from the
States at the same time as a 1,000-man increase in the 14th's roster was
authorized. The two events gave a noticeable boost to many of the lagging
projects throughout Luzon. On Bataan, which was still low on the military-
projects list, only work on the Mariveles and Limay docks and Bataan air

field was authorized. Between December 10 and 23, Gen. MacArthur ordered the preparation of a string of temporary landing fields from central Luzon to the tip of Bataan, thus facilitating, at least, the completion of the peninsula's first two airstrips, Bataan and Cabcaben.

It was not until after the December 23 withdrawal order that engineer units, as they reached the peninsula, were put to work on the important frontline and coastal defense positions. Now, work began at near-frantic pace on the neglected but vital network of roads and trails that would be needed to help insure a successful defense. Along the chosen battleline, fields of fire were cut and cleared, foxholes and machine gun positions dug, barbed wire strung, and mines laid. A late December boost to the under-manned engineers came with the formation, right on Bataan, of the 301st P.A. Engineer Regiment (which was later split to form the 201st and 202d Battalions). They were composed of about 500 army stragglers and American civilian mining engineers who had sought refuge on the penin-sula. Most of the regiment's officers came from within its ranks of mining engineers, who were given temporary commissions in the U.S. Army.

Under the able command of Brig. Gen. Hugh Casey, engineering ac-complishments remained as varied as they were numerous. Aside from struggling under the handicaps of too little time, too few trained men, and equipment shortages, the job was still somehow done. Along with the ever-continuous, top-priority work on roads and bridges, urgent calls for help went out whenever supply failed to meet demand. But the miracles were forthcoming. A shortage of hand grenades, for example, brought about the development by the engineers of the "Casey Cookie." It was a half-stick of dynamite stuffed with nails and glass into a hollow joint of bamboo, then sealed with cement. For accuracy, usually against enemy snipers, it was sometimes launched from a homemade bow. Although its record in com-bat remains questionable, it did serve its purpose from time to time. Another important improvisation made by the engineers was antitank mines. They were made out of small wooden boxes stuffed with four or five pounds of dynamite, a flashlight battery, and the appropriate wiring. Although classified as antitank mines, in practice most of them could be detonated by foot soldiers as well as an unsuspecting animal, usually a carabao, that had wondered into the minefield. Later, when some of the 20,000 made were placed into boxes constructed out of green lumber, the sun, as it dried out the wood, forced the boxes to warp enough to actually explode the mines prematurely. Gun mounts for machine guns salvaged off wrecked or unflyable aircraft were also forged for use as infantry and anti-tank weapons by the engineers. Bolo knives for use in the dense Bataan jungle were also a scarce but important item. The engineers hand-shaped and honed over 1,000 from spring leaves taken off wrecked vehicles. The problem of dust on Bataan Field brought on a successful experiment by

Not one bridge was left standing by U.S. engineers for Japanese use on the road leading down Bataan's east coast.

Col. Wendell Fertig, Chief Bataan Construction Engineer. Remembering a method once used to keep dust down on a clay tennis court back home, he simply applied a mixture of water and waste molasses from a Bataan sugar refinery to the runway. It worked.

With the early February arrival of a small, blockade-running inter-island ship loaded with unhusked rice, the engineers dismantled and successfully relocated five rice-threshing mills from central to southern Bataan. Also, by early February, they had appropriated and relocated a civilian sawmill on the southern tip of the peninsula. As long as the supply held out, the mill produced close to 25,000-board-feet of lumber per day. Behind the eastern half of the first main battle line on Bataan, the engineers built about 50 dummy-gun positions out of stove pipe, bamboo, and lumber. To attract enemy fire, small charges of dynamite were set off from time to time.

As the army on Bataan began to dig itself in, the most critical need soon became barbed wire. Nearly 20 tons were salvaged from two barges sunk off Corregidor and Cabcaben. This effort got the barbed wire removed from the critical list.

Wherever possible, engineers built earthen dams across rivers on or near the MLR, creating natural defense barriers to the enemy. In mid–February, following the Japanese invasion of the Bataan west coast, which resulted in what was called the battle of the Points, engineers went to work clearing cliffs of foliage to better facilitate observation of the beaches below. Before they were through, over 80,000- square yards of cliff-face was estimated to have been denuded of growth. More and more, as time went on, engineer units either formally or through trial by fire became "combat" engineers. In the end, although fighting as infantrymen, their last order, to destroy all equipment that could be of use to the Japanese, came to them as engineers. It may very well be that their "last order" was indeed the last order to be successfully carried out on Bataan.[2]

Bataan Quartermaster and the Supply Situation

Readers of American military history must look long and hard to find the occasion of an American military defeat. Equally, they may have to go back to the Mexican War to find a time when an American army was long in the field without adequate food and medicine. Unfortunately, the Bataan campaign was an occasion of both defeat and lack of supplies. In studying it, one can easily surmise that it was more the lack of food and medicine rather than an efficient enemy that brought the army on Bataan to its knees. Why this was allowed to happen will not be discussed here. What will be said is that prewar planning and priorities, set up by Gen. MacArthur, brought on an irrevocable supply deficit that helped seal the fate of the Bataan garrison long before the fight started.

When, in late December 1941, it became necessary to withdraw into and make a stand on Bataan peninsula, either the supplies themselves were not available or, when they were, the transportation to get them there was lacking. In either case, Bataan came up far short of a proposed six-month supply of food and medicine. No sooner had the gates been closed behind the last of the Fil-American troops as they entered the jungled peninsula than the astonishing discovery was made that without further supplement the 75,000-man army on Bataan along with some 25,000 civilian laborers and refugees, at full ration, would have only enough food to last 20 days.

Three steps were immediately taken in an attempt to ease the critical situation: first, the entire command, including Corregidor personnel, were put on half-ration, which represented a cut in calories from 4,000 to 2,000 per man per day; second, frantic efforts were made to procure ships, crews, and supplies in Australia to run the Japanese blockade of Philippine waters. Lt. Gen. George Brett, U.S. Commanding General in Australia, was given an unlimited source of funds by President Roosevelt to be used in this pursuit. Because of the high risk involved, however, very few ships or crews could be found. In the end, only four were able to break through, and then with only enough food to barely fill a two or three day ration requirement for the hard-pressed troops on Bataan; third, although probably the most successful, yet like everything else, limited, was an all-out attempt made by the Quartermaster to live off the land, so to speak. Although many freshly harvested stacks of unthreshed rice (palay) covered the rice fields throughout the Islands at this time, 90 percent of Bataan's rice grew in the enemy-controlled northeast corner of the peninsula. Through the courageous efforts of local Filipinos and Philippine Army raiding parties, about 30,000 pounds of rice were plucked from behind the lines, brought back, threshed, milled, and issued. Even the rice mills themselves were dismantled under the very nose of the enemy, rebuilt near the southern tip of the peninsula, and used effectively until the palay ran out in mid–February. With additional help from blockade-runners, the daily issue of rice stayed near 14 ounces per man per day throughout the battle. As cursed as it was by the Americans, rice remained the only adequate food source throughout the battle.

Another important food item, particularily to the American diet, was fresh meat. The slaughtering of local livestock during the campaign by the veterinary corps, up to mid-March, amounted to approximatley 30,000 pounds per day. Local livestock consisted of about 3,800 carabao (Philippine water buffalo and beast of burden), over 300 cavalry and pack horses, and approximately 80 pack mules. Also, a couple of hundred head of cattle and about 100 pigs smuggled across the bay in small boats from Cavite Province during the campaign were slaughtered. In early March, when forage for the corralled animals ran out, the remaining 500 were slaughtered, taken to Corregidor's large cold storage plant, and frozen. From here, three times a week, the meat was prepared, sent by boat to Bataan, and then by truck to units throughout the peninsula. Although unavoidable, this method of distribution remained far from being satisfactory. Most combat units in isolated jungle positions at the far end of the distribution line were the last to be served. Some even had their ration delivered by pack mule. Some would find their meat ration crawling with maggots by that time, as the tropical fly's egg would hatch within a half-hour after it was laid. In most cases, after removing the legless fly larva, the food was eaten anyway.

Fresh fish, as a meat supplement, and one preferred by the Filipinos, was quite abundant early in the campaign. With fishing villages lining Bataan's quiet eastern shoreline, encouraging local Filipino fisherman to risk tending their traps at night for money was easy. For the first three weeks of the campaign, as much as 12,000 pounds of fish were caught nightly. A sudden realization by the Japanese of what was going on, however, brought a quick, early February end to the supply of fresh fish.

As long as flour lasted, bakeries were set up at different spots along the east coast. The only permanent ovens, which were used until late January, were at the tiny fishing village of Puerto Rivas on the northeastern Bataan

A Filipino baking bread at one of the three Quartermaster bakeries maintained on Bataan until flour ran out in mid–March.

coast. Temporary field bakeries were set up at Limay, Lamao, and Cab-caben. Remaining in operation until late February, they provided about 25,000 pounds of bread a day to American and Philippine Scout units, in an attempt to maintain the American ration balance for as long as possible. Frontline Filipino troops had one advantage over those in the rear areas: At night, Filipino soldiers would often make their way across the lines into nearby barrios. There they would buy or trade for food from markets, occasionally grab up a loose pig or chicken, and maybe bring back a sack of rice. Also, the Filipino's willingness to seek supplement from the local flora and fauna helped him to maintain his health. Most Americans were reluctant to experiment with local edibles. Although not as tasty or appetizing as American foods, they did, however, supply many of the important vitamins not offered in the day's ration. Along with monkey and iguana, the Filipinos also ate python (indigenous in some number to the rugged west coast), its eggs, and dog.[3]

The Bataan Ration: The controversial "Bataan Ration," implemented in early January 1942, represented barely half the usual peace-time ration of 4,000 calories or 71 ounces of food per man per day. Although ordered, if the 2,000-calorie daily Bataan ration was ever issued, it was probably short-lived and to the better-off rear-area troops. According to records, the ration, from the first day's issue to the last, receded steadily

Private Avon Sherman and Lt. H. H. Roberts enjoy what was soon to become a rarity on Bataan—doughnuts—from one of the three field bakeries on the peninsula that continued to operate until flour ran out in mid–March.

until bottoming out in late March at near 1,000 calories, or 17 ounces. Bottoming out at the same time from the ration's effects was, of course, the starved and struggling Bataan Army. The disadvantage of the ration, regardless of the number of calories it offered, was its disregard of caloric and vitamin balance for the sake of quantity. Although unavoidable, it soon had most of the command suffering from malnutrition. Since rice was the most plentiful food, it became the basic part of the diet. As long as it remained available, the Americans' rice issue was supplemented by canned salmon or fresh meat (carabao) and bread. General Wainwright commented that "young carabao [wasn't] so bad, particularily if you [had] some kind of seasoning handy. But," he hastily added, "Bataan seemed to be a land reserved for carabao veterans." From Henry G. Lee's poem "Bomb Raid" comes a description of a typical issue of the Bataan Ration:

> Eight ounces of rice per man and four of bread
> Just two of milk and one small salmon can
> For every fifteen men.

The Filipino issue offered about four ounces more per meal of rice along with some fish or occasionally a little meat. Any consistent addition to the ration was usually due to a resourceful or foresighted mess sergeant who had brought as much food into Bataan with him as he could beg, borrow, or steal. Surprisingly enough, within many small units, these supplements were large enough to last throughout the entire 90-day campaign. Less-balanced supplements came from wild pig, monkey, or iguana, usually captured by the starving, ever-scavenging Bataan soldier. Little that was edible, in fact, escaped notice for long. Lieutenant John Bulkeley and his PT boat crew, for example, got tired of eating rice and salmon one day and "ate a tomcat" that had been bothering them at night. "We boiled it to get all the good out of it," said Bulkeley, "and it wasn't bad. All dark meat—reminded you a little of duck." Although battlefield successes against the Japanese were many, the behind-the-lines battle with the Bataan Ration remained a losing one throughout the campaign.[4]

Transportation: The short-notice problems existing within all units of the Bataan Defense Command did not escape the notice of the Motor Transport Service and Col. Michael Quinn. The most critical shortage was of trucks, whose role on Bataan was acknowledged to be vital. Even the Philippine Division was not exempt from such shortages. Far worse off, however, was the recently mobilized Philippine Army, which had been allotted just 20 trucks per 7,500-man division. Existing transportation fell far short of its needs. To alleviate the problem, Col. Quinn was able to lease nearly 1,000 trucks from dealers in Manila when the war broke out. The only problem was that many were without bodies and cabs, which were hastily added.

For the Philippine Army, privately owned transportation companies, by past agreement, were to supply its divisions in case of emergency with as many buses as needed. It was therefore not unusual to see open-sided, multicolored buses on Bataan with such names as Pambusco, Raytranco, Pastranco, and others barely vivible through layers of red Bataan dust. A shortage of the traditional army jeep within the Philippine command again put the squeeze on the resourcefulness of the needy. Staff vehicles ranged from the few command cars that did arrive just prior to the outbreak of hostilities, to a wild array of nonmilitary vehicles: Fords, Chevys, Chryslers, Cadillacs, La Salles, Packards—you name it and you probably would have seen it underneath a coat of red Bataan dust and olive-drab paint. The manner of requisition for many of the vehicles is best left unexplained, although most of them were leased or purchased from private dealers as the need occured before and in the early days of the war.

Despite all of this, the number of motor vehicles on Bataan still remained insufficient. In emergencies, commanders of needy combat units were allowed, at first by priority and later by order, to commandeer vehicles to fill their immediate needs. As this practice continued, however, it began to spread to noncombat units which, with little excuse, would hijack not only the vehicle, but its load as well. In fact, hijackers, who were usually Filipinos, considered a confiscated truck filled with anything edible as really hitting the jackpot. Although much curtailed by the mid–January rationing of gasoline and closer checkpoint scrutiny by military police, the practice continued throughout the campaign.

An early January check on the amount of gasoline stored on Bataan, based on the anticipated period of need, put it at the acceptable figure of 500,000 gallons. However, careless allotment, which averaged out to nearly 14,000 gallons a day during the first half of the month, quickly brought about a tight rationing program that slashed the daily issuance figures to between 3,000 and 4,000 gallons of gasoline. Major Clarence Bess, an operations officer with the II Corps, wrote, "At first the gasoline ration was fixed at three gallons of fuel per day for the necessary administrative vehicles. It was then lowered to three gallons per week per vehicle." The engineers also felt the pinch on petroleum products. For the first time, jobs involving the use of fuels, usually diesel, were either cancelled or cut by as much as 80 percent. Several hundred gallons of precious gasoline were salvaged by engineers from wrecked and beached barges around the peninsula. Yet, so critical had the shortage of fuels become, that in some cases, engineer tasks were later estimated by the number of gallons of diesel fuel or gasoline it would take rather than by their importance to the defense. Priorities were established entirely on fuel estimates. A 300- or 400-gallon job, for example, would lose out to a 100-gallon job. These restrictions, although controlling the unnecessary use of vehicles, forced tight limitations on their authorized uses as well. Even the gasoline-powered generator used to supply power for the important Bataan to Corregidor radio and message center was restricted in its use. Hospitals could offer no ambulance service. Even the vital ration trucks sometimes found themselves unable to complete runs because of an empty tank.[5]

The Bataan Hospitals and the Medical Situations

Aside from the medical detachments assigned to individual combat units, provisions were made for the establishment of a general hospital on Bataan just prior to the December withdrawal into the peninsula. The site chosen was near the barrio of Limay along the east coast. The buildings were tin-roofed barracks used by Philippine Scouts before the war. Shortly, a second hospital, known variously as Field, General, or Base Hospital No. 2, was established in the jungle near the Real River, some three miles west of Cabcaben. Although functioning entirely out of tents, the location of the hospital amid the thick jungle and intermingling clumps of bamboo provided it with a great natural concealment from the air. Its open-air wards offered an additional plus. Foxholes could be dug, in many cases, right under the patients' beds. Nurse Lt. Juanita Redmond, described the nurses quarters at No. 2 as "consisting of half-shelters strung through the trees, and while we at No. 1 had some sort of crude shower arrangement . . . the girls at No. 2 did their bathing and laundry in the creek."

The function of the hospital at Limay of taking all battlefield casualties requiring surgery ceased late in January following the general withdrawal to positions on the second MLR. Because of its close proximity to the new line, it was moved up the Mariveles Road, past the turn off to Hospital No. 2, to an area known as Little Baguio. Here it remained to the end as Hospital No. 1. Luckier than Hospital No. 2, which inherited no permanent structures at all, the new No. 1 was able to move into barracks and sheds formerly occupied by a prewar motor-pool unit. Water was nearby, the air relatively cool, but the natural cover provided Hospital No. 2 by the jungle was missing at Little Baguio. Conceding its visibility from the air, it was, however, liberally marked with huge red crosses as a precaution against being accidentally bombed by the Japanese.

The hospitals were staffed by about 40 doctors, both military and civilian, of various professional skills, 50 or 60 American and Filipino nurses, and about 200 medics, orderlies, and technicians. Due to the lack of laundry facilities, traditional hospital whites had long since given way to big, baggy, army-green or khaki coveralls, which, of course, did little for the morale of the appearance-conscious nurses. Once they accepted this, however, air corps Capt. Dick Fellows, in command of the Philippine Air Depot near Bataan Field, suddenly found himself "very popular with all the nurses." Seems he had the only small-sized coveralls to be found on Bataan.

By March the two hospitals were literally bursting at their seams, having taken in over three and a half times their designated capacities of 1,000 patients each. Restrictions were immediately placed on all admissions. From then on, to be admitted, a man had to be in serious or critical condition. Minor wounds or wounds that could be handled by corps or division hospitals were not eligible for general hospital treatment. Even when "qualifying," patients often had to wait between eight and ten hours from the time when they were made ready for collection and the time they were finally admitted. With the premium on fuel and transportation vehicles, the hospitals themselves offered no ambulance service, which, in turn, gave the arriving wounded the appearance of being victims rather than patients. It was possible, in some cases, that a wounded man's journey from the distant front started on the back of a pack mule. From there, after fresh dressings and the decision to send him on, it was likely his next three hours or so were

spent painfully bouncing along a chewed-up, dusty stretch of Bataan road
on the floor of an open-sided commercial bus. It was not unusual for some
of the more isolated Philippine Army troops to have spent as many as 24
hours in transit from frontline outposts. Captain and doctor Alfred Weinstein of the Bataan hospital staff wrote of the wounded men's ordeals, "they
had lain in their foxholes and first aid stations for days until they [could be]
carried by hand litter or mule pack over mountains and through swamps
to where ambulances could navigate." By the time they reached the
hospital, "their wounds stank to high heaven and crawled with fat maggots."6

Medical Problems

Malaria: During the first two months of the battle, the spread of
malaria in the mosquito-infested jungles of Bataan was kept at a con-
trollable level. Unfortunately, by the end of February, the supply of quinine
dwindled to the point where it no longer could be given as a preventive except to those actually stricken by the disease. Every effort imaginable was
made in an attempt to supplement the shortage. There was little success.
Although quinine in powder form remained available, its bitterness made
it unpalatable. Immediately, the effects of the disappearance of the drug as
a prophylaxis was felt. On the seventh day after its use was restricted, nearly
500 men qualified for admission to hospitals suffering from the disease.
This daily admission rate continued rising until it reached the staggering
figure of 1,000 by the end of March. Within the combat units, particularly
Filipino, over 70 percent of the men would contract malaria before the
surrender.

As if malaria by itself wasn't enough, a particular strain of the disease,
indigenous mostly to the low-lying swamps and forests of central Bataan
through which Fil-American positions on the final MLR ran, also took its
toll. Technically known as estivo-autumnal malaria, to most it was simply
known as dreaded, man-killing, cerebral malaria. A man bitten by this
mosquito usually went out of his mind within five days, on his way to dying
an agonizing death. Although there were many known cases on Bataan,
mostly among the more exposed Filipino troops, the mosquito was fortunately not selective when choosing its victim. The Japanese, just after the
fall of Bataan, were struck with an epidemic that not only put 10,000 in the
hospitals and killed some 500, but almost brought about a postponement
of the invasion of Corregidor.

Gangrene and Gas Gangrene: The malnourished condition of the
starving Bataan soldier, combined with the high incidence of combat-
related wounds, rendered his body nearly incapable of fighting off infection
once it set in. Added to this was the fact that the Bataan soil was inundated

with gangrene bacteria, making it not only a constant threat to the untended or unhealing wound, but conducive to the occurrence of gas gangrene as well. Gangrene in its gaseous state, which could be readily identified by its sickeningly sweet odor, also became highly contagious. Special isolation wards had to be built out in the jungle away from other patients, while experiments were conducted to find a cure. With penicillin not yet available and the on-hand supply of antitoxin soon exhausted, the infected patient usually found himself in the capable hands of doctors Tony Adamo and Earl Wilson at Hospital No. 1. These men, "under the stress of emergency," found a way to stop the gas gangrene infection. The wounded arm or leg was laid open usually to the bone, the infected tissue removed, the wound cleansed, and left open to the air. "The response to this treatment was dramatic," wrote Dr. Weinstein. Most of the time, "soldiers lost their toxicity in 12 to 24 hours. Their pulses slowed, their blood pressure rose, they lost their mental confusion, and took nourishment with gusto."

Dysentery: The dire lack of training in the practical use of sanitary precautions within the inadequately prepared Philippine Army units soon found many of the permanently bivouacked troops on Bataan suffering from various forms of dysentery. The noxious combination of open, poorly placed latrines, unchallenged hordes of flies, and the drinking of unpurified water remained the leading causes. Men suffering from the disease found themselves seeking relief as often as 40 times a day. This, needless to say, minimized their ability to function in the combat zone. Effects of the Philippine dry season also put great demands on men's water requirements. In the tropics, wrote Dr. Weinstein, a man "goes raving mad in a couple of days without water. The few watering points and water trucks [on Bataan] were totally inadequate. The lister bags issued to each company were not plentiful enough when the outfit was deployed to cover a half-mile of line. The chlorine for them soon ran out. It was not possible at all times to boil water because of the danger of campfires attracting dive-bombers and enemy artillery. Thirst-crazed men drank water they knew to be polluted from carabao wallows and stagnant mountain pools. At least 30 percent of the troops had bacillary dysentery, 10 percent amoebic dysentery, and the rest some variety of worm infestation of the bowel." Those patients suffering most critically from the disease were eventually moved into one of the field hospitals. "Because of our dysentery patients, who had to make as many as 50 visits to the latrine in a day," wrote Lt. Redmond, "[the latrine] could not be placed very far from the wards."

The Bataan Diet: Aside from combat and mosquito-related cases, most of the suffering within the army on Bataan originated from dietary deficiencies. In January, all of Bataan was placed on a half-ration that by mid–February became a "dwindling" half-ration and by mid–March, a mere quarter. Captain Alan Poweleit, surgeon with the Provisional Tank

Group, recorded in his diary on March 9 that the rations issued that day "were little better than a fourth of what a person should have normally." With the critical shortage of food came, of course, the imbalanced diet. Important vitamin deficiencies, particularly of Vitamin B, which led to edema and beriberi, affected all of the troops, whether at the front or in rear areas. A soldier suffering from malnutrition not only lost the physical stamina to persevere, but usually the emotional will as well. He not only lost the ability to fight off the sickness and disease, but also the facility to combat it once it struck. Within the last 20 days of the battle, unit commanders typically reported the combat efficiency of their troops to be at barely 40 percent, some even less.[7]

Communications

Communications, or the lack of them, have supplied the margin of difference in battles throughout history. It would be so on Bataan, as well. Effects of the extremely dense Bataan jungle on an army seriously short of necessary signal equipment to begin with magnified communication difficulties. These can perhaps be best understood by taking note of comments made by one of Gen. MacArthur's operations officers, Col. James V. Collier. After an inspection tour of "every division and regimental C.P." on Bataan, Collier reported that the "damned jungle hides and swallows everything. Communications don't exist. Messengers get lost. Divisions can maintain only marginal contact with regiments. Some regiments can't find their battalions. We came across companies that didn't know to whom they belonged. It's a mess!"[8]

APPENDIX C

Refugees

The presence of nearly 25,000 refugees within the confines of the peninsula, most within the bounds of the three relocation camps along the Real River above Cabcaben, added greatly to the already critical supply problem. The situation, of course, was one of great concern to the army. First, the military could use all the volunteer civilian labor it could get. Second, the army maintained total responsibility of feeding and caring for the entire refugee population, regardless of their willingness to contribute to the labor needs. It was, therefore, not easy to entice civilians to work for money, since there was little or no food to be bought, or to work for food alone since they were being fed by the army anyway. Also, working for the army increased the possibility of being shot at or bombed by the Japanese and took away the apparent security of the camps tucked in along the edge of the Real River. Yet jobs were offered, and although the labor force usually proved inconsistent and unreliable, the jobs remained filled most of the time. Both the quartermaster and the engineers offered jobs for almost as many as wanted to work. In response, over 1,500 drivers were added to the overburdened transportation service, forming the bulk of 24 provisional truck companies that operated throughout the entire campaign.[9] Major Clarance Bess of the U.S. 31st Infantry's Service Company commented that the "native drivers must receive praise for the gallant service they performed. The 70 of them were organized into a platoon composed of four sections. They identified themselves with the company, and except for one man, did not request or desire relief from any hazardous duty."[10] Other quartermaster-related jobs included the establishment and maintenance of cemeteries, salvage and reclamation of equipment, and loading and unloading of supplies at distribution points and dumps. Engineer needs put civilians to work on roads and air fields and in construction and repair of military installations, buildings, air raid shelters, and hospitals. The hospitals, in fact, had very little trouble attracting and keeping the usually inconsistent volunteers. The added inducement of extra rations and a chance to work with one's hands kept the response to hospital jobs high. Since most of the jobs around the hospitals were pick-up in nature, the Filipinos, with their trusty little bolo knives and an endless supply of local bamboo, made everything from brooms to double and triple-decker beds to hospital wards themselves. For convalescing patients, a crutch and cane factory was actually put into operation, employing 30 or 40 people. In the end, as the army on Bataan went, so did the civilian refugee. When Bataan fell, fewer than 10 percent of the civilians remained unaffected by malaria, dysentery, or malnutrition.[11]

Troop Morale

It was, of course, necessary that the morale of the army on Bataan throughout the long seige remain high. Unlike most history-making American armies, however, this one was trapped. All efforts, therefore, were channeled towards making the encircled garrison believe this condition was temporary. Spurred by early campaign victories, for about 75 of the 90 day long battle, this remained relatively easy. In "Abucay Withdrawal," Henry G. Lee made reference to Gen. MacArthur's promise of reinforcements:

> "The time is secret but I can say
> That swift relief ships are on the way
> Thousands of men and hundreds of planes—
> Back in Manila before the rains!
> With decorations and honors, too."
> MacArthur said it, it must be true.

American confidence in their country's ability to "bail them out" of the Bataan predicament continued strong up to the mid–March news of Gen. MacArthur's escape to Australia. With the General's "abandonment" came the almost unbelievable realization that all efforts by the United States to save the Philippines had desisted. From that moment on, morale on Bataan began its irretrievable plunge to the bottom, where it remained in wait for the obvious end.

So unassailable had morale on Bataan remained up to that time that even the collapse of the free world around them—of Wake Island, Guam, Java, Malaya, and Singapore—failed to shake it. The Japanese, perhaps having realized this, concentrated their efforts on disrupting and splitting the command through the Filipinos. Few stones were left unturned or tricks untried in these efforts. Propaganda directed toward the Filipino soldier came frequently and in all forms. Leaflets, radio broadcasts over radio KZRH, Manila, and even broadcasts over public address systems set up on the battlefield were used. Captain (later Col.) Carlos Romulo on one of his trips to the Bataan front witnessed one of the Japanese "sound-truck" broadcasts. "Out of the night," he wrote, "came a woman's voice, sweet and persuasive. In sentimental words it announced the dedication of a program to 'the brave and gallant defenders of Bataan.' Songs followed, quavering through the forest. They were selected to arouse nostalgia to the breaking point in a boy facing death and longing for home. 'Home, Sweet Home,' 'Old Folks at Home'—these were the kinds of songs that the Japanese broadcast in the dead of night, alternating heartbreak with horror. . . . For the first time, I realized what the boys were enduring, spiritually, physically, and mentally in the foxholes of Bataan." Attempts were made to build up hatred in the Filipinos for their American comrades. Incidents occurring at the time of the Spanish-American War and later with the American army of occupation were dug up. Others attempted to show discrimination between Americans and Filipinos. Were not the Americans paid more and fed better but exposed less on the battlefield? Was not this war between Japan and the United States and not the Philippines? After all, were the Japanese not fighting to build an "Asia for the Asiatics"?

One of the more widely circulated leaflets dropped among Filipino troops was a "free pass" through the Japanese lines to freedom. Printed on one side were the words TICKET TO PEACE, or TICKET TO ARMISTICE. On the back was a set of instructions telling the desiring bearer how to put it to use.[12]

On occasion, copies of one of the three most influential prewar Manila newspapers, controlled by then, of course, by the Japanese, were dropped over the lines by plane. Along with exploiting Axis success and Allied failures throughout the world—of which there were many at that time—attention was also directed toward the country's peaceful return to normalcy under Japanese rule.

In the end, the question was, Could the Japanese sever the bonds of trust and friendship between the Filipino and the American? Wasn't it really America's fight? Maybe. But it was the Filipinos' countryside and villages and cities that were indifferently being destroyed in its wake. It was their women who were being raped and their families who were being starved and mistreated. It was forcing an existence and a way of life on a country which was already living and happily functioning under the guidance of the United States until 1945, when it would become an independent Philippines. The Filipino loyalties to comrade and country would not break or waver. They would instead look upon their achievements on Bataan with great pride and dignity, without giving the question of "did they belong there?" a second thought. In fact, when the end came on Bataan, it would be the Filipino who would be the last to believe it, not the American.

To counter Japanese propaganda, a radio program, ordered and named personally by Gen. MacArthur as the Voice of Freedom, originated three times a day from Corregidor. Captain (later Col.) Carlos Romulo and his staff of writers kept troops up to date on war news, news from home, and on the heroic feats and deeds of their own comrades on Bataan. "The Voice of Freedom," commented Gen. Wainwright, "played us some swing tunes and told us on Bataan that help was on the way. When we first heard that, some of the men wept with joy." In addition, a single-page mimeographed newspaper, known as the *International News Summary,* was put into circulation from the same Press Relations Office on Corregidor. It was distributed as a daily supplement to the Voice broadcasts. After early battle success against the Japanese, a small caption appeared daily at the bottom of its only page: MEET YOU IN MANILA IN 90 DAYS, the next day, in 89 days, then 88, etc. Unfortunately, the "mile-long convoy" constantly referred to in the paper and over the Voice of Freedom broadcasts failed to reach Bataan in time to supply its army with the reinforcements necessary to make the Manila rendezvous.[13]

A second mimeographed sheet, emanating from a Bataan naval headquarters tunnel in Mariveles, was also started. Its twice daily circulation rate of 200, although later cut to a single edition due to a paper and ink shortage, was distributed two to three copies per American unit. The entire discourse of this four or five page release came from news broadcasts monitored from the outside world by the powerful navy radio receivers located near Mariveles on Bataan.[14]

Response to the efforts made to keep the news-starved troops informed became immediately obvious. Newspapers were read and passed on again and again until dog-eared and unreadable. Some men were known to have hitchhiked and walked as far as ten miles to get a copy. Radio locations throughout the command became popular gathering places during the Voice of Freedom broadcasts, especially in the evenings after issue of the day's end ration. In addition to the voice broadcasts, a program identified as Freedom for the Philippines originated at 6 P.M. nightly from shortwave station KGEI in San Francisco. Like the Voice of Freedom, it was received with mixed feelings. Some men branded its especially prepared scripts as propaganda. But to most, they offered the only link with the outside world, a link that for some, at least, made it seem not quite so far away.

The Weather and Its Effect

The weather of the Philippine dry season of 1942 had a torturous effect of its own on the confined army on Bataan. It was particularly tough on those in the combat zones, whose sufferings, unlike many of the rear area troops, were magnified tremendously by the extremes of poor diet, inadequate mosquito protection, and the unendurable weather.

December, climatically, is the Philippine's most ideal month, with temperatures and humidity both, by Western standards, at near-liveable levels. However, by mid-January, the time the Bataan campaign opened, the dry season had begun. Weather that offered no rain, daytime temperatures that consistently rose above 90 degrees, and worst of all, humidity that remained near 100 percent made for a very uncomfortable and exhausting existence. Major Stephen Mellnik commented on the before-the-war effects of the dry season climate on Americans. With daily temperatures rarely below 82 degrees and humidity over 92 percent, "few Americans dared to work outdoors between 10 A.M. and 4 P.M. when the temperature and humidity exceeded 98. Men gasped for breath during the hot season and prayed for cooling rains."[15] As if that wasn't bad enough, of the heat encountered on his first trip to Bataan in early January, Col. Carlos Romulo wrote that "Instantly our clothes were wet through. I have traveled around the world four times and spent considerable time in the tropics, but never have I encountered anything like the heat of Bataan. . . . We were told it was the hottest summer in the history of the peninsula."

In sharp contrast to the oppressive heat of the day, the China Sea–cooled nighttime temperatures also affected the troops. Men, before the night was over, needed a blanket to avoid the chill that moved in over Bataan with the setting of the hot Philippine sun. This again, however, was a necessity not always available to troops in frontline positions.

The countryside at this time, accordingly, became brown and dry, leaving most of the battle-torn roads, although continuously under repair by the engineers, mere dust-colored ribbons winding in and out of the jungle. Suffocating clouds of red "Bataan dust" trailed vehicles everywhere, settling on foliage, buildings, and bivouacked troops along the edges of the road. Colonel Carlos Romulo wrote that men even had to wear "gas masks as protection against the all-prevailing dust." In fact, after four hours of bouncing over the roads of Bataan, he "burst out laughing" at the two Filipino officers accompanying him. "They looked like albinos,"he said. "Pallid dust caked their hair and uniforms and skins." Dust-tails created by vehicles moving along the roads became such ideal targets-of-opportunity for the ever-lurking Japanese Air Force, that travel was limited as much as possible to predawn and dusk hours. Later, after noting the tendency of Japanese pilots to take three-hour lunch breaks, midday movement of troops and supplies was cautiously resumed. By three o'clock, however, whether at its destination or not, traffic was halted and the road cleared until dark.[16] With reference to the unpleasant roads, Henry G. Lee made the following mention in his poem, "Abucay Withdrawal":

> The road is rutted and sometimes steep
> And the heavy dust lies ankle deep;

It covers the grass with a film of gray
And dulls the green where jungles sway.
Hard on the flank of the twisting road,
And every car with its hasty load
Raises a choking, blinding cloud,
That hangs in the air like a dirty shroud

NOTES

The main sources for each chapter are listed with the usual explanatory notes. The authors of the following books, which were of great value, will occasionally be listed in this section by their author's name. They are Gen. Jonathan Wainwright, *General Wainwright's Story;* Allison Ind, *Bataan—The Judgment Seat;* Juanita Redmond, *I Served on Bataan;* Alfred A. Weinstein, *Barbed-Wire Surgeon;* Carlos P. Romulo, *I Saw the Fall of the Philippines;* Lt. Col. William E. Dyess, *The Dyess Story;* and Col. Ernest B. Miller, *Bataan Uncensored.*

Special mention must be made of the contribution to this book by Dr. Louis Morton, whose massive work, *The Fall of the Philippines,* written in 1953 for the United States Army in World War II series, which served as an indispensible "bible" on the U.S. Army's strategic and tactical role in the campaign, as well as an excellent chronology of the battle. Most of the otherwise undocumented details in this book should be credited to Morton.

Introduction

1. Maj. Ernest L. Brown, "Operations of the 57th Infantry, Abucay, January 1942." Monograph prepared for the U.S. Army Infantry School, Ft. Benning, Georgia, 1947. Hereafter, Brown.

2. Lt. Col. Adrianus Van Oosten, "Operations of the First Battalion 45th Infantry in the Battle of the Toul Pocket." Monograph prepared for the U.S. Army Infantry School, 1948. Hereafter, Van Oosten.

3. Maj. Eugene Conrad, "Operations of the 31st Infantry." Monograph prepared for the U.S. Army Infantry School, 1947. Hereafter, Conrad.

4. Col. William E. Brougher, *South to Bataan—North to Mukden.* Hereafter, Brougher.

5. Col. Russell Volkmann, *We Remained.* Hereafter, Volkmann.

6. Maj. William E. Webb, "Operations of the 41st Infantry in the Defense of the Abucay Line." Monograph prepared for the U.S. Army Infantry School, 1950. Hereafter, Webb.

7. Interview with Col. Ambrosio P. Peña, Bataan veteran and retired chief historian, Philippine Army. Hereafter, Peña.

8. Col. Ambrosio P. Peña, *The 1st Regular Division.* Hereafter, *1st P.A. Div.*

9. Col. Ambrosio P. Peña, *Bataan's Own* (the story of the Second Philippine Division formed on Bataan and made up of former Philippine Constabulary). Hereafter, *2nd P.A. Div.*

10. Abie Abraham, *Ghost of Bataan Speaks.* Hereafter, Abraham.

11. Interview with Frank Hewlett, United Press correspondent on Bataan. Hereafter, Hewlett.

12. Lt. Sheldon Mendelson, "Operations of the Provisional Air Corps Regiment" Monograph prepared for the U.S. Army Infantry School, 1947. Hereafter, Mendelson.

13. Cmdr. E. L. Sackett's unpublished paper, "History of the USS *Canopus.*" Hereafter, *Canopus* diary.

Chapter One

1. *2nd P.A. Div.*

2. Two U.S. Air Force studies: "Army Air Action in the Philippines and Netherlands East Indies, 1941–42"; and "Summary of Air Action in Philippines and Netherland East Indies, 7 December 1941–26 March 1942." Hereafter, USAF studies. Also, diaries of 24th Pursuit Group activities on Bataan by majors Ben S. Brown, David L. Obert, and Stewart W. Robb. Hereafter, 24th Pursuit diary.

3. *Canopus* diary.

4. Brig. Gen. Charles Drake, "No Uncle Sam," unpublished paper. Hereafter, Drake.

5. USAF studies.

6. Stewart Holbrook, *None More Courageous.* Hereafter, Holbrook.

7. USAF studies.

8. Gen. Douglas MacArthur, *Reminiscences.* Hereafter, MacArthur.

9. Robert L. Underbrink, *Destination Corregidor.* Hereafter, Underbrink.

10. Walter Edmund, Interview with Lt. Gen. R. K. Sutherland, 1945. Hereafter, Sutherland interview.

11. *Engineers of the Southwest Pacific,* volumes I and II. Hereafter, *Engineers SW Pacific.*

12. Ibid.

13. Holbrook, Underbrink.

14. Brown, and Maj. John E. Olson, "Operations of the 57th Infantry at Abucay, Jan. 1942." Monograph prepared for the U.S. Army Infantry School, 1948. Hereafter, Olson.

15. Holbrook.

16. Olson.

17. Holbrook.

18. Interview with Manuel Mabunga.

19. Olson.

20. Ibid.

21. Webb, and Maj. William Nealson, "Operations of Provisional Battalion 41st Division at Abucay, January 1942." Monograph prepared for the U.S. Army Infantry School, 1948. Hereafter, Nealson.

22. John T. Boyt, Col. Stewart's grandson. Interview with author.

23. MacArthur.

24. Holbrook.

25. USAF studies.

26. Ted Buenafe, *Wartime Philippines.* Hereafter, Buenafe. Also, Benjamin Gray, *Rendezvous with Destiny.* Hereafter, Gray.

28. Maj. Louis Besbeck, "Operations of the Third Battalion, 45th Infantry at Abucay Hacienda, January 1942." Monograph prepared for U.S. Army Infantry School, 1947. Hereafter, Besbeck.

29. USAF studies.
30. 24th Pursuit diary.
31. Col. Uldarcio Baclagon, *They Served with Honor.* Hereafter, Baclagon.
32. MacArthur, Underbrink
33. Conrad.
34. Maj. John I. Pray, "Action of Co. G, 31st Infantry at Abucay Hacienda, January 1942." Monograph prepared for U.S. Army Infantry School, 1947. Hereafter, Pray.
35. 24th Pursuit diary
36. Lt. John D. Bulkeley "Summary of Operations—Motor Torpedo Boat Squadron Three, December 7, 1941–April 7, 1942," unpublished paper. Hereafter, Bulkeley. Also, Robert J. Bulkley *At Close Quarters: PT Boats in the U.S. Navy.* Hereafter, Bulkley. Brig. Gen. Steve Mellnik, *Philippine Diary 1939—1945.* Hereafter, Mellnik.
37. Bulkeley, Holbrook. Also, W. L. White, *They Were Expendable.* Hereafter, White.
38. January 16, 1942 Action Report of Capt. John Wheeler, 26th Cavalry, and Edwin P. Ramsey's book *Lt. Ramsey's War.*
39. White.
40. Peña.
41. Besbeck.
42. Maj. Henry Pierce, "Operations of Co. L, 45th Infantry at Abucay Hacienda, January 1942." Monograph prepared for U.S. Army Infantry School, 1950. Hereafter, Pierce.
43. Conrad.
44. Pray.
45. Besbeck.
46. Frank C. Waldrop, *MacArthur on War.* Hereafter, Waldrop.
47. 24th Pursuit diary.
48. Ibid.
49. Webb.
50. Pierce.
51. Maj. Everett Mead, "Operations and Movements of the 31st Infantry Regiment." Monograph prepared for U.S. Army Infantry School, 1948. Hereafter, Mead.
52. Gray, Baclagon.
53. 24th Pursuit diary.
54. Bataan Diary of Lt. Thomas P. Garrity. Hereafter, Garrity.
55. Maj. Alfred Santos, "The First Regular Division, PA, in the Battle of the Philippines." 1947 U.S. Army School of Logistics paper. Hereafter, Santos.
56. Garrity.
57. Maj. Clarence Bess, "Operations of Service Company, 31st Infantry, January 5–April 9, 1942." Monograph prepared for U.S. Army Infantry School, 1948. Hereafter, Bess.
58. Mead.
59. Bess.
60. Mead.
61. Besbeck.
62. Waldrop.

Chapter Two

1. Peña.
2. White, Bulkeley.
3. 24th Pursuit diary.
4. Baclagon.
5. William F. Hogaboom, "Action Report: Bataan," *Marine Corps Gazette,* 1946. Hereafter, Hogaboom. William Prickett, "Naval Battalion at Mariveles," and "The Naval Battalion on Bataan," *Marine Corps Gazette,* 1950, 1960. Hereafter, Prickett. Dwight R. Messimer, *In the Hands of Fate: The Story of Patrol Wing Ten.* Hereafter, Messimer.
6. White, Bulkeley, Bulkley, Holbrook.
7. Hogaboom.
8. Messimer.
9. Clark Lee, *They Call It Pacific.* Hereafter, Lee.
10. Hogaboom, and Diary of Col. Paul D. Bunker. Hereafter, Bunker.
11. 16th Naval District War Diary, 8 December 1941–19 February 1942. Hereafter, 16th Nav. Dist. diary.
12. 24th Pursuit diary, USAF studies.
13. Bunker, Hogaboom.
14. Lee.
15. Hogaboom.
16. 16th Nav. Dist. Diary, and Lt. Cmdr. John Morrill, *South from Corregidor.* Hereafter, Morrill.
17. Holbrook.
18. 16th Nav. Dist. diary.
19. Hogaboom.
20. *Canopus* diary.
21. *2nd P.A. Div,* Baclagon.
22. Baclagon.
23. Samual A. Goldblith, "The 803rd Engineers in the Philippine Defense, Military Engineers, 1946." Hereafter, Goldblith.
24. *2nd P.A. Div.*
25. Col. Harold K. Johnson, "Anyasan and Silaiim Points," 1947. U.S. Army School of Combined Arms monograph. Hereafter, Johnson.
26. Dyess.
27. Goldblith.
28. Lt. Col. Thomas Dooley, "The First U.S. Tank Action in World War II," 1948 U.S. Army Armor School monograph. Hereafter, Dooley.
29. Dyess.
30. Ibid.
31. Dyess, *Canopus* diary.
32. Lee.
33. Johnson.
34. Ibid.
35. 24th Pursuit diary, USAF studies.
36. Bulkeley, White, Holbrook.
37. 24th Pursuit diary.
38. Johnson.
39. Underbrink.
40. 24th Pursuit diary.

41. Ibid.
42. Gen. Richard Fellows. Interview with author. Hereafter, Fellows. Walter D. Edmonds, *They Fought with What They Had.* Hereafter, Edmonds. Also, Underbrink.
43. Lee.
44. Waldrop.
45. James K. Eyre, "Early Japanese Imperialism and the Philippines, U.S. Naval Institute Proceedings, 1949."
46. Norman Lauchner. Interview with author.
47. Messimer.
48. Dooley.
49. Johnson.
50. 24th Pursuit diary; Allison Ind, *Bataan—The Judgment Seat.* Hereafter, Ind.
51. Lee.
52. 24th Pursuit diary; Ind.
53. Garrity.
54. Maj. Achille Tisdelle, "Diary of Major A. C. Tisdelle," *Military Affairs,* 1947. Hereafter, Tisdelle.
55. Baclogan.
56. 24th Pursuit diary; Ind; USAF studies; Edmonds.
57. Peña.
58. Garrity.
59. Baclogon.
60. Col. Lee Vance, 26th Cavalry Diary. Hereafter, Vance. William E. Chandler, "The 26th Cavalry—Battles to Glory," *Armored Cavalry Journal,* 1947. Hereafter, Chandler.
61. Vance.
62. Johnson.

Chapter Three

1. Volckmann.
2. Ibid.
3. Santos, Baclagon.
4. Brougher.
5. Santos, Baclagon.
6. Van Oosten.
7. Holbrook; John Toland, *But Not in Shame.* Hereafter, Toland.
8. Toland.
9. Brougher.
10. Maj. Beverly Skardon, "Operations of Company A, 92nd Infantry." Monograph prepared for U.S. Army Infantry School, 1947. Hereafter, Skardon.
11. Baclogon.
12. Santos.
13. *1st P.A. Div.*
14. Van Oosten.
15. Ibid.
16. Brougher.
17. Skardon.

18. Cameron W. Forbes, *The Philippine Islands.*
19. Waldrop, Holbrook.
20. Hewlett.
21. *2nd P.A. Div.*
22. Van Oosten.
23. Skardon.
24. Toland.
25. Baclagon.
26. Waldrop.
27. Ibid.
28. Ibid.
29. Peña.

Chapter Four

1. Waldrop.
2. Ind.
3. Alvin C. Poweleit, *USAFFE.* Hereafter, Poweleit.
4. Volckmann.
5. Lee.
6. Lee, White.
7. White, Bulkeley, Holbrook.
8. Underbrink.
9. Edgar P. Whitcomb, *Escape from Corregidor.* Hereafter, Whitcomb.
10. Lee.
11. Underbrink.
12. Conrad.
13. Peña.
14. Mendelson.
15. Ibid.
16. Garrity.
17. Baclagon.
18. Kai Martin. Interview with author.
19. Poweleit.
20. Lt. Henry G. Lee, "Company History—HQ and MP Company's of Philippine Division," unpublished diary. Hereafter, H. G. Lee.
21. Lee.
22. White, Bulkeley.
23. Fellows.
24. Dyess, Ind, Edmonds, 24th Pursuit diary, USAF studies, and Samuel C. Grashio, *Return to Freedom.* Hereafter, Grashio.
25. White, Bulkeley, MacArthur, Bulkley.
26. James Wall. Interview with author.
27. Whitcomb.
28. Fellows.
29. Garrity.
30. Bataan diary of Col. Richard C. Mallonee. Hereafter, Mallonee.
31. Poweleit.
32. Mallonee.
33. Mead.

34. Drake; Capt. Harold A. Armold, "The Lessons of Bataan," *Quartermaster Review*, 1946. Hereafter, Armold. Frank Hewlett, "Quartermasters on Bataan Performed Heroic Feats," *Military Affairs*, 1949. Hereafter, *Heroic Feats*. Louis Morton, "The Battling Bastards of Bataan," *Military Affairs*, 1949. Hereafter, Morton.

35. Dr. W. H. Waterous, "Reminiscenses of Dr. W. H. Waterous Pertinent to World War II in the Philippines," unpublished paper. Hereafter, Waterous.

36. Lt. Col. Arthur C. Fischer, "Operation Malaria." *Great Untold Stories of World War II* (Author unknown).

37. Whitcomb.

38. Conrad.

39. Mallonee.

40. John J. Beck, *MacArthur and Wainwright*. Hereafter, Beck.

41. Military History Branch, Philippine Army publication, "Japanese Plan of Maneuver in Final Battle of Bataan." Hereafter, Final Plan.

42. Ibid.

43. Brougher.

44. Final Plan; John Toland, *The Rising Sun*. Hereafter, *Rising Sun*.

Chapte Five

1. Waldrop.

2. Mallonee.

3. Tisdelle.

4. Webb.

5. Edwin P. Hoyt, *The Lonely Ships*. Hereafter, Hoyt.

6. Underbrink.

7. Tisdelle.

8. Wyatt Blassingame, *Combat Nurses of World War II*. Hereafter, Blassingame.

9. Ibid.

10. Poweleit.

11. Hoyt; James H. and William M. Belote, *Corregidor: The Saga of a Fortress*. Hereafter, Belote.

12. Tisdelle.

13. *2nd P.A. Div.*

14. Tisdelle.

15. Mellnik.

16. Conrad.

17. Mead.

18. Baclagon.

19. Gray.

20. Drake.

21. Conrad.

22. Belote.

23. Peña.

24. Gen. Richard Fellows, "The Last Flight into Bataan," *Daedalus Flyer*, 1986. Hereafter, Last Flight.

25. Bess.

26. Conrad.

27. Toland.

28. Conrad.
29. Ibid.
30. Chandler
31. Ibid.
32. Tisdelle.
33. MacArthur, Toland, Beck.
34. Karl C. Dod, *The Corps of Engineers: The War Against Japan.* Hereafter, Dod.
35. Last Flight.
36. Grashio.
37. *2nd P.A. Div.*
38. Chandler.
39. Ibid.
40. *2nd P.A. Div.*
41. Bunker.
42. Chandler.
43. Whitcomb.
44. Mallonee.
45. Robert W. Levering, *Horror Trek.* Hereafter, Levering.
46. Jerome B. Leek, *Corregidor GI.* Hereafter, Leek.
47. Whitcomb.
48. Calvin E. Chunn, *Of Rice and Men.* Hereafter, Chunn.
49. Tisdelle.
50. *Canopus* diary.
51. Chunn.
52. *Canopus* diary.
53. Chunn.
54. Ibid.

Chapter Six

1. Whitcomb, Blassingame, Holbrook.
2. Blassingame, Holbrook.
3. Morrill.
4. Leek.
5. Levering.
6. Tisdelle.
7. Salvador P. Lopez, "When Bataan Fell," *Voice of the Veteran,* 1971.
8. Tisdelle, Mellnik.
9. Chunn.
10. Bunker.
11. Blassingame.
12. Chunn, Mellnik.
13. Chandler.
14. Waterous.
15. *1st P.A. Div.*
16. Brougher.
17. Col. Virgilio Cordero, *Bataan y la Marcha de la Muerta.*
18. H.G. Lee.
19. Reynaldo Perez, "Escape," *Voice of the Veteran,* 1971.
20. Dyess; Stanley Falk, *The March of Death.*

Appendix B

1. Dooley.
2. *Engineers SW Pacific,* Dod, 16th Nav. Dist. diary, Goldblith.
3. Drake, Morton, Armold, *Heroic Feats,* and Alvin P. Stauffer, *The Quartermaster Corps: Operations in the War Against Japan.*
4. Ibid.
5. *Engineers SW Pacific,* Dod, Drake, *Heroic Feats.*
6. Weinstein, Redmond, Waterous.
7. Ibid.
8. The Signal Corps, Volume II—The Test December 1941–July 1943.
9. Buenafe.
10. Bess.
11. Buenafe.
12. Peña.
13. Mellnik.
14. Peña, *Canopus* diary, and John Hersey, *Men on Bataan.*
15. Mellnik.
16. Ibid.

BIBLIOGRAPHY

Abraham, Abie. *Ghost of Bataan Speaks.* New York: Vantage Press, 1971.

Baclagon, Col. Uldarico S. *They Served with Honor.* Philippines: D. M. Press, Inc., 1968.

Beck, John Jacob. *MacArthur and Wainwright.* Albuquerque: University of New Mexico Press, 1974.

Belote, James H., and William M. Belote. *Corregidor: The Saga of a Fortress.* New York: Harper and Row, 1967.

Blair, Clay, Jr. *Silent Victory.* Philadelphia: J.B. Lippincott, 1975.

Blassingame, Wyatt. *Combat Nurses of World War II.* New York: Random House, 1967.

Brougher, Brig. Gen. W. E. *South to Bataan—North to Mukden.* Athens: University of Georgia Press, 1971.

Bulkley, Robert J. *At Close Quarters: PT Boats in the U.S. Navy.* Washington, D.C.: U.S. Government Printing Office, 1962.

Carroll, Gordon. *History in the Writing.* New York: Duell, Sloan and Pearce, 1945.

Chunn, Calvin E. *Of Rice and Men.* Los Angeles: Veteran's Pub. Co., 1946.

Cordero, Virgilio N. *Bataan y la Marcha de la Muerte.* Madrid: Afrodisco Aguado, 1957.

Craven, Wesly F., and James L. Cate. *U.S. Army Air Forces in World War II: Volume I—Plans and Early Operations, January 1939 to August 1942.* Chicago: Chicago University Press., 1948.

Dod, Karl C. *The Corps of Engineers: The War Against Japan.* Washington, D.C.: U.S. Army, 1946.

Dyess, Lt. Col. William E. *The Dyess Story.* New York: G.P. Putnam, 1944.

Edmonds, Walter D. *They Fought with What They Had.* Boston: Little, Brown, 1951.

Engineers of the Southwest Pacific: Volume I—Engineers in Theater Operations, 1941–45; Volume II—Engineer Supply. Washington, D.C.: U.S. Government Printing Office, 1947.

Falk, Stanley L. *The March of Death.* London: Robert Hale, 1964.

Floherty, John J. *The Courage and the Glory.* Philadelphia: J.B. Lippincott, 1942.

Forbes, W. Cameron. *The Philippine Islands.* Cambridge, Mass.: Harvard University Press, 1945.

Gasei. *Philippine Expeditionary Force.* Manila, P.I.: Watari Group Information Department Publications, 1943.

Grashio, Samuel C., and Bernard Norling. *Return to Freedom: The War Memoirs of Colonel Samuel C. Grashio, USAF.* Tulsa, Okla.: MCN Press, 1982.

Gray, Benjamin A., *Rendezvous with Destiny.* Manila, P.I.: Philippine Education Co., 1965.

Griffin, Marcus. *Heroes of Bataan.* Carlsbad, N.M.: Privately printed, 1968.

Hersey, John. *Men on Bataan.* New York: Alfred A. Knopf, 1943.
Holbrook, Stewart H. *None More Courageous.* New York: Macmillan, 1942.
Hoyt, Edwin P. *The Lonely Ships.* New York: David McKay, 1976.
Ind, Allison. *Bataan—The Judgment Seat.* New York: Macmillan, 1944.
Karig, Cmdr. Walter, and Welbourn Kelly. *Battle Report: Pearl Harbor to the Coral Sea.* New York: Farrar and Rinehart, 1944.
Lee, Clark. *They Call It Pacific.* New York: Viking Press, 1943.
Lee, Henry G. *Nothing but Praise.* California: Murray and Gee, 1948.
Leek, Jerome B. *Corregidor G.I.* California: Highland Press, 1948.
Levering, Robert W. *Horror Trek.* Ohio: Horstman Printing Co., 1948.
MacArthur, Gen. Douglas. *Reminiscences.* New York: McGraw-Hill, 1964.
Mellnik, Brig. Gen. Steve. *Philippine Diary 1939—1945.* New York: Van Nostrand Reinhold Co., 1969.
Messimer, Dwight R. *In the Hands of Fate: The Story of Patrol Wing Ten.* Annapolis, Md.: Naval Institute Press, 1985.
Miller, Ernest B. *Bataan Uncensored.* Minnesota: Hart Publications, Inc., 1949.
Morison, Samuel Eliot. *The Rising Sun in the Pacific.* Boston: Little, Brown, 1947.
Morrill, Lt. Cmdr. John and Pete Martin. *South from Corregidor.* New York: Simon and Schuster, 1943.
Morton, Louis. *The Fall of the Philippines.* Washington, D.C.: U.S. Army, 1953.
Peña, Col. Ambrosio P. *Bataan's Own.* Philippines: Munoz Press, Inc., 1967.
_____. *The First Regular Division.* Philippines: 1953
Poweleit, Alvic C., *USAFFE.* Privately printed, 1975.
Ramsey, Edwin and Stephen Rivele. *Lieutenant Ramsey's War.* New York: Knightsbridge, 1990.
Redmond, Juanita. *I Served on Bataan.* Philadelphia: J.B. Lippincott, 1943.
Reports of General MacArthur: Japanese Operations in the Southwest Pacific Area, Volume II—Part I. Washington, D.C.: U.S. Government Printing Office, 1967.
Romulo, Carlos P. *I Saw the Fall of the Philippines.* New York: Doubleday, Doran, 1942.
The Signal Corps: Volume II—The Test, December 1941–July 1943. Washington, D.C.: U.S. Government Printing Office, 1957.
Stauffer, Alvin P. *The Quartermaster Corps: Operations in the War Against Japan.* Washington, D.C.: U.S. Army, 1966.
Sunderman, Maj. James F. *World War II In the Air—The Pacific.* New York: Bramhall House, 1962.
Toland, John. *But Not in Shame.* New York: Random House, 1961.
_____. *The Rising Sun.* New York: Random House, 1970.
Underbrink, Robert L., *Destination Corregidor.* Washington, D.C.: Naval Institute Press, 1971.
Volckmann, Russell W. *We Remained.* New York: Norton, 1954.
Wainwright, Gen. Jonathan M. *General Wainwright's Story.* New York: Doubleday, 1946.
Waldrop, Frank C. *MacArthur on War.* New York: Duell, Sloan and Pearce, 1942.
Weinstein, Alfred A. *Barbed-Wire Surgeon.* New York: Macmillan, 1948.
Whitcomb, Edgar D. *Escape from Corregidor.* Chicago: Henry Regnery, 1958.
White, W.L. *They Were Expendable.* New York: Harcourt, Brace, 1942.
Williams, Ted. *Rogues of Bataan.* New York: Carlton Press, 1979.

Articles

Armold, Capt. Harold A. "The Lessons of Bataan." *Quartermaster Review* (Nov.–Dec. 1946), 12–16.
Baldwin, Hanson W. "The Fourth Marines at Corregidor." *Marine Corps Gazette* (Nov. 1946–Feb. 1947).
Brougher, William E., "Baggy Pants." *Reader's Digest* 68 (Jan. 1946), 75–78.
Chandler, William E., "The 26 Cavalry—Battles to Glory." *Armored Cavalry Journal* (March–Aug. 1947).
Eyre, James K. "Early Japanese Imperialism and the Philippines." United States Naval Institute Proceedings (Nov. 1949).
Fellows, Richard W. "The Last Plane into Bataan," *Daedalius Flyer* (1986).
Fischer, Lt. Col. Arthur C. "Operation Malaria," *Great Untold Stories of World War II.*
Goldblith, Samual A. "The 803d Engineers in the Philippine Defense," *Military Engineer* (Aug. 1946), 323–324.
Hewlett, Frank. "Jap Snipers in Bataan Hide Behind Own Paint," *Los Angeles Times* (February 20, 1942).
————. "Quartermasters on Bataan Performed Heroic Feats," *Military Affairs* (Summer 1949), 107–113.
Hogaboom, William F. "Action Report: Bataan," *Marine Corps Gazette* (April 1946), 27–31.
Johnson, Lt. Col. Harold K. "Defense Along the Abucay Line," *Military Review* (Feb. 1949).
Lopez, Salvador P. "When Bataan Fell," *Voice of the Veteran* (memorial edition, 1971), 2–4.
Morton, Louis. "The Battling Bastards of Bataan." *Military Affairs* (Summer 1949), 107–113.
Perez, Reynaldo. "Escape," *The Voice of the Veteran* (memorial edition, 1971), 13–17.
Prickett, William F. "Naval Battalion at Mariveles," *Marine Corps Gazette* (June 1950), 40–43.
————. "The Naval Battalion on Bataan," *Marine Corps Gazette* (Nov. 1960, 72–81.
Tisdelle, Maj. Achille C. "Diary of Major A. C. Tisdelle." *Military Affairs* (Summer 1947), 135–146.
Wheeler, Capt. John. "Action Report 26 Cavalry—January 16, 1942," *Life* magazine (March 23, 1942).

Unpublished Sources

Papers

Bulkeley, Lt. John D. "Summary of Operations—Motor Torpedo Boat Squadron Three, December 7, 1941—April 10, 1942."
Drake, Brig. Gen. Charles. "No Uncle Sam" (paper on Quartermaster operations and activities on Bataan).
Interview with Lt. Gen. Richard K. Sutherland at GHQ, Manila, June 4, 1945, by Walter D. Edmonds.

"Japanese Plan of Maneuver in Final Battle of Bataan." Military History Branch, Armed Forces of the Philippines, 1953.

Sackett, Cmdr. E. L. "History of the USS *Canopus.*"

Waterous, Dr. W. H. "Reminiscenses of Dr. W. H. Waterous Pertinent to World War II in the Philippines."

Diaries

Diaries on 24th Pursuit Group activities on Bataan by majors Ben S. Brown, David L. Obert and Stewart W. Robb.

16th Naval District War Diary: 8 December 1941–19 February 1942.

Bataan Diary of Lt. Thomas P. Garrity, U.S. Army Air Corps liaison officer with Gen. Wainwright. (Published in *Los Angeles Times,* June–July 1942.)

Bataan Diary of Col. Richard C. Mallonee, senior instructor of the Philippine Army's 21st Field Artillery Regiment.

26th Cavalry Diary of Col. Lee C. Vance, commanding officer, 26th Cavalry Regiment, Philippine Scouts.

Diary of Col. Paul D. Bunker, Seaward Defense Commander, Corregidor.

Histories

Lee, Lt. Henry G. "Company History—HQ and MP Co. of the Philippine Division."

USAF Studies

"Summary of Air Action in the Philippines and Netherland East Indies, 7 December 1941–26 March 1942."

"Army Air Action in the Philippines and Netherland East Indies, 1941–42."

Monographs

Written for the U.S. Army Infantry School, Fort Benning, Georgia:

Besbeck, Maj. Louis B. "Operations of the Third Battalion, 45th Infantry (P.S.) at Abucay Hacienda, January 1942" (1946–47).

Bess, Maj. Clarence R. "Operations of Service Company, 31st Infantry (U.S.), 5 January–9 April 1942" (1947–48).

Brown, Maj. Ernest L. "Operations of the 57th Infantry (P.S.), Abucay, January 1942" (1946–47).

Conrad, Maj. Eugene C. "Operations of the 31st Infantry (U.S.)" (1946–47).

Mead, Maj. Everett V. "Operations and Movements of the 31st Infantry Regiment (U.S.)" (1947–48).

Mendelson, Maj. Sheldon H. "Operations of the Provisional Air Corps Regiment" (1946–47).

Nealson, Maj. Williem R. "Operations of a Provisional Battalion, 41st Division (P.A.) at Abucay, January 1942" (1947–48).

Olson, Maj. John E. "Operations of the 57th Infantry (P.S.) at Abucay, January 1942" (1947–48).

Pierce, Maj. Henry J. "Operations of Company L, 45th Infantry (P.S.) at Abucay Hacienda, January 1942" (1949–50).

Pray, Maj. John I. "Action of Company G, 31st Infantry (U.S.) at Abucay Hacienda, January 1942" (1946–47).
Skardon, Maj. Beverly N. "Operations of Company A, 92d Infantry (P.A.)" 1946–47).
Van Oosten, Lt. Col. Adrianus. "Operations of the 1st Battalion, 45th Infantry (P.S.) in the Battle of Toul Pocket" (1947–48).
Webb, Maj. William E. "Operations of the 41st Infantry (P.A.) in the Defense of the Abucay Line, January 1942" (1949–50).

Written for the U.S. Army School of Logistics:
Santos, Maj. Alfred. "The First Regular Division, Philippine Army in the Battle of the Philippines" (June 1947).

Written for the U.S. Army School of Combined Arms:
Johnson, Col. Harold K. "Anyasan and Silaiim Points" (1946–47).

Written for the U.S. Army Armor School:
Dooley, Lt. Col. Thomas. "The First U.S. Tank Action in World War II" (May 1948).

Interviews

Boyt, John T. Interview with author.
Fellows, Brig. Gen. Richard. Interview with author.
Lauchner, Norman. Interview with author.
Mabunga, Manuel. Interview with author.
Martin, Kai. Interview with author.
Wall, James. Interview with author.

INDEX

13, 105; 3d Battalion 104; Navy: Naval Battalion 101, 103, 105, 107, 113, 116, 117, 118, 122, 125, 148; Patrol Wing Ten 148; Philippine Army: 1st Division 8, 31, 81, 162, 167, 169, 173, 175, 177, 319, 321, 325; 1st Infantry Regiment 8, 32, 69, 173, 174, 325; 1st Battalion 167, 170, 175, 319; 2d Division (Philippine Constabulary) 8, 19, 85, 98, 247; 1st Infantry Regiment, 1st Battalion 8, 102, 108, 126, 153, 154; 2d Battalion 8, 101; 3d Battalion 8, 101, 135, 136; 2d Infantry Regiment, 2d Battalion 181, 184; 4th Infantry Regiment 277, 281, 283, 284; 11th Division 6, 7, 8, 162, 166, 167, 169, 174, 177, 182, 193, 199, 233, 277, 319, 321; 11th Infantry Regiment 169, 174, 175, 180, 247; 2d Battalion 182; 12th Infantry Regiment 137; 21st Division 6, 45, 47, 51, 79, 88, 191, 254, 256, 257, 258, 259, 260; 21st Infantry Regiment 52, 78, 79, 254; 22d Infantry Regiment 254; 23d Infantry Regiment 254; 21st Field Artillery Regiment 222, 229, 239; 31st Division 6, 8, 46, 47, 48, 78, 81, 87, 138, 185, 187, 205, 278, 281; 31st Infantry Regiment 185, 273; 32d Infantry Regiment 77, 188, 272, 273; 33d Infantry Regiment 182, 187, 188, 251, 252, 262, 263, 266, 268; 31st Field Artillery Regiment 32, 69; 41st Division 6, 8, 34, 38, 44, 76, 89, 191, 206, 248, 256, 258, 262, 263, 322; 41st Infantry Regiment 34, 45, 76, 77, 187, 190, 248, 252, 254, 263, 264, 265, 266, 268; 42d Infantry Regiment 34, 191, 248, 249, 251, 254, 262, 263, 266; 43d Infantry Regiment 34, 36, 48, 49, 50, 52, 53, 57, 191, 248, 251, 254, 262, 263, 266; 41st Field Artillery Regiment 241, 256; 51st Division 6, 34, 35, 37, 38, 46, 47, 49, 50, 51, 53, 69, 78, 87, 170, 185; 51st Infantry Regiment 36, 37, 44, 45, 49, 50, 51, 52, 57, 72, 73; 53d Infantry Regiment 36, 37, 44, 50, 52; 51st Combat Team (CT) 179, 182, 184, 190, 261, 273; 71st Division 6, 8, 31, 163, 325; 72d Infantry Regiment 321; 71st Field Artillery Regiment 116; 71st Engineer Battalion 133; 91st Division 6, 8, 31, 162, 163; 92d Infantry Regiment 175, 179, 181, 185; 2d Battalion 69; 91st-71st Division 84; 201st Engineer Battalion 269, 278, 337; 202d Engineer Battalion 269, 337; 301st Field Artillery Regiment 141, 191, 335, 337

Upper Pocket 177, 181, 182, 183, 184

U.S. Navy Section Base, Mariveles 133, 283, 289, 298

USAFFE 21, 38, 143, 149, 196, 230, 231, 233, 333

USAFFE Headquarters, Corregidor 24, 56

USFIP 232, 239, 333

USS Canopus (also "Old Lady") 12, 21, 22, 23, 53, 122, 123, 133, 139, 296, 298

USS Permit 209

USS Quail 119, 121, 304

Vance, Col. Lee 163, 274

Vanderboget, Col. Carlton 225

Van Oosten, Maj. Adrianus 4, 170, 179, 180, 185

Velasco, Cpl. Ramon 162

Villamore, Capt. Jose 155

Voice of Freedom 24, 74, 154, 192, 226, 285, 308, 313, 351, 352

Volckmann, Lt. Col. Russell 7, 166, 167, 199

Wachi, Lt. Gen. Takeji 231, 232

Waco 258, 279

Wainwright, Lt. Gen. Jonathan M. 24, 29, 30, 31, 32, 36, 51, 53, 60, 65, 67, 81, 83, 85, 86, 127, 132, 133, 134, 162, 166, 169, 170, 171, 173, 183, 187, 197, 199, 200, 220, 221, 222, 223, 229, 230, 233, 246,